MILITARY HISTORY FOR THE MODERN STRATEGIST

MILITARY HISTORY FOR THE MODERN STRATEGIST

AMERICA'S MAJOR WARS SINCE 1861

UPDATED EDITION

MICHAEL O'HANLON

BROOKINGS INSTITUTION PRESS
Washington, D.C.

Published by Brookings Institution Press
1775 Massachusetts Avenue, NW
Washington, DC 20036
www.brookings.edu/bipress

Co-published by Rowman & Littlefield
An imprint of The Rowman & Littlefield Publishing Group, Inc.
4501 Forbes Boulevard, Suite 200, Lanham, Maryland 20706
www.rowman.com

86-90 Paul Street, London EC2A 4NE

The Brookings Institution is a nonprofit organization devoted to research, education, and publication on important issues of domestic and foreign policy. Its principal purpose is to bring the highest quality independent research and analysis to bear on current and emerging policy problems.

Composition by Westchester Publishing Services
Typeset in Sabon

British Library Cataloguing in Publication Information Available

Library of Congress Cataloging-in-Publication Data Available

ISBN: 978-0-8157-4067-4 (pbk. : alk. paper)
ISBN: 978-0-8157-4068-1 (ebook)

∞™ The paper used in this publication meets the minimum requirements of American National Standard for Information Sciences—Permanence of Paper for Printed Library Materials, ANSI/NISO Z39.48-1992

Contents

Preface to the Updated Edition

After a year of speaking with amazing audiences around the United States about the hardback version of this book and the wars covered within its pages, I have become even more convinced that military history can teach us so much. It can inspire us with its tales of human heroism, strong will, and selfless dedication. It can and should sober us about the human potential for depravity, even in modern times, as we are now witnessing in Russia's attack on Ukraine. It can teach tactical lessons about battle, as well as broader campaigns and strategy, that may be of use for future conflicts and for deterrence. History tells us how we got to the world we have today and thus how to try to understand it. As more of a strategist and defense analyst than a true historian, I would like to express my gratitude again to those who make history their passion and their profession and whose combined works provided the grist for this book.[1]

Military history can also offer a warning about the cardinal sin of the strategist: overconfidence. Leaders, especially aggressors, tend to have theories of rapid victory in mind when they launch attacks, but their theories are rarely realized in practice on the battlefield. As I argue in the conclusion of this book, wars tend to be longer, costlier, and bloodier than expected by those who start them. That is often because, as Clausewitz warned, the fog of war makes even the simple things more difficult. Moreover, when quick wins do not transpire, humans tend to double down. Normal citizens and soldiers often do so because they have seen friends and relatives die. Consequently, they wish to avenge or redeem their deaths, which may give them a distorted view of the causes as well as the importance of the conflict.[2] Political leaders, especially aggressors, often persist because they are often too stubborn and heartless to admit a mistake. We see this in the contemporary world in Ukraine—a war that had already bogged down a year ago, when the first edition of this book was published, despite expectations in the Kremlin, the CIA, and elsewhere that it would go quickly. As I write these words in late 2023, however, there is still no end in sight. It is also worth bearing in mind another lesson or observation from my concluding chapter: Outcomes in war are not preordained. Conflicts take many unexpected twists and turns. Regardless of what the Ukraine conflict looks today, it may look quite different down the road. At the moment, despite the drones and satellite links and smart-phone apps that are part of this conflict, the fighting reminds me of the Western Front in World War I, from 1915 to 1917, more than any other war covered in this book. But it is worth remembering that even that front cracked and then disintegrated in 1918—initially to the benefit of the Germans but later to that of the Western allies, including the Americans.

When I first penned this book (mostly during the Covid shutdown), I chose seven conflicts that were America's largest and generally most consequential, but I left out the American Revolution. I did so because only 2.5 million people lived in the colonies in 1775, so most battles involved thousands rather than tens or hundreds of thousands of troops. Another reason I did so was because the technologies of the day as well as the way battles were fought had little apparent relevance for the modern strategist. I also left out the War of 1812, the U.S.-Mexico War, and the Spanish-American War since they were modest in scale (as one indication of scale, each of these four wars cost between $2 billion and $10 billion as expressed in today's dollars).[3]

With this new edition, I attempt to make partial amends. The Revolutionary War, in particular, is important enough to merit treatment in a book that, among its other purposes, seeks to capture the major struggles in America's first 250 years of existence. It was, in fact, the original, and perhaps even the only, existential struggle in the country's history, for the very creation of the United States hinged on its outcome. Only the Civil War, which threatened to divide the country in two, and World War II, which had the potential to rip the entire planet apart and perhaps even lead to a direct attack on the mainland of the United States if Hitler had realized his greatest dreams, could possibly claim to be in the same category of vital importance. And moreover, relative to the size of the country at that time, the Revolutionary War was, in fact, large, with a substantial fraction of the adult population ultimately serving. As such, I have chosen to discuss it at modest length in this preface. I also offer brief observations on the three other conflicts in U.S. history that led Congress to declare war: the War of 1812, the U.S.-Mexico War of 1846–1848, and the Spanish-American War of 1898.

Thematically and methodologically, my approach here as in the original book is to focus on overall strategy as well as the campaign level of analysis. Military campaigns are sequences of battles, maneuvers, and operations that typically occur over a period of weeks, months, or years, and over geographic zones of hundreds or thousands of miles, with a logical, overarching goal linking them together. In these pages, individual battles receive less attention except in the way they fit into larger campaigns. This approach keeps history at the level of the forest rather than the trees and keeps the focus on big ideas, key concepts, and overall strategy.

The Four Main Campaigns of the Revolutionary War

The Revolutionary War can be largely captured in four main campaigns. Each one typically lasted one to two years and took place over a geographic zone generally spanning about one to three colonies or states. Indeed, they might be called the New England campaign, the upstate New York campaign, the New York City/New Jersey/Pennsylvania campaign, and the Carolinas/Virginia or Southern campaign. Sometimes, there were swings of momentum and shifts in objectives within a given campaign—and as such, some scholars might argue that it would be more accurate to think of the war as including five or six or seven campaigns. But for the sake of simplicity, and because much within each theater did remain logically continuous throughout the period in question, I stick with four.

The first campaign centered on Boston starting in April of 1775. In general, it went the rebels' way. A second campaign centered on the river and lake systems going northward up the Hudson River to Lake George and Lake Champlain and then to the St. Lawrence River, with its cities of Montreal and Quebec. This campaign started very badly for the rebels, especially at Quebec on New Year's Eve 1775–1776, but it finished very well for them near Saratoga in September and October of 1777. A third campaign began on Long Island in the summer of 1776 and then continued onward in a great chase through Manhattan, New Jersey, and across the Delaware River toward Philadelphia, with various back-and-forth movements. Britain dominated the opening phases of this campaign, but as it progressed, General George Washington found a way to trade space for time, slowing down the British effort even as General William Howe and his Redcoats retained the upper hand. The fourth campaign, the Southern campaign, was waged mostly in the Carolinas and mostly over the 1780–1781 period. It began well for the British crown but of course ended disastrously for them, leading to what proved to be the conclusive fight in Yorktown, Virginia, in the early fall of 1781 (it would take two more years for the war to end formally).

Campaign-level analysis is admittedly not quite a complete way to understand the conflict. Notably, for much of the war, there were engagements involving rebel forces, British forces, and native Americans (fighting on both sides, depending on tribe and time and location) in New York, Pennsylvania, and over to Indiana and Illinois. Most of these, except some in central New York State, were largely disconnected from the four main geographic campaigns delineated above. Some other battles, such as the unsuccessful U.S.-French effort to liberate Newport, Rhode Island, from British rule in the summer of 1778 (though the Brits pulled out themselves in 1779), do not quite fit into the four-campaign narrative, either,[4] but for understanding the main efforts of the two sides and ultimately the chief determinants of the war's outcome, the four-campaign framing is not only parsimonious but generally solid.

There were also important naval components to the war. Some factored importantly into the four main campaigns: General Howe's big troop movements from Boston to New York and later from New York toward Philadelphia, contests along the Hudson and Lake Champlain, General Washington's crossings (of the Delaware and the Hudson, most famously), the seizure of Charleston by British forces, and the definitive boxing in of General Cornwallis at Yorktown. There was also an ongoing maritime conflict that was not particularly limited in time or space and thus not really a central part of any of the four campaigns. This maritime conflict included British efforts to box in the colonies' economies through naval blockade of ports, John Paul Jones's remarkable challenges to the British Navy in the latter's home waters in 1778 and 1779 (including aboard the fabled *Bonhomme Richard*, named by Jones in honor of Benjamin Franklin), and rebel privateers' often-successful efforts to seize British shipping (while getting wealthy off the booty).

The Brits managed to hold several cities—taking Boston in 1775 (but only temporarily), New York and Newport in 1776 (remaining in the latter for four years and in the former for the duration of the war), Philadelphia in 1777 (also just temporarily), Savannah in 1778, and Charleston in 1780. Yet fairly early in the saga, it had become clear that this war would not be primarily a contest over metropolitan areas.[5] America was a vast land with a spread-out population; its 2.5 million people were fewer than a fourth of those in the British Isles, and Britain also had mercenary forces known as Hessians on its side. Britain was also an extended and overcommitted empire, however, fighting a revolutionary people in a faraway place.[6]

The first campaign began in the Boston suburbs on the morning of April 19, 1775, after British Redcoats reached Lexington following a nighttime march toward Concord. It was a skirmish that left eight patriots dead. "The shots heard round the world," as the battle was coined, also left the surrounding countryside, and the Minutemen, awakened, alerted, and incensed. As British troops neared Concord with the intent of destroying its rebel military stores, they were surrounded on various sides and ambushed by rebels hiding behind trees and hills and houses. British forces withdrew toward Lexington, where they were reinforced by more forces coming from Boston. On the way back to Boston, however, they still lost nearly 300 of their 1,800-strong force to death, injury, or capture.[7] The war was now truly underway.

The next big battle took place at Breed's Hill, next to Bunker Hill, just north of Boston on the Charlestown peninsula. There, rebels established a position with just over 1,000 troops on June 16. Redcoats rowed out to meet them and ultimately drove them away the next day—but only after fierce fighting that left some 1,000 out of roughly 2,500 British troops as casualties. Losses were also heavy for the rebels but substantially fewer, at around 400. Even in tactical defeat, the patriots gained a further boost of morale and confidence.[8] During these same days of mid-June, meanwhile, the Continental Congress created a Continental Army, placed George Washington in command, and authorized the raising of ten companies of soldiers to complement all the various state militias that also contributed to overall rebel strength.

As summer turned into fall, the goals of the belligerents started to crystallize. The rebels hoped to drive the Brits out of Boston, despite knowing that they could cause trouble elsewhere. The British crown hoped to squash the rebellion in the city where it had largely been borne in the belief that such a defeat might deflate the revolutionary movement writ large. The next big move took place not in Boston, however, but around Lake Champlain in New York. Early in the war, in May of 1775, rebels had seized Fort Ticonderoga and its artillery with ease. Then, the following winter, when lakes froze and snow fell, the guns were sledded across New England all the way to Boston. Showing considerable logistical and engineering creativity, the rebels under General Washington quickly and stealthily placed them in improvised fortifications on Dorchester Heights, south of Boston, on the night of March 4. That brought rebel cannons within range of British positions in the city center, and the move proved the game changer. Understanding his predicament, General Howe chose to relocate rather than fight. He departed with his troops and some loyalists for Nova Scotia on March 17, where he then spent the spring receiving reinforcements from Britain, building up his forces, and planning the next move.[9]

The second campaign involved the waterway system defined by the broader Hudson River Valley and extending up to Lake Champlain and then into Canada to the St. Lawrence River. It began after rebel forces successfully seized Fort Ticonderoga on the southern part of Lake Champlain (still a good distance from Canada) and began threatening Quebec and Montreal. Part of their calculus was based on the hope that such a foray could persuade anti-British forces in Canada to join with the revolutionaries from the thirteen colonies, ideally leading to Britain's eviction from all of North America. Recently appointed General Washington thought it might be useful, therefore, to threaten Canadian targets. The Continental Congress was initially not so sure, wondering if a negotiated agreement with London might still be possible and thus preferring to avoid anything that smacked of offensive warfare. Congress eventually changed its position, however, in part due to King George III's August 23, 1775, declaration that the colonies were in a state of rebellion, but the combination of political indecision with slow military preparation augured badly for the scheme's ultimate prospects. Rebel forces moved northward into Canada, with a bit more than 1,000 men, at the very end of August—and with winter soon to loom.[10]

The overarching rebel concept for the move into Canada was to take control of the St. Lawrence River, its main cities of Montreal and Quebec, and perhaps, through a snowball effect, all of Canada. Everything happened too slowly, however, allowing the Brits just enough time for the necessary reinforcements to arrive.

The rebels did moderately well at first, but only very slowly—needing two months to take Fort St. John's en route to Montreal. Montreal fell faster; the Brits had far too few soldiers there to hold it, and now the race was on for Quebec. By late December, some 300 men under General Richard Montgomery had made their way to the fortified city after their start in upper New York, while another 600 under Colonel Benedict Arnold (with Daniel Morgan and Aaron Burr among his notable subordinates) had arrived via an arduous overland and partially amphibious route further east starting in Maine. Together attacking Quebec during a snowstorm on December 31, 1775, they were unable to defeat the wily British defenders, who by this point had improved their position, their fortifications, and their supplies considerably. General Montgomery was killed, Benedict Arnold was wounded, and the assaulting party suffered a major defeat. Then it became a competition of which side could build up forces faster. For the rest of that winter and the following spring, rebel forces sought to strengthen their ranks with additional reinforcements, but enough Brits (and Hessians) arrived to keep the balance favorable to the crown. Ultimately, the rebel forces gave up their efforts to take Quebec, as well as their positions in places like Montreal, and returned home.[11]

Thus, if these opening months of fighting in the Canadian theater in the spring of 1776 were treated by themselves as a complete campaign, the result would clearly be scored as a British win, but the tide would turn dramatically the following year.

Out of fear that rebel forces might again come north, London maintained a separate military command for Canada and diverted scarce resources there. That set the stage for what ultimately occurred at Saratoga in the fall of 1777. When British forces later sought to sail northward from New York and move southward from Canada in a coordinated assault to create a divide in the colonies along that same Hudson/Lake Champlain seam, they failed catastrophically. Their overall strategy was dubious, and the separate commands did not plan or coordinate very well.

In this second phase of the Hudson/Champlain/Canada campaign, the British goal was to sever New England from the rest of the colonies on the premise that New England was the hotbed of revolution. If it could be isolated (even partially) from the other colonies, they thought, insurrectionists to the south, who had less revolutionary fervor than the New Englanders, might become discouraged and give up the struggle. London always held out hope in this phase of the fight that many if not most colonists were in fact loyalists and could be persuaded to come back around to support the crown with the right mix of incentives.

British General John Burgoyne, coming south from Canada by land and by lake with something shy of 10,000 personnel (and wagons full of creature comforts for himself), had plans to take Albany. There, he would be met by Redcoats moving northward along the Hudson from New York City. But none of that happened. Burgoyne succeeded in his first major task of reclaiming Fort Ticonderoga, making clever use of high ground nearby to threaten the rebel positions and force their evacuation of the fort in early July 1777, but he then found himself unable to handle all the challenges of the complex topography of the region, including rebel ambushes and delaying tactics that made good use of the hills, forests, lakes, and marshes (rebels often felled trees to block paths, for example). Patriot ranks were reinforced by various militias over the course of the spring and summer, as Commander in Chief Washington recognized the importance of the theater for the overall war and directed reinforcements as well as some of his best commanders to the vicinity.[12] Fighting took place further west in the state, too, with native Americans from the Iroquois nation often part of the action (mostly but not entirely on the British side).

The campaign culminated in two battles at Freeman's Farm and Bemis Heights near Saratoga in the early fall of 1777. There, rebel forces under General Horatio Gates made good use of the natural terrain combined with smart defensive tactics to stymie the British forces' attack and ultimately to force their surrender on October 17, as their provisions dwindled and their sense of isolation grew.[13] That was largely because the expected assistance coming from New York, under General Henry Clinton, proved too little too late for the Redcoats. In fact, Clinton's forces never made it more than about halfway up the Hudson.[14] Burgoyne had to surrender his entire army, or what was left of it.

That spelled the end, more or less, of the second campaign. By now, the Americans had established momentum in the overall war as well (despite the recent loss at Brandywine, as discussed below). Soon thereafter, persuaded after Saratoga that the rebel cause was worthy of its support, France would join the war.[15] As historian Kevin Weddle put it, "For the British, Saratoga was not merely a battlefield defeat; it was a strategic, operational, and tactical catastrophe."[16]

Clinton would try again to control the Hudson in 1779, by then as overall commander of British forces. Even with Benedict Arnold's turncoat assistance to the Brits at West Point, however, where Arnold kept fortifications weak and told his erstwhile adversaries where and how to attack, Clinton would again fail.[17]

The third campaign, overlapping with the Hudson/Champlain/ Canada campaign but following the New England campaign, started in New York City in the summer of 1776—just as fateful things were happening on the political front, with the Declaration of Independence signaling that there would be no going back on the fight now. The British organized the largest force of the war, with estimates of total manpower in the New York area as high as 45,000, including soldiers, Hessians, and sailors. They slowly prepared to attack the general New York area while keeping their specific intentions secret. General Washington had some 20,000 men in all under his command in the region. Taking advantage of their dominance of the waterways, and good amphibious techniques, the Brits came ashore in southwestern Long Island, across from Staten Island, with considerable speed and aplomb. Some 20,000 Brits landed to face about half that number of rebels, roughly half of Washington's total force.[18] The fact that Washington had rightly surmised they would go to New York still didn't make the defense of that geographically complex, sprawling, and somewhat more British-friendly city anything but a long-shot proposition.[19]

The British decisively carried the day in the campaign's first major engagement, which took place just east of Manhattan on Long Island. Doing a better job than General Washington of figuring out the topography, they were able to flank rebel defenses through a pass known as Jamaica Road and deliver a serious battering to Washington's troops. John Adams observed that, "In general, our generals were outgeneraled."[20] Rebel casualties reached about 1,500, while British losses were only a quarter as great. The Brits then patiently starting laying siege to remaining rebel positions on Long Island with the intent of annihilating the remainder of the forces. The situation appeared dire, but then Washington salvaged most of his army and some of his reputation with a brilliant and stealthy nighttime redeployment back over the water to Manhattan— even as British warships dominated the general maritime zone.[21]

Although complete disaster for the rebels was averted, more British victories would follow, first in Manhattan, then at points north and west. Washington realized he could not hold the main developed parts of downtown Manhattan, but he hoped to hold onto Fort Washington in northern Manhattan as well as Fort Lee across the river in New Jersey—

two positions that, together, were intended to deny Britain easy use of the Hudson, even though the rebels never proved capable of achieving that goal. Neither could they, it turned out, withstand direct sieges. British forces, who had come ashore in Manhattan in mid-September, forced the surrender of Fort Washington in mid-November, and some 3,000 rebel soldiers became British prisoners. Before that, the Brits had pursued Washington northward, engaging him at White Plains, New York, at the end of October and getting the better of that fight as well. They also forced the evacuation of Fort Lee on the New Jersey side of the Hudson on November 20. The rebels were reeling; Washington's reputation and even his self-confidence were suffering. The likelihood that General Howe and the Brits would next make a beeline for Philadelphia, or destroy Washington's army along the way, seemed all too real.[22]

Yet somehow a silver lining eventually emerged for the rebels from these terrible three months of fighting in and around New York. As Washington biographer Ron Chernow put it, these defeats "had shown [Washington] the futility of trying to defend heavily fortified positions along the seaboard and forced him out into the countryside, where he had mobility and where the British Army, deprived of the Royal Navy, operated at a disadvantage."[23] Late 1776 became a key turning point, if not yet on the battlefield then in how Washington viewed the war, and how he thought strategically. The Brits also may have squandered their momentum. As famed historian Joseph Ellis put it, "Based on what we now know about the military history of the American Revolution, if the British commanders had prosecuted the war more vigorously in its earliest stages, the Continental Army might very well have been destroyed at the start and the movement for American independence nipped in the bud."[24] Fortunately, Washington figured out how to prevent the British from fully regaining that momentum.

After assembling an armada of wagon trains and horses to transport supplies for the large army, Howe sent British and Hessian forces southward after Washington (who managed to get the bulk of his forces back across the Hudson River following the limited fight at White Plains).[25] General Cornwallis pursued Washington and his few thousand remaining fighters, who were unable to find the kind of support from local militias that they had hoped for. The beaten-up rebels at least managed to burn enough bridges to keep the pursuing British from closing the gap.

In December, Washington and his rebel forces reached Trenton. They confiscated all nearby boats so the chasing Brits would not be able to use them and then crossed the Delaware River—buying themselves a few weeks of good defensive position (at least until the Delaware froze). Their goals were to protect themselves while also potentially creating a shielding force to protect the original home of the Continental Congress in Philadelphia (though out of caution, Congress temporarily relocated to Baltimore on December 13).

As British forces reached the vicinity and considered their options, Washington struck. He used some of his force to cross the Delaware back to the New Jersey side on Christmas night, leading to the first Battle of Trenton on December 26, in which rebel forces got the better of their adversary. Washington did it again a couple days later, leading to the second Battle of Trenton on January 2, 1777. After that second offensive, Washington snuck around British forces, going north and east to strike a garrison at Princeton on January 3. His forces defeated the small British position there, too—most nearby British forces, under Cornwallis, were still encamped in Trenton. Washington then moved his exhausted forces northwest into safer country to set up what became their winter positions.[26] The combination of good defense with a little opportunistic and clever offense kept rebel forces motivated and British forces off guard. These attacks also helped keep the rebels supplied, after they confiscated goods from the Brits at Trenton and Princeton. These three battles combined may have produced as many as 3,000 British/Hessian casualties, including killed, wounded, and captured.[27]

Then winter set in fully, interrupting the fighting. Washington's Continental Army camped at Valley Forge, facing tough conditions, but with the help of a Prussian officer named Baron von Steuben, they trained and improved considerably during this period. Meanwhile, the British tried to figure out their next move. At their own winter headquarters, they suffered ambushes from rebel forces as they foraged for food and were otherwise kept off balance.

Not until the warm weather came did the Brits develop a new plan of attack. They first returned to New York, then loaded up on ships to sail southward all the way to the Chesapeake Bay—to then sail northward toward Philadelphia and disembark. By the late summer, they were approaching the city by land. When Washington came out to meet them, the result was the Battle of Brandywine, one of the war's biggest fights as measured in troop strength, on September 11, 1777. In that single-day engagement, British forces again successfully outflanked the patriots and Howe again outgeneraled Washington, causing perhaps 900 rebel casualties to an estimated 550 for British forces. Philadelphia fell to the British later that same month (though only temporarily, as it turned out, since the British withdrew the next year).

To gain this prize, General Howe had taken some 15,000 Redcoats out of the overall troop strength the Brits had based in New York City, which left General Clinton with only about 7,000 troops and unclear instructions—a combination that proved fatal for British hopes along the Hudson.[28]

In Howe's mind, at least, he got his win in Philadelphia. But given the limited strategic importance of Philadelphia, or any single American city, for that matter, and in light of the fact that the Continental Congress could again relocate safely before British troops arrived (this time going to York, Pennsylvania), the sum total of these events was no decisive win for the British. After all, they already held the city of New York, along with Newport, at this point (and would later hold Charleston, South Carolina, as well as other coastal cities) yet were unable to translate such gains into strategic victory.[29]

Indeed, the Brits themselves seemed to recognize as much in 1778. That year began with the momentous decision by France to ally with the rebels and support their cause of independence. In June, Britain and France wound up formally at war. Now, the Brits had other things to worry about in other places; they would have to economize in the fight against the American rebels. As a result, they decided to vacate Philadelphia and return to New York. Rebel forces, learning of the British retrograde action, set out in pursuit from Valley Forge. Among the major results was the Battle of Monmouth on June 28, effectively fought to a draw but nonetheless crystallizing solid support for General Washington's leadership in the young United States—a strength and depth of support he would never again lack.[30]

In this third campaign, the overall British campaign goal had seemed to be the destruction of General Washington's army first and foremost, leading to collapse of the rebel cause. Washington's own goals trended toward a strategy of attrition—or erosion—or at least survival of his army, trying to avoid pitched fights in the interest of preserving the rebels' modest fighting strength.[31] In this broader sense, the third campaign ended with the advantage going to the rebels. By the summer of 1778, the northern regions of the country entered into a period of limited fighting as more of the action for the rest of the war shifted to the south.[32]

The fourth and final campaign was the British attempt to control the southern part of the colonies, perhaps with the hope of thereby generating more momentum throughout the colonies. They were initially successful at Savannah and nearby locations in late December of 1778 and thereafter, culminating in the taking of Charleston in the spring of 1780. But the tables turned by late 1780 and early 1781, and then disaster struck later in the year.

Again, the British hope in this southern campaign was to find and empower a silent majority of loyalist subjects of the king. Even though that had not worked out so well up north, perhaps it could work in the Carolinas and Georgia. The Brits also hoped to put the economic squeeze on the rebels by depriving them of ports, crucial for exports. The theory may have had a kernel of logic behind it, but it would not succeed overall. Loyalists were not as numerous as they had hoped, and rebels proved to be a dedicated lot. Brutal tactics on both sides intensified emotions and prolonged the fighting.

Famed leaders like Alexander Stewart and Banastre Tarleton on the British side, and Nathanael Greene, Daniel Morgan, William Hill, Thomas Sumter, and Frances Marion on the rebel side, commanded the efforts. Many engagements were in remote areas and fought between small units, resembling guerrilla warfare at times.[33]

The British had earlier tried and failed to take Charleston in June of 1776. Specifically, they sought to destroy or seize Fort Sullivan on Sullivan's Island in the Charleston Harbor, but poor British seamanship, palmetto wood's forgiving ways when struck by cannon fire, and what turned out to be a lack of strong Tory support in the immediate environs doomed the attempt to capture the fort or compel its inhabitants to surrender.[34]

The Brits did much better on their later try. The key success was in Charleston. Rebel forces there under General Benjamin Lincoln were ultimately trapped and forced to surrender on May 12, 1780. Some 5,500 rebels were taken prisoner, the most to be captured on the American side during the entire war. As spring and summer unfolded, British forces built on this initial coastal success and established a series of outposts throughout much of South Carolina, where rebel forces now seemed genuinely disheartened if not outright defeated.[35]

But the rebels proved relentless. In October, at Battle of Kings Mountain near Charlotte, North Carolina, British forces suffered a defeat. They had perhaps extended their range, as well as their ambitions, too fast and too far. They also continued to have unrealistic expectations about the level of likely Tory support and too much contempt for the rebels, who proved more resolute and tenacious than believed. The rebels also benefited from a local topography of forests and swamps and rivers that many of them, as locals, knew well.

In the following months, the Americans continued to raid British outposts and conduct clever small-unit maneuvering and ambushing. The hybrid mix of militia and Continental soldiers was led by General Nathaniel Greene, with other illustrious subordinate commanders.[36] British forces, meanwhile, sought a decisive engagement. They got one— but the result was not to their liking. They finally caught up with a large chunk of rebel forces, resulting in the Battle of Cowpens, South Carolina, in January of 1781. American forces performed magnificently. Author Lawrence Babits wrote a book about the battle called *A Devil of a Whipping*, a phrase that came from the American commander Daniel Morgan's own summary of that short but momentous fight. Morgan's forces employed excellent tactics, including multiple, disguised fighting positions and feigned retreats, as well as the clever and timely use of horse cavalry to complement his infantry.[37]

British forces did a bit better at Guilford Courthouse in March. That engagement could be called a tactical victory for the Redcoats since the rebels ultimately retreated. But at a strategic level, the outcome was perhaps closer to another strategic setback for the British, if not an outright defeat, given the costs in troops that were hard for Cornwallis to replace.

Because his strategy was not working in the Carolinas, Cornwallis became consumed by visions of greater glory in the Old Dominion, so he headed to Virginia with much of his army by May—relegating the Carolinas to a secondary zone strategically. In so doing, however, he left himself precariously placed in a region where, as it turned out, the French and not the British would be able to establish crucial naval superiority.

Of course, that was the fateful move. After General Cornwallis frittered away much of the warmer months in 1781 in the Virginia countryside on various raids and small-scale operations, he ultimately let himself be trapped, with no escape by land or sea, at Yorktown, Virginia, in 1781. Seeing where he was headed, General Washington and his French counterparts Lafayette and Rochambeau seized the opportunity. They sent ground reinforcements to pin Cornwallis down while Admiral Francois de Grasse bottled the British up and closed off possible escape routes on the Chesapeake Bay. With roughly a two-to-one advantage in ground strength with 17,000 troops, as well as naval superiority, they lay siege to the British position. Cornwallis was forced to surrender his 8,000-strong forces to Washington on October 19, 1781, in what proved the last big battle of the war, even if final resolution of the conflict did not come until two years later in 1783.

A few overarching words about the war are in order. First, in terms of root causes, while there was certainly a very real dispute between the colonies and London over the form of government, individual liberty, and taxation without representation, the war was not simply a dispute over whether monarchy or democracy was the better form of government. Many colonists simply did not welcome being ruled by a faraway power. Some of the ensuing rhetoric about individual rights and liberty and freedom, while sincere, was also opportunistic and convenient. It stoked the embers of passion for an independence cause that many wanted anyway but for less lofty reasons. Given how many of the founding fathers were slaveowners, their commitment to liberty was sincere at one level but conditional at another; given how light the British touch generally was on most colonists prior to the development of their revolutionary fervor, the grievances that the colonists developed as they turned into rebels were sometimes exaggerated. Moreover, much of the decisive effort in the war was provided by European monarchies whose help the colonists gladly accepted when it was finally offered—by France in 1778, by Spain in 1779, by the Dutch in 1780—even though the war was purportedly against monarchy. Beggars can't be choosers, and the colonists were not wrong to seek such aid, but the war was not only about lofty principles, however important they indeed were.

Thinking in terms of the weaponry of war and tactics of the day, this was a war of muskets and artillery as well as cannons on land and sailing ships, with heavy cannons, at sea. But it preceded the Napoleonic revolution with the latter's focus on the mass-conscript army and industrialized production of weaponry. Rebel troop strength, militias plus regular army, may have peaked at around 40,000, with a total of 100,000 or more fighting against the Brits at some point during the war, and the largest number in a single battle reaching about 20,000 (in New York City in 1776 and in Saratoga in 1777). Rebel fatalities may, in rough numbers, have totaled 4,000 to 5,000 over the course of the war, though some estimates are higher; British, Hessian, and loyalist losses were also likely in that same general range.[38]

Railroads and the telegraph did not yet exist. Communications were often by horseback, but most soldiers moved by foot (though supply trains were pulled by horse, and there was certainly some cavalry, or "dragoons").

Most American soldiers were local militia, not members of the Continental Army. Conscription was employed, but with lots of abuses, workarounds, perverse incentives, and undesirable effects as a result. It took time to build a viable fighting force, and leaders like Washington were often frustrated with the quality of their troops, especially in the war's early stages.[39] British soldiers came from the home country but also, as mercenaries, from Hesse (in modern Germany) and other places.

As for General Washington, as Russell Weigley argued in his masterpiece *The American Way of War,* he was a fascinating blend of tradition with improvisation. He wanted to command a somewhat traditional army, in organization, training, and even tactics, yet he also came to realize, especially during the course of 1776, that his strategic approach had to be largely defensive.[40] The (misnamed) Battle of Bunker Hill in June of 1775, and more generally the successful siege of British forces in Boston over the following months that led to their redeployment to Nova Scotia (and later New York) on March 17, 1776, raised rebel hopes. But the battles to defend New York in the summer of that year were unsuccessful and costly. The ensuing retreat through New Jersey showed a more successful path to survival (and thus, eventually, possible victory), especially when Washington figured out how to combine an overarching campaign of withdrawal with limited, tactical offensives across the Delaware in the winter of 1776–1777. With his smallish and often ragged forces, he could not win the big slugfests against the British, and therefore he could not protect the colonies' major cities or even reliably win major engagements fighting on the tactical defensive. He had to be elusive and cherish his army itself more than the territory or people he was protecting—since there was a decent chance he could keep his army going indefinitely, but only a modest chance he could win any given big battle.[41] He also needed to look for ways to use other tools, like the rebels' small navy (and a large number of privateers acting with government permission), to harass and bleed British shipping and resupply efforts.[42] In that basic strategic outlook, he had some commonalities with twentieth-century proponents of people's war and insurgency like Mao and Ho Chi Minh—or with Fabius Maximus of ancient Rome.[43] Yet there were ultimately successes for the rebels in big fights, too, at Saratoga in 1777 and Yorktown in 1781, and Washington knew how to take advantage of these opportunities when he saw them.

The case of the Revolutionary War also affirms the first two broad observations about America's major conflicts that I offer in the conclusion to this book. First, outcomes in war are rarely if ever preordained, and major shifts in momentum often occur—sometimes without much warning. Second, war is usually harder and bloodier (and longer) than expected. Regarding the first observation, there were several major swings of momentum during the American Revolution: the British departure from Boston followed by big success in New York; Washington's retreat in New Jersey in late 1776 followed by his bold crossings of the Delaware and attacks at Trenton and Princeton around the turn of the year; Benedict Arnold's and Horatio Gates' big victory for the rebels at Saratoga in October of 1777; the British seizure of Charleston in 1780 and subsequent successes in the South Carolina countryside that spring and summer, followed by defeat at Kings Mountain in late 1780, Cowpens, and (for all practical purposes) Guilford Courthouse in early 1781; and, of course, defeat at Yorktown in the fall of 1781. The battle of Saratoga followed by the French entry into the war probably together represented the main overall turning point; prior to that time, British victory looked very plausible if not likely.

As my Brookings colleague Robert Kagan notes, we learn history looking backward, but it is made moving forward. What can seem destined to be in retrospect was often not so foreseeable or inevitable at the time.

Second, the idea that a simmering struggle between the British crown and colonists that had taken a few lives here and there during the first half of the 1770s would explode into an all-out war lasting years and killing thousands was a shock. And in the early months, there were still hopes for a negotiated peace of some sorts, as well as an initial reluctance on the colonists' part to build a sizeable standing army with long-term enlistments.[44] Independence was not declared until fifteen months into the fighting. When the shooting began in April of 1775, few would have prognosticated that the war would drag on until 1783. Indeed, the American Revolution lasted longer than any American high-intensity war until at least Vietnam, and it caused casualties that relative to the size of the population at the time were exceeded in American history only by the Civil War and World War II. It was, indeed, harder, bloodier, and longer—by far—than most expected.

The Main Campaigns of the Three Declared Wars of the Nineteenth Century

Not every war is equally long or hard, of course, even those that are officially declared by majority votes of both houses of Congress. There were three such wars in the nineteenth century (in addition to the massive but undeclared Civil War, operations against the Barbary pirates, and frequent fighting against native Americans). They were the War of 1812 (and 1813 and 1814 and a little bit of 1815), the U.S.-Mexico War of 1846–1848, and the "splendid little war"—as Secretary of State John Hay described it—the Spanish-American War in the spring and summer of 1898. To study these wars as an American is sobering. They were, in effect, all wars of choice for the United States; the country was never at serious peril when it chose to enter into them. In the case of the U.S.-Mexico War, in particular, the conflict was due to rather aggressive action by Americans against their southern neighbor, resulting in a huge land-grab. They are among the reasons that historian Robert Kagan called the United States a "dangerous nation" during this time period—and they are worth reflecting on for those who might have thought that America has normally been a peaceful nation.[45] Whether one can make a case for these wars or not, they were certainly not the result of peaceful mindsets of U.S. leaders. None of that is to deny a very noble and crucial role for the United States in world affairs over the course of its two and a half centuries of existence, but the more important contributions to the well-being of the global order occurred in the twentieth century (and perhaps to some extent the twenty-first)—not the nineteenth.

The War of 1812 was not short, but it was not particularly protracted, either, especially since it ended with no clear military victory or culminating achievement by either side. Nor was it nearly as bloody as some wars—even if it could certainly be brutal at times. Although the stakes became rather high, with some Americans wanting to take Canada from Britain, and some Brits perhaps hoping to reverse the outcome of the Revolutionary War, the engagements were generally limited in space and time.[46] The United States may have lost somewhat more than 2,000 killed in action, and several thousand more wounded, out of a population that had grown to more than 7 million by the time of the 1810 census.[47]

Although it became the first declared war in U.S. history, it was not a necessary one. Yes, there had been insults and harm done to Americans in preceding years by the British policy of impressment—stopping American ships on the high seas to arrest British sailors who had deserted. Various tariffs and boycotts were also applied by London against American commerce in the context of the British-French warring in Europe and Britain's desire to impede normal commerce with France so as to weaken it economically and militarily. But some of these problems were being mitigated by negotiation even as Congress chose, at President James Madison's request, to declare war. The dangers and costs of war were certainly much worse than what the United States was suffering due to British policies before June of 1812.[48] There was a certain recklessness in starting a war when negotiations were producing results and when, as historian Henry Adams wrote some seventy-five years later, "No serious preparations for war had yet been made when the war began."[49] The competing Federalist party, and much of the region of New England, were strongly against the war from the start (and throughout). Moreover, the Treaty of Ghent that ended the war left borders and the maritime policies that had produced the disputes unchanged, making the war seem all for naught to many.[50]

Thinking again in terms of military campaigns, one can identify three during this war.[51] The first was the series of skirmishes, raids, and lake battles across the northeast region of the United States near the border with Canada, especially from the general region of Detroit eastward across the Great Lakes and the Niagara River all the way to Lake Champlain. These fights lasted throughout the war and generally produced aggregate stalemate, despite wins and losses and some heroics—like Oliver Hazard Perry's victory in the Battle of Lake Erie on September 10, 1813, for the Americans.[52] The American goal here was to grab as much of Canada as possible to create leverage against Britain—or even to keep the seized territory and expand the nation, at least in the minds of some war hawks like Kentucky senator Henry Clay.

The second of three campaigns was ongoing throughout the war, with various twists and turns. It consisted of the general pattern of maritime engagements in Atlantic waters throughout the war, near U.S. coasts, for the most part. Sometimes the action was out at sea, but the British also used their naval superiority to conduct raids at various points along the eastern seaboard. They included the sacking of Washington, D.C. (with the burning of the White House and Congress) in August of 1814 and the subsequent attack on Baltimore that produced what became our national anthem, "The Star-Spangled Banner," in September. The goals were both to punish the Americans and to apply economic pressure, in the hope that the Americans would back down; when Napoleon abdicated in the spring of 1814 in France, Britain had more means available to pursue such operations. These engagements produced a British advantage (despite some American success with raiding and privateering) and considerable reductions in U.S. exports as well as a big budget deficit. They did not, however, cause enough economic pain to induce surrender in a large and economically well-endowed continental country like the United States.[53]

The third campaign was the fight in the south, culminating in Andrew Jackson's historic defense of New Orleans in early 1815 that gave a nice final chapter to the fighting from an American perspective. However, it is perhaps fitting for such an ambiguous and seemingly pointless war that perhaps its greatest battle victory for the Americans came after the war was over—since the decisions for compromise and peace had already been made by the time of that fight (even if word had not yet reached Louisiana).[54]

If the War of 1812 was a war of choice, that was true in spades of the U.S.-Mexico War of 1846–1848. In many ways, it was the most naked land grab against a foreign country in American history. Former general and president Ulysses S. Grant, writing in his memoirs around 1885, regarded the war "as one of the most unjust ever waged by a stronger against a weaker nation."[55] On the other hand, some would call it virtually inevitable since it concerned territories that seemed a natural extension of the United States to most Americans, even though they seemed an important (if remote, sparsely inhabited, and faraway) part of Mexico to Mexicans.[56]

The U.S.-Mexico War began when an ambitious, land-hungry United States made a move to annex Texas roughly a decade after that polity had successfully fought for its independence from Mexico. Mexico itself had been free from Spain only since 1821. It was dominated militarily as well as politically for much of its first quarter century by Antonio Lopez de Santa Anna, the president of Mexico multiple times as well as the nation's top general (once he returned from exile) in the war against the United States.

President James Polk made the decision to provoke and then prosecute the war, but he was far from alone among Americans in his thinking on the issue. The immediate stated cause of the war was a dispute over where the Texas-Mexico border should be drawn, but the real stakes were much greater. When fighting began, Congress promptly gave Polk the declaration of war that he requested in May 1846 by overwhelming majorities in both houses. Just as Polk wished, even if he did not admit as much when asking Congress for permission to fight, the war resulted in massive land acquisition by the United States—not only Texas but also New Mexico, Arizona, other parts of today's southwest, and California—clearly the primary goal of the United States.

The war can be fairly well divided into three discrete military campaigns because distances were so great that combat theaters rarely overlapped. First, the United States wanted the larger version of Texas (all land north of the Rio Grande). Second, it wanted all the land that is today in the southwestern and western states mentioned above. And third, after failing to persuade or coerce Mexico into selling it most or all of these lands in 1845, it wanted to seize enough of the heart of Mexican territory that it would have leverage in eventual peace negotiations so as to coerce Mexico to give it the land it really wanted.[57] President Polk dissembled about having such goals when asking Congress for a declaration of war, instead framing the need for military action as a response to a Mexican ambush (that the United States had effectively induced by crossing into disputed territory). But his goals were territorial from the start.[58]

The first large campaign was led by Zachary Taylor and would help propel him to the presidency in the election of 1848. He moved southward to seize the disputed parts of Texas and then chunks of northern Mexico that could be used as bargaining chips in future peace talks. Like all major campaigns in this war, logistics were very challenging given the harsh climate and topography. Most soldiers moved on foot, though cavalry and dragoons were mounted. Horses, mules, and wagons were also generally needed to bring along food, water, ammunition, and artillery. Communications of the day were slow and by courier on horseback or, sometimes, by ship.

Taylor's initial battles took place in early May of 1846 at Palo Alto, where just over 2,000 Americans relied principally on artillery to defeat a Mexican force of almost 4,000, and in a follow-up battle that turned into a rout for the Americans at Resaca de la Palma, near the Texas-Mexico border.[59] With all that momentum, and after receiving reinforcements, Taylor then crossed the Rio Grande later in May and prepared to move south. That led to the Battle of Monterrey in late September and then, with General Santa Anna assembling a huge force of more than 20,000 to try to drive the Americans back home, the Battle of Buena

Vista in late February 1847. Both resulted in U.S. victories, though the first was a tough fight that produced more U.S. than Mexican casualties—some 500 Americans killed and wounded out of a force about 6,000 strong compared to Mexico's losses of perhaps 350 to 400 out of a force numbering just over 7,000.[60] The Buena Vista victory was better executed and more impressive, given that U.S. forces were considerably outnumbered in that fight, perhaps roughly 5,000 Americans to 15,000 Mexicans—yet the American forces suffered only about half as many casualties as did Mexican troops.[61] That win did not, however, lead to any further noteworthy battles, as attention on both sides was shifting southward to a new combat theater where the war would be effectively decided in September.

Before getting to that decisive campaign, though, there are the battles in the West to consider. There were some fights in New Mexico, but most were in California. Like Taylor's campaign, these battles began in 1846. American forces included three types of fighters: an organized overland military expedition, ship-based sailors and marines, and adventurers of various stripes. The organized overland force was led by Stephen Kearny, who departed from Fort Leavenworth, Kansas, in the spring of 1846 and proceed westward, ultimately reaching Santa Fe via that town's namesake trail. Once a bit west of Santa Fe, Kearny decided to proceed with only a small fraction of his original 1,600-strong force. He finally made it to San Diego after surviving the Battle of San Pascual in December of 1846, and there, he joined forces with previously shipborne American military personnel under Admiral Robert Stockton, whose forces had already helped take control of key towns in northern California earlier in the year. In those efforts, American troops were sometimes assisted by adventurers like Kit Carson as well as John Fremont of the U.S. Topographical Engineers, who had rounded up sixty armed men and traveled to California looking for action as soon as late 1845.[62] The consolidation of U.S. control of California reached a key milestone in January of 1847, when Stockton and Kearny, starting from San Diego with a combined strength of perhaps just over 500 personnel, took Los Angeles after victories in the Battle of San Gabriel and the Battle of La Mesa.[63]

The culminating campaign of the war took place in the spring and summer of 1847. It was led, as with the Zach Taylor campaign, by an aging and famous general, Winfield Scott. He had begun the war as the nation's top general, based in Washington—but he was always itching to get into the action. Finally, he persuaded Secretary of War William Marcy and President Polk to put him in charge of what was expected to be, and what would indeed prove to be, the war's decisive effort.

With some 10,000 to 12,000 soldiers, Scott gained important help from the navy for what began as a huge amphibious operation, staged initially out of New Orleans, to come ashore in Veracruz, east of Mexico City, in March. A successful siege of that city made possible the ascent into the Mexican highlands toward the nation's capital. After Veracruz, a notable early battle was fought at Cerro Gordo in mid-April. There, army engineers achieved a remarkable engineering feat, building paths through mountainous terrain that was believed impassable by the Mexicans—thus setting up an effective surprise attack. The U.S. victory was decisive even though American forces were outnumbered against Santa Anna's army by roughly 8,500 to 12,000.

The decisive battles for Mexico City would, however, have to await reinforcements arriving from the United States. Thus, they would not begin until late summer, after Scott had spent most of the summer in the town of Puebla to Mexico City's east.[64] By August, Scott's strength reached about 14,000, and he felt ready to move, even though the combined enemy forces were by then more than twice as large. The battles of Contreras and Churubusco took place on August 20, devastating Santa Anna's armies; Mexican casualties, killed plus wounded, were estimated at around 4,000, with U.S. losses only a quarter as great. After a short-lived truce lasting the last week of August and first week of September, the Americans continued their assault. They took the fort of Chapultepec on September 13, inflicting nearly 2,000 more Mexican casualties while again suffering perhaps only a quarter as many themselves. Santa Anna chose to flee, allowing Scott to take control of Mexico City the next day.[65]

Finally, rounding out the century—and the list of all of America's declared wars, including the three discussed in this preface and the two world wars—was the brief Spanish-American War of 1898. It was surely less consequential than all the other wars I've discussed, with the possible exception of the War of 1812, but not inconsequential by any means. The liberation of Cuba was the initial concern, but American imperial ambition metastasized during the war, even as President William McKinley initially sought to put a damper on it. Seizure of the Philippines, Puerto Rico, and Guam from Spain, as well as the acquisition of Hawaii, became goals—and realities—as well.[66]

Cuba had resisted Spanish rule for decades, and America had resented Spain's presence for a long time as well—less out of territorial ambitions than out of jealousy a European power would still hold such sway so close to U.S. shores. To a certain extent, Americans also had concern for the well-being of Cubans. Seeking to pressure Spain into concessions, the United States deployed a warship, the U.S.S. *Maine,* to Cuban waters in early 1898. A deadly explosion on the ship on February, probably, as it turns out, caused by an accident rather than a Spanish mine, provided the United States with all the pretext it needed to launch a war against Spain.[67] Congress declared war in late April during a period in which it also appropriated additional funds for military forces, equipment, and operations.[68] President McKinley's administration proceeded to enlarge the army from some 25,000 to 200,000 soldiers over the ensuing months.[69] The process of building a large army so fast ran into inevitable roadblocks and was far from smooth—but it does seem to have improved as the conflict progressed, even though by mid-August, a bigger and better American army would no longer be needed against Spain.[70]

In this short war, the distinction between battle and campaign was largely erased. The first fighting occurred in Manila Bay on May 1, when Commodore George Dewey destroyed the local Spanish armada. A couple of months later, the United States would annex Hawaii, partly to counter growing Japanese influence there and partly out of perceived need to have a way-station for reaching the Philippines as well as other parts of Asia. "Manifest Destiny" was invoked to justify the move.[71]

The main theater, however, was Cuba. In late April, U.S. warships sailed for the vicinity with the intent of establishing a blockade, cutting undersea telegraph cables out of Cuba, and preparing to intercept any Spanish naval reinforcements that might be forthcoming—notably, as it turned out, those under Admiral Pascual Cervera. The action turned to ground combat in Cuba in June and early July, when Americans teamed up with Cuban revolutionaries to conduct their attacks. There, U.S. forces that included Teddy Roosevelt's volunteers, the fabled volunteer "Rough Riders," won the battles in, around, and for Santiago on the island's east side, including the Battle of San Juan Hill on July 1.[72] U.S. naval forces under Admiral William Sampson then destroyed Cervera's ships in Santiago's main harbor as they sought to flee for the open ocean on July 3.[73]

The action then moved to Puerto Rico between July 25 and August 9, where American forces enjoyed a rapid success against the Spanish units based there. The grounds were thus established for the signing of a peace treaty by which Spain ceded Puerto Rico and Guam to the United States and granted Cuba independence (after what would be a period of U.S. occupation), with its pain lessened somewhat by a cash transfer of $20 million. Negotiations over the treaty continued through the fall, and the Treaty of Paris was signed on December 10, with ratification in the two countries early in the new year.[74]

After the fighting in Puerto Rico, the United States then won the Battle of Manila. It would take more time to formalize the peace, but the fighting was all over by mid-August, less than four months after America's declaration of war.

That is, all the fighting against Spain was over. The ultimate U.S. decision to replace Spain as imperial owner of the Philippines contributed to the outbreak of a guerrilla war that lasted officially until 1902 (and unofficially until much later, with occasional skirmishes for years to come). The battles were difficult and inconclusive for a time and lasted far longer than the Spanish-American War itself. More than 1,000 U.S. soldiers would die in the fighting by 1902; even larger numbers died from disease, and larger numbers yet of Filipinos died over the years in the fighting. Fortunately, the United States would not try its hand at such large-scale colonial rule again.[75] Fortunately as well, despite many errors along the way in its occupation of the Philippines, the United States had a relatively light touch politically in how it administered the country—and thus probably did not wind up poisoning its long-term relationship with that nation as much as many colonizing powers did with their erstwhile colonies.[76]

Two Final Thoughts

Walking through the four wars discussed here reminds us that not all wars are equally long or hard. The Revolutionary War was both long and hard, especially when the population and wealth of the colonies are remembered. The other three wars, especially the Spanish-American War, were not so prolonged or costly, whether in absolute terms or against the expectations that contemporaries held as the conflicts began. In the twentieth and twenty-first centuries, the United States has also used military force in limited ways.

Nonetheless, the observations that I offer in the conclusion remain valid. War is *often* longer, harder, and bloodier than expected—and because there is no going back or attempting a do-over once conflict begins, the long and sanguinary conflicts should be weighted more heavily than the ones that turn out to be easy when assessing the nature of human warfare. By arguing that war is often, even usually, worse than prognosticated, I am not proposing an iron law of history or political science so much as a warning. Even if actual wars turn out to be much more painful than expected only one-half or two-thirds of the time, that is still a very high ratio—and it should serve as a stark warning to anyone who would consider launching a major military endeavor (or even a modest one).

Second, even for the four wars considered here, another observation from the book's conclusion is correct: Wars take unexpected turns, and outcomes are usually not preordained. The Revolutionary War could have gone either way, especially until Saratoga. The War of 1812 did not really need to end in stalemate. Winfield Scott's taking of Mexico City depended on some excellent engineering work by the U.S. Army and clever surprise attacks; had his approach to the Mexican capital failed, it is not clear if the American public would have supported doubling down on the war effort to try again. It may be hard to imagine how Spain could have defeated the United States in 1898, but perhaps I am just not imaginative enough. In any case, for the wars treated here, three out of four do seem to have been up for grabs during much of their respective durations.

If only Putin had thought more about such matters, and such lessons from history, before his invasion of Ukraine in 2022. To the extent we can influence them, let us make sure that the Chinese do so as well. All should remember these lessons, in fact—even we Americans, for as the rest of this book shows as well, we have often downplayed the unpredictability and the difficulty of war in our own history.

Preface and Acknowledgments

This is a book about the big questions of modern American military history: why did wars happen, what were their main phases, how were they fought and won or lost—and could their outcomes have plausibly been different? It also seeks lessons to inform anyone in the United States or elsewhere who is fascinated by questions of strategy, whether at "grand" levels of national purpose or at more specific military levels.

The wars considered here have generated huge literatures already. Throughout this project, and throughout my life, I have been an admirer and consumer of history. I would like to express my gratitude to those professionals who make it their lives' work—as well as my preemptive acknowledgment for undoubtedly missing important dimensions of some of the literature. Moreover, historians through their rigorous research and their analytical excellence continue to improve our understanding of past wars. To take just the example of World War II: in relatively recent years we have learned that blitzkrieg was less tank-centric than often previously understood, that strategic bombing was less effective than expected in weakening the industrial output of America's adversaries, and that aircraft carriers were less dominant overall in the naval warfare of that era than often believed. In writing this book, I was the beneficiary of these and many other profound and important insights produced by the history discipline.

All that said, my goal here is specific and, I hope, complementary to most previous works: to explain the wars' key causes, major campaigns, dynamics, and outcomes conceptually and succinctly. Military history is often extremely detailed. That makes sense. It is the courage, sacrifice, and drama of individuals and peoples trying to achieve victory and avoid defeat and death that inspires and fascinates us at the human level. But the general reader or busy policymaker may also want a more conceptual, and concise, treatment of modern U.S. history's major wars. This book attempts to provide that resource. It begins with the conflict that for the United States marked the beginning of industrialized and large-scale combat, the U.S. Civil War. It examines each world war, then Korea and Vietnam, and concludes with Iraq and Afghanistan.[1]

The narrative here emphasizes what is often termed the operational or campaign level of war. It seeks to link military operations, wartime objectives, and grand strategy. I hope that approach makes it a useful contribution to the literature, together with the fact that it brings the reader into the year 2022, and thus is more contemporary than some earlier surveys of conflicts over the ages. In these ways, it indeed presents military history for the modern strategist.

Individual battles are certainly discussed, too. But the priority is to explain how they fit into a sequence of battles and other events typically lasting multiple months over a given geographic region. Think, for example, of General George McClellan's peninsula campaign that began with a major troop movement by boat down the Chesapeake Bay, designed to seize Richmond during the spring and early summer of 1862 in the U.S. Civil War. Or consider General Robert E. Lee's efforts from late summer 1862 through mid-1863 to take the fight to the North at Antietam and Gettysburg, or General Ulysses S. Grant's laborious but ultimately successful year-long effort to mount a campaign against Lee's armies in Virginia starting in the spring of 1864. Germany's attacks on northern France in the world wars are other salient examples, as are the American island-hopping campaigns during the approaches to Japan in World War II, or General Douglas MacArthur's Inchon landings followed by his fraught decision to move northward toward the Yalu River in the Korean War.

The main purpose of this book is to chronicle, analyze, and reflect upon modern American military history. In that sense, it is a primer. But it is also a primer with a purpose. The central lessons of the book center on the persistent and dangerous proclivity of decisionmakers to display naivete, as well as overconfidence, about the likely courses, costs, and outcomes of war. Vladimir Putin has delivered the world a signature example of this flawed human tendency with his ill-fated aggression against Ukraine. That war began on February 24, 2022; Putin probably expected it would end within days, and certainly by "V-E Day" in Russia on May 9. As of this writing in the summer of 2022, sadly, the conflict continues. Russia's early hopes for a knockout blow against the government, and perhaps even an annexation of much or most of the country, have joined the litany of countless other cases in history in which aggressors began wars with breathless enthusiasm and unwarranted optimism for quick, easy wins.

The danger of overconfidence may increase when policymakers have not recently experienced a cataclysmic event in their own lifetimes or careers. It also grows when the advent of new technologies creates exciting new possibilities for military planners—yet often with accompanying downsides or vulnerabilities that are underappreciated at the time decisionmakers choose to go to war. It also seems most likely when decisionmakers misunderstand or underestimate their potential adversaries—and the human tendency to become more committed to a war, rather than less, once family and friends begin to die at the hands of an enemy. Indeed, to continue with the contemporary Russian example, prior to launching his brazen invasion of Ukraine, Putin had become accustomed to relatively easy wins in places such as Crimea and Syria in recent years, had taken great pride in his military modernization effort of the previous decade that had produced highly-touted new missiles among other weaponry, and had developed a contempt for President Volodymyr Zelensky of Ukraine—as well as the very concept of Ukraine as a truly independent and sovereign nation.[2]

Overconfidence is not always a problem, to be sure. Nor does it typically afflict each party to a major war equally. Perhaps both Union and Confederate sides were naïve about the likely costs of war in 1861, for example; so were most if not all of the belligerents in World War I. But world leaders who chose not to confront Hitler as he violated the terms of the Versailles Treaty, reoccupying the Rhineland and otherwise revving up his military machine and ambitions, were arguably well aware of the potential for enormous devastation that could result from another massive conflict so soon after World War I. The caution of Western leaders did nothing to prevent, and inadvertently may have helped cause World War II (the Munich meeting of 1938 with Hitler, Prime Minister Neville Chamberlain of Britain, and Prime Minister Edouard Daladier of France is often cited as the moment of maximum appeasement of Hitler, though by then it was already becoming too late to stop him in many ways, as discussed below). Their completely sober and rational expectations about the costs of war may have actually worsened their crisis response, making them less willing to confront Hitler at a time when he may still have been partially deterrable (perhaps).

In other conflicts, for example, the United States in Operation Desert Storm against Saddam's Iraq in 1991, as well as the invasion phases of the conflicts in Afghanistan and Iraq starting in 2001 and 2003 respectively, expectations were that war would be much harder than it proved—or, at least, that the initial battles would be harder, as the entireties of those operations obviously did wind up very difficult.

Thus, my observation about the prevalence of overconfidence in war is intended neither as an iron law of political science nor as an admonition to all policymakers to approach crisis management with fear and trepidation. There have been times in human history when accepting the risks and costs of war made sense for at least one party, at a strategic and also even a moral level, compared with the alternative. There have also been numerous times when strengthening deterrence, rather than seeking compromise, has been the crucial ingredient in averting war. There will be such cases in the future, too. I certainly favor strong and credible American and allied strategic postures in today's world, built on military as well as economic and other elements of what U.S. secretary of defense Lloyd Austin and I, among others, have called "integrated deterrence." To invoke concepts pioneered by the late Robert Jervis, the trick for the United States and other powers is to strengthen deterrence without collectively spiraling into arms races, escalatory crisis management paradigms, and any tendency toward itchy trigger fingers.[3]

In an era of nuclear weapons, the warning about overconfidence seems particularly appropriate. Because this book is about military history for the modern strategist, it is worth underscoring the past proclivity of many leaders to downplay the likely costs of war and exaggerate their own country's prospects of rapid battlefield success. None of the wars analyzed here happened by accident. But most happened with a good deal of naivete, or at least extreme hopefulness, on the part of numerous participants.

A corollary observation or theme is that the outcomes of most wars the United States has fought since 1861 could quite plausibly have been different. The Confederacy could have outlasted the North in the Civil War. Germany's Schlieffen Plan in 1914—which will be discussed at length later—might have achieved its goal of the rapid conquest of France. Germany and Japan might have left the Soviet Union and the United States out of their crosshairs in World War II, and had much better prospects for achieving more limited but still quite grandiose objectives. The Korean War could have, and in fact did, go either way (or both ways). The list goes on. It is too easy when reading history, and knowing the results of past wars, to slip into the facile or even subconscious assumption that most outcomes were meant to be—that is, overdetermined by the larger forces of history. Such thinking is incorrect.

In all of this, leaders matter greatly. The American Civil War would not have happened the same way, or perhaps even at all, without specific figures like Lincoln, Lee, and Grant. The world wars would not have unfolded similarly absent Kaiser Wilhelm II and Hitler, Czar Nicholas II and Joseph Stalin, Woodrow Wilson and Franklin Roosevelt and Winston Churchill—the lists go on. Leaders matter. So do innovators, at the level of technology, tactics, and operational concepts in war.

Another theme centers on geography. The advanced, densely populated, closely spaced, and heavily industrialized countries of Europe brought us both world wars, with Japan important as well. The roles of Russia and the United States were much different, but also heavily influenced by their geography. It gave them strategic buffers, as well as large resource bases—but not such great separation from other nations as to preclude their crucial involvement in the main fights of each saga. Just like the case with world leaders, geography still remains crucial today, even in an era of global communications and of intercontinental-range weaponry.

A third matter for the modern strategist studying history to reflect upon concerns the role of alliances in the outbreak and conduct of war. When alliances are shaky or undependable, or nonexistent, conflict seems more likely. World War I and World War II both featured a number of nebulous or conditional security pacts involving several of their main protagonists; these failed to deter conflict. For its part, the United States was disengaged militarily from Eurasia, and thus also failed to wield meaningful deterrent power. By contrast, World War III has not occurred throughout the period when the United States has been engaged with firm security commitments, strong alliances, and forward-deployed military forces. America's wars since 1945 have generally occurred in places where U.S. alliances and commitments did not exist or apply.

Military preparedness is important, for deterrence in particular, as several cases of deterrence failure discussed in this book underscore. National resoluteness in the face of an ambitious and aggressive adversary is important too in order to reduce the chances that aggressive would-be adversaries will themselves become overconfident about their odds of successful attack. But restraint, and caution, are crucial attributes for policymakers as well. When they are not present, crises can quickly escalate. The outbreak of World War I should be as much on our minds as that of World

War II, and the conflicts had very different types of causes. For the particular case of the United States today, as I have previously argued in my 2021 book, *The Art of War in an Age of Peace*, Washington should center its grand strategy on a concept of "resolute restraint," with equal emphasis on both of those words. We should be resolute in defense of core and key interests. We should however be reluctant to take on additional security commitments, and should generally manage any great-power crises that may erupt with a top priority on de-escalation and rapid war termination.

The likelihood of foolish and unnecessary decisions to choose war as an instrument of policy often grows when leaders are not thoughtful students of history. By contrast, when they develop historical models and analogies—as when Kennedy administration officials thought about the outbreak of World War I during the Cuban Missile Crisis—they often display greater wisdom, provided that they not fixate on single cases or precedents.[4] History can offer inspiration, from the courage and wisdom of those who have gone before. It can also offer many vivid cautionary tales. But it needs to be invoked with considerable care and nuance, requiring that it be systematically studied and debated. There is no single and simple lesson of history that should automatically guide future behavior or strategic decision-making by the leaders of today and tomorrow. That is why the modern strategist must have a good, textured, and balanced working knowledge of military history to do her or his job well.

There is a clear warning for the present day in these pages. How to avoid overconfidence in one's own strategic community, and to discourage it in the minds of would-be adversaries? With Russia's resurgence and China's rise, to say nothing of a nuclear-armed North Korea and other challenges, this message is especially timely. The words of Holocaust survivor Viktor Frankl capture the dilemma well: "So, let us be alert—alert in a twofold sense: Since Auschwitz we know what man is capable of. And since Hiroshima we know what is at stake."[5]

In my experience, military history is underappreciated in much of American academia, especially in many political science departments and policy schools. Knowledge about major past wars is often either presumed or considered relatively unimportant, or viewed principally as data for statistical analyses. As a community, we need to do better at teaching, and discussing and debating, military history for the modern strategist. This book, I hope, will constitute a modest contribution in that direction.

In a related vein, I owe an enormous debt of gratitude to those political scientists who *do* value history—many of whom have been my professors, colleagues, and friends—as well as to other inspirations from other
walks of life. A number of people read much or all of the book and provided absolutely invaluable feedback, though remaining mistakes are all
my responsibility, of course. My profound gratitude goes out to John Allen,
Dick Betts, Steve Biddle (who provided an extremely thorough and helpful review of the manuscript), Richard Bush, Kurt Campbell, Eliot Cohen,
Conrad Crane, Walter Cronkite (all three of the generations I've been
blessed to know), Ivo Daalder, Ray Della of Canandaigua Academy in an
earlier life, Hal Feiveson (such a crucial mentor and great friend to me),
Michele Flournoy, Lawry Freedman, Aaron Friedberg, Mike Green, Bob
Jervis, Bob Kagan, Fred Kagan, Kim Kagan, Jim Mattis, Stan McChrystal, David Miller of Hamilton College, Jim Miller, Michael Neiberg, my
father, Edward O'Hanlon, Dave Petraeus, Barry Posen, Ken Pollack (with
his unbelievably attentive reading of most of the book), Yelba Quinn, Alejandra Rocha, Chris Schroeder, Steve Solarz (what an avid reader and
great mind), Jim Steinberg, Bob Swartout, Steve Swartout, Woody Turner
(a lifelong friend whose fascination with and knowledge of history is exemplary, and who did much to inspire me to attempt this book), Richard
Ullman, Steve Van Evera, Steve Walt (who told me after general exams to
keep reading history), Paul Wolfowitz, Katherine Zimmerman, and at
Brookings, Bill Finan (a real hero of the place), Suzanne Maloney (with
her selfless, exemplary leadership), Melanie Sisson, Strobe Talbott, Caitlin Talmadge, Adam Twardowski, Tom Wright, Cole Beaty, Jack Bradley,
Alejandra Rocha, and Lily Windholz, and an anonymous reviewer.

Applying history's lessons to today, American strategists and policymakers must prevent a potential adversary from becoming overconfident
about its ability to defeat the United States in war. We need to prevent
such theories of victory from dominating the decision calculus of key foreign actors. That would require, among other things, doing what we can
to disabuse a would-be attacker of any realistic belief that it could exploit major vulnerabilities in our command, control, communications and
reconnaissance systems, our forward military bases and big assets, our
computer networks, and the domestic infrastructure that would help move
and support U.S. and Allied forces. We cannot let an enemy think that by
finding and striking a modern-day Achilles heel it could knock the United
States out of a war long enough to create a fait accompli and perhaps persuade us not to fight thereafter. We also need to be as clear as possible

about what we would really fight to defend, without trying to defend too much, either.

By the same token, the United States needs to avoid developing over-confidence in its own prowess. The size of the U.S. defense budget, the excellence of its technology, the remarkable qualities of its men and women in uniform, and the strength of American alliances position the nation very well in today's global order. But they would hardly make it easy or straight-forward for the United States to defeat Chinese or Russian aggression in places close to the borders of those nations. The Pentagon has plans today for waging war quickly and early in the so-called contact and blunt phases of conflict—right after a limited adversarial action might begin, say over the Senkaku Islands in the East China Sea, or shipping lanes in the South China Sea, or Taiwan, or the Baltic nations in Europe. I worry that such thinking could, if misapplied, lead to military plans that resem-ble Germany's Schlieffen Plan of World War I—an elaborate and escala-tory concept for combat operations that requires a quick decision to go to war even when provocations are modest and information is murky.

The U.S. Department of Defense, and government as a whole, needs to develop capabilities—and avoid vulnerabilities—that enhance deterrence by preventing an adversary from perceiving any crucial vulnerability in America's defense posture, or its political will. Thus, there are lessons here for the technologist and tactician and military planner, as well as the higher-level strategist.

We must ensure that no foe develops overconfidence in its ability to defeat the United States. But America itself also needs to avoid overcon-fidence about its own ability to wage war decisively and successfully. One of military history's purposes must be to remind us of such principles, es-pecially in times of rapid technological and strategic change.

ONE　　　*The American Civil War*

The American Civil War is a tragic tale of combat that decimated and nearly destroyed the young United States. More than 10 percent of the country's total population served. Union military strength peaked at around 700,000, and over the course of the war some 2.5 million served in its ranks. Respective Confederate figures were 40 to 50 percent as great. Some fifty major battles and another hundred smaller fights were waged over a period of almost exactly four years.[1]

Roughly three-quarters of a million combatants on the two sides died. Those losses came out of a combined American population only a tenth of today's, just over 30 million. Thus, deaths in the war constituted about 2.5 percent of all Americans of the time—and of course a far greater percentage than that among young men. The percentage was higher still among white Southern men, who were outnumbered more than 3:1 in this struggle, and suffered about three-fourths as many estimated total fatalities. (The prewar population of the United States was roughly 20 million in the North, including border states, and some 9 million in the South of whom about 3.5 million were slaves, with the remainder in western territories.)[2] Hundreds of thousands more were severely injured or maimed.[3] Those fatality totals probably exceed the *aggregate* American losses in both world wars, Korea, Vietnam—and every other war in U.S. history, all added together. Even though the adjusted budgetary cost of the Civil War was closer to that of Operation Desert Storm than to the world wars or Korea, Vietnam, Iraq, and Afghanistan—in the range of $100 billion, by contrast to $400 billion for World War I as well as Korea, roughly $1 trillion or more for Vietnam, Iraq, and Afghanistan (each), almost $5 trillion for World War II—its human toll in terms of American casualties was enormous.[4]

Modern strategists and policymakers need to have a working knowledge of the American Civil War—not only to understand the nation's history, but

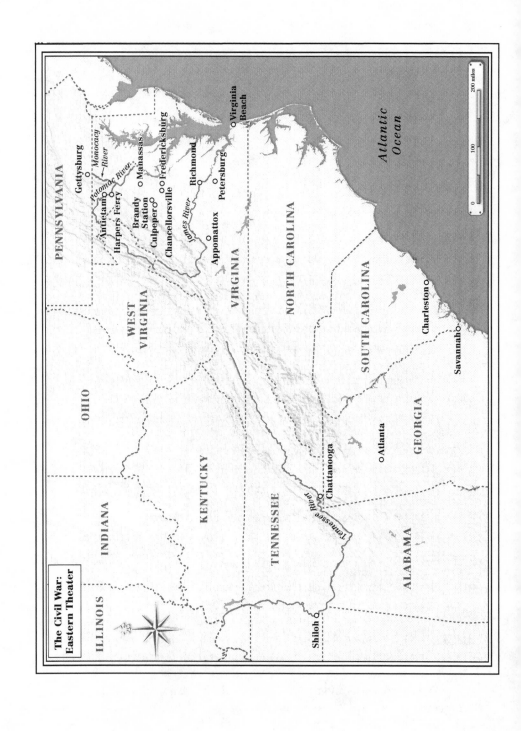

The Civil War:
Eastern Theater

ILLINOIS

INDIANA

OHIO

KENTUCKY

WEST VIRGINIA

TENNESSEE

VIRGINIA

NORTH CAROLINA

SOUTH CAROLINA

GEORGIA

ALABAMA

PENNSYLVANIA

Atlantic Ocean

Gettysburg

Monocacy River

Potomac River

Antietam
Harpers Ferry

Brandy Station
Culpeper

Manassas

Fredericksburg

Chancellorsville

Richmond

James River

Petersburg

Appomattox

Virginia Beach

Charleston

Savannah

Atlanta

Chattanooga

Tennessee River

Shiloh

200 miles
0   100

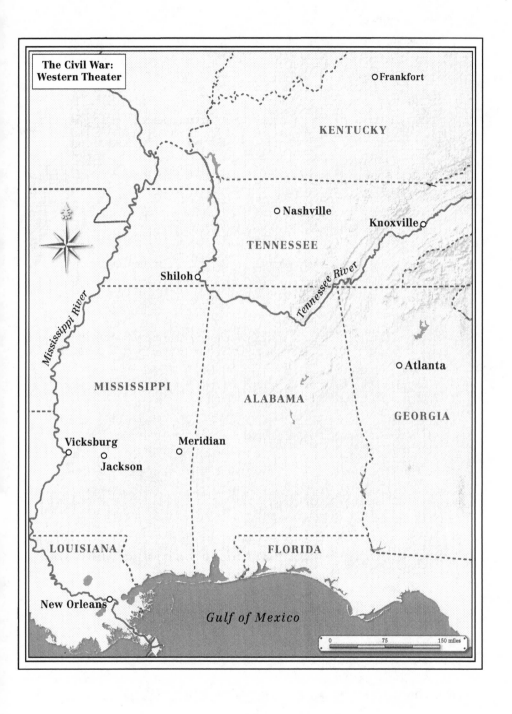

The Civil War:
Western Theater

o Frankfort

KENTUCKY

o Nashville

Knoxville o

TENNESSEE

Shiloh o

Tennessee River

Mississippi River

o Atlanta

MISSISSIPPI

ALABAMA

GEORGIA

Vicksburg   Meridian
   o   o
   Jackson

LOUISIANA   FLORIDA

New Orleans o

Gulf of Mexico

0   75   150 miles

to draw lessons about the nature of modern warfare. The American Civil War was arguably the first modern conflict of history—waged on an industrial scale, using a wide range of new and rapidly evolving technologies, and involving the whole of society. Napoleon's wars had displayed some of these characteristics but not all of them.

The duration and the huge costs of the war were not anticipated by virtually anyone. Had they been foreseen, even recognized as possible, perhaps war would have been avoided or undertaken in a much different way. To a large extent, the nature of the war probably should have been foreseeable. Some related technologies of modern warfare—and their effects on exposed human flesh—had been battle-tested already in the Crimean war of the previous decade. Moreover, the willingness of Confederate forces to wage a war of attrition in the hopes of wearing out Union patience and will was far from unthinkable, given the passions that surrounded the issues at hand. Nor was it completely irrational, in the sense that it had some chance of ultimate success—even if was morally regrettable and extremely risky. Nor, once the basic immoral decision to divide the nation to protect slavery had been made, was such a military concept focused on enemy attrition and will itself immoral. The primary way in which the South fought the North—the targeting of Union armies, mostly on Confederate territory—comported with most elements of just-war theory, even if the broader war was not just.

It would admittedly have been very difficult to avoid the conflict, given how deeply America's original sin of slavery had become interwoven with the economy and culture of the South, and hence the politics of the United States. The American Civil War was in the eyes of many participants an existential struggle for what they held most dear: for many Southerners, their economic system and their very way of life, as well as their powerful sense of local and regional identity; for many Northerners, the existence of the Union together with commitment to the principles of human equality and human rights articulated in America (if not implemented) ever since the Declaration of Independence was written.

Yet leaders of both North and South also went to war with an overconfidence about their prospects for rapid success, politically or militarily. This simple observation, developed further below, is perhaps the single most important lesson that the American Civil War holds for current policymakers and strategists. It is a warning about the unpredictability of war, as well as the tragic tendency of human beings to believe they can control it much more than generally proves to be possible. It does not mean the North was wrong to fight the war, or that Abraham Lincoln was anything other than America's greatest president in the nation's history. It does suggest that even people who believe they are following noble pursuits can wind up in horribly sanguinary conflicts.

To understand the chronology of the war, it is important to understand the period leading up to the spring of 1861. How could the nation find itself engaged in existential conflict of brother against brother, sister against sister, friend against friend, father against son—and do so with so little awareness of how devastating the conflict could be in military, economic, and human terms? Thus, an equally central part of the story of the American Civil War is what happened in the months just before and after the first shots were fired at Fort Sumter, South Carolina, in April 1861. It is during this period that key military preparations were made—or were not made, as the case may be—revealing prevalent expectations for a relatively short war.

The Weapons of War, Character of the Conflict, and Strategies of the Protagonists

The American Civil War is a military story about foot soldiers, horses, railroads, ships moving troops and enforcing blockades, the telegraph, improvements in rifles as well as rifled artillery, and mass-mobilizing societies. The railroad, telegraph, and rifle in particular ushered in a type of revolution in military affairs in this period.[5]

Less impressive was the state of medical care for those who were hurt or sick. Capacity for mobile medical care was sorely lacking. The wounded were treated with methods that predated the understanding of microbiology and bacteria (and drank a little whiskey before any necessary amputations, if they were lucky enough that it was available). Heroic efforts by innovators in field medicine such as Florence Nightingale, in the decade before during the Crimean War, and Clara Barton during the Civil War itself, could only partially mitigate these glum realities. Disease often ravaged troop concentrations more than enemy fire did.

Railroads were used for large movements of troops and supplies like never before in warfare. They were far more available than in the past—with 30,000 miles of track nationwide when the war began (in contrast to only one-tenth as much as recently as 1840).[6]

Ships were used in important ways as well. For example, after Nashville, Tennessee fell to the North in February 1862, it became a major staging and supply base for Union forces in the broader theater throughout the war, ultimately receiving some 200 shiploads of supplies, as well as dozens of daily railcar arrivals.[7] Horses were used to pull supply wagons on roads and to outfit cavalry on both sides, which served as the eyes and ears and "special forces" of the respective armies (analogous to today's drones, reconnaissance aircraft, satellites, and electronic intelligence platforms). Most soldiers walked, with shoes if they were lucky.

Battlefield communication was generally conducted by men on horseback, as well as signal flags. Strategic communication with national capitals and between major military commands was by telegraph whenever working lines could be maintained or established and protected. These links helped bring in reinforcements from distant locations at key junctures in various battles and ensure adequate logistics support. They were generally not used by Washington or Richmond to micromanage tactical decisions and operations.

The key weapons of war were artillery and muskets. Rifled muskets, used with so-called Minié balls, used a grooved barrel to create spin—resulting in greater accuracy than earlier bullets, though the degree of improvement remains debatable.[8] Breech-loading rifles, which did not require a soldier to stand up to place a new cartridge with bullet and powder charge down the muzzle of the gun made their debut too, with Union forces in particular. Weapons like Sharps and Spencer rifles, the latter capable of holding seven bullets in a single magazine, played a growing role during the conflict as well.[9]

Naval warfare began to enter an era of major change during the Civil War. The signature battle was the duel between two partially armored ships, the *Merrimack/Virginia* on the Confederate side and the *Monitor* on the Union side. They fought to a standoff on March 9, 1862, after pounding each other incessantly but ineffectually with the guns of the day. Mines and fledgling concepts for submarines and torpedoes also made their appearance, all to limited effect.[10] Observation balloons saw action too, but again, played only a niche role overall.[11]

Key elements of successful defenses utilized trenches that were often quickly dug when an engagement could be anticipated. The shovel arguably became more important than the bayonet as the war progressed.[12]

Effective tactics often involved using surprise and speed to attack an enemy from the flank or rear. In such situations, the adversary's defensive preparations would be less useful, its soft underbelly of logistics support more exposed, and its vulnerability greatest to "enfilade" fire—by which artillery could aim in the right general direction and be fairly confident of hitting enemy troops regardless of exact range.[13] Yet artillery preparations of the battlefield before a wave of soldiers charged an established defensive position on foot could usually only do so much. The fuses of the day were not up to the task of precisely detonating rounds at trench lines, battlefield reconnaissance capabilities were limited, and artillery gunners could be targeted by snipers with rifles if they tried to get close.[14]

The war lasted almost exactly four years—and almost exactly overlapped, hardly coincidentally, with the Lincoln presidency. It had, broadly speaking, two major theaters and several major ebbs, flows, and turning points. In the eastern theater, General Robert E. Lee led Confederate forces for most of the war, and a succession of generals, culminating with George Meade and Ulysses S. Grant, led Union forces. The two sides faced off throughout the struggle in regions encompassing Richmond, peninsulas to the east, the Shenandoah Valley to the west, forest and farmland throughout—including, of course, parts of Maryland and Pennsylvania as well.

In the broadly defined western theater, which included the area from Kentucky and Tennessee to Mississippi and Louisiana, and even Arkansas and Missouri in more limited ways, Union forces had ups and downs but made more consistent progress. They established increasing control along the Mississippi River, culminating in the taking of New Orleans in 1862 as well as the ultimately successful siege of Vicksburg in 1863. The two theaters ultimately converged, as Union positions in southeastern Tennessee allowed for General William Tecumseh Sherman's attacks on Atlanta and then his "March to the Sea."

Most battles were in daylight hours. They typically lasted one to three days. It was usually harder even for winners to fight longer than that, or to consolidate victories with rapid follow-on maneuvers and operations, given the intensity and bloodiness of the combat.[15]

The main military goal of the Confederacy was to endure long enough on the battlefield to convince Union leaders, or failing that Union voters, that it was not worth the trouble of forcibly reunifying the country. It almost worked. Even if it could be couched in defensive terms, this concept of victory often went along with an offensive mindset, in terms of campaign plans and battle tactics, by Confederate generals including Lee, Stonewall Jackson, and J. E. B. "Jeb" Stuart (of those three, only Lee survived the war). Confederacy President Jefferson Davis, himself a West

Point graduate and former U.S. secretary of war, also subscribed to "offensive-defensive" thinking.[16] The history of Napoleon's wars, with their great decisive battles in the early 1800s, influenced the Confederate leaders' theories of successful warfare.[17] They also hoped to gain international recognition for the Confederacy, and create a momentum that would have psychological effects in both North and South, with convincing victories. This approach ultimately failed, of course, for the South. Still, it must be acknowledged that several of these Confederate generals were tactically very clever, often leaving small defensive forces to guard established positions and then using maneuver and ruse to create favorable conditions for their attacks.

The initial wartime goal of the Union involved forcing the South to take on the role of aggressor. That would, Lincoln hoped, make pro-Union Southerners think twice about sustaining something so radical as a secessionist war. It would also attempt to maximize sympathies in the North, border states, and foreign countries for the Union cause. In other words, Lincoln was quite Clausewitzian in his basic thinking, naturally recognizing the interplay between politics and military operations. Of course, the sequence of events had a different prevalent interpretation in the South; Jefferson Davis, in reflecting on how the North portrayed the events at Sumter, wrote that "it was cunningly attempted to show that the South, which had been pleading for peace and still stood on the defensive, had by this [bloodless] bombardment inaugurated a war against the United States."[18]

Once that more political approach failed, however, Union war aims changed and escalated. They then included threatening Richmond in the belief that taking the South's capital might effectively destroy the Confederacy. They also included weakening main Southern forces to the point where they could no longer resist the North's terms. The first approach viewed the Confederate capital as the South's center of gravity; the second saw Confederate forces as the main objective. They were often pursued simultaneously, largely because threatening Richmond tended to induce Confederate armies to try to block the Union advances—and fight. A complementary Union objective was an attempt to strangle the Southern economy with military operations from the Mississippi to main Atlantic and Gulf ports (through blockade) to the major railroad networks of the South. Indeed, the head of all Union forces at the war's start, General Winfield Scott, advocated prioritizing this approach over ground warfare, and called it the "Anaconda" strategy. Lincoln himself believed, from fairly early on in the war, that destroying Lee's army was the center of gravity of the war effort, so he included Anaconda in the Union strategic plan but did not rely principally upon it.[19] Grant also viewed Confederate forces—Lee's, as well as those in other theaters—as the main focus of his own strategy once in overall command of Union forces starting in March 1864.

Grant and Sherman became the signature successful generals of the Union war effort. For Grant, the key to success was understanding his overall numerical advantage and the difficulty of Lee's position in pro- tecting Richmond as well as his own forces. Thus, Grant was relentless in the campaign of 1864–1865, even when he experienced tactical frustra- tions and defeats. For Sherman, the crucial insight was understanding the power of maneuver, in a different kind of geographic theater. In threaten- ing Atlanta in 1864, he sought advantageous places to fight, largely avoid- ing direct attack against entrenched Confederate units. Later, he chose to break free from his dependence on the railroad, plowing through a large swath of Georgia and then the Carolinas while living off the land (and destroying much of what his men could not consume). His methods raise difficult questions about whether the ends justify the means in such a war of national survival; I do not attempt to resolve such questions here, only to flag them in the context of a broader historical discussion.[20]

There were also many mediocre generals on both sides. That was partly because politics often playing a role in their selection—especially (though not exclusively) on the Union side, and especially in the war's early years.[21] Sometimes, the military officers on opposing sides knew each other well from their educations at West Point, or from common service in the army, including in the U.S.-Mexico War of 1846–1847. The relatively easy com- bat experiences in that earlier campaign may have contributed to the over- confidence that many brought to the Civil War in the early going. About a quarter of the U.S. Army officer corps defected to the South and fought for the Confederacy.[22] A number of them were excellent. As historian Bruce Catton put it about the best Confederate generals, "They fought all-out. If they hit at all they hit with everything there was. They had an exultant ac- ceptance for the chances of war. They fought as if they enjoyed it, and they probably did. The Army of the Potomac [in the early years] just was not getting that kind of leadership."[23] Eventually, however, the Union army would—and then, its huge advantages in manpower and materiel would finally carry the day. But that day would be a long time coming.

Overconfidence, Naivete, and the Path to War

To say that leaders, and citizens, in North and South were overconfident about their respective prospects for rapid victory is not to say that Americans took the possibility of civil war lightly. There was a passion and a gravity to political debate in the years leading up to the conflict of a type rarely rivaled in the history of the United States. Both sides, North and South, had long anticipated the possibility of an existential struggle for the nation rooted in the "peculiar institution" of American slavery. Slavery has been described as the nation's original sin. Not only did it bother many at a moral level—with varying degrees of guilt, to be sure, since many of the very individuals who were troubled by slavery also owned slaves. But already, they anticipated how it could divide the nation, by race and by region.

The pace of discord picked up in the ten to fifteen years before the Civil War began. Slavery and states' rights issues increasingly dominated the politics of the United States. They resulted in, among other things, the Fugitive Slave Act of 1850, which was designed to help slaveowners retrieve escaped slaves from the North; the Kansas-Nebraska Act of 1854, which superseded the 1820 Missouri Compromise and allowed more all-out competition over where slavery might spread; the 1857 Dred Scott decision rejecting numerous constitutional and legal rights for blacks; the Abraham Lincoln-Stephen Douglas Senate debates of 1858; and of course the fateful presidential election of 1860. The territorial acquisitions resulting from the 1846–1847 U.S.-Mexican War intensified the discord. As new territories prepared to become states, they threatened to change the balance of power between slaveholding and free states, with ominous portents for the future for both sides. Secession talk became more prevalent as a result. The division of the nation seemed possible.[24]

Still, most of the churn and angst of the 1840s and 1850s had little to do with preparing for actual war. The debates were more political and more philosophical. Indeed, much of the abolitionist movement was pacifist and idealistic. Even as the possible use of violence became more thinkable to some as the 1850s unfolded, the debate was couched largely in lofty and abstract terms, such as Frederick Douglass's argument in an 1859 editorial that accepted the possibility of war if necessary, because "If speech could end slavery, it would have been done long ago."[25] For their part, most secessionists did not anticipate a robust Northern military response, should they make good on their aspirations for separation.

Even as actual secession approached toward the end of the 1850s, few expected a long war. Violence was increasingly a part of the story, to be sure—as in Kansas, between partisans of pro-slavery and anti-slavery groups; with the infamous 1856 caning in the U.S. Capitol of Massachusetts Senator Charles Sumner by Congressman Preston Brooks of South Carolina; and in abolitionist John Brown's zealous and violent 1859 raid at Harpers Ferry, West Virginia (still part of Virginia at that time), which led to his hanging. But the notion of a major war was far from most people's minds. For example, to the extent that fears of violence grew in the South, it was largely the worry that the kind of vigilantism organized (badly) by John Brown at Harpers Ferry could spread, not that federal armies would come to impose their will and occupy the South.[26] As Confederate President Jefferson Davis wrote in his memoirs, in 1861, "there was a prevailing belief that there would be no war or, if any, that it would be of very short duration."[27] While Davis did not share this view, he also failed to foresee the carnage to follow, having spoken of it costing "thousands of lives" when in fact the eventual toll reached three-quarters of a million.[28] Lincoln's main concern was to check slavery's spread but at the same time to find any way possible to avoid secession, and war, even at the price of tolerating slavery indefinitely in the South.[29] Militia movements gained greater appeal, but this was at the individual state level, and did not amount to serious and coordinated military preparation.[30]

As the presidential transition from James Buchanan to Abraham Lincoln took place on March 4, 1861, Union army forces remained fewer than 20,000, spread across the nation's vast territory, with no more than 4,000 east of the Mississippi.[31] Indeed, as James McPherson wrote, "The strongest armed forces during the winter of 1860–1861 were the militias of seceding states."[32] The Union army only had two officers who had commanded as much as a brigade in battle before and both were over 70 years old. Its general-in-chief, Winfield Scott, was 74 years old and showed his age, with a proclivity for falling asleep during conferences. The army had no general staff, no strategy, and no plans for how to mobilize larger forces.[33] It also began the war with no intelligence organization.[34] The War Department had 93 employees. Naval forces were not much more ready for battle.

West Point cadets of the day studied more math and engineering than strategy or Carl von Clausewitz, the great Prussian scholar of the century. Images of easy or at least fast and glorious conquest in the U.S.-Mexico War probably influenced their collective thinking too much. As historian and strategist Russell Weigley has argued, the most popular military text of the day, written by an important future Union general, failed to conceptualize strategy properly—viewing it more as preparation for a great battle than a plausible overall path to victory.[35] The historian Stephen Ambrose wrote that, "Like most Americans, the cadets assumed the war would consist of one gigantic battle, with the winner marching on and capturing the loser's capital."[36] The Civil War predated the development of modern computational methods for predicting combat dynamics and outcomes But no one even seemed to sketch out intuitively what might happen if two large forces of relatively comparable size and equipment fought all-out against each other until one side's armies were rendered largely ineffective.

In some sense, military preparations in the North could not get too far ahead of the politics of the situation. Not wanting to provoke secessionists, Lincoln had not tried to build up Northern armies in the early weeks of his presidency.[37] He directed his energies toward trying to prevent war—or at least giving the South the last clear chance to avoid it. As he said to adviser John Hay in April of 1861, "My policy is to have no policy." Lincoln and his old nemesis, Stephen Douglas, met at the White House on the very day—April 14, 1861—when the Union flag came down as Fort Sumter surrendered to Confederate forces. At their meeting, in a twist that was ironic given their earlier policy disagreements about the future of slavery, it was Douglas who recommended the more robust approach. He suggested that Lincoln, who was planning to ask Congress for funds for 75,000 troops, instead ask for funding for 200,000. While far from cavalier about what was happening to the nation, Lincoln himself did not grasp where any war might be headed—or how he might, as commander in chief, successfully prosecute it.[38] Like many, he saw secession as a faddish insurrection driven by a vocal minority within the new Confederacy. Once deftly put in its place, that minority would, according to this view, quickly be suppressed politically by wiser and more numerous Southern supporters of the Union—a silent majority, if you will.[39] In January of 1861, just before becoming president, he told a visitor, "I cannot see that more than two or three regiments will be required to execute all the United States laws in disaffected States."[40] As Lincoln had said campaigning for president in the summer of 1860, "The people of the South have too much of good sense, and good temper, to attempt the ruin of the government. At least, so I hope and believe."[41]

Lincoln hardly took the idea of war lightly, of course, and believed the South could give a good fight if combat really ever began.[42] But neither Lincoln nor his advisers were seriously contemplating what the nature of any war might be, or what strategy and associated effort might be needed to win it, before the war began. Lincoln had other things to worry about. The fundamental identity, purpose, and character of the nation were at stake.[43] He also remained anxious throughout not to make the secessionists believe they were at risk from the Union so as to avoid giving them a pretext to act first and thereby create a *fait accompli*, and to avoid fanning sympathies for secessionists in the crucial border states of Delaware, Maryland, Kentucky, Missouri, and what was to become West Virginia. As he said in his first inaugural address on March 4, 1861.

> There needs to be no bloodshed or violence, and there shall be none unless it be forced upon the national authority. The power confided to me will be used to hold, occupy, and possess the property and places belonging to the government and to collect the duties and imposts; but beyond what may be necessary for these objects, there will be no invasion, no using of force against or among the people anywhere.[44]

As he later reflected in his second inaugural address on March 4, 1865: "Neither party expected for the war, the magnitude, or the duration, which it has already attained."[45]

It is hard to blame Lincoln for not spending hours poring over war plans or conducting detailed wargames (none of which existed in any case). He was working doggedly on the politics of the war—and the politics were integral to its military dimensions too. The question of whether the five border states would remain cohesive as well as inside the Union, and whether unionists within the Confederacy itself might force an end to the secession and the conflict, had crucial implications for how any combat would go. Yet the inattention to military preparedness is still striking. Even in Lincoln's July 4, 1861, address to Congress, when the president asked for funding for 400,000 more troops to make this "contest a short and decisive one," he still used the phrase of "suppressing the rebellion" to indicate his instincts, or at least his hopes, about the nature of the campaign that lay ahead.[46] The use of the term "rebellion" was largely based on Lincoln's consistent, steadfast refusal to recognize the legality of secession or the standing of the Confederate states. But his choice of verb implied an expectation of a relatively short effort. Yes, he did in these months authorize the construction of a new factory to produce arms, in Illinois.[47] So his expectations were not of a "cakewalk." But the true nature of what lay ahead was hardly evident to the president.

One further telling indicator of this situation was the choice for head of the War Department. As a consolation prize of sorts for a poorly regarded but influential man named Simon Cameron, who had wanted to be secretary of the treasury, Lincoln instead gave him the choice of running the War Department or Interior Department. Lincoln did not evidence a strong preference. Sadly for the Union, Cameron chose the former. He wound up leading the Department of War throughout the rest of 1861 even as allegations of fraud and corruption surrounded his leadership, bogging down the North's military preparations when it was crucial that the Union move full speed ahead. In the words of Lincoln biographer David Herbert Donald, "The appointment suggested how far Lincoln was from thinking about war."[48]

The seceding states were also more focused on the momentous decision of seceding, and forming a Confederacy, then preparing for a protracted war that might ensue from those acts. When the Southern states seceded, they did not declare war. Instead, they asked only to be left alone to pursue their chosen way of life. Hence the durability, even in the South today, of the expression the "war of northern aggression." That proud and self-righteous sense of self-determination and aggrievement contributed to the South's Pollyannaish views of its prospects in any war against a group of states with more than three times the white population of the South's own. Many Southerners felt their culture possessed greater gallantry, virtue, and martial skills than did peoples of the North. Virginia's proud heritage as the birthplace and home of numerous presidents, together with its considerable economic power, reinforced the narrative. Southerners also expected a certain amount of help from abroad, largely out of a belief that the world needed their cotton more than would prove to be the case, as other supplies were to be found in other countries such as Egypt and India.

Robert E. Lee may have been more realistic in his expectations about the likely course of the looming war. But he was an exception; as his aide Walter Taylor put it, Lee "alone, of all those then known to me . . . expressed his most serious apprehensions of a prolonged and bloody war," and, "looked upon the vaporific declamations of those on each side who proposed to wipe their adversaries from the face of the Earth in ninety days as bombastic and foolish."[49] Still, Lee appears to have believed the South had a good chance to prevail and retain its new independence—at least until the aftermath of the Battle of Gettysburg in July 1863.

These common Southern attitudes of superiority and resulting overconfidence were only reinforced in the war's early going, such as the Confederate victory, discussed further below, over underprepared Union forces at the First Battle of Manassas on July 21, 1861.[50] In addition, as Shelby Foote noted, "The South had the proud example of the American Revolution, where the odds were even longer against those in rebellion."[51]

None of this is to say that America was inherently a peaceful place in the nineteenth century. That was the period when the nation, initially covering just a swath of the eastern coastal region of North America, expanded from sea to shining sea. Often violence was part of the equation— first in the revolt against the British, continuously against Native Americans, ultimately against Mexico as well as Spain. The historian and strategist Robert Kagan has called America in this period a "dangerous nation." But the combined violence levels, and military mobilizations, of all of these other struggles were minuscule to modest in comparison with what was coming in the Civil War. At no time in its history until the world wars did the United States have anything remotely like the size and scale of its armed forces during the Civil War. Total estimated American fatalities for each previous conflict, and each subsequent one until World War I, typically numbered in the low thousands.[52] As James McPherson put it, "In 1861 many Americans had a romantic, glamorous idea of war." Another of his elegant encapsulations, describing the Confederate mobilization of 1861, was that "expecting a short and glorious war, Southern boys rushed to join the colors before the fun was over."[53]

Whatever overconfidence or naivete about the likely future course of battle that existed at war's outset did not last that long after the shooting started. Although Ulysses S. Grant acknowledged that he and many others expected a relatively short war at least until the battle of Shiloh in Tennessee in April 1862, both sides were building up for protracted war by that point, with major mobilizations of soldiers and production of weaponry.[54] Indeed, by the late summer of 1861, General McClellan's proclivity for extreme caution, and thus delay and procrastination, became at least as injurious to the Union cause as any overconfidence. But one cannot reread and relive the years leading up to 1861 without noticing that neither side seems to have had the slightest idea what war could really bring.

To be sure, once the horrors began, both sides showed remarkable spine. Many Americans from all walks of life served in this terrible war.[55] On both sides they found powerful motivation in ethics, religion, attachment to their respective cultures and ways of life, and the common conviction that the stakes of this conflict warranted a great deal of sacrifice if necessary.[56] Yet great sacrifice on the battlefield is not what they, or their leaders, generally expected at first. Indeed, with perhaps some slight dramatization, Bruce Catton tellingly captured the early-war mood among most soldiers:

> The army had been gay when it went out. The point that is so easy to overlook nowadays, when all of the illusions about war have been abraded to dust, is that those young men went off to war eagerly and with light hearts, coveting the great adventure which they blithely believed lay just ahead. They went to war because they wanted to go, every man of them, and the obvious fact that in their innocence they did not have the remotest idea what the reality was going to be like does not change the fact. The bounty jumpers and the drafted men had not yet appeared. This was the army of the nation's youth, consciously trying to live up to its own conception of bravery, convinced that a soldier marched forward into high romance; an army with banners that postured pathetically and sincerely as it followed its own boyish vision.[57]

Shelby Foote had a similar observation:

> For all the talk of States Rights and the Union, men volunteered for much the same reasons on both sides: in search of glory or excitement, or from fear of being thought afraid, but mostly because it was the thing to do. The one characteristic they shared beyond all others was a lack of preparedness and an ignorance of what they had to face . . . All shared a belief that the war would be short, and some joined in haste, out of fear that it would be over before they got there.[58]

It is hard to believe that the war would have begun the way it did, if at all, had there been more prescience about the likely nature, duration, and cost of combat. Perhaps Lincoln would have chosen not to reinforce Fort Sumter, which was arguably one of the only plausible immediate catalysts to war in 1861, since Lincoln had pledged in his inaugural address not to use force against the South, again, saying even *after* the secession of seven states and formation of the Confederacy that "there needs to be no bloodshed or violence; and there shall be none, unless it be forced upon the national authority."[59] And perhaps he should have given General Winfield Scott's "Anaconda" strategy of squeezing the South economically, through blockade and control of coasts and rivers, a real chance before undertaking large-scale ground combat. Perhaps the North would have built up a real army before initiating hostilities so haphazardly.

Most of all, perhaps Southern states would have been content to stay within the Union even if they lost the opportunity to spread slavery to new states. To be sure, they could never have been confident that the abolitionist cause would not grow in strength and target slavery where it already existed in the South more frontally. They had also developed not only a distinct economic model, based largely on slavery—though most Southerners were not major slaveowners—but also a social system and way of life that differed fundamentally from much of the rest of the country. These distinctions may have become more rather than less palpable over time.[60] But compared with what ensued—and with what could have been realistically forecast, at least in broad brush—the decision to risk war over slavery looks not only unethical but foolish.

With these broad ideas and context in mind, I now turn to a short summary of the war, year by year, just as I will do in subsequent chapters. In each case, the focus is not on the details of individual battles so much as the campaigns and strategies that stitch the battles together and explain their broader purposes.

The Battles of 1861

The shooting in the American Civil War started at Fort Sumter in Charleston, South Carolina on April 12 and April 13, 1861—roughly a month after Abraham Lincoln's inauguration as the nation's sixteenth (and first Republican) president. Some federal forts in secessionist states had already been lost, but Lincoln insisted on the principle that as U.S. president he should have control over all of them. So he sought to make a stand at Sumter, and planned to resupply it as provisions dwindled. Anticipating the arrival of supplies by sea, the Confederacy struck first, bombarding the fort until surrender became necessary. Fortunately, the exchange of fire, mainly from the Confederate side, caused no fatalities (though an artillery salute to the Union flag after surrender led to an accident that took two soldiers' lives).[61] The battle did lead to a hardening of pro-Lincoln and pro-Union sentiment in the North. Even former Lincoln nemesis Stephen Douglas made an impassioned speech imploring support for the Union (only weeks before his death as it turned out). Robert E. Lee, for his part, declined the Lincoln administration's offer to become general in chief of Union forces, resigned his commission in the U.S. Army, and soon joined

Confederate forces. The Union later confiscated Lee's Arlington, Virginia home for delinquent taxes, eventually turning it into a graveyard that would later earn the name Arlington National Cemetery.[62]

The secession process had in fact begun with South Carolina exiting the Union several months before—on December 20, 1860, after the election of Lincoln but during the Buchanan administration. The process continued early in the new year with the departure of six more states from the Union—Mississippi, Florida, Alabama, Georgia, Louisiana, and Texas—all by February 1. The formal formation of the Confederacy happened later that same month. Arkansas, North Carolina, Virginia, and Tennessee would join in the spring and early summer.

Lincoln's approach was designed to force the Confederacy to fire the first shot of the war with the hope that it would either not do so or at least not be able to reinforce the narrative that the North was the aggressor in the conflict. As noted earlier, Lincoln suspected that there was a silent pro-Union sentiment even in the South, and that once the folly of going to war was recognized, peace and a return to the Union might follow.[63] All of this was undertaken with an eye toward restoring the Union quickly if possible by playing the politics right in both sections of the country. This proved to be largely wishful thinking in regard to the South.

However, Lincoln's strategy was much more successful in galvanizing Northern sentiment in support of war. He also had his eye on the slave-holding border states that had not opted for secession but could do so at any point. As he famously quipped, while he certainly hoped that God was on the Union's side, "I must have Kentucky."[64] For reasons of geography Lincoln certainly needed Maryland, too. One of his great strategic successes was to keep the border states in the Union camp throughout the next four years.

In the following months, there were several other limited engagements between Southern and Northern forces. Most were where North met South geographically. Battles at Wilson's Creek in Missouri in August and Ball's Bluff near Leesburg, Virginia in October went the Confederate way. However, starting in July, Union forces drove Confederates out of what was soon to become the new state of West Virginia, and resisted various southern efforts to retake territory there afterward.[65] These battles, plus Virginia's secession from the Union, created the necessary legal preconditions for the formal process of creating West Virginia. They also gave the 34-year-old General George McClellan, until recently a railroad leader and not a war planner, his initial successes. Those brought him to the attention of Washington, setting the stage for his rapid ascent—first as commanding general of the Army of the Potomac, then also for a time as general-in-chief of U.S. armies—shortly thereafter.[66]

The first large fight of the war, however, was the First Battle of Manassas (or Bull Run) on July 21. By this point, Richmond, Virginia, was the capital of the Confederacy—succeeding Montgomery, Alabama, with that distinction. Thus, Jefferson Davis could take the train to watch the fight, just as a key contingent of Southern troops could arrive by train to take part in it. Both sides by this point had organized substantial fighting forces with which they sought control of key terrain and transportation arteries in the general theater of Washington, DC, northern Virginia, and environs. Union forces, aware of the concentration of Confederate troops some 30 miles from the nation's capital, set out from Washington to confront them.

Both sides tested the other's mettle here. In the aftermath, both also began to appreciate that this conflict would be a real struggle with lots of hard fighting. As the famed Lincoln biographer Carl Sandburg wrote, "The Battle of Bull Run, Sunday, July 21, 1861, was to a large and eager public a sort of sporting event, the day and place of combat announced beforehand, a crowd of spectators riding to the scene with lunch baskets as though for a picnic."[67] But any sense of carnival-like atmosphere quickly dissipated. As the famed Civil War historian Shelby Foote wrote, "Few of the romantic preconceptions as to brilliant maneuver and individual gallantry were realized."[68] About 20,000 men fought on each side, producing an estimated casualty count of about 600 dead and 1,000 or so additional wounded on each side. General Irvin McDowell led the Union forces. General Pierre Beauregard had field command for the Confederates, with General Joseph Johnston in overall command. Other individuals that would become famous in the course of the war were involved there too, including Ambrose Burnside, William Sherman, and Oliver Howard on the Union side and "Stonewall" Jackson as well as Jeb Stuart on the Confederate.

Northern forces enjoyed early success in the battle, due to a clever early-morning tactical maneuver and attack. They might have won had they exploited their initial advantage (or carried out the attack a day or two sooner). But Confederate generals adjusted to initial setbacks, repositioned forces, benefited from just-in-time reinforcements, and also fought with temerity. Indeed, it was here that Stonewall Jackson got his nickname, for the doggedness with which he and his brigade held their ground. Many

Union forces, by contrast, performed poorly when the going got tough, especially those whose original ninety-day enlistments were already about to expire. A number raced back toward the relative safety of Washington, DC in the aftermath of the setbacks. As a result of the poor Union performance, General McDowell was fired and replaced with the young and arrogant McClellan.[69]

The outcome reinforced a Southern belief in the inherent superiority of its warrior culture and the righteousness of its cause. However, it had in fact been a close-run thing and very far from a certain victory. And not all Union forces collapsed in the aftermath of battle by any means.[70]

There were several, often underappreciated successes for the North in 1861 in other places beyond the future West Virginia. Notably, the North's naval blockades began to produce results. The blockades began in the summer of 1861. The Union navy discovered that it could use rifled artillery on steam-propelled ships sailing along unpredictable trajectories—thereby reducing vulnerability to Confederate fire from land—to attack and defeat some Southern forts, especially on barrier islands and the like. Seizures of islands and small ports started in August in North Carolina and continued southward, reaching Port Royal, South Carolina that November and points further south, into Florida, over the ensuing winter and into early 1862. With this approach the North could develop refueling stations and bases for enforcing the blockades on Confederate soil even when there was no chance of holding the nearby mainland territories.[71] Such attacks had their limits. They were not successful against stronger land bastions, like the port of Charleston, which was bombarded unsuccessfully on April 7, 1863, and never conquered by subsequent attacks from the sea (it only fell in 1865, as General Sherman's armies approached—more on that later).[72] Still, these attacks gave the North a much more effective base network from which blockade operations could be undertaken and sustained.[73] Those operations ultimately cut cotton exports more than tenfold relative to prewar levels, even if it took a while to achieve that effect.[74]

Otherwise, 1861 was largely a year of mobilization and preparation for the big campaigns that were soon to follow. This process involved recruiting large numbers of soldiers on both sides, with various incentive systems and various terms of service ranging from three months to three years. Conscription was not yet in effect for either government. Several hundred thousand soldiers were formed into units on each side that year. The Confederacy, with fewer than one-third as many white men of military age as the Union, nonetheless came close to keeping up with the North in manpower—more effectively than at any subsequent time in the war. The North was hampered by legislation that initially only allowed three-month enlistments; as noted, it was led by an incompetent secretary of war in this period.[75]

Mobilization also involved ginning up industry for production of weapons and other key materiel. On these fronts, the North had huge advantages. In 1860, for example, it had produced a whopping 97 percent of the country's firearms and more than 90 percent of shoes, iron, locomotives, and other key elements of a major war effort. Financing, the military buildup led, among other innovations, to the creation by Washington of the first federal income tax in the United States.

The Confederates attempted to compensate by developing some industry, buying supplies abroad to the extent some weapons could get through the naval blockades, and seizing weapons in federal arsenals on their territory. The chief of the Confederacy's Ordnance Bureau, Josiah Gorgas, won plaudits for his efforts. But the odds were stacked steeply against the South, initially and throughout the next four years.[76]

In addition to his careful calculations about how to keep the border states within the Union, Lincoln also succeeded in keeping European powers out of the fight, despite their appetite for Southern cotton (and lingering resentments in some quarters over the outcome of the Revolutionary War). To do so, he had to quietly back down in a crisis of the Union naval forces' own making. In November, the U.S.S. *San Jacinto* stopped a British vessel, the *Trent,* in the Caribbean region and detained two Confederate envoys who were headed to Great Britain and France. Britain threatened war if the detainees were not promptly given into British custody. When Lincoln was challenged on his decision to release them, he retorted, "One war at a time."

1862 and the Slog of War

The year 1862 was when it became abundantly clear that the American Civil War would not be short or easy by any stretch of the imagination. It was also the year that, implicitly or explicitly, the strategies of the two sides started to come into focus. Gone were the heady days of hoping for quick knockout punches. More serious concepts were needed.

For the South, the goal—if probably not to capture Washington, or Lincoln, realistically speaking—was still to play good enough defense to protect Richmond and the main territories and armies of the Confederacy, while hoping that cunning and élan could create battlefield victories that would sap the Northern will to fight. This approach almost worked.

For the North, the gradually crystallizing objective—at least in Lincoln's mind, if not yet in those of many of his generals—was to employ its huge advantages in manpower and materiel to wear down the South, even if the quick and decisive win did not happen and even if some battles were lost. More successful in 1862 were elements of General Winfield Scott's Anaconda strategy. Union forces sought to chop up the Confederacy into multiple pieces that would be cut off from each other and the outside world, and achieved relatively early successes in Tennessee as well as the broader Mississippi River region. The Union had enough structural factors in its favor that, as time went on, the realities of battlefield conditions increasingly augured its success—provided that it could find the right commanders in battle and sustain the political resolve to finish the fight.

Consider the western theater first. The most important action occurred along and near major rivers—especially the Mississippi, but also the Tennessee and the Cumberland—as well as the Ohio River. The latter three rivers flow either west or north into the Mississippi, making them all part of the same overall network. The rivers were important for military as well as economic reasons. They constituted transportation arteries through a large and forested area where road and rail networks were less densely developed than in the east. A key initial Union stronghold was Cairo, Illinois on the banks of the Mississippi River where the Ohio River joined it (just across the Mississippi River from Missouri).

Throughout this entire region, along a line stretching from the Appalachian Mountains to the Ozarks of Missouri, Confederate forces numbering some 50,000 were under the command of General Albert Sidney Johnston. Union forces along the same stretch slightly exceeded 100,000 and were under two commands: that of Henry Halleck from Missouri to the Cumberland River, and that of Don Carlos Buell from the Cumberland eastward. General Halleck, cautious by disposition, benefited from the services of a bolder subordinate officer who had recently rejoined the U.S. Army after leaving it in a cloud of some disrepute (regarding drinking) in 1854—Ulysses S. Grant.

Most initial forces, and military leaders, were of uneven and generally mediocre quality. Initial recruiting in the war tapped into patriotic fervor and often employed cash incentives. But almost all recruits were green regarding military matters. In the course of 1862, this reality became increasingly apparent, and the volunteer system also started to reach the limits of what it could deliver in terms of manpower. Thus, in the spring of 1862, the Confederacy resorted to a fairly comprehensive conscription act that required military-age men to serve up to three years. The Union followed in the spring of 1863, though with a less comprehensive and more loophole-ridden conscription act of its own.

As 1862 started, then–Brigadier General Grant helped devise a plan to attack Fort Henry on the Tennessee River along the Kentucky-Tennessee border, using combined army and navy forces and approaches. The attack, in February 1862, identified a weak spot far forward in the Confederate position, and succeeded. This should have been no big surprise, as Confederate General Albert Johnston was attempting to protect a defensive perimeter across all of Kentucky with a very modest force. Whatever the political logic of making the attempt to demonstrate commitment to all parts of the new Confederate polity, the task of holding a 300-mile line along the Tennessee-Kentucky border with just 50,000 troops was herculean. Indeed, Union forces soon achieved an additional, if more difficult, success at nearby Fort Donelson on the Cumberland River.

As the spring of 1862 began, Confederate forces under Albert Johnston ultimately retreated southward, just below the Tennessee-Mississippi border to the town of Corinth, Mississippi.[77] There, Confederate forces under the general command of General Beauregard were reinforced with 15,000 troops arriving from New Orleans and from Mobile, Alabama under the command of Braxton Bragg. The resulting force of more than 40,000 was large enough not only to regroup but also to hatch a plan for a counterattack moving northward. Hence ensued the Battle of Shiloh, the largest of the war to date, on April 6–7, 1862. Southern forces had moved northward into Tennessee, near a port called Pittsburgh Junction, where Grant had brought his forces to join up with those of General Buell in preparation for an assault on Southern forces at Corinth.

Union forces were not prepared for the possibility of an attack against their own encampments. They were not dug in or otherwise particularly concerned about the possibility of defending themselves in that location, which they considered only a way station on their general southerly movement. Thus, Union forces were quite surprised when the South attacked. The ensuing fight took place near a country church that gave the battle its name and its place in Civil War lore. The weather during the night between the two days of battle was horrible. Grant nonetheless found the indoor shelter area that had been arranged for him—which was doubling as a field hospital—too depressing, so he sought a place outside in the rain to smoke a cigar. There, General Sherman found him and said, "Well, Grant, we've had the devil's own day, haven't we?" To which Grant famously replied, "Yes, lick 'em tomorrow though."[78] Whatever his underlying sense of confidence, however, this was also the battle that persuaded Grant that the war would be long and hard.[79]

Day two did go better for Union forces. With the overnight arrival of Buell, the combined Union forces were able to hold off the assault and eventually drive the smaller Southern forces back from where they had come. Losses were large on both sides. Out of combined forces of nearly 100,000 (perhaps just over 50,000 for Union forces, around 40,000 for the South), total casualties including killed and wounded numbered at least 20,000.[80] General Albert Johnston was hit in the leg by a bullet and bled to death soon thereafter, making him the highest-ranking casualty on either side in the entire duration of the war.

The outcome at Shiloh set up Union forces to continue their general southward thrust. General Halleck, his total strength now at 100,000 troops, moved on the Confederate positions near Corinth, a crossroads where two important railroads met. Confederate reinforcements arrived, too, and produced a total force in the area of some 70,000 troops. But they were a rather motley crew, and afflicted by the outbreak of disease as well. They ultimately had to evacuate the city in late spring. Now, the Union was positioned on the Confederacy's only major east-west railroad artery, the Memphis and Charleston, as well as the other railroad traversing Corinth, the Mobile and Ohio.

Memphis and New Orleans also fell in April 1862, the latter to the fabled 60-year-old David Farragut of War of 1812 fame. In New Orleans, Union forces profited from their naval capacities—combined with the fact that the South could spare few troops for the direct defense of New Orleans given all the other threats posed by Union forces. The overarching Union goal in the west was to put multidimensional pressure on the South, and its economy—again, consistent with the idea of cutting the Confederacy up into a number of blockaded pieces that would eventually be strangled into submission. Already, in the west, Union commanders were starting to think and act in theater-wide campaign terms, recognizing their aggregate advantages in men and materiel and pressing on even when they encountered tactical setbacks.

In the taking of New Orleans, Farragut used his small armada of shallow-keeled ships to run the gauntlet of guns on the Mississippi River below the city. The fighting was intense for a stretch of time and space, and featured rams, sea mines, and other new features of contemporary naval warfare. In the end, all but a few smaller Union vessels made it through, opening up a route to the city for ships carrying 15,000 ground troops.[81] Baton Rouge was taken by the Union as well. The squeezing was occurring in multiple directions by now.[82]

So 1862 was a very promising year for Union forces in the western theater of combat. Comprehensive victory there was still a ways off, however, and would have to wait until the following summer. Union forces still had to contend with long logistics lines, Confederate raids that went as far north as Kentucky, disease, and other challenges. They did not gain any further momentum in the rest of the year.

The one remaining big battle in the western theater—starting on New Year's Eve and continuing into January 2, 1863—was fought to a standstill in central Tennessee around the Stones River and Murfreesboro. There, the two sides, under General William Rosecrans for Union forces and General Bragg for the Confederates, sought to strengthen their control of respective parts of that key state. This battle followed an earlier and related one in the fall of 1862 near Perryville, Kentucky.[83] The net effect was that Kentucky remained on the Union side.

Meanwhile in the Virginia theater, things were more challenging, and 1862 proved a very tough year. If Shiloh signaled that the war would be tough, the Virginia campaign that spring and early summer proved it beyond any reasonable doubt.

This is not to say that everything went badly for the North in the eastern theater. Union forces did begin, for example, to display impressive use of transport and logistics capabilities. The efforts of the Army quartermaster general, Montgomery Meigs, and of Lincoln's new secretary of war, Edwin Stanton, were beginning to produce results. Meigs had been in his job since June 1861; Stanton replaced the poorly regarded Simon Cameron in January 1862 and became a strong Lincoln ally. Under Meigs, competitive bidding for army supplies became commonplace. Standardized clothing sizes were introduced (for the first time anywhere); new methods of making shoes were devised; and what became known as pup tents were invented to make for easier transport. These kinds of innovations were of paramount importance for a military often campaigning with 100,000-plus men in two separate theaters, and far away from home territory, consuming many hundred tons of supplies a day.[84] And by this point in the war, the Army of the Potomac was better organized too, under its new commander, Major General George McClellan.

However, McClellan was less successful at battle than at organization. Already in early 1862, McClellan showed signs of the traits for which he later became infamous, seemingly unwilling to risk his reputation by taking the fight to the enemy until he had a type of overwhelming superiority that he never attained. As his biographer Stephen Sears put it, "When making war, General George Brinton McClellan was a man possessed by demons and delusions."[85] Already sensing difficulties, Lincoln relieved McClellan of his position as general-in-chief of the U.S. Army in March of 1862, though Lincoln left him as commander of the Army of the Potomac for what would be a fateful spring and summer.

McClellan's main campaign plan for 1862 was put into motion in March. Seeking to attack Richmond from the eastern flank, after traveling down the Chesapeake Bay by ship, he managed to land more than 100,000 forces on the peninsula between the James and York Rivers in Virginia. Again, the maritime dimension to the conflict was important. An inconclusive fight between the CSS *Virginia* versus the U.S.S. *Monitor* preceded this operation; the former had to pull back to Norfolk after the battle, and therefore could not threaten shipping in the bay.[86] Neither ship survived the year; the *Virginia* was scuttled in May as Norfolk fell to Union forces, and the *Monitor* was lost at sea when being towed southward for a blockade assignment. (Both sides built successor ships over the course of the next three years.[87])

McClellan's seaborne transport operation involved 400 ships and went quite well, accomplishing the movement within two weeks.[88] The Union plan, after coming ashore, was then to approach Richmond by land via Yorktown and Williamsburg. Those attacking forces were to be joined by perhaps another 35,000 under the command of General Irvin McDowell, marching south from Fredericksburg, Virginia. Together, Union forces would marshal about twice the total number of Confederate forces who under General Joseph Johnston's command were defending Richmond. But the plan did not come to pass—and frustration soon ensued for the campaign plan writ large, as McClellan's forces suffered several setbacks and then effectively ran out of gas for any further campaigning, even once they were reasonably close to Richmond. McClellan demonstrated that he did not have the verve or toughness that would ultimately be needed to win this war. Despite considerable superiority in numbers, he tended to avoid attack, and even dug in for a month (basically the whole month of April) near Yorktown when he became convinced that Union forces were outmanned by Confederate forces when the latter were in fact considerably less numerous.

In fairness, there is nothing wrong with being a little extra sure before proceeding—especially when one's side has the preponderance of overall power.[89] McClellan also sought to use maneuver and an unexpected approach to Richmond to avoid the kinds of pitched battles against prepared fortifications that were the bane of so many other Civil War generals. Again, there was a certain logic in his thinking.[90] Intelligence was bound to be inexact, as well; we toss around exact figures for the dispositions of the respective forces fighting Civil War battles in history books, but there was nothing so precise about the real-time estimates available to commanders.

However, in this case McClellan was contributing to a sense of Northern inertia that, when juxtaposed with the politics of the Union, risked giving the Confederacy a path to victory. The South could increasingly envision a way to win: effectively run out the clock on the North's patience and will to continue the fight. Indeed, in his headier moments, Lee may have aspired not just to run out the clock but to deliver a knockout strike against McClellan's whole army. Lee was actually disappointed that, for all of his defensive successes in the 1862 campaign, he could not achieve that glorious and decisive counteroffensive with his outnumbered total force of some 80,000 soldiers.[91]

President Lincoln himself showed deference to McClellan—more than the general usually demonstrated to his president. Lincoln even offered, metaphorically, to "hold McClellan's horse" if that was what it took to help the general deliver success.[92] Alas, such patience and humility on the part of the commander in chief were not to be rewarded. McClellan often allowed himself to be outmaneuvered by weaker forces, and often sat back to lick wounds after tough fights rather than pursuing the campaign. These traits gave General Lee the recourse of dividing Confederate forces even when they were smaller to begin with—knowing that McClellan would usually not detect or exploit the resulting opportunities, and often surprising Union forces with maneuver and unexpected attack from unforeseen directions.

How this played out in the spring and summer of 1862 is roughly as follows.

First, President Lincoln, perhaps too cautious himself in this case, changed his mind on sending General McDowell's forces overland to reinforce McClellan. This resulted from a masterstroke by Lee. He sent General

Stonewall Jackson, with 17,000 soldiers, to undertake a complex series of maneuvers through the Shenandoah Valley in western Virginia, on foot and even on train, producing five victories against combined forces twice as large. These successes created the perception of a danger to Washington, DC that led Lincoln to tell McDowell to stay put, denying McClellan the added strength he expected to go after Richmond and General Lee. (Jackson's forces did ultimately arrive in the Richmond theater, however—in time for the "Seven Days' Battles.")

This change affected McClellan's total numbers and it also seems to have affected his confidence in the basic plan of attack. The unexpected development, plus soggy conditions where his forces came ashore near Yorktown, made for a slow approach toward Richmond. Confederate forces had time to prepare positions, create credible feints, and take advantage of their superior knowledge of the local environment. Combat ensued east of Richmond at so-called Seven Pines at the end of May and at the Seven Days' Battles a month later.

This is not to say that Union forces collapsed at any point in the campaign. In fact, while the Confederates showed considerable chutzpah, it is hard to say that Lee won the engagements. The Seven Days' Battle produced 30,000 total casualties, with more on the Confederate side. Nonetheless, McClellan decided in the aftermath to give up his ambitions of defeating Lee or taking Richmond, with the result that even Union tactical successes somehow still amounted to strategic defeat for the north.[93] Fearing that Lee might have 200,000 troops under his command, multiples of what he actually possessed, McClellan persuaded himself that no prompt follow-up action made sense.[94]

Ironically, the outcome of this fighting near Richmond in the spring and early summer of 1862 also may have amounted to a form of strategic defeat for the *South*—what renowned Civil War historian James McPherson called the "profound irony" of these early successes of Robert E. Lee. Suppose that McClellan had succeeded in taking Richmond in that campaign, convincing Davis and his government to abandon the fight. Had the Civil War, and secession, ended at that relatively early moment, slavery might have been preserved, and the eleven states of the Confederacy might have kept their "peculiar institution" for years or decades to come. At that juncture, the North's war aims had not yet escalated to undoing slavery within the territories of the Confederacy itself.[95]

McClellan's forces withdrew under orders of General-in-Chief Henry Halleck in August in the same basic way they had arrived. A new 50,000-

plus Union force, called the Army of Virginia, was formed under General John Pope. But General Lee again sent Stonewall Jackson north, with a modest force of only 12,000 this time, to challenge Pope before he could threaten the fertile Shenandoah Valley. Reinforcements soon doubled Jackson's strength, while help for Pope from McClellan's forces was limited, and slow to arrive.[96]

Parts of Jackson's and Pope's forces fought a modest battle in early August at the evocatively named Cedar Mountain, just south of Culpeper in northern Virginia. (For those not familiar with the area, it is north of Charlottesville and Richmond, west of Fredericksburg, and east of the Shenandoah Valley). The inconclusive outcome set up the Second Battle of Manassas or Bull Run on August 29–30. As had been the case in his earlier Shenandoah Valley campaign, Jackson's disciplinarian ways, aggressive maneuvering, and fast marching sowed confusion in Union ranks. General Jeb Stuart's cavalry added to the North's uncertainties and anxieties. General Pope and other Union leaders were unsure about the location of enemy armies, including General James Longstreet's late-arriving forces. Again, Lee had gambled that he could divide his modest-sized forces, leaving only a small fraction to guard the Richmond area, and counting on Union hesitancy to be his ally. In the end, some 54,000 Confederate troops defeated 63,000 Union forces—the former suffering some 9,500 casualties, and the latter, some 14,500 including those killed and wounded and captured.[97] Still, Jackson showed less tactical aggressiveness in battle than during his remarkable maneuvering and marching, and so Pope managed to survive with his army intact.[98]

By this point in the war, Lincoln had decided to free slaves in rebellious states by edict, reasoning that his position as commander-in-chief gave him the prerogative to do so against a rebellious Confederacy. But battlefield circumstances left Lincoln, for the moment, unable to issue his Emancipation Proclamation that would legally free all slaves in the secessionist states. Lincoln felt he needed a victory to make such an edict credible and powerful. He would soon have a better opportunity.

After Second Manassas, Lee set his sights on Maryland—the first of his two great gambles to take the fight into Northern territory. He moved his forces across the Potomac to the vicinity of Frederick, Maryland (not to be confused with Fredericksburg, Virginia—and near the current Camp David, about 25 miles south of the Pennsylvania border and 25 miles or so east of Harpers Ferry, West Virginia). His ambitions in moving into the North were to create a psychological sense of crisis among

Union supporters, gain access to supplies in the verdant fields of Maryland and/or Pennsylvania, reveal any latent pro-Southern sympathies among Marylanders, and perhaps achieve foreign recognition of the Confederate government if the South then seemed to be headed for victory (recognition then possibly helping ease the burden of the North's economic blockades). He would fail on each count.

After learning that there were Union forces near Harpers Ferry, Lee set out in that westward direction to do battle. But the much-maligned General McClellan had managed to stitch together surviving Union forces into a newly reorganized Army of the Potomac to defend Northern territory. Then he got a stroke of luck when a Union soldier found a copy of Confederate battle plans in an abandoned campsite. This allowed McClellan to position his forces smartly in northwestern Maryland near Sharpsburg and Antietam Creek in a way that might help him divide and defeat Lee's troops. The initial clash on September 17—the bloodiest single day of the war—went largely the Union's way. Casualties were comparable on both sides, at roughly 11,000 for the South and 12,000 for the North (with a total of some 3,600 killed and almost 20,000 wounded or captured, between the two sides). But the Union could afford the losses more easily, as it brought some 60,000 troops to the fight against the South's 45,000— and it was the South which had ambitions for a big follow-on maneuver that had to be discarded thereafter.[99] It was enough of a victory to allow Lincoln to issue the preliminary version of the Emancipation Proclamation several days later, to be officially effective on January 1, 1863, and freeing all slaves within the territories of those states in rebellion.

Alas, it was only a partial victory. McClellan's innate caution led him to conduct only sequential, somewhat limited attacks on the big day of battle, rather than using his advantages in force size and battlefield intelligence to go for the decisive kill. In a damning critique, the military historian Russell Weigley wrote:[100]

[McClellan] not only failed to perceive the opportunity presented by the high ground in Lee's rear, but where he did fight he conducted three consecutive uncoordinated assaults, each of them broken into a further series of uncoordinated advances. Thus he permitted Lee all day to shift his scarce troops from one threatened point to another. Meanwhile, McClellan never used his own reserves. Moreover, he never felt the pulse of the battle, because while he positioned himself on high ground east of the Antietam so he could view the fighting west of the stream from a distance, he was never close enough to the action to develop the sense of ebb and flow and thus of the decisive moment for a climactic effort that the greatest military commanders have always gained—even in the twentieth century—from leading at the front.

McClellan also failed to pursue Confederate forces afterward, when he had a chance to trap them on the north side of the Potomac and defeat them in detail, element by element, the following day. As a result, Confederate forces soon escaped southward to home turf and relative sanctuary.

In November 1862, Lincoln diagnosed McClellan with a case of the "slows"—epitomized in late October when McClellan claimed that his horses were still tired (a month after Antietam, their last real action). Lincoln also admonished him directly, saying "My dear McClellan, if you don't want to use the Army I should like to borrow it for a while." Honest Abe relieved him of command and replaced him with General Ambrose Burnside.[101]

Burnside promptly took up pursuit of Southern armies with the goal of moving forward on the path to Richmond. On December 13, Burnside's 115,000 troops encountered Lee, Jackson, Longstreet, and others—and their combined strength of almost 80,000—near Fredericksburg, Virginia. But what ensued was some of the worst tactical generalship of the whole war. Exposed Union forces marched in headstrong fashion straight into enemy positions benefiting from higher ground and a protecting stone wall near an open field—failing to account for the accuracy, volume, and lethality of Confederate fire. The result was catastrophe, and an effective end to the campaign for the year. Union casualties approached 13,000 to the South's total of just over 5,000. Soon, Burnside had himself been relieved of command as well.[102]

In the aftermath, the North fell into a collective funk in many ways. That was true despite the partial success at Antietam, and the general progress that year in the western theater. Yet these partial and debatable successes could not outweigh the overall frustrations of campaigns in Virginia, and the difficulties of developing perceptible strategic momentum in the war more generally. Taking the whole picture together, the famed biographer of Grant, Bruce Catton, wrote of a "winter of discontent" in the North.[103]

1863: From Chancellorsville and the Wilderness to Gettysburg, Vicksburg, and Chattanooga

The year 1863 was the midpoint of the Civil War. There had been fighting for roughly one and a half years before it; there would be another 15-plus months of combat after the year was over. While it proved in many ways the major inflection point of the conflict, especially with the nearly simultaneous Union victories in early July in Vicksburg and Gettysburg, it would not create the kind of momentum that made victory for the North inexorable. Indeed, Lincoln later came close to losing reelection in 1864 over frustrations with the campaign a full year after those milestone successes in the eastern and western theaters. Thus, the best way to view 1863 on balance is simply as the midpoint of a terrible saga that nearly tore the country in two for good—and that still could have throughout that whole year, and beyond. If there was a more promising sign, barely visible through the fog of war and of mass slaughter on both sides, it was the emergence of Ulysses S. Grant and his relentless style of campaigning as the new hope for the Union. But in the course of 1863, Grant was not yet in overall command.

As January and February unfolded, the winter of despair continued. General Grant, as part of his ongoing efforts to take Vicksburg—an endeavor that would ultimately succeed in midyear, but only after lengthy preparations and a long siege—described the situation as follows:[104]

> This long, dreary, and, for heavy and continuous rains and high water, unprecedented winter was one of great hardship to all engaged about Vicksburg. . . . Troops could scarcely find dry ground on which to pitch their tents. Malarial fevers broke out among the men. Measles and smallpox also attacked them. . . . Visitors to the camps went home with dismal stories to relate; Northern papers came back to the soldiers with these stories exaggerated. Because I would not divulge my ultimate plans to visitors, they pronounced me idle, incompetent and unfit to command men in an emergency, and clamored for my removal.

Yet even in these times of woe, the situation was gradually developing in a favorable direction, at least in the western theater. Grant's engineers and logisticians were figuring out how to position, supply, and prepare a powerful force for an ultimate siege of the city, despite harassment to their supply lines, soggy footing in many places, and the difficulty of moving downriver in the face of the Confederacy's shoreline guns. Even if some in the North demanded Grant's head, his superiors supported him, giving him the time he needed for the complex logistical operations. As Grant wrote, "With all the pressure brought to bear upon them, both President Lincoln and General Halleck stood by me to the end of the campaign. I had never met Mr. Lincoln, but his support was constant."[105]

To circumvent Mother Nature as well as Confederate positions, Grant finally marched his forces on the west (Louisiana) side of the river, starting above Vicksburg and winding up south of it. He then ordered naval vessels to run the gauntlet of Confederate guns along the Mississippi in Vicksburg, benefiting from the 4-knot southward current to minimize time in the most intense killing zones. Once safely below the city, they then transported his soldiers back to the eastern side. The emotion with which Grant described finally finding a way ashore on high ground south of Vicksburg by the end of April of 1863 is palpable. It feels at least as great as anything he extolled after winning actual battles in the war; it also demonstrates how Grant thought in terms of extended campaigns, perhaps even more than individual battles:[106]

> When this was effected, I felt a degree of relief scarcely ever equaled since. Vicksburg was not yet taken it is true, nor were its defenders demoralized by any of our previous moves. I was now in the enemy's country, with a vast river and the stronghold of Vicksburg between me and my base of supplies. But I was on dry ground on the same side of the river with the enemy. All the campaigns, labors, hardships and exposures from the month of December previous to this time that had been made and endured, were for the accomplishment of this one object.

As the British strategist and historian J. F. C. Fuller put it, admiringly, "Four months of ruses and feints, of wrestling with swamps, bayous and forests, of labours seldom equaled in war, were the fog which covered his landing."[107] With these positions established, the siege of Vicksburg could soon begin. That involved digging trench lines a few hundred yards from Southern positions, fortifying and protecting them, and then gradually extending the trench lines forward as Confederate defenses were battered and supplies depleted.

Getting into siege position was far from the end of the story, however. Realizing that time was working against them, the Confederates attempted to change the dynamics in the broader region. General Joseph Johnston sought to muster a force that could harass Grant's flanks, interfere with his supply lines to the east and north, and otherwise provide relief to the Vicksburg contingent of Confederates. But the Union responded very effectively. Grant temporarily brought his own forces to join with those of General Sherman against Johnston. Grant did so without normal lines of communication and resupply to support his forces—recognizing that he needed to eliminate the threat from the east, and destroy the rail line connecting Vicksburg to Jackson, to be in a strong position for the eventual siege of Vicksburg. Again, he was thinking in campaign terms. This effort foreshadowed Sherman's March to the Sea, also accomplished by cutting loose from traditional and secure supply lines—and in Grant's case, he was doing so when local enemy forces were even more potentially threatening to his own.

Grant's troops received reinforcements during this period, ultimately exceeding 70,000 in number as the final assault was prepared. With the aid of underground explosions to crater key parts of the enemy's defensive perimeter on June 25 and July 1, the city was taken. With this attack successful, Confederate General John Pemberton accepted Grant's fairly tough yet humane terms of surrender on the symbolic date of July 4.[108]

Back east, however, the going continued to be very tough for the North in the year's early months. As General Joseph Hooker plotted next moves in the inevitable aspiration to take Richmond, Lee did it again. Although outnumbered 2:1 in the theater, he divided his forces in preparation to go on the attack near the so-called Wilderness (which would surface again as an important battle site a year later).

The Battle of Chancellorsville, centered on the period from May 1 through May 4, 1863, was the immediate result. All the brush and complex terrain gave the home team a major advantage. Hooker was unable to profit from his advantages in mass and firepower. Through maneuver and surprise, the South won a battle with smaller forces by going on the tactical offensive. Usually that was a perilous approach given the weaponry and tactics of the day. The key tactic was a stealthy maneuver through dense forest that brought large numbers of Southern forces into a position from which they could strike the flank and rear of Union forces. Any Union aspirations for advances southward for the foreseeable future were effectively halted as a result of this fight.

The South suffered some 12,500 casualties all told out of a force of around 60,000. The North, with 130,000 soldiers, lost 17,300.[109]

But again, these kinds of victories were not a type that the South could afford very often. Losing Stonewall Jackson, mistakenly shot in the arm by Southern forces, leading to amputation and soon death, was bad enough. As Lee put it, even before Jackson had died, "He has lost his left arm; but I have lost my right arm."[110] A week later, those words would ring even more true when Jackson died. Beyond Jackson, losing a higher percentage of a smaller force—even if successful in maneuver, and in style points—was no huge achievement. As Russell Weigley perceptively argued, "Even in his greatest battle, Lee had imposed on the scarcest and most indispensable Confederate resource—the lives of Confederate soldiers—a cost that could foreshadow only a downward spiral of Southern military fortunes."[111]

Now Hooker's days as commander of the Army of the Potomac were numbered too. He was soon replaced by General Gordon Meade, who took over just in time for Gettysburg and stayed in that position for the duration of the war. Thus, over the first two years of the Civil War, the Army of the Potomac had four commanders fired—McDowell, McClellan, Burnside, and Hooker. John Pope was also relieved of command of the Army of Virginia, during the period in 1862 when that distinct body existed, after defeat at the Second Battle of Manassas/Bull Run. (Over the course of the war, Scott, McClellan, Halleck, and Grant all had the position of general in chief, but only McClellan held that position and general of the Army of the Potomac simultaneously for a stretch of time).

And then came Gettysburg. It is remarkable to think just how far north this battle occurred. Lee was showing the Union that he could operate on Northern territory, that he could forage off the land just as Northern armies sometimes did in the South (and as Sherman would, to great effect, the following year), and that he could even pose a hypothetical threat to the nation's capital. His goals were as much political—shocking the North into deciding the war was not worth it, strengthening antiwar political elements in the Union, perhaps persuading some European states to see the Confederacy as an established fact and thus recognize it—as military.

Lee started his march into the North in June, with the cavalry-dominated Battle of Brandy Station near Culpeper, Virginia an early part of the broader campaign. There, sensing movement in Confederate forces, Union cavalry tried to head off what they wrongly thought was a possible threat to Washington, DC. In fact, what they had seen was part of Lee's early preparations for the movement north and west. Eventually, after Lee again crossed the Potomac and moved forward, Gettysburg, some 75 miles north of Washington, DC, became the place for the fight. It was there that the bulk of Union forces recognized what was happening, had time to react, and positioned themselves. As a crossroads and hub, Gettysburg turned out to be the place where multiple roads and thus multiple units would converge.

A great debate occurred in the Confederate ranks about the nature of the fight to come, which the South could have attempted to avoid if it had wished. Much of this is elegantly caricatured in one of the great historical novels of modern times, *The Killer Angels*. The book features a debate between General Lee and the more defensively inclined General Longstreet over warrior and martial culture—and whether Lee should attack Union forces there, or bypass their positions and try to lure them into attacking him (perhaps on the way to Washington, DC). A master campaigner, who knew how to read his opponent and take advantage of defense preparations when they worked to his advantage and take risks, Lee also had an almost mystical faith in the importance of the offensive. In this warrior attitude he was far from alone, among generals of his day. As Lee biographer Emory Thomas put it, "He wanted to carry the war into the enemy's country and thus defend the Confederacy from Pennsylvania instead of in Virginia. And regardless of what Lee said or wrote to Jefferson Davis, what Lee did make clear was his desire to fight a climactic battle on Northern soil. He still sought a showdown, a battle of annihilation that would end the war in a single afternoon."[112]

In fairness, Lee had to worry about supply lines, and could not have wandered about Pennsylvania and Maryland too much (or dug in for too long) without risking shortages. But that does not mean he had to ignore the realities of 1860s military technology, and his own relative dearth of soldiers, and plunge head-on into established Union positions as he did. Among the worst Southern mistakes were Pickett's charge across a large and open field in the face of Union fire, as well as the unsuccessful attempt to storm and capture Little Round Top at the southern extent of the main battlefield, where Confederate generals hoped to be able to enfilade (or fire along the main axis) of Union positions on Seminary Ridge.

Both armies limped away from the Gettysburg fight. Neither was destroyed or incapacitated, though casualties were very heavy—perhaps 28,000 or more than one-third, of the Southern force of around 77,000, and about 25,000 out of a larger Union force of some 93,000. But Lee clearly could not take too many more episodes of that same character, and his northern foray effectively ended with this battle. As such, however it is scored tactically, Gettysburg amounted to a major Union strategic success.[113] Indeed, Lee felt so defeated and so physically fatigued in the aftermath that he offered his resignation, although President Davis rejected it. Meanwhile, Union forces in the east did not seek to pursue any advantage they may have gained at Gettysburg with a major southern movement for the rest of the year. There were various skirmishes between elements of Meade's and Lee's forces in and around Culpeper, the Rapidan and Rappahannock Rivers, Bristoe Station, Broad Run, Mine Run, and other notable towns and landmarks in northern Virginia. But no major or decisive battles or maneuvers occurred for the rest of the year in that theater.

If Vicksburg represented a major Union win in the so-called western theater, and Gettysburg a significant (if defensive) success in the east, another theater became important in the latter half of 1863—in eastern Tennessee. The ongoing competition between the forces of generals Bragg and Rosecrans for control of that pivotal state as well as northern Georgia had not yet produced results of major strategic import. As summer wound down, the two generals attempted to strengthen their forces, solidify logistics lines (especially for Rosecrans, since he was operating in enemy territory), and consider next moves. Rosecrans hoped eventually to put pressure on the eastern Tennessee/northern Georgia region, where Confederate rail lines connected different parts of the region and where Atlanta could eventually be threatened as well.

But those goals were not to be realized right away. What resulted instead was the Battle of Chickamauga in northwestern Georgia on September 19–20, 1863. Union forces wound up with control of Chattanooga, Tennessee in the aftermath, but with no prospect of moving beyond—if they could even hold that position. Chickamauga, fought near a small river (called a "creek") of that name, was a very intense and bloody affair, with the Northern Army of the Cumberland losing perhaps 16,000 out of 57,000 troops and the Confederates under General Braxton Bragg losing 18,500 out of 66,000.

Union forces lost in the sense of losing ground they once held, and finding themselves in a perilous position that, fortunately for them, Bragg failed to exploit fully. Yet they also suffered somewhat fewer casualties than the South. Indeed, as famed historian Russell Weigley put it, echoing his comments about Chancellorsville, "More victories like Chickamauga would be as fatal to the Confederacy as a few more Gettysburg defeats." In geographic and campaign terms, the real outcome of the battle was still indeterminate, and would depend on future events. Although the Union held Chattanooga after the battle, as Weigley continued, "Bragg now occupied the heights commanding Chattanooga, notably the point of Lookout Mountain to the southwest and Missionary Ridge to the east, to make the conquered city more a prison than a prize for the Army of the Cumberland."[114]

Those future events began to take shape when General Grant, previously commander of the Army of the Tennessee, was put in command of the broader western theater in October, in what was now called the Military Division of the Mississippi. That meant he also assumed responsibilities for the fighting throughout the state of Tennessee as well. The Confederate siege of Chattanooga, which had squeezed Union forces in the city between the river to the north and enemy positions to the south and left them on only partial rations, became his immediate concern. Grant arrived there six days after assuming this new command, on October 23, to oversee subsequent operations. Four of his divisions were sent on a slow rail journey from Vicksburg toward Chattanooga, repairing track as they went; they were to join up with the Army of the Cumberland in Chattanooga, and with additional reinforcements arriving, also by rail, from the Army of the Potomac.[115] Generals Grant, Hooker, Sherman, and Rosecrans would all be on the scene eventually.

Before all the Union forces had arrived, in order to open up supply lines and break the siege, Grant approved a plan to cut a bee line through a region where the Tennessee River winds up and down, back and forth. Using ruse and darkness to create a fait accompli before Southern forces could move to head off the operation, Grant and his generals succeeded in this effort in the last days (and nights) of October.[116] The winding part of the river was now bypassed by an overland shortcut, "the Cracker Line," that the Union could protect. Again, Grant showed an appreciation for the campaign-level conduct of war—as well as his previously demonstrated ability to combine riverine and overland operations in a single effort.

Then, in late November, Grant undertook a more general and offensive effort to drive Confederate forces off the high ground near Chattanooga, including Missionary Ridge and Lookout Mountain, and secure the area more thoroughly. The ensuing fight lasted from November 23 to November 25 and involved an impressive uphill charge into (poorly situated) Confederate positions. The higher-altitude combat became known evocatively as the Battle above the Clouds.[117] Overall for the three-day engagement, Union losses out of an initial force of some 56,000 troops totaled around 6,000. Bragg's smaller force of 30,000 lost perhaps 7,000. Even more important, the victory decisively lifted the siege and consolidated Union control of the area, setting up the famous southward campaign of General Sherman in 1864.[118]

As mentioned earlier, perhaps the largest story of the second half of 1863 was the emergence of Grant as the inspirational leader, if not yet the commander, of the Northern war effort.

Grant had his foes, not least of them General John McClernand, a "political general" whose clout Grant had had to weaken over time in the Vicksburg campaign. McClernand wrote President Lincoln seeking to smear Grant even after that victory was won. As renowned Grant biographer Bruce Catton put it, "McClernand obviously was threatening to restate the old charge that General Grant now and then drank more than his situation required."[119] In fact, if Grant had a flaw, it was probably not his drinking. Lincoln was famously reported to have said in response to that same charge being leveled against Grant on a different occasion that someone should figure out what brand of whiskey Grant drank so that the president could send bottles to all of his other generals. Rather, Grant's temptations for ambitious horsemanship landed him unconscious and in bed for several weeks in early September of 1863 after a riding accident near New Orleans.

But Grant recovered from the incident and assumed command of the Military Division of the Mississippi, being accorded that position by Secretary of War Edwin Stanton—the two meeting in person, for the first time in their lives, to seal the deal in Indianapolis, Indiana. And then, Grant was able to head to Chattanooga in the manner described.[120]

After Chattanooga, Grant did not sit on his laurels. He immediately began looking for opportunities to continue southward, even if it would not be until the following year when Atlanta could be prudently approached and attacked. In this regard, Grant was thinking in broader campaign terms, as well as of overall strategy for winning the war. As Catton put it, in a chapter entitled "The Enemy Have Not Got Army Enough," Grant "had at last reached the point where he could see that final triumph for the Union depended on crowding a beaten foe without respite, permitting no breathing spell in which the weaker antagonist could regain his balance and repair damages—using the superior power of the North, in short, to apply unrelenting pressure of a sort the Confederacy had not the resources to resist."[121]

Taken together, Grant's battlefield successes and growing reputation led Lincoln to make Grant general-in-chief in March 1864—after a session in Washington, DC, that was *their* first meeting as well. Lincoln expressed his confidence in Grant clearly and decisively in a letter to the secretary of war, in which he wrote, "You and I, Mr. Stanton, have been trying to boss this job, and we have not succeeded very well with it. We have sent across the mountains for Mr. Grant, as Mrs. Grant calls him, to relieve us, and I think we had better leave him alone to do so as he pleases." Grant once remarked that of all the visitors to his various battlefield camps, Lincoln was the only person in proper position to ask about Grant's campaign plans, and the only person who did not actually ask. That is not to say, of course, that Lincoln became a mere spectator to events.

Even with this clear vote of presidential confidence and the associated authorities that came with it, most of the balance of the year was to be a long chapter for Grant. Victory hardly seemed ensured throughout it.[122] The next year would be very hard, especially until Atlanta fell to Sherman's forces in early September 1864.

1864 and 1865

The remaining fifteen-plus months of the Civil War can be lumped together because, especially in the crucial eastern theater, they included a single extended military campaign that lasted just under a year. Meade and Grant progressed gradually southward toward Richmond—ultimately flanking and gradually starting to encircle it—and toward Lee's army. In the end, both Richmond and Lee's army fell within days of each other. That fact leaves somewhat unresolved for strategists and historians the long-standing question as to which should be viewed as the Confederate center of gravity—the capital or the main Confederate army.

However, through the summer of 1864, it looked as if the South might still win the war. Indeed, the famed 1990 PBS documentary by Ken Burns on the Civil War described the summer of 1864 as the low point of the entire war saga for the North.[123]

The South's main remaining path to victory in 1864 again involved a mixture of military campaigning with politics. A pure military win was not possible and was perhaps not necessary, either. The effective strategy was to tire out the Union—not so much its army, but its leaders and its voters—such that Abraham Lincoln would not be reelected in November of that year. Then, a new U.S. president might agree to a peace deal, with or without a reestablishment of the whole nation, and certainly without the abolition of slavery.

Even in military terms, in fact, the Union still faced challenges, despite its advantages of 3:1 or more in most realms of manpower, industry, and materiel. First, with so much of the western theater now under Union control, through Tennessee and into the broader Mississippi Valley in particular, many forces were needed just to protect logistics lines. For the most part, Union forces continued to depend on railroads and rivers to transport huge amounts of provisions. Sherman had not yet employed his tactics of largely living off the land, which he would eventually make use of that summer, and few other Union leaders had found ways to reduce their supply requirements.

Second, many of the three-year enlistments that built up the Union army back in 1861 were expiring as the spring and summer of 1864 unfolded. Many soldiers seemed to fight less hard in their waning weeks of service. Only a bit more than half of the outgoing three-year enlistees could ultimately be induced to reenlist. Conscripts could be used to plug gaps in personnel requirements, but their dependability and quality were open to question. All in all, Grant estimated that only one in five of new enlistees he saw that year proved to be proficient soldiers. As Bruce Catton wrote, "The Civil War armies had been built on the volunteer system and this system had long since collapsed because it had been asked to carry too much. Once it brought in the country's best men and now it brought in its worst, and army commanders who used to prefer volunteers to conscripts now wanted conscripts if they could get them."[124] Then there was the ongoing problem of the "political generals" who owed their positions to connections and often performed poorly on the battlefield.[125]

Thus, as armies moved out of winter quarters on opposite sides of the Rapidan River in north-central Virginia in the early spring of 1864—not long after Grant became general-in-chief in early March—there would be no rapid victory. In fact, many of the memorable battles of the Civil War in the Virginia theater were prosecuted over the next seven, bloody, inconclusive weeks: the Wilderness, Spotsylvania, Cold Harbor, Petersburg. At least Lincoln finally had a general who would not pull back to lick his wounds or otherwise relent after a tactical setback.[126]

Union forces began the spring campaign with somewhat more than 70,000 forces to Lee's 40,000 or so. The ratios of force totals stayed similar throughout the fight, growing to 110,000 versus 60,000 in Cold Harbor, for example. Ratios of casualties were similar, too, with Union forces losing far more soldiers. Grant's strategy and campaign plan were both much better than the typical tactics employed by Northern forces in these battles. In the week of early May that included the Wilderness and Spotsylvania attacks, Union forces lost some 32,000 killed, wounded, or missing to the South's 18,000 or so. These were staggering, devastating numbers, and even though many of the losses could be replaced, the net effect was to create considerable gloom in the North, already tired by years of combat. By the end of June, the total losses in the spring campaigns for the Union were 65,000, to the South's 35,000.[127]

As the fighting continually moved southward, eventually reaching Petersburg below Richmond, the signature event of the summer was the successful detonation of a huge underground mine that Union forces had gradually tunneled under Confederate defenses over a period of weeks. Alas, this event was followed by a completely unsuccessful exploitation of the enormous crater and the temporary hole in southern lines, that it created. On balance, this period and the ensuing summer were not happy ones for the Union. Grant's doggedness did not translate into quick victories, and by summer, his geographical progress slowed, too.

Even secondary efforts in the eastern theater, as with Union forces under General Philip Sheridan in the Shenandoah Valley, were frustrating. "Mosby's Raiders," mounted on horses and taking advantage of their knowledge of the region, harassed their flanks and rear area in a form of irregular or what might now be called hybrid warfare. After crossing the Potomac and prevailing in the Battle of the Monocacy River near Frederick, Maryland, in July, General Jubal Early even managed to get enough Confederate forces across the Potomac to approach within a few miles of Washington, DC, before finding the capital's fortifications too much to breech.[128] Sounds of the fight tempted a tall gentleman in distinct stovepipe hat to venture out for a closer inspection until a Union soldier told the unrecognized President Lincoln to "get down, you damn fool, before you get shot."[129] Reportedly, Lincoln chuckled and did as he was told. Only later that fall after a prolonged campaign by General Sheridan in the Shenandoah Valley that foreshadowed Sherman's March to the Sea in intent and character was this Confederate army route into Union territory finally closed off for good.

With all the frustrations, and all the death, witnessed in 1864, the national mood was poor. That summer, Lincoln's reelection prospects accordingly did not look good—and it appeared that the Southern strategy, such as it was, still might just work. The very same George McClellan who had struggled in command of Union forces a couple years before seemed poised to defeat Honest Abe at the ballot box come November.

Yet, even though it was hard to see at the time, dynamics were tilting increasingly in the North's favor. Grant was close to Richmond, and was able to supply his forces and replace his losses. Meanwhile, Lee's army was suffering too, and was enjoying less and less strategic depth from which it could garner supplies or to which it might retreat as Union forces constantly kept the pressure on. Again, from an overall campaign perspective, Grant was succeeding, and appears to have known it, even as he and the Army of the Potomac were arguably losing most of the individual battles.

Politically, though, what saved Lincoln's presidency—and thus, perhaps, the Union—that fall was not the Army of the Potomac, but developments further south. Near Atlanta, after a summer of patient maneuvering, General Sherman was making headway. General Joseph Johnston and then General John Hood's Confederate forces had been able to maintain defensive positions protecting the city and fend off various probing attacks, fighting hard only when in advantageous defensive positions as at the Battle of Kennesaw Mountain on June 27, where the Confederates won a lopsided tactical victory. But their luck eventually ran out.

Atlanta fell on September 1, 1864. Sherman's clever maneuvering finally paid off, as he moved at Atlanta from an unexpected direction south of the city. Sherman, not in a mood to take care of civilians or to burden his logistical lines with the necessity of sustaining an occupation force for Atlanta, then had the city evacuated.

The entire national mood in the Union soon changed. Lincoln won the 1864 election on November 8 with a commanding Electoral College advantage of 212 to 21 over McClellan.

Then, after having his supply lines harassed by the remnants of Hood's forces, Sherman and his 60,000 soldiers finally received permission from Grant, Stanton, and Lincoln to break free of supply lines in an eastward march. The goal in Sherman's words was to "make Georgia howl." They then cut a swath of land over the 285 miles to Savannah and the sea. Carrying their ammunition with them, but otherwise seizing resources from the local economy for sustenance, Sherman's troops spent the last six weeks or so of 1864 on one of the most consequential marches in military history. With the Confederate economy already floundering, even as the Union economy boomed, Sherman effectively denuded a swath of land some 25 to 60 miles wide through the heart of the Deep South, all the way to Savannah, with only scant Southern resistance along the way.[130] Jefferson Davis, perhaps not entirely unfairly, nicknamed Sherman the Attila of the American Continent, though in this case the property damage was much worse than the direct loss of life.[131]

In a less famous but at least as important and even more difficult march, Sherman and his legions subsequently spent the winter doing the same kind of thing to the Carolinas. Again, this was the Anaconda strategy at work, but with a distinctly Shermanesque twist. Hood, meanwhile, turned toward Tennessee, where he sought to find some way to salvage a victory in a different theater and start to drive Union forces out of the middle theater of the conflict. But General George Thomas's 60,000 forces defeated Hood's 40,000 in Nashville near the end of the year.[132]

Back in the eastern and northernmost theater, things had, as noted, slowed a bit. Grant turned more of his attention to the Shenandoah Valley, seeking to make sure that future threats to the Union and to Washington could no longer emanate from that region, and to deprive the Confederacy and its armies of a fertile breadbasket. General Sheridan rallied his forces to salvage success at the Battle of Cedar Creek on October 19, 1864, and more broadly the campaign in that theater gradually went the way of the Union.

Around Richmond, battle dynamics and movements appeared slow. Perhaps Grant's armies there were tired from the brutal spring and early summer campaign. He also seemed to be thinking in terms of applying pressure against Lee from all directions, including contributions from Sherman and Thomas as they finished their previous campaigns elsewhere— meaning that the effort would naturally need to await early 1865. Still, the gradual constriction continued. Grant continued to turn southward and westward to challenge supply lines including, he hoped, the Weldon Railroad and Southside Railroad. There were battles in places like Boydton Plank Road, Chaffin's Bluff, Hatcher's Run, and Peeble's Farm. Late summer, fall, and winter operations by Union forces gradually closed off more roads, and soon another railroad, and ensured the robustness of the Union positions against any possible Confederate attack.[133]

As winter progressed and the war's last spring approached, Lee mulled his options. He thought about breaking out of his encirclement to, in effect, abandon Richmond and go help forces under General Joe Johnston fight Sherman in the Carolinas. That approach would have conceded Richmond (with the hope that Jefferson Davis and his government could get out first), in effect retaining the Army of Northern Virginia as the main surviving manifestation of the Confederacy. But it was not to be. After Union forces routed General John Gordon's forces east of Petersburg, they did the same to Pickett's division southwest of the city—and the die was cast. Lee could not escape.

Lee's total strength now equaled only about 35,000 soldiers, and his ability to evade the tightening noose around him was disappearing fast. Lee sent a note to Jefferson Davis to abandon Richmond on Sunday April 2. President Lincoln visited the vanquished city soon thereafter, as Lee fled westward in a movement that Union forces soon contained—forcing the surrender at Appomattox on Palm Sunday, April 9 (and five days before the fateful assassination of Lincoln on Good Friday, April 14). After a long debate over whether Richmond or Lee's army was the true center of gravity, and proper military focus for Union forces, in this war, both the city and the army had fallen within a week of each other.[134]

Some fighting continued for a brief time elsewhere. But on May 10, Jefferson Davis was captured in Georgia (he would spend two years in detention before being released), and other Southern efforts to retain hope had also evaporated. The war was finally over.

Mistakes Made and Lessons Learned

Debate among historians about the major decisions made in the American Civil War has continued for more than 150 years and will surely go on for centuries to come. But for the modern strategist, which issues, questions and takeaways are most compelling for today?

Many crucial debates about this epoch are political and ethical, concerning as they do secession, slavery, and the basic experiment of American democracy. But for the modern military strategist, seeking to distill lessons that have broader applicability for warfare, several more specific questions should also concern us:

- Was McClellan too cautious in the Virginia campaign, especially in 1862?
- Did the North have the right overall strategy of pursuing Lee's armies, and trying to bear down on Richmond, while also applying the "Anaconda" concept for economic pressure? Could a more patient and resolute implementation of the latter approach have obviated the need for many of the frontal assaults that wound up characterizing the conflict?

- Did the South have the right overall strategy—trying to win, in effect, on the conventional battlefield?
- Was Lee too aggressive, especially in his efforts to move into Union territory?
- Did generals on both sides send too many soldiers to their deaths in frontal assaults that the technologies of the day made increasingly ill-advised?
- Did the Union need to maintain the long logistics lines on which it depended for its preferred style of warfare?

It is worth reflecting on some of these specific questions before taking a broader view and asking which lessons from the Civil War should really inform our thinking today.

There can be little doubt that, early in the war in the Virginia theater, Union generals exhibited much less elan, tactical and campaign-level creativity, and good judgment than did their Southern counterparts. The Union's preparations in terms of recruiting and training soldiers and equipping them properly were also a bit chaotic in the war's early months—Russell Weigley wonders, for example, why it took longer to train Union troops than it took to train Vietnam-bound troops a century later.[135] So yes, it is hard to rave about northern performance in the war's first phases.

Regarding Lee, and Southern strategy more generally, although Lee is often celebrated for his tactics, his overall military legacy is surely much more mixed. He almost certainly preferred the offensive too much, given the technologies of the day, as well as the force disparities and war goals of each side. He wound up in too many slugfests that, even if he won more than his share, could not realistically maximize the advantages of the Confederacy—or mitigate its weaknesses, as a well-regarded U.S. Marine Corps document forcefully argued back in 1997, before Lee's legacy took an even more substantial beating in recent times.[136] Arguably the way that General Joseph Johnston sought to trade space for time—generally avoiding pitched fights against Sherman unless Johnson saw that his own forces were in virtually unassailable position, as at Kennesaw Mountain—would have been a better concept for Southern forces overall. It might have drawn out the war and with it, Northern patience, and political will. And it would have had precedent on North American soil in the basic strategy of George Washington during the Revolutionary War. This is what Grant also believed, when asked after the war if there was any strategy the South could have followed more successfully.[137]

Other elements of strategy have been fiercely debated, as well. The British historian J. F. C. Fuller argued that the Union made a major mistake in focusing on the Virginia theater as the center of gravity of the Confederacy.[138] Fuller would have advised focusing on the narrow swath of land between Chattanooga, Tennessee, and Atlanta, Georgia, since two major railroad lines traversed the area, linking the southern and western parts of the Confederacy with Virginia and the Carolinas. By severing that connection, he argued, Union forces would have created the conditions for a more effective squeezing strategy by delinking the three aforementioned states from the rest of the South.

So yes, if the North had gotten going faster, it might have won faster. If Lee had behaved more like the Vietcong, or even George Washington, he might have lasted longer in the field—and maybe even outlasted Northern patience and will. If the North had adopted a "Chattanooga strategy," or given the Anaconda strategy more time to work, perhaps it could have avoided some of the slugfests of the Virginia theater and elsewhere. There are lots of ways the war could have gone differently, and some might well have reduced the carnage.

Yet the mistakes need to be understood in the context of a hugely devastating and tragic civil war for which the nation was underprepared intellectually, materially, and institutionally. Upon reflection, I am not persuaded that they were the main reasons the Civil War went so tragically.

Take for example the critique that the North was slow to organize its forces, and wasted much of 1861 in the effort. True enough. But with a better approach, all that would have likely resulted is a couple months' worth of quicker preparation for the campaigns of 1862. Consider again the comparison with America's mobilization for Vietnam. In that latter conflict a century later, the institutional U.S. military was already large when the 1960s began—already on a Cold War footing, only a decade removed from the massive Korean War effort. The military of 1861, by contrast, had been tiny—and very political—and it lost many of its top technocratic officers to the Confederacy once secession occurred. A period of inefficient response was inevitable. Again, as Clausewitz argued, in war everything is simple, but even the simple things are hard—especially when you have never done them before on anything close to the necessary scale.

The argument that many generals of the day, even including its most storied, failed to appreciate the effects of rifles and better artillery—insisting on charges across open fields against entrenched defenders anyway—is partly correct. But in a large fraction of battles, attacking generals attempted to use maneuver to avoid such desperation measures whenever they could. They sought to flank and enfilade enemy forces such that they could fire lengthwise along the opponent's main positions. Or they sought to isolate and break enemy formations into pieces that could be overwhelmed individually. I do not know how to estimate the fraction of casualties caused by such headstrong and largely obsolete offensive charges. But a reading of the main battles of the war does not make me think the number reaches 50 percent of all losses. Only a few battles, such as the Union attacks at Fredericksburg in December 1862 and Pickett's Charge at Gettysburg in July 1863, strike me as truly stupid in retrospect.

Yes, in purely military terms Lee probably should have avoided going on the tactical offensive as often as he did. Yet without glorifying Lee, his actions do have a certain logic. The historian Jay Winik has pointed out that Lee and Jefferson Davis seriously contemplated, in the early weeks of 1865, a strategy that would give up Richmond and turn Lee's forces into a form of guerrilla resistance—but in the end they could not quite bring themselves to a decision that would, in their minds, run so counter to sustaining the Southern civilization and way of life that they loved.[139] Lee's attempts to invade the North also had an understandable political logic of seeking to weaken the Union's morale and its will to fight.

What about McClellan's purported pusillanimity? The general always seemed to expect more from Washington, or other commanders, or anyone else he could criticize. He always had an excuse for why he could not move, or sustain a fight, or prevail in many engagements. Certainly, the pompous general's letters and public statements—together with the fact that he ran against Lincoln in the 1864 election and did so with a view of the Confederacy that now seems akin to appeasement—have placed him in a bad light in history. Wouldn't the war likely have been much shorter if he had not been in command?

All the critiques of McClellan seem fair (and one wonders why a statue of him still stands near Dupont Circle in Washington, DC). More specifically, had McClellan seized the moment in 1862, his logistically impressive peninsular campaign might well have succeeded in reaching Richmond—perhaps even leading to an early end to the war.

It is worth remembering, however, that McClellan was not the only Union general in charge of the eastern theater to favor caution. McDowell before him, at Manassas, and Burnside as well as Hooker after him, were similarly disinclined to move fast. None followed up uncertain battlefield outcomes with potentially decisive follow-on action. Part of this may have reflected, as Russell Weigley has argued, a certain preoccupation with the great battle rather than with the sustained and multi-pronged theater-wide campaign, though such interpretations remain contentious among Civil War historians.[140] For those of us who see the battles of the day with 150-plus years of good information about the opposing forces at our fingertips, it is worth remembering that part of the difficulty of fighting them well arose from the poor state of battlefield intelligence. As Clausewitz wrote about intelligence—and this certainly applied to the Civil War as much as to the battles that he knew well from the Napoleonic campaigns earlier in the century—"Many intelligence reports in war are contradictory; even more are false, and most are uncertain."[141]

In any case, it is common in war for the best available commanders not to be easily identified. Sometimes the wartime experience itself provides the real test and the real filtering—and that process takes time. Moreover, McClellan did have real strengths in terms of organization, logistics, and morale building among his soldiers, all traits that Lincoln appreciated.[142] (And his idea from August 1861 of building an army of almost 300,000 to march decisively on Richmond, then continue to points further south, was not entirely crazy given the materiel advantages enjoyed by the North.[143]) Looking back, we take Grant's virtues of doggedness, persistence, and underlying confidence almost for granted. But they were perhaps at least as unusual a set of qualities as the earlier generals' tendencies toward caution.[144]

It is not unnatural or even obviously unwise for an economically superior, yet underprepared and unready power, to take its time in fighting a weaker adversary. That this plodding style of Union war making might now be recognized as mistaken does not make it categorically foolish for the conditions and circumstances of the day.

Moreover, the several dozen major battles of the American Civil War were absolutely brutal. Losses were enormous. When one considers that casualty levels after one to three days of fighting were often 15 to 30 percent of initial forces, it is also easy to understand why winners did not always rapidly pursue losers. They were themselves too broken and weary to do so, especially given the logistical and other requirements of carrying out follow-on attacks against a retreating adversary. As Russell Weigley writes about Lincoln's frustration with General Meade, for failing to pursue Lee after Gettysburg, "It was as unfair an assessment as Lincoln ever made."[145] Yet in another sense Lincoln was correct, if the pursuit could have ended the war, and the carnage, sooner.

In short, in reflecting on these and other decisions or policies that occurred within the conflict itself, once it was underway, the war was likely to be protracted and devastating. Both sides defined it in existential terms. Each had strong, even fervent commitment to its cause. Both had enough weaponry, and strategic depth, and other assets and resilience, to make a quick victory by the other implausible. Yet neither had been preparing for war very well for long, given the hopes that political compromise could avoid such a horrible civil war. Big mistakes were virtually inevitable.

Thus, the crucial mistake was not, for either side, in waging the war badly. It was waging it at all. The mistakes of McClellan, or Lee, or anyone else pale in comparison to the horribly disastrous decision by the South in particular to wage the war in the first place.

The likely difficulties of the saga should have been foreseeable—even before the realities of actual combat made that conclusion obvious in retrospect. Clausewitz had been writing about the horrors and complications of war in recent decades—and he had plenty of evidence on his side, at the time of his writings and in subsequent conflicts like the Crimean War of the 1850s. Romanticizing war, even in defense of a noble and popular cause, is always a mistake—and the leaders of the day should have known as much.[146]

The war may have seemed existential to many Southerners—and thus unavoidable, whatever its costs. But no one was threatening genocide against the other and in fact no one was insisting on any near-term change to existing ways of life. Thus, from another perspective, the war was not really existential—especially when considering its horrors. The immediate stakes were about the expansion of slavery, not its perpetuation in places where it already existed. I do not doubt that many Southerners viewed the war as essential to saving their way of life—but the fact that they had this mindset does not prove it was correct. Given the likelihood of military defeat in a large-scale war, it would have been wiser to accept the eventual risks to their way of life of staying within the Union.

A serious look at the correlation of resources between North and South should have challenged even those who extolled the martial virtues of the South that they could really have prevailed. Their theory of victory relied on Northern irresoluteness in the face of a war that the North would find too burdensome even as the South found it entirely sustainable. The theory was not demonstrably implausible on its face—but it was too optimistic.

The South deserves main blame for the Civil War, on ethical and political and military levels. But one can challenge Northern thinking, too.

Perhaps Lincoln was himself overconfident. Perhaps he should have attempted a different and more deliberate version of an Anaconda strategy, without the land battles—trying to squeeze the South into gradual submission. We know that it is difficult to use sanctions and other instruments of economic warfare to force major change in a polity's behavior quickly. It is also possible that, absent a direct overland threat to their polity, Southerners might have gone after the Union positions in coastal islands and ports that enabled the blockade to be somewhat effective. Yet even if such a patient and risky Union strategy had taken a decade or more to achieve its goals, might that have been preferable to the carnage that resulted from war? It is not clear that Lincoln or most other northern defenders of the Union even seriously considered such an approach. Perhaps they should have.

As the great Australian historian Geoffrey Blainey noted, leaders going into war usually expect to win, and they usually expect to win relatively fast. This unfortunate human tendency needs to be identified, understood—and systematically challenged.

As RAND scholars Alain Enthoven and K. Wayne Smith wrote in their classic book on military analysis, *How Much Is Enough,* it is always important when contemplating or planning war to envision both optimistic *and* pessimistic possible outcomes.[147] This simple verity is frequently forgotten—but that is no excuse for the insouciance with which many entered into the American Civil War. Contingency planning for difficult wartime circumstances was not in vogue on either side of the Potomac in the 1850s and early 1860s.

The lessons for today are several. The most important is that we would be highly optimistic, and indeed reckless, to count on quickly winning any war against a major power, or for that matter even many modest powers. It is easy to become intoxicated by belief in the righteousness of one's cause, or the martial qualities of one's military, or the cleverness of new military technologies and tactics—and expect rapid, decisive victory. History in general, and certainly the American Civil War in this particular case, suggests otherwise.

But by the same token, we should worry that a future adversary might develop an overly optimistic theory of victory against *us*. Perhaps President Xi Jinping of China, or a successor, might think that with his country on the rise, and with many materiel advantages due to the country's massive population and industry, it can prevail against the United States— especially in a conflict near China's shores and far from our own, say over Taiwan or the South China Sea. Perhaps President Vladimir Putin of Russia, or a successor, might conclude like Robert E. Lee that a dramatic maneuver into NATO territory (like the Baltic states) is the best way to compensate for overall strategic weakness, just as Lee attempted to take the war into Maryland and Pennsylvania in 1862 and 1863 (and even have a subordinate try again in 1864). Next, we will examine a conflict that should have been much more influenced and informed by the lessons of the American Civil War than proved to be the case. That conflict is World War I.

TWO | *World War I*

W orld War I was sparked by the killing of Archduke Franz Ferdinand, heir to the Hapsburg throne within the Austro-Hungarian Empire, in the city of Sarajevo on June 28, 1914. Austria-Hungary had recently annexed Sarajevo and the rest of Bosnia-Herzegovina in 1908, angering Serbs and their Russian supporters. Gavrilo Princip, who would be arrested and convicted for the crime, dying five years later of tuberculosis while in prison, was the assassin. But he did not act alone. He was trained and supported by "Black Hand" elements in Serbia, the small independent country to the east that sought to expand its territory to include more of the broader Serbian diaspora in the region, including in Bosnia-Herzegovina. Serbia was a country rife with nationalism as well as internal political intrigue.[1]

The war began because Austria-Hungary chose to punish Serbia for the Sarajevo assassination through a punitive military raid. Germany supported its ally Austria-Hungary in that goal. But Russia, having been embarrassed by previous setbacks for its allies and interests in recent years in the Balkans, and worrying about its future access to the Turkish Straits, chose to resist. Those earlier setbacks included not only the annexation of Bosnia-Herzegovina by Austria-Hungary, but also the outcomes of the Balkan conflicts of 1912 and 1913. Over the course of those two struggles, which drove the Ottomans from their hold on most of southeastern Europe, Serbia grew in size. But it also had to curtail its territorial ambitions for access to the Adriatic Sea—after being issued an ultimatum not to pursue those aspirations by Austria-Hungary.[2] In 1914, Russia was determined to defend more doggedly and successfully its fellow Orthodox Christians, even at the risk of general war. Indeed, its war plans called for full mobilization against not only Austria-Hungary, but also Germany— and it would shortly follow through on those plans. In this context, Germany chose to begin combat with an attack on Russia's ally *France*. That

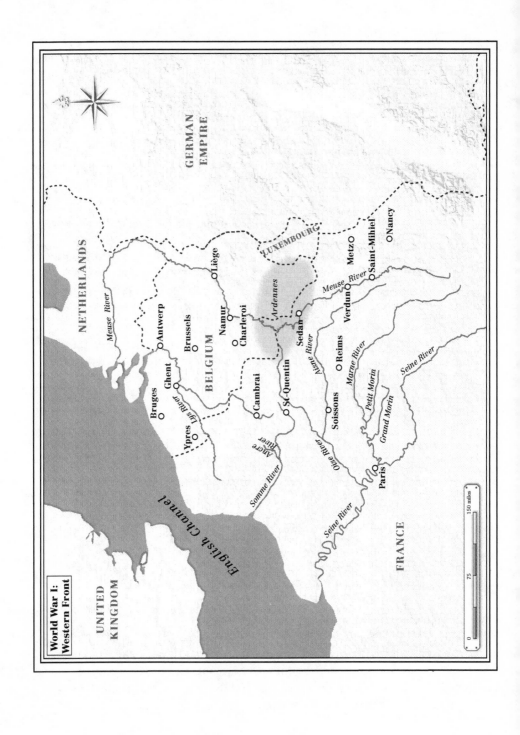

World War I:
Western Front

UNITED
KINGDOM

NETHERLANDS

GERMAN
EMPIRE

Meuse River

Liège

LUXEMBOURG

Antwerp

Brussels

Namur

Charleroi

Ardennes

Metz

Saint-Mihiel

Nancy

Meuse River

Verdun

Sedan

Bruges

Ghent

BELGIUM

Cambrai

St-Quentin

Aisne River

Reims

Marne River

Ypres

Lys River

Ancre River

Somme River

Oise River

Soissons

Petit Morin

Grand Morin

Seine River

English Channel

Seine River

Paris

Seine River

FRANCE

0   75   150 miles

World War I:
Eastern Front

FINLAND

SWEDEN

Baltic
Sea

GERMAN
EMPIRE

Saint Petersburg

Narva

Riga

Libau

Dvinsk

Moscow

Kovno

Königsberg

Tannenberg

Vilna

Grodno

Minsk

RUSSIA

Przasnysz

Warsaw

Łódź

Radom

Brest-Litovsk

Pinsk

Pripet
Marshes

Lublin

Cracow

Jaroslaw

Gorlice

Przemyśl

Rovno

Lvov

Tarnopol

Kiev

Stanislau

Budapest

AUSTRO-
HUNGARIAN
EMPIRE

Alps

Carpathian Mountains

Kishinev

Odessa

Nikolaiev

Sarajevo

Belgrade

SERBIA

MONTENEGRO

ITALY

ALBANIA

Bucharest

ROMANIA

Danube River

BULGARIA

Sevastopol

Black Sea

Tyrrhenian
Sea

Ionian
Sea

GREECE

Aegean
Sea

Gallipoli
Peninsula

TURKISH EMPIRE

Adriatic Sea

Dvina River

Vistula River

Bug River

Dnieper River

Dniester River

Prut River

Danube River

Drava River

Sava River

0   300   600 miles

was because of Berlin's two-front Schlieffen Plan that necessitated moving west first, and securing a quick victory against France, before turning attentions eastward toward the more ponderous Russian military machine. France was known in Berlin to have ambitions against Germany, not least to avenge losses in earlier wars. That helped the German proponents of war make their case that it made more sense to go first rather than wait to be attacked.

After five weeks of bluster, mutual consultation, secret diplomacy, public threats, and military preparations, as well as limited attacks by Austria-Hungary against Serbia, major hostilities began on August 4. The German assault went through neutral Luxembourg and Belgium into northern France. Russia soon attacked Germany and Austria-Hungary on the eastern front, in and around present-day Poland.

Thus, a tragic yet isolated political assassination led to a global catastrophe. World War I was surely among the most consequential mistakes made by humans in all of history. It was a collective failing, particularly of European leaders and of the European state system of the day, at a time when Europe was the center of geopolitics and global economic and military power. Vigorous historical debate continues about which countries were most to blame. Few would let Germany off the hook as a major cause of the conflict. Russia, too, was very aggressive and more bent on furthering national ambitions than resolving or mitigating any crisis. But France and Great Britain were hardly innocent; they had established much of the hypercharged sense of rivalry and imperialism that set the broader context in which World War I began.[3]

The war killed 10 million people directly. The major European participants typically each lost 1 to 2 million dead, plus even larger numbers of wounded, many maimed for life. These losses came out of national populations that totaled about 40 to 65 million each (except Russia, with an estimated 170 million).[4] By contrast, the American Civil War, itself considered absolutely devastating to society, took some 750,000 lives out of a total U.S. population of just over 30 million. World War I was two to three times as lethal on a per capita basis for most of its main European participants. And its flawed peace set the stage for a second world war that would be several times again more deadly.

There were many causes of World War I. But, consistent with a central theme of this book—and of much military history over the ages—the prevalence of overconfidence was extraordinary. So was naivete about the likely consequences of combat. A half century after the American Civil War, militaries had not really grappled with the likely characteristics of warfare in an era of rapid-fire and very lethal weaponry.

Hypernationalistic and militaristic outlooks in key countries contributed greatly to the outbreak and continuation of the war. As just one example, in Germany a popular book written by General Friedrich von Bernhardi just before the conflict began was entitled *Germany and the Next War*. Respective chapters explained the right to make war, the duty to make war, and the necessity of making war.[5] More generally, many in this period viewed war as somehow ennobling, inspiring, edifying.[6]

Incestuous monarchies contributed too. Incredibly, at the outbreak of the conflict, both the German and British heads of state, Kaiser Wilhelm II and King George V, were grandchildren of (the deceased) Queen Victoria, as was the wife of the czar of Russia. The czar was himself a cousin of the kaiser. Rather than familiarity breeding affection, here it bred rivalry, and often contempt, among this group of leaders.[7] Indeed, it was an unimpressive group of leaders in general, in all the main countries at issue. It is hard to find any greats among them. Even those who attained acclaim in later years, notably Winston Churchill, were arguably more part of the problem than the solution in World War I. Perhaps the most impressive figure of the day, who believed in reforming his own country to treat minorities like Serbs more kindly, was the very heir to the throne of Austria-Hungary whose assassination sparked the war. Another admirable individual was King Albert of Belgium. But the bravery that he and his small army displayed in defending their territory against foreign invasion could not stop the German military juggernaut (it may have helped slow it enough to buy France meaningful time, however). Woodrow Wilson kept the United States out of the war until 1917 because he understandably saw guilt on all sides, and then tried to create a strong League of Nations after the war in an attempt to prevent future such catastrophes. But given his failure in this latter effort, and the general problems with the Treaty of Versailles, it is hard to see him as a major hero.[8]

The fact that the "Great War" occurred in an era otherwise characterized by some of humanity's greatest achievements in engineering, science, transportation and communications, economics, and human well-being makes the tragedy all the more unthinkable. The scientists and intellectuals of the day were far ahead of their contemporaries in political and military spheres.

Germany, Austria-Hungary, and initially Italy formed what was called the Triple Alliance. France, Britain, and Russia made up the so-called Entente. Italy later wound up on the Entente side. The remaining elements of the Ottoman Empire, centered on modern Turkey (and sometimes referred to here by that latter name as well), joined Germany and Austria-Hungary. The U.S. entry into the war in 1917 on the Entente side more than compensated for the departure of Russia, as the latter's government fell that year, with the nation descending into revolution and civil war and no longer able to mount meaningful military resistance.

Geographically, the war can be thought of as occurring in four main zones. The first was of course the famous western front, a relatively limited space in northern France and Belgium where a modified version of the Schlieffen Plan was put into action in the late summer of 1914.[9] Trench warfare soon ensued. Each year after 1914, new attempts were made by one side or the other to break the stalemate and push the respective trenches some modest distance either south and west or north and east. But only in 1918 did lines move very much.

The second main area of battle was the broader region of Central Europe where the Austro-Hungarian Empire, Russian Poland, Russia itself, modern Ukraine, and Germany came together. This battle zone ultimately extended to Serbia and other Balkan states, and to Italy.

The third arena was made up of places around the world where colonial and imperial holdings brought the various European powers plus Japan into contact as they sought to protect or expand their conquests. These areas included parts of sub-Saharan Africa, northern Africa, the Mediterranean extending over to the Turkish Straits, the Arab Middle East, and parts of coastal China. Sometimes, colonized peoples were required to fight on behalf of their colonizers, whether close to home or on the European front. Notably, for example, some 1.3 million Indians would serve in the British army in World War I, with some 74,000 losing their lives.[10] Many Africans from areas under British and French rule served, too.

The fourth and very important combat zone was the Atlantic Ocean and the seas of northern Europe, where blockades and counter-blockade efforts first put Britain at risk but over time severely weakened Germany. It was largely the combat that occurred in this area over the war's first three years that finally brought an angered United States into the war after too much of its shipping and too many of its people were lost to unrestricted German submarine activity.

As with the American Civil War, much of World War I can be simplified into study of several dozen key battles. And just as with my treatment of that earlier conflict, it can be understood by breaking the struggle down year by year, as undertaken below. But first, several aspects of the backstory and backdrop to the conflict should be highlighted.

The Strategic Context and the Alliance System of Early Twentieth-Century Europe

The roots of World War I derived from several hundred years of the European state system and its increasingly nationalistic, competitive, and imperialistic characteristics, all combined with the march of technology and the ongoing modernization and industrialization of the major economies.[11] The 1648 Treaty of Westphalia, as well as the so-called Concert of Europe of the nineteenth century—cooperation among the great powers to dampen or resolve problems that arose—are often credited with confining conflict within certain parameters. But those years were hardly peaceful, within and beyond Europe's borders. The Westphalian system did not prevent Britain and France from fighting each other frequently, from North America to sub-Saharan Africa to the region around Egypt and the Nile.[12] And there continued to be important wars in Europe in the nineteenth century—in 1853–1856 in Crimea, pitting Russia against France, Britain and the Ottoman Empire; in 1866 between Prussia and Austria; in 1870–1871 between Prussia and France.

The more specific origins of the Great War arguably date from the end of the 1870–1871 conflict. That was when Germany, having just wrested Alsace and Lorraine from France, emerged as a cohesive and increasingly powerful state.

Military rivalries became much worse from the 1890s onward, after the departure of Chancellor Otto von Bismarck in Germany, who had been a voice for relative restraint and calm (at least after Prussia/Germany won its wars and forged a nation in the 1860s and early 1870s). Germany as well as Italy, latecomers to the great games, wanted their shares of the overseas colonies and spoils. Yet that was not easily achieved. Despite having just carried out a naval buildup, Germany did not feel it was gaining ground in the imperial competition—losing out to France for control of Morocco in 1911, for example.[13]

Germans, including Chief of General Staff Helmuth von Moltke, also began to fear that growing Russian power and tightening British-Russian ties would leave it worse off in the years to come. Moltke and others with this view began to advocate preventive war so that Germany could weaken rivals. Some may have favored acquisition of strategic real estate in Europe, for example ports in Belgium and northern France, as a result of any such war, as well.[14] German military leaders were consistently in favor of the use of force, over Morocco or Bosnia or other issues, and against France, Britain, and Russia, in the decade leading up to 1914. As Stephen Van Evera put it, speaking of Germany's top officers, "They called for war in every crisis during 1905–1914."[15] That perspective ultimately led to using the Austro-Hungarian attack on Serbia, and resulting Russian aggression in the east, as a pretext for attacking *France* preventively.

Indeed, in the two years before war broke out, Kaiser Wilhelm II's letters, dispatches, diplomatic engagements, and other conversations are laced with references to the desirability as well as the inevitability of general war. They were often couched in racial terms, depicting a contest of Germanic versus Slavic and Latin peoples—with territorial ambitions for Germany and its allies extending from the English Channel to the eastern Mediterranean.[16] Stunningly, near the end of his life, the kaiser (who abdicated in 1918 and moved to the Netherlands, where he died in 1941) celebrated Hitler's initial victories as vindicating and realizing his own goals, and celebrated Germany's generals, who had led the campaigns, with these words: "Educated by Schlieffen they put the plans he had worked out under me into practice along the same lines as we did in 1914."[17] It is for this reason that the famed, if controversial, German historian Fritz Fischer argued in the 1960s that Germany was the main guilty party in causing World War I—and why many eminent modern historians and strategists such as Stephen Van Evera of MIT agree with him.[18]

I do not disagree with these critics of Germany. But like many historians, I also see the early Russian aggression against both Austria-Hungary and Germany in the war's early days as unnecessarily escalatory. At a minimum, Russia's full mobilization and preparation for attack on both Germany as well as Austria-Hungary handed Berlin the pretext it wanted to launch general war. Russia had concerns that Austria-Hungary, after defeating and possibly deconstructing Serbia, would move onward to seize control of access to the Black Sea through the Turkish Straits (the Dardanelles and Bosporus), and that Vienna as well as Berlin would then gain the ability to squeeze the Russian economy.[19] But that is a fairly indirect and hypothetical concern on which to base a direct assault on the core territories of two neighbors. Nor were Paris and London innocent. The worldwide imperial ambitions, and conquests, of France and Britain in previous decades did much to create a hypercharged nationalistic competition among the great powers of Europe. France also had an aggressive military concept, Plan XVII, to go along with a grand strategy that aspired to reclaim territories that had been lost to Prussia and the young German state several decades before. Germany deserves a special blame but is far from the only guilty party. These critiques of other powers do not lessen Germany's guilt; assigning responsibility for the outbreak of World War I is not a zero-sum analytical exercise in which a certain amount of blame is apportioned. What is staggering is just how many mistakes were made in many different places. Put differently, several countries had credible ways to stop this war before it began, and none of them did.

If some nation-states were consolidating and strengthening in the nineteenth and early twentieth centuries, other empires were weakening. Centrifugal as well as centripetal forces were at work—and sometimes, both at the same time. Austria-Hungary was simultaneously hungry for conquest and expansion, like the stronger states of Europe, while being very worried about its ability to hold together an empire of some nine main nationalities. The Ottoman Empire, though still substantial, was near the end of its multicentury decline. Its shaky hold on territory created opportunities for other imperialistic countries—but also mutual fears among many that some other foreign powers would gain control, say of the Turkish Straits, at their own nation's expense. That created the potential for conflict. As Barbara Tuchman wrote in her World War I classic, *The Guns of August,* "For ten centuries, Russia had yearned for Constantinople, the city Russians called Czargrad that lay at the exit of the Black Sea. That narrow and famous sea passage, called the Dardanelles, fifty miles long and nowhere more than three miles wide, was Russia's only year-round egress to the rest of the world."[20] Perhaps an opportunity to seize the area might soon present itself. More forebodingly, perhaps Germany and Austria-Hungary would seek to control it.

European leaders failed to heed the warnings set down on paper just a few decades before by the great Prussian soldier and scholar, Carl von Clausewitz, who wrote about the fog of war and escalatory dynamics. Or perhaps they listened too much to, and misunderstood, passages of *On War* (published in 1832) in which Clausewitz described war as a continuation of politics and policy by other means. That adage can be interpreted (correctly) as a recognition that few if any wars arise out of nothing, or follow a purely military logic, or continue until the enemy is literally annihilated.

Dangerously, however, it can also be misunderstood as somehow legitimating war and suggesting it can be confidently controlled. Clausewitz could also be misunderstood in his advocacy of "decisive battle." To be sure, such successful showdowns are to be preferred over wars of attrition. But aspiring to such successes does not always bring them about.[21] Clausewitz's warnings about the advantages of fighting on the defensive should have given more pause to any such offensive-minded interpretation of his ideas.[22] Alas, to the extent he was read, he was read quite selectively.[23]

Leaders also failed to reflect adequately on what the great scholar of ancient Greece, Thucydides, had observed about the attractions and dangers of war. In book one of his *History of the Peloponnesian War,* the great struggle pitting Athens and its allies against Sparta and its own allies, Thucydides famously noted that humanity's main motives for engaging in combat boiled down to fear, greed, and honor.[24] Greed and honor seem to have been particularly on display in the early years of the twentieth century. Thucydides wrote of the "Melian dialogue" in which strong Athens laid down the law for the lesser power of Melos, noting that in international politics, the strong do what they will and the weak do what they can.[25] A much strengthened Germany wanted its place in the sun, in Europe and globally. France and Britain, already masters of many lands beyond their own, did not want to share the glory and honor they had already achieved.[26]

Perhaps because the European wars of recent experience had been generally brief, notably the Prussian-Austrian War of 1866 and the Prussian-French War of 1870–1871, too much faith was placed in the idea that war would remain limited in the future. Europeans of the day might have been wiser to study the American Civil War than their own most recent conflicts (the turn-of-century Boer War in southern Africa showed some of the same attributes as the Civil War).[27]

Some of the key European leaders who are on record believing war would be short include, to name just a few, German Chancellor Bethmann Hollweg, German Chief of the Naval Staff Admiral Bachmann, Lord of the Admiralty Winston Churchill, British Chancellor of the Exchequer and future prime minister Lloyd George, and Russian War Minister General Soukhomlinov. The list goes on.[28] The kaiser told departing German troops in August 1914 that they would be home "before the leaves have fallen from the trees." Not everyone was so rash—in fact, the respective chiefs of the French and German militaries, General Joseph Joffre and General

Helmuth von Moltke, foresaw long battles of attrition. But they did not adjust anything about their war plans or grand strategies accordingly. Lord Kitchener, in Britain, was also pessimistic about the likely length of a war and in his case actually did something about it, demanding (once combat actually began) that Britain immediately plan for a long war involving millions of British troops.[29] But such voices of caution were relatively few.

The above depicts what was happening in a number of individual countries, and in the minds of a number of men, as 1914 approached. But just how an isolated crisis in faraway Sarajevo could lead to world war remains hard to fathom. The ripple effects due to varying types of alliance relationships were remarkable.

None of the key alliances were designed to undergird what might be called defensive grand strategies. Because the European powers had spent previous decades, and centuries, seeking to gobble up territory—whether on the periphery of Europe, or in the Americas or Africa or the Middle East or South Asia and littoral Asia—they did not want security treaties that required truly good behavior on their own part. Bismarck's Germany was the (partial) exception for a while, but he left office in 1890. Rather, even when seemingly defensive in specific purpose, the alliances were designed to provide a license for aggression elsewhere—and they were increasingly reinterpreted in such offensive terms as 1914 neared.

To be specific, in 1879, Germany and Austria-Hungary established a dual alliance pledging mutual defense in the event of an attack by Russia. They created it after the earlier Austro-Prussian War of 1866, in which they had been adversaries, and the subsequent formation of the Austro-Hungarian Empire (with a single monarch but two separate governments) in 1867. The German chancellor of the day, Otto von Bismarck, intended the alliance to have a defensive character. But that changed after his retirement. Indeed, by the time 1912 had arrived, German chancellor Bethmann Hollweg told his parliament that Germany was required to help Austria-Hungary if the latter wound up in a war with Russia, regardless of which country had caused the war in the first place.[30] Thus, the alliance became more potentially offensive in purpose.

Indeed, the problem was much worse than that. As Berlin saw it, if Germany had to fight Russia in support of Austria-Hungary, France would likely attack from the west—out of opportunism, a chance to regain previously lost territories, and fear of what Germany could subsequently do to France if victorious against Russia. Berlin was not without basis for such fears. Thus, Germany might just as well attack France first itself.[31]

That tragic logic led to the development of the Schlieffen Plan over the years. By 1913, von Moltke went so far as to eliminate for planning purposes the option of a one-front war against just Russia.[32] In the crisis of 1914, Germany and Austria-Hungary were, despite occasional flirtation with more conciliatory approaches, encouraging each other toward escalatory policies including full mobilization and war.[33]

In 1882, Italy joined Germany and Austria-Hungary to form the Triple Alliance. They agreed that if any one of them were attacked by *two* states (not just one), the others would provide assistance to the aggrieved party. The Triple Alliance remained in place into the early 1900s even as Italy's commitment to it weakened. Notably, Italy reached secret agreements with France in 1900 and 1902 that neutered much of Italy's commitment to Germany and Austria-Hungary. It also signed a secret accord with Russia in 1909 to constrain competition in the Bosporus and Dardanelles region of the Ottoman Empire as well as Tripoli and Cyrenaica in today's Libya.[34] Ultimately, taking advantage of the Triple Alliance's specific stipulations that made the alliance binding only in the event its members were themselves attacked, Italy chose not to join the war in 1914 on the side of its belligerent allies.[35]

It is worth noting that, in 1887, Germany and Russia signed a short-lived "Reinsurance Treaty" in which they pledged not to fight each other—unless Germany attacked France or Russia attacked Austria-Hungary. In other words, it was designed to apply under defensive circumstances, not cases in which Berlin or St. Petersburg chose to initiate hostilities. It lasted only until 1890, however, because Chancellor Otto von Bismarck's successors did not see the wisdom of Bismarck's mutually restraining and largely defensive arrangements.[36] Bismarck was motivated largely by his desire to ensure that France could not and would not attack Germany to avenge its defeat in 1870–1871. His successors, tragically, often had more ambitious goals, within Europe and globally.[37] Later, in 1905, Germany's Kaiser, Wilhelm II, made a provisional pact with Czar Nicholas II by which Russia and Germany would become allies. But the agreement, borne of improvisational personal diplomacy between monarchs, was opposed by other German officials and did not take root.

Germany and Britain also toyed with the idea of an alliance of sorts under Kaiser Wilhelm II and Prime Minister Lord Salisbury around the turn of the century.[38] Ultimately, however, they wound up more rivals than strategic partners, for example in Germany's opposition to Britain's Boer War in southern Africa.[39]

Germany and Britain did cooperate, along with Russia, in helping defuse the Balkan crises of 1912–1913. However, Russia wound up regretting the outcome. It resolved to do better by its Serbian allies (and itself) the next time around.[40]

In 1891, Russia and France began to form a pact in which they pledged to counter any military mobilization by one or more Triple Alliance countries with their own mobilizations. Their alliance was formalized in 1894.[41] However, the terms were secret. Moreover, they were not entirely clear even to the signatories. Paris and St. Petersburg often differed in their views of which crises around the world should require the one to come to the other's assistance.[42] Over time, the situation evolved. Specifically, in the two years before World War I began, France increasingly signaled that it would have Russia's back in any crisis beginning in the Balkans, and their militaries tightened their collaboration in developing joint plans. Presumably this view in France arose not from altruism toward faraway Russians but out of geostrategic ambition and opportunism. This was largely the result of the views of Raymond Poincare, who was French foreign and prime minister starting in 1912 and president from 1913 through war's end. (A number of prime ministers followed over the course of the war, the last being Georges Clemenceau.)[43]

In the late nineteenth century, Great Britain had an understanding with Italy and Austria-Hungary about managing their common interests in preserving stability and thereby limiting opportunities for Russia in the Mediterranean.[44] However, after dallying with the idea of joining Germany, Austria-Hungary, and Italy in their Triple Alliance around 1901, Britain eventually chose to ally with France and Russia.[45] It formed an Entente Cordiale with France in 1904 and then signed the Anglo-Russian Convention of 1907. Britain also formed an alliance with Japan in 1902, mainly focused on ensuring an open-door policy toward China.[46]

The pacts between Britain, France, and Russia did not amount to a mutual-defense security system, however.[47] For example, the Anglo-Russian pact focused on avoiding confrontation in Persia, Tibet, and Afghanistan—where Russian and British competition had been intense for many years. (There was also rivalry in China, the Bosporus, Dardanelles, Black Sea, and Mediterranean Sea.)[48] Britain's commitment to France was shaky enough that Germany was still trying to talk London out of intervening in any continental war in late July 1914.[49]

In summary, from 1871 to 1914, Germany came into being, strengthened as a country, became Europe's industrial powerhouse, and gained an ambitious leader in the form of Kaiser Wilhelm II.[50] Meanwhile, German leaders thought that France would surely look for an opportunity to re-take Alsace and Lorraine, after losing them to Prussia in 1870–1871. France's doctrinal commitment to the offensive reinforced that view in Berlin. Germany's decision to embark on a major naval buildup under Ad-miral Alfred von Tirpitz, starting around 1897, coming on top of its strong industrial growth and demographic boom since unification in 1871, created a growing tension between Germany and Britain as well. Yet Rus-sia's growing strength after 1905 made Germany feel time was not on its side. Russia had a huge population of almost 170 million, two and a half times the size of Germany's. Although boasting only about 40 percent the per capita income of France or Germany, Russia's economy had been growing reasonably fast for a generation and very quickly—5 percent a year—from 1909 through 1913.[51] France and Britain, competitors for so long on the world stage, managed to dampen their competition with an agreement in 1904 by which the former would have primary sway in Mo-rocco, and the latter in Egypt. Even as they scaled back the intensity of rivalry with each other, they conceded little space in this competition to Germany, except begrudgingly in a few places like Samoa and Cameroon. Berlin may have increasingly worried about its long-term access to cru-cial raw materials for this and other reasons.[52] The weakening of the Ottoman Empire meant that the Balkans experienced strategic turbu-lence, and the future control of the Turkish Straits was uncertain as well.[53] Finally, the France-Russia and Germany-Austria-Hungary security pacts became more binding and unconditional, and less focused on defense, while the British commitment to the Entente remained shaky.

The Weapons and Other Technologies of the War

In some ways, the key technologies of World War I were not so different from those of the American Civil War. Small arms, artillery, railroads, and telegraph/telephone lines played roles in the former not entirely dissimi-lar from those in the latter. So did the shovel! And the horse. The bicycle began to be used in military reconnaissance as well.[54]

To be sure, there were differences. The small arms of World War I fea-tured the machine gun, automating and amplifying the effects of rifled bar-rels that already made the fate of any man on foot approaching a pre-pared enemy position highly fraught. They also benefited from the advent of smokeless gunpowder that made it much harder to ascertain the location of a sniper or other enemy soldier. Artillery grew enormously in size and explosive yield; recoil absorption technology and delayed-action fuses improved artillery accuracy and effectiveness as well. Artillery could also be fired much more rapidly; as historian Hew Strachan wrote of the French 75-millimeter field gun, "By placing the barrel on a slide and by absorbing the recoil with buffers, the 75mm could fire up to twenty rounds per minute without being repositioned after each round."[55] Barbed wire was added to the battlefield mix. Shovels were still used to dig trenches, yes, but the trenches became deeper, more multilayered, and interconnected. They were often reinforced with concrete, and often complemented with deep dugouts where troops could ride out artillery barrages.[56]

Telegraph made its mark. Radio began to be used in limited ways as well, though telephone was more prevalent in land warfare (telephone and telegraph cables were often cut to deny their use by the adversary). But much communication was still by flag or other rudimentary means; the fledgling radio technologies of the day were limited in availability and dependability.[57]

Generals sometimes moved around in cars. And one key reinforcement of troops from Paris to the Sixth Army in the Battle of the Marne in September 1914 used Paris's taxi fleet for tactical redeployment! But, overall, motorized vehicles were rather few and far between.[58] Trains, however, were at the center of the action, with enormous capacity in some key parts of the European battlefield.

Aircraft played a role in World War I. This was the era of early dogfights and of "aces" like the Red Baron. But massive bombardment of enemy positions by aerial means had not yet arrived; for their effects on the ground, aircraft were more important for observation and for targeting. Lighter-than-air zeppelins caused some damage, and some terror, with bombings of cities, even if only limited physical and human damage (for example, fewer than 1,500 people were killed in this way in Britain over the course of the war).[59] Still, airpower's role was expanding quickly as the war reached its conclusion—auguring a much greater role in all future combat.[60] By the end of the war airpower was affecting the tactical battle considerably.[61]

Tanks also made their debut in this war. By the end they were making a positive difference for Allied forces. Chemical gas also made its tragic arrival on the modern battlefield in World War I as well. It was used extensively through much of the war. However, these innovations did not fundamentally change the offense-defense balance, or otherwise hasten appreciably the end of the saga.[62] For example, while thousands of tanks were produced by war's end, many were too heavy, slow, and prone to breakdown to be optimal for the muddy battlefields of northern Europe; refinement based on technological advances, and lessons learned from their use in battle, would be needed before they could reach their heyday in World War II.[63]

Metal-hulled and steam-propelled ships had come into their own fully by World War I. England continued to dominate in this realm, based in large measure on its commitment to having a navy that exceeded in size the world's next two navies combined in aggregate numbers of ships. Huge ships dedicated to powerful, long-range bombardment and known as Dreadnoughts came to be the central element in the fleets of the day. Once the war began, submarines and antisubmarine warfare platforms engaged in a crucial battle of the Atlantic that was central to the war's outcome.[64] Various types of mines were a big part of the action too, often with devastating effects.[65]

In the American Civil War, major battles typically involved roughly 50,000 to 100,000 personnel on a side. In World War I, the figures were often several times as great. This was a war of mass conscription and mass mobilization. The German forces of 1.5 million men who were to fight on the western front were six times larger than the Prussian forces that fought France in 1870.[66] By war's end, at least several million individuals had served from each major belligerent, making for a grand total of some 65 million veterans.[67]

Although the common image of World War I fighting is of largely static trench warfare—and that was indeed the reality for most of the war on the western front—that was not the reality in other places. Even in France and Belgium, the war began with a fast-moving circular motion of German armies through neutral Belgium and into northern France that almost kept to the original schedule of trying to defeat France comprehensively within some forty days. Tactical movement was on foot, but troops could cover 15 to 20 miles a day if not engaged in heavy fighting, so the main action did advance fairly rapidly at times.[68] War involving Russia, Austria-Hungary, Germany, Italy, and smaller states in central Europe featured a good deal of maneuver.

Strategies and War Plans

What were the fundamental aims of the main players as war loomed in 1914? And what war plans had the players developed to pursue these objectives? Unlike the period before the Civil War in the United States, this was an era of much planning and preparation in the armed forces of major nations. Unfortunately, rather than sensitize planners and leaders to the uncertainties and potential pitfalls of war, the planning seems to have begotten even more overconfidence; these strategists fell in love with their insights and intellectual innovations. They tended to forget the dictum of Helmuth von Moltke ("von Moltke the elder" as history often identifies him) from 1871 that no plans survive first contact with main enemy forces.[69] Moreover, some key strategic goals evolved or crystallized only in the war's early months as well.

Austria-Hungary wanted to punish Serbia for what was in effect state-sponsored murder. Beyond simple vengeance, its strategic objective was to discourage any further attempts by Serbs to expand their influence or borders in areas where the broader Serbian diaspora lived. Some leaders in Vienna may have even aspired to dismember or dismantle Serbia.

Russia, by contrast, wanted to favor the interests of its allies and proxies in the region. It had general ambitions of its own for greater influence in the Balkans, Bosporus, Dardanelles, and Mediterranean—and fears of losing that terrain to competitors.

For Germany, the main strategic goal was to defeat and decimate the French army to such an extent that it could dictate the terms of peace. That might even have included annexing a substantial fraction of northern French territory and otherwise leaving France unable to challenge its hegemony in western continental Europe. It also worried about Russia's rise and had some preventive war aims in an eastern direction as well—though the German grand strategy by which any military victories against Russia would be translated into a more stable long-term peace remained somewhat unclear.

France would likely have been happy for an outcome that defeated Germany and won back Alsace-Lorraine. Great Britain was less interested in border adjustments in continental Europe than in preventing the emergence of a dominant German state, including one that might pursue naval and therefore global ambitions as well—Britain being the world's top imperialist power at the time, with the largest overseas empire and greatest navy.

As 1914 approached, Italy had of late developed some opportunistic territorial ambitions of its own, centered in southeastern Europe as well as northern Africa.

For the Austro-Hungarian, Russian, and Ottoman empires, any territorial concerns or ambitions at the start of the war turned into existential struggles for survival by the end. Those struggles were generally unsuccessful, at least for the regimes that began the war in power.

For the United States, the main initial goal was to stay out of the war. The eventual aspiration was to end the war rapidly and then remake the world order so that something similar could never happen again. Of course, the United States failed to achieve any of these goals, except the objective of helping the Entente win relatively quickly once it chose to enter the military engagement. Ultimately, President Woodrow Wilson's concept for a League of Nations, painstakingly negotiated in Paris by the president himself over roughly six months after the armistice, was defeated in the U.S. Senate, and tough reparations were imposed on Germany at Versailles despite Wilson's druthers as well.[70]

These broad goals of the belligerents were reflected in their war plans. Yet the war plans might best be understood as a combination of mobilization plans and initial operational concepts. They were not as strong for anticipating possible subsequent phases of the fight. As military strategies they were generally incomplete. As grand strategies that would somehow guide their nations toward successful and stable postwar peace arrangements, they fell dramatically short.[71]

The most famous example was Germany's long-standing Schlieffen Plan, which had been in development for some two decades before World War I broke out (Schlieffen himself retired in 1906 and died in early 1913). It assumed axiomatically that in any future European war, Germany and Austria-Hungary would fight both France and Russia. It prioritized a massive attack through neutral Luxembourg and Belgium against France. The idea was to use most of the German army on the "right wing" (or northernmost and then westward side, from Germany's perspective) to seek a decisive effect against the bulk of France's army within some six weeks of the start of the war. The defeat and surrender of that army was Germany's main war objective. After most German forces were used for this great counterclockwise movement into the heart of France, and victory thus presumably achieved, many of the victorious troops could be put on trains and rushed to the eastern front in time to handle a more slowly mobilizing Russian army.[72] Thus, regardless of the immediate cause of the war, Germany had to strike France first—before France could attack it (as, in fairness, it might well have done), before Russia could mobilize, even before Belgium could preemptively blow up all its key bridges on major transportation arteries once it saw an attack coming—and win fast in the west.

In the end the Schlieffen Plan almost worked. But in military planning, one must always also ask what can go wrong, and what are the consequences as well as the possible redresses if Murphy's Law prevails. Field Marshal Alfred von Schlieffen and his colleagues did not really do so.

Nor did their peers in most other countries. Planners elsewhere were also quite competent in calculating mobilization and transportation schedules for what had become stunningly large military forces.[73] In the late nineteenth and early twentieth centuries, militaries across Europe developed war colleges, conducted staff rides to survey battlefields, carried out war games, and paid elaborate attention to the use of railroads and roads as well as other logistical matters in preparing for war. The ensuing plans were generally very detailed, and precisely timed, at the level of logistics. Sometimes, they focused on how to maneuver within a given hypothetical battle. Nonetheless, the plans did not tend to survive first contact with the enemy in time of war. Although European states were starting to institutionalize military planning in this period, they did not do a great deal of what would today be called "red-teaming." There were no real Plan Bs.[74]

The groupthink was not absolute. Notably, not all Germans truly believed in the Schlieffen Plan's logic. The "old field marshal," Helmut von Moltke, as well as his nephew and namesake, "von Moltke the Younger" who succeeded Schlieffen as chief of staff, both suspected that war could be hard and long. The latter was worried enough about weaknesses in the plan to shift some forces within the broad German front from Schlieffen's cherished right (or westernmost) wing back to the center and left. Schlieffen's Plan had envisioned that fifty-three of the seventy-two German divisions in the western theater would go into the right wing. But Moltke the Younger watered that concentration down. And once the war began, he took four divisions to reinforce his eastern flank in fighting Russia while keeping seven divisions in Belgium to deal with the unexpected resistance there. As it turned out, even the smaller force that went into France partially outran its supply lines.[75] Meanwhile, benefiting from internal lines of communication, France could reposition forces by train to counter Germany's initial successes. Taken together, logistical constraints and shifting battlefield requirements reduced the chances of a decisive early German win.[76]

France, inspired by Napoleonic thinking about great victorious battles, had a certain fetish for the attack. The concepts of *élan vital* and *offensive à outrance* (excess) captured the essence of the prevailing philosophy. General Ferdinand Foch and Chief of Staff General Joseph Joffre were among its champions.[77] The basic belief was that confidence, boldness, and courage would carry the day in battle. In addition, France depended more heavily than Germany on its active forces, so striking hard and early was crucial. France had decided that in any future war, it should attack Germany with all its might, before Germany could reach full strength. The result was Plan XVII. It anticipated a rapid thrust eastward—perhaps to Alsace and/or Lorraine, perhaps elsewhere, with the final decision to be made by General Joffre as he took stock of the initial phases of any German attack—despite the presence of well-prepared German defenses.[78] Joffre's goals were to be opportunistic in terms of territory as French forces, with whatever British and Belgian help they might receive, principally sought the defeat of the German army.[79]

Britain was highly ambivalent about getting involved in combat in continental Europe. And as noted, its commitment to France was provisional. Thus, it is hard to say that it truly possessed war plans. That said, within the respective military circles of the two countries, London had been gradually clarifying its willingness to send about seven divisions or some 150,000 soldiers of its relatively small standing army to France in the event of war. But whatever the war planners favored, many politicians in Britain held tight to the idea of "splendid isolation" and preferred not to make any commitment to fight in defense of the Entente.[80]

Russia's commitments to France were slightly stronger. In the years leading up to World War I, after many consultations between general staffs, Russia eventually promised France that in the event Germany assaulted France, it would attack Germany with several hundred thousand troops within fifteen days of mobilization. Accordingly, it started to improve its rail lines into the part of Poland that it then controlled as sovereign territory. Russia had augmented its military forces and concentrated more of its energies in Europe after losing a war against Japan in 1905 and undergoing major internal political reforms in that same time period. A crucial decision it made in war planning was not to develop a real option for fighting just Austria-Hungary alone. It persuaded itself that any war would necessarily also lead to conflict with Germany and turned that assumption into a self-fulfilling prophecy with a mobilization plan that had little capacity for partial efforts. Russian planners had designed a full-mobilization concept that was inflexible, failing to countenance the possibility that a partial mobilization would precede it.[81]

Because France depended on Russia for crucial help, it felt hard-pressed to criticize the czar for his decision to punish Austria-Hungary over the Sarajevo and Serbia matters. Indeed, it may even have encouraged Russian action, believing that the crisis provided an opportunity to settle old scores with Germany. Thus, the details of war plans, while often developed by military organizations in some separation from their respective governments, wound up reinforcing the path to war—not only in Germany, but in Russia and France (and elsewhere) as well. To be sure that allies would get the help they needed in the event of war, they wound up indulging each other's worst instincts rather than challenging them. This perverse dynamic worsened the capacity for good decision-making during crises.

As noted, Austria-Hungary's initial goal was of course to punish and weaken Serbia—and perhaps to break it up.[82] Vienna's specific war plans involved three main concentrations of forces: a modest capability to deal with Serbia or other threats to the south, a larger force to face Russia, and a swing force to reinforce either effort as need be.[83] If Russia wound up in combat against Germany, the latter would need Austria-Hungary's help, and fast—since the presumption was that Germany would be focused mostly on the western front in the war's early weeks. So Vienna needed flexibility, and quick responsiveness, if it was to uphold its alliance obligations. Austria-Hungary's rail networks were relatively weak, however, and thus its capacity for any such rapid repositioning of forces was limited.[84]

The intentions of small and neutral Belgium were unclear; its neutrality obviated the need for formal war plans, since it was not considered acceptable to imagine any country violating that neutrality. But in the end its small army of six divisions fought hard against the Germans.[85]

The United States did its utmost to stay out of the war, or even out of wartime preparations. As President Woodrow Wilson put it in 1914, "Every man who really loves America will act and speak in the true spirit of neutrality." Part of the motivation for the rhetoric of neutrality was America's complex ethnic makeup—with large numbers of immigrants from various countries in Europe that were now at war with each other, including many German-Americans (and Irish-Americans, who were not exactly pro-British or pro-Entente as a group).[86] Wilson's attitude, and that of most Americans, changed over time. A notable accelerant was the sinking of the luxury British passenger liner *Lusitania* on May 7, 1915—with some 1,200 individuals perishing, including 128 Americans—by a German U-boat. The U-boat was part of an "unrestricted submarine warfare" campaign that sought to interdict any and all shipping that might carry supplies to the Entente powers. But the change in U.S. attitudes took time.[87] Despite a gradual growth in pro-defense and anti-Germany sentiment, the war did not even dominate the 1916 U.S. presidential election campaign, which pitted Wilson against Republican Charles Evans Hughes. Some prominent voices, such as former president Teddy Roosevelt, former secretary of state and senator Elihu Root, and former Secretary of War (as well as future secretary of state and war) Henry Stimson, favored sterner measures. But Wilson campaigned on the motto "he kept us out of war" and only occasionally hinted at the possibility of any direct American military intervention through the fall of 1916.[88]

Wilson directed the secretary of war and the secretary of the navy to develop plans for expansion in late 1915. With Congress's support, he then translated these into law and policy in 1916. Still, in 1916 the U.S. Army was only 286,000 strong. Not until May 2017 was a Selective Service Act passed and signed into law.[89] When World War I began, the United States did not really have any war plans.

In summary, Russia and Germany had escalatory plans for future war. Any conflict was assumed to spread, both in the number of participating nations and the geographic scope of the fighting. Conflict mitigation and military de-escalation were not seen as priorities. And Austria-Hungary, with its plan for punishment of Serbia, was prepared to set the whole thing in motion. Countries emphasized early and rapid mobilization and envisioned decisive battles occurring in the opening weeks or, at worst, months of warfare.

War plans were typically very secret. They were hidden not only from publics and adversaries, but often from allies. They were even hidden from other parts of the various militaries' own respective governments. This tendency toward stove-piping and secrecy was witnessed in the autocratic and authoritarian countries of Russia, Germany, and Austria-Hungary, where the monarchs controlled foreign policy and decisions on war and peace.[90] More surprisingly, this tendency was also evident in the parliamentary democracies. For example, French Chief of Staff General Joseph Joffre and his civilian counterparts in the defense ministry had virtual free rein over military policy.[91] In Britain and Germany, the army did not even share war plans with the navy![92]

The Path to War in 1914

World War I began because Austria-Hungary decided to punish Serbia for helping sponsor the assassination of the heir to its throne, partly to deter any subsequent secessionist movements or struggles within its multinational empire. But Russia was unwilling to see its ally attacked by a chief rival, so threatened war itself, with a strong suggestion that it would target not only Austria-Hungary but also Germany. Germany, aware of that possibility, saw little reason not to invoke the strange and reckless logic of its Schlieffen Plan and its concept for a staggered two-front war. France, hoping that general war could serve its strategic and territorial interests, thought more about making sure Russia would come to its aid— by quickly launching war against Germany on the eastern front—than about trying to defuse the crisis.

Britain contributed to the problem by discarding any leverage it may have had to deter Germany from attacking France. Mostly through Foreign Minister Edward Grey, it repeatedly confounded everyone when asked to clarify the conditions under which it might fight. Would it be in response to any German attack on France, for example, or only a German violation of Belgian neutrality in the process of attacking France? The kaiser, aware of the many rivalries between Paris and London, seems to have hoped that perhaps Britain would not fight at all.[93] Some of the fault was London's, as Grey sought to be too clever by half in his subtle, noncommittal posturing and maneuvering. Perhaps he and other British leaders, including Prime Minister Henry Asquith (who was British head of government for the first two years of the war, later being succeeded by David Lloyd George in 1916), did not even know themselves how they would respond in the event of war.[94]

One last time, the kaiser Wilhelm II reassessed whether Germany should really attack France in a preventive war. But by August 1, the Schlieffen Plan's initial preparatory phases had already been put into motion. It was effectively too late—or so claimed Chief of General Staff Helmut von Moltke, and the kaiser was ultimately unwilling to overrule him. Even though the kaiser as monarch of Germany had extraordinary powers, there came a point at which his impulsive improvisations could not reverse the rigidly scheduled wartime operations that he himself had allowed to be planned and codified.[95] Indeed, in all the key countries, military organizations had considerable sway in devising war plans and communicating with Allied peers—civil-military relations did not robustly or reliably include strong civilian control of the respective nations' armed forces.[96]

After the June 28 assassination, the chronology of events over the next five weeks looked like this. The first few weeks were not so intense or foreboding. On July 5, the Kaiser privately promised support to Austria-Hungary in the crisis, and even encouraged Vienna to be very tough with

Serbia. At that point, any Russian attack was considered a possibility but not a given.[97] The Kaiser then left for his yacht for a three-week summer sail. On July 23, Austria-Hungary issued an ultimatum to Serbia, demanding investigation and punishment of networks like the Black Hand within Serbia that were believed to be linked to the assassination. Distrusting the Serbs, Vienna insisted on playing an oversight role in those investigations. In fact, compared with plausible alternative demands, the ultimatum was rather mild, as it did not propose any dismemberment of Serbian territory, permanent infringement of sovereignty, or payment of indemnities. It was partly accepted by Belgrade on July 26. Yet Serbia attached enough conditions and caveats, including the rejection of any right of Austria-Hungary to be part of investigations, that Vienna chose to view it as a rejection of its terms.[98]

Things heated up fast. On July 28, Austria-Hungary declared war on Serbia and on July 29 conducted a small attack on Belgrade. On July 29, Russia announced a partial mobilization of its forces, those in the interior of the country and not along the border with Austria-Hungary. The next day, however, both Austria-Hungary and Russia went to full and general mobilization. On July 31 Germany issued an ultimatum to Russia to stand down.[99] Berlin may well have been secretly grateful for the Russian mobilization decision, however, because it appears Germany had already committed to its own mobilization and, thus, to war on both fronts.[100] As such, Russia's move simply made Germany look (to some) more like victim than aggressor, but did not persuade Berlin to do anything it was not already intending. Germany then went to general mobilization itself.

Because Germany's plan for attacking France required surprise in the opening movements into Belgium, a German decision to mobilize was tantamount to a decision to go to war. Alas, officials in other countries, and many German leaders themselves, did not understand that fact. Initial positions inside Belgium had to be seized before surprise was lost, lest the whole Schlieffen Plan and its foolishly exquisite timing and choreography be put in jeopardy.[101]

Later the same day, France also announced general mobilization—although it also maintained a 10-kilometer (more than six-mile) pullback of its forces from the Franco-German border to avoid risk of inadvertent war. Rather than ratcheting down tensions itself, however, Berlin ratcheted them up. Still, on August 1, it issued Paris a remarkable demand that German forces be allowed to garrison French forts along their common border for the duration of a war in the east that was now inevitable. France of course declined to comply. The kaiser then tried a Hail Mary. He sent a telegram to King George V stating that if Britain would guarantee French neutrality, Germany would not attack France. London did not accept the proposed terms and thus the invasion preparations continued. On the evening of August 1, German troops crossed into neutral Luxembourg. At the same hour, the German ambassador to St. Petersburg passed a note to the Russian foreign minister that declared war.[102]

Barbara Tuchman's incomparable prose captures the moment brilliantly:[103]

> With their relentless talent for the tactless, the Germans chose to violate Luxembourg at a place whose native and official name was Trois Vierges. The three virgins in fact represented faith, hope, and charity, but History with her apposite touch arranged for the occasion that they should stand in the public mind for Luxembourg, Belgium, and France.

(Tuchman certainly had a way with words in general. She also once said, in reflecting back on her career and many accomplishments, "If I had taken a doctoral degree, it would have stifled any writing capacity."[104] Ouch!)

On August 1, Britain had not yet been ready to clarify its commitments to France. But Winston Churchill mobilized the nation's navy in anticipation of such an eventuality.[105] On August 2, Berlin issued an ultimatum that Belgium allow its territory to be used temporarily by German troops in a form of "benevolent neutrality." King Albert and his government refused that demand early the next morning, with the small Belgian army continuing its mobilization that had begun July 31.[106] On August 3, Berlin declared war on France. That same evening in London, British Foreign Minister Grey made his prescient and haunting comment that "The lamps are going out all over Europe; we shall not see them lit again in our lifetime."[107]

German troops crossed the Belgian border the next day, on August 4. By the end of that day, Britain and Germany were at formally at war with each other, too—Berlin having refused Britain's ultimatum to reverse its violation of Belgian neutrality, a neutrality that had been guaranteed in 1839 by several powers, including both Britain and Germany. Concern about possible German hegemonism in continental Europe may have driven British decisionmaking as much as anything, but the violation of tiny Belgium's neutrality was a politically crucial linchpin for the war in

London.[108] Austria-Hungary declared war on Russia on August 5. By August 12, Britain and France were also at war with Austria-Hungary.[109]

The Guns of August (and Autumn) in 1914

As German forces entered Belgium on August 4, resistance began, and with it so did World War I. The equivalent of several German divisions met a single Belgian division, out of the small country's grand total of six, in battle near the city of Liege. The Belgian division benefited from the natural barrier of the Meuse River (and the ability to destroy some bridges before the Germans reached them), as well as a system of fortresses built around Liege on both sides of the river. Crossing the river en masse required neutralizing that system, which included a dozen individual subterranean fortresses to protect the city and transportation arteries (a similar system had been built at nearby Namur). The single Belgian division fought hard but could only do so much against overwhelming odds and was withdrawn after two days of fighting.

The separately garrisoned forts held on for a time. Only with the deployment of new and gigantic artillery, broken down into pieces for transport by wagon on roads, and then reassembled, could German forces ultimately achieve this objective. The 12-inch shells fired over some 2 miles' distance were gradually "walked up" to the target, as initial misses were observed and subsequent shots corrected. By mid-month, the fortresses at Liege were largely in pieces, and the garrison forces intimidated and demoralized. On August 17, only two days behind schedule, the main mass of German forces could begin its southward move toward France. By August 24, the same kind of attack had happened at Namur, and the German juggernaut continued onward.[110]

The German violation of Belgium was bloody and brutal at times. It involved several massacres of civilians, including the deliberate killing of some local political leaders and priests. It also included the tragic destruction of much of the ancient city of Louvain—library, museums, architecture, inhabitants—in a rampage starting August 25 that lasted nearly a week.[111]

Brussels was occupied on August 20. But the small, fierce, courageous Belgian army had been withdrawn further north, to near Antwerp, and it survived to continue the fight as part of the broader Allied coalition.

Starting August 14, French forces began their own offensive into Lorraine after a smaller probing attack into Alsace a week before. This was in effect implementation of their own long-prepared Plan XVII, an offensive concept that revealed French thinking in this period was far from purely defensive in operational or in strategic terms. France had long wanted back land lost to Prussia more than 40 years before and sought to reclaim it once the war had begun. With several axes of advance French units crossed the French-German border and pushed into territory that Prussia had taken from France in 1870–1871. German forces initially offered only limited resistance, deliberately allowing French forces to extend their supply lines and their flanks into German territory—before mounting a severe counterstroke that decisively repelled the French attempt. Parallel French efforts through the Ardennes forest were similarly unsuccessful after faulty French intelligence underestimated the strength of the proximate German forces.[112]

Indeed, the French had a bad start to the war in general, in these August engagements that are often collectively known as the Battle of the Frontiers. Beyond failing in these offensives, they reacted slowly and poorly to the German attack through Belgium. Again, near the Meuse River, where it meets the Sambre River west of Liege, they failed to hold their ground in battle on August 21 and had to retreat. (This fight is often known as the Battle of Charleroi, Belgium.)

Some five divisions of British troops had arrived on the continent starting August 10. With their recent combat experiences in Africa, the British troops constituted a more professional and battle-tested force than the large conscription armies of the continental powers. They had been holding their own rather well despite their small aggregate size, as was seen in combat August 23 near the town of Mons. But they too had to retreat once the French pulled back, lest their flanks be exposed—thereby leaving unprotected supply lines, support structures, communications channels, and field commanders vulnerable to sudden attack. The German campaign, though slowed by Belgian resistance, was doing reasonably well with its overall plan and schedule. The Battle of the Frontiers had gone very much to the German net advantage to date.

That said, no main French or British combat formations had been comprehensively defeated. While it was now clear that there would be no rapid French victory, it was not yet clear that the Schlieffen Plan would succeed. And in fact, it would not.

In the last ten days of August and the first few of September, French and British forces successfully carried out what historian John Keegan called "The Great Retreat." German troops were at their heels, having first crossed into France on August 24, around 150 miles from Paris. General

Joffre ordered a repositioning seventy-five miles southwest of Mons along the Somme River, with his own new headquarters to be on the Seine. Although Joffre's *offensive à outran*ce concept had failed, he kept his calm—along with his leisurely lunches and ironclad commitment to a full night's sleep—and devised an effective backup plan.

Joffre realized that, despite the early setbacks and huge losses, France had many remaining advantages if it could only reposition and restructure its forces. France's five main armies were intact. The First and Second Armies held their positions firmly in the east (despite having failed in their earlier offensives); the Third, Fourth, and Fifth moved southward while maintaining cohesion. A new Sixth French Army was formed to contest the German westernmost or right wing. It was created largely out of elements no longer needed for the First and Second that were shipped by train from the east to the country's center.[113] (Germany's armies were likewise numbered with a simple logic, with the First army being the most westward, the Seventh the most eastward. An "army" typically included several corps, and a corps would often have two divisions within it.)[114] Although France had lost chunks of its territory that were important for industry and mining, the overall geography of the situation was still acceptable for its existential prospects. The forts in the east were intact; the waterways of the Seine River system had not been crossed or taken by German forces; internal lines of communication increasingly favored France as it set up a critical mass of troops north of Paris. Meanwhile, supply lines would grow increasingly lengthy and uncertain for invading German forces. Joffre was also a hands-on commander who visited forces in the field to encourage them—and to decide when to fire commanders who had performed poorly. By contrast, von Moltke was more removed and on balance less effective in this second stage of the war.[115]

As the retreat played out, a number of small to midsized battles ensued as British and French forces sought to slow the Germans while ensuring their own movement southward. (British forces were reinforced modestly, by a division and a half, in late August.) Fights occurred at Landrecies, Maroilles, Le Cateau, Guise/St. Quentin, Nery, and elsewhere.

By September 5, after marches that often entailed movement of 15 to 20 miles a day by soldiers typically carrying 60-pound packs in the blazing late-summer sun, the so-called Battle of the Marne began. In fact, the main fighting was along and near its various tributaries, not the Marne itself. The main river flows generally westward from eastern parts of the country in an arc-like fashion, looping first northward and then somewhat southward before flowing into the Seine near Paris.[116] Over the next week one of the more consequential battles in the entire war was soon to take place in this general sector.

With the French and British repositioning complete, Joffre and British General John French together commanded 459 battalions to Germany's 262 in the westernmost area of the fight. German headquarters oversaw the operation in faraway Luxembourg.[117] Other estimates of the military balance at this time put the Entente advantage at thirty-six divisions to fewer than thirty for Germany. (Incidentally, at this stage of the war, each division typically included twelve battalions of infantry, each with 1,000 soldiers, as well as twelve batteries of artillery, each with six guns—making for a total of about 15,000 soldiers per division.)[118] Some 2 million troops were arrayed there between the two sides. More than 100,000 would soon be casualties.[119]

The Schlieffen Plan called for Germany's First Army, the westernmost force, to stay west of Paris and sweep below it before turning eastward. Instead, the commander of that First Army, General Alexander von Kluck, took advantage of his command prerogatives to change the plan. He swung his forces eastward when they were still north of Paris, believing he would there find the flank of a badly weakened French force centered around its Fifth Army.

That was not to be. Crucially, France's new Sixth Army under General Michel-Joseph Maunoury, part of the new Armies of Paris under General Joseph Gallieni, went on the attack. The French forces were able to find and attack the flank of von Kluck's army by virtue of good intelligence—first, maps with German battle plans were found on a dead German officer, and then aerial reconnaissance confirmed the change of German direction.[120] Parts of this French force were famously rushed to the key area of battle by a fleet of some 600 Paris-based Renault taxis ferrying a total of 3,000 infantrymen, though the actual military significance of this deployment is disputed.[121]

In addition, the British forces under General John French (confusingly named!) rallied and returned to the fight. That was after the British commander had grown demoralized by the initial performance of France's army and the Great Retreat southward and therefore pulled his forces well out of the action, rather than risk their destruction. But General French ultimately found his mettle—thanks in part to a personal chewing out by the secretary of war, Field Marshal Lord Kitchener. The British forces subsequently, and somewhat luckily, found the seam between two German armies—von Kluck's First and von Bulow's Second—thereby implicitly threatening both with flanking attacks.

The Miracle on the Marne resulted, as Entente forces turned the tide of the battle and thus the war. Yet the success did not happen overnight. Throughout several days of fighting, it still seemed possible that Germany might be successful in encircling, trapping, and destroying much of the main French army.[122] Everyone was trying to outflank everyone else. Multiple armies on each side were involved. Trench warfare was not yet a major thing. Reconnaissance and communications were mediocre enough, and different commanders were independently minded enough, that the battlefield was complex and very fluid.

But the advantages of numbers and geography ultimately saved the French and British.[123] So did the fighting spirit of the French soldier. As General Alexander von Kluck said about his worthy adversary on September 9, "But that men who have retreated for ten days . . . that men who slept on the ground half dead with fatigue, should have the strength to take up their rifles and attack when the bugle sounds, that is a thing upon which we never counted; that is a possibility that we never spoke about in our war academies."[124] Historian Holger Herwig argues that it was the most significant land battle of the twentieth century because it prevented a rapid and decisive German victory and set in place the dynamics that would soon ensure a long war.[125]

Germany then did a reassessment of the defensibility, exposure, and logistical sustainability of its forward positions. The key player was a midgrade envoy from von Moltke's headquarters, Lieutenant Colonel Richard Hentsch, who combined authority from headquarters with knowledge from visits to several armies in the field and a reputation for brilliance. He found the German positions exposed, vulnerable, and unsustainable and counseled a pullback to a more defensible position.[126] Obligingly, German forces then retreated somewhat to a parallel river located somewhat farther north within France, the Aisne. By the end of the second week of September, using its impressive engineering and digging capabilities, Germany had established a new continuous trench line through much of northern France. But its hopes for a quick victory were over.

Sensing opportunity, French and British forces moved north and went on the attack in the latter half of September. German forces probed and tested here and there, too. All of this was to little net avail.[127] Just as France's hopes for a quick victory had failed a few weeks before in Alsace, Lorraine, and the Ardennes, so did Germany's and Schlieffen's similar hopes evaporate in the general region of northern France defined by the Marne and Aisne Rivers.

The only remaining area where stalemate might be broken was in Flanders, Belgium, near the sea. There, the monthlong First Battle of Ypres ensued, from October 19 until November 22. The various parties, including Belgian divisions and British Indian forces, attempted to find means of successful attack in what was still open country. Each hoped that a breakthrough penetration, or a successful flanking, might win the "race to the sea"—thus setting up the possibility for decisive results across the broader theater. Each was to be disappointed. There were various back-and-forths, including a decision by Belgium to flood part of the battlefield to impede German troop movement. The ultimate results were inconclusive.[128] Finally, cold weather and exhaustion effectively ended the fighting season. At this stage in the war, Germany had the advantage in artillery, Britain in the professionalism and marksmanship of its main soldiers, France in geography and generalship—but most of all, the defense had the advantage, as long and narrow trench lines took hold of the northern European landscape.[129]

As 1914 neared a close on the western front, the gravity of what had just happened began to settle in. Huge losses—nearly a quarter million dead for Germany, some 300,000 for France, 30,000 each for Britain and Belgium—had been suffered out of a total of some 4 million total troops on the battlefields. Continuous trench lines had been established along a sliver of land 475 miles long from the North Sea to Switzerland. The deadly effects, especially against exposed foot soldiers on the attack, of the technologies of modern war had been revealed. Yet those trench lines would be tested time and time again over the next four years, generally to very little effect.[130]

In the eastern theater of war, the fighting of 1914 was also intense, and also involved swings of fortune for the various parties. But it played out over a larger geographic zone and did not produce quite the same kind of stalemate by the time the year was over.

The main course of the eastern campaigns of 1914 went like this. Austria-Hungary initiated hostilities against Serbia, which proved inconclusive. Despite Serbia's small size and relative backwardness, it was able to withstand the attacks. That was partly because of its very relative backwardness—since roads and rail lines were relatively few in the difficult topography, rapid military maneuver and conquest were difficult. Serbia was also able to muster 400,000 troops once everyone was mobilized, not a mean feat for a small nation.[131] Russia then entered the war, against both Austria-Hungary and Germany. It did so through that part of Poland that was under its sovereign control at the time—a sort of peninsula sticking into the unfriendly seas of Germany and Austria-Hungary. Russia's Polish protrusion meant that it faced Germany on two sides: East Prussia to the north, and another part of Germany known as Silesia to the west. Russia also faced that region of Austria-Hungary known as Galicia to the south (yet further south were the Carpathian Mountains, and then the open plains of Hungary).

Russia believed itself strong enough to take on both countries at the same time due to the small fraction of Germany's armies that were available in the east at that juncture, as well as the fact that Austria-Hungary was distracted in battle in the Balkans. This was true even though Russia's vast expanses, mediocre infrastructure, and slow mobilization schedule meant that it would have only a fraction of its forces—which could eventually total some 135 divisions all told (and somewhat larger divisions at that)—available in the war's opening weeks.[132] It did muster an initial overall advantage of nineteen divisions against nine German divisions at the outset of fighting, and of seventy-one divisions to Austria's forty-seven in the Galicia region.[133] However, Russia's numerical advantages were partly checkmated by logistical disadvantages; Russia suffered from an asymmetry in rail lines, which were sparse in Russian Poland but plentiful in East Prussia.

Two separate Russian armies took parallel and staggered and badly coordinated paths into East Prussia. They went on different sides of the so-called Masurian Lake region and its difficult topography. Not only were the two main Russian armies in poor communications with each other at the higher level of headquarters, but when each army attempted to speak with its own subordinate commands by radio, Germany was fortunate enough to make some key signals intercepts and figure out the enemy plan of attack. Germany also was more successful in its aerial reconnaissance, which required not only getting planes into the air in the right areas and right weather conditions but making reasonable assessments of the size and dispositions of whatever enemy forces were detected below.

That said, Russia had some initial success. On August 17, the northernmost of those Russian armies, under General Paul von Rennenkampf, initiated its attack against German forces. On balance, Russia gained the upper hand in this opening fight and German forces withdrew. But Rennenkampf felt himself badly enough bruised, and logistically enough challenged, that he did not pursue the retreating Germans. Even though the outcome of this first fight was a modest Russian win, it set the stage for a big defeat to come.

A couple days later, Russia's other main army charged with invading Germany, under the command of General Aleksandr Samsonov, made its way to the vicinity of Warsaw. It was to be the southern pincer to complement Rennenkampf's northern army. But here German advantages in intelligence, together with command boldness in the new leaders that von Moltke sent to lead the operation, Generals Erich von Ludendorff and Paul von Hindenburg, led to a bold and decisive action. Confident that Rennenkampf would not in fact pursue the retreating German forces, the new German leadership team of Hindenberg and Ludendorff decided on a daring plan. Gambling, they put many of the German forces that had been fighting in the north on trains inside of German territory. (These were rail lines with different gauges than those in Russian Poland, by the way—meaning they were, practically speaking, not available to the Russians, unless Russia could somehow confiscate German train cars, or regauge the rail lines.) Those German forces were shipped southward to where they could help in the battle against Samsonov.

The result was a devastating encirclement and annihilation of much of Samsonov's forces beginning August 25, reaching full scale on August 26 and lasting roughly a week in what has become known to history as the Battle of Tannenberg. Estimated Russian losses included some 50,000 dead and wounded, and as many as 92,000 prisoners. The battle's name comes from a nearby town in East Prussia (today within Poland and called Stebark) with historical importance in the German military mind, as German ancestors known as the Teutonic Knights had lost a battle to Polish and Lithuanian forces there some five centuries before.[134] Half a millennium later, the Germans had their revenge, of sorts—even if against a somewhat-different enemy. Samsonov is believed to have committed suicide deep in the forest in the aftermath of his defeat, given how crushing it became, reportedly lamenting just before taking his own life that he would never be able to face the czar again, having let him down so.

As historian Dennis Showalter put it, in reflecting on what the Battle of Tannenberg meant for Germany in particular—not only at the time, but well into the future as well:[135]

Tannenberg was the only battle of World War I that could be directly compared with the great victories of history. It had a beginning, a middle, and an end, coming over a relatively short span of time. It was an undisputable victory, the only one of its kind Germany could show for four years of war.

Then, in the second week of September, German forces drove Rennenkampf out of East Prussia in the Battle of the Masurian Lakes. It was a less decisive rout, but it did complete the job of restoring sovereign control of national territory.[136]

Russia fared much better against the less impressive forces of Austria-Hungary. Between August 26 and September 10, and ending with the Battle of Lemberg, Russia achieved a major victory—exacting huge losses on the Austro-Hungarian forces and driving them deeply into their own territory. Austria-Hungary's hot-headed and often careless Conrad von Hotzendorf, chief of the general staff, had allowed his armies to become separated, exposing their flanks as their logistics lines lengthened with their movements northward. The result was catastrophic.[137] Austria-Hungary was lucky that its heavily fortified city of Przemysl, a major transport and logistics crossroads, was able to hold out against an ensuing Russian siege for some six months. For three decades, a huge construction project had been undertaken there, producing some thirty-five individual forts over a 30-mile circumference that enclosed the city.[138] That bought the main army time to regroup at least partially—though it never really could do so completely, so heavy were its losses in the war's early weeks. As an additional consequence of its early defenses, Austria-Hungary ultimately had to defer much of its main campaign of vengeance against Serbia until later in the war.[139]

In these fights on the eastern front, armies were generally in motion when they came into contact. This was for the most part not yet trench warfare. The fighting was intense, and the human cost of war was enormous. Indeed, counting all casualties and prisoners, Russia and Austria-Hungary were each to lose more than 1 million soldiers in 1914.[140] In addition to the Masurian Lakes, a number of geographic reference points and military obstacles gave shape to the battlefield, including the Vistula and San Rivers, as well as the Carpathian Mountains.

Unlike the situation in France and Belgium, major battles continued on the eastern front well into the fall and then winter. In October, some fifty-five Russian divisions fought against thirty-one Austro-Hungarian and thirteen German divisions on the approaches to Warsaw in the central region of Russian Poland. Russia won this one. The Germans eventually pulled back a good deal, though they retained a slice of the western part of Russian Poland. Austro-Hungarian forces suffered a severe defeat in the battle and withdraw back to home territory near Cracow.

A second battle of Warsaw took place in November, with somewhat better results for Germany and Austria-Hungary. Battles around the city of Lodz, further west, occurred in November and December. Fighting also continued along the Russian border with Austria-Hungary near Cracow and around the Carpathian Mountains. There was also a key battle south of Poland between the towns of Limanowa and Lapanow in Galicia (then part of Austria-Hungary) in December. There, Austria-Hungary checked Russian ambitions to continue further southward into its territory—in what has been described as its last real victory of the entire war, save those in which Austria-Hungary was the junior partner to Germany. It fared less well in mountain fighting against Russia later in the winter.[141]

None of the resulting changes of territory or losses of men and materiel were particularly conclusive at a strategic level, however. The most important net effects of battle in the east, in fact, may have been the impact it had on the western front. When Germany sent two corps of troops eastward to help in the fight against Russia, it further weakened Germany's right wing and thus further damaged the already-faltering prospects of the rapid defeat of France that Schlieffen had envisioned. Without a rapid victory in the west, no big swing of forces for the east could occur, and the fights would go on in both sectors.

Even further east, Japan seized German possessions in China in the city of Tsingtao and neighboring vicinities. Tokyo also decided to take a number of island chains in the western Pacific. The United States was ultimately unable to reverse these Japanese grabs in peace negotiations after the war, but of course Japan's ambitions would only expand in the years thereafter.[142]

Finally, to the east and south, the Ottoman Empire entered the war in support of Germany and Austria-Hungary. That decision may not have been inevitable. But a fluke of history made it happen anyway. At the war's outset, two German ships were caught in the Mediterranean, unable to get home. They made a run for Turkey instead, to evade Entente forces. There, the ships were flagged as Turkish naval vessels. With German officers still commanding them, the ships proceeded northward over the course of the autumn, and ultimately fired on Russian positions along the northern littoral of the Black Sea on October 28. In a sense, therefore, Germany had duped Turkey into joining the war on its behalf, when the Ottomans had not quite made up their mind about whether to stay neutral.

Largely as a result, Russia declared war on Turkey in early November, with France and Britain soon following.[143]

1915 and 1916

The next two years of the war can be compressed into a single narrative. And perhaps even a single word: futility. To be sure, there were considerable attempts at military innovation, but they tended to help the already strong defense even more than the offense. There were continued efforts on all sides to ramp up their commitment to the war even further, for example on the industrial front. But rather than create breakthroughs, this effort only intensified the fighting and multiplied the carnage. As historian Theodore Ropp put it, about this overall period (on the western front), "in spite of heroic sacrifices, of new hopes as fantastic as the old ones, the lines did not move more than ten miles for twenty-eight months . . ."[144]

On the western front, fighting was characterized by occasional yet always unsuccessful efforts by one side or the other to break the stalemate. A few massive and generally long battles made their way into the history books as a result—Ypres (again), Verdun, the Somme. In the east, Germany gained the upper hand against Russia by swinging more of its forces into that theater. Yet geography and Russia's size prevented decisive action. And finally, from Gallipoli to Mesopotamia in what is now Iraq, the Entente sought new avenues of attack that might avoid the trench lines of the western front, and might profit from the Entente's advantages at sea and along many of Europe's flanks. These campaigns all failed strategically, even if there were some localized successes in places like the Middle East. More needs to be said about all of these dynamics, but they are nonetheless the overarching stories of these two largely stalemated years of the war.

On the western front, there was a break between 1914 and 1915 due to the onset of winter—as well as the need to recover from the sheer enormity and calamity of what had just occurred in the previous months' fighting. But over the ensuing months, Britain geared up for war and, along with Canada and Australia, sent many more forces to France and Belgium. France also mobilized many more forces and ginned up its industry. Together, the Entente Allies developed an offensive mentality that went beyond earlier concepts with Plan XVII. After all, France needed such an attitude, and strategy to have any hope of gaining back its occupied territory—which included half or more of its coal, iron, and steel production.[145] It also hoped for a way still to win back Alsace and Lorraine.

These offensive goals were not achieved. Tacticians formulated new ideas for fighting, but their results tended to be much more helpful to the defense than the offense. No big breakthroughs would result. Defensive improvements included deeper trenches—with additional, parallel trenches for fallback positions, often on the downslope of any nearby hills so as to reduce vulnerability to artillery fire by the attacker. The trenches also included concrete emplacements for machine-gun positions, barbed wire, and buried telephone lines for more reliable communication between established positions.

There were attempts to improve offensive weaponry and tactics as well. Attackers hoped that unexpected concentrations of forces in certain sectors, greater amounts of available ordnance, and better coordination of artillery using "rolling barrages" with the movement of foot soldiers would give enough of a boost to the offense to make a difference. Some of these ideas would eventually produce better results by 1918, but generally not at this point in the war. Longer barrages were not particularly effective against dug-in troops, for example. These bombardments also gave warning to the attacked side to bring reinforcements to the area. When the attacker completed its preparatory actions, and sent forward its troops, defenders were generally ready to open up on the exposed infantry with machine guns and their own artillery.[146] Later in the war, when the effectiveness of counterbattery artillery improved, rolling barrages were used more consistently to precede infantry attacks. Infantry units were also given autonomy in decisionmaking and in weaponry when they did attack. Both led to improved results.[147]

Some ideas were more creative. For example, attackers tried tunneling to place explosives under enemy positions. This could work well locally, after great effort, as at the Second Battle of Ypres with fighting near Neuve-Chapelle in the spring of 1915. But it did not produce breakthroughs of theater-wide significance.[148]

Second Ypres is also where German forces introduced the use of poison gas to the World War I battlefield.[149] Initially, it was not reliable or potent enough to help attackers much, especially as defenders learned to take simple precautions such as wearing wet handkerchiefs over their noses and mouths, which helped against water-soluble chlorine gas.

Later that year, in the nearby Artois region (near the very northernmost tip of France, contiguous to Flanders), the British and French attacked again, and failed again. The French also attempted an unsuccessful assault further east in the Champagne region, northeast of Paris and west of

Verdun. The goal had been for the eastward-bound Artois penetration to meet up with the northward Champagne movement and cut off a large chunk of German armies between them. It was not to be, as defense trumped offense. There were notable fights at Loos, Souchez, Soissons, Festuburt, Tahure, La Folie (aptly named), and La Main de Massiges. As John Keegan wrote, "It had been a doleful year for the Allies on the Western Front, much blood spilt for little gain and any prospect of success postponed until 1916."[150] By this point, at the end of 1915, France in fifteen months of fighting had already suffered more than half the casualties it would incur over the course of the entire war.[151]

Tragically, 1916 would not go much better on the western front (even if casualty rates would decline somewhat). It was the year of two gargantuan attempts at head-on assault, one by each side. The first, at Verdun, across from Lorraine (more or less due east of Paris), was launched by the Germans on February 21. It featured a massive artillery bombardment; the Germans enjoyed an advantage in heavy artillery and sought to exploit it. A million rounds fell the first day, typically from 150-millimeter shells (roughly 6 inches in diameter), though some of the huge guns used in Belgium in August 1914 were employed as well. By contrast, the preferred French artillery at this stage of the war was still the 75-millimeter gun, of greater use against exposed individuals than bunkers or other fortifications. At least 40 million artillery rounds would be used there by the belligerents over the course of the year.[152] The battle wound up lasting through the spring and into summer—indeed, to some extent, virtually the entire year. The brainchild of Chief of Staff General Erich von Falkenhayn, it was designed to break the French spirit by profiting from the sheer intensity of the firepower brought to bear. Airpower, largely for reconnaissance, and poison gas were also important ingredients in the fight on both German and French sides.[153] Indeed, airpower had become important enough by this point in the war that General Philippe Petain, head of the French Second Army and charged with the defense of Verdun, said, "If we're chased from the skies, then it's simple, Verdun is lost."[154]

Verdun was the war's longest single battle, and a massive tragedy. As historian Paul Jankowski wrote,

When Falkenhayn later claimed that he had intended solely at Verdun to bleed the French white, a heretical pretension that would indeed set him part from his compatriots and that would damn him in the eyes of posterity, he sounded as implausible as Douglas Haig, commander of the British Expeditionary Force, who contended after the Somme in 1916 and after Passchendaele in 1917 that attrition had been his lone objective as well.[155]

Ultimately, both bled each other severely, with each side suffering some 375,000 total casualties over the course of the nearly year long fight.[156] Attrition strategies do sometimes work in war. But in the years 1915–1917, they typically produced horrible devastation for little territorial gain.

Over the summer, French forces went on the offensive at Verdun. In the course of the fall they would gradually retake much of the land that Germany had seized in the battle's opening weeks and months. (French forces would retake yet more nearby land in August 1917, and the American Expeditionary Forces would ultimately launch their Meuse-Argonne offensive centered at Verdun in late September 1918—more on all that below.) As the battle's futility became apparent, Falkenhayn would lose his command in August 1916, being replacing by General Paul von Hindenburg.[157]

The other big battle of 1916 on the western front took place more or less due north of Paris, roughly halfway to Belgium, along the Somme River. It was conceived largely by British General Douglas Haig, who by now had replaced French as commander of the British Expeditionary Force (BEF). Fighting began in late June, with a week of artillery bombardment. Then, infantry went on the assault.

The Battle of Somme was also a disaster. Almost 20,000 British soldiers were killed on the first day, July 1, of the four-month saga near the Somme, with almost another 40,000 wounded. Yes, there was more preparation and more firepower in these attacks; strictly speaking, they were not exact replicas of previous efforts. There were also adjustments such as a greater attempt by British and French forces to synchronize their artillery barrages with the subsequent movement of infantry. But again, most changes in tactics helped the defender more than the attacker. Trenches were dug even deeper, with more of them further back from front lines, and complemented with protective dugouts far below the surface. The soldiers manning trenches had also learned they could often survive very intense bombardment even if it seemed the world was about to end while they had to endure it.[158]

As Peter Hart of the Imperial War Museum in London wrote:[159]

The expression "front line" was something of a misnomer. In fact it was a fully realised trench system consisting in itself of three lines about 200 yards apart, linked together by communications trenches and incorporating fortress villages. The trenches were extremely well constructed with the plentiful provision of deep dugouts with multiple exits up to 40 feet deep. . . . In front of them were two belts of tangled barbed wire that were up to 30 yards wide. The houses of the villages had been fortified, largely by the use of reinforcing concrete, and the extension of existing cellars to form an underground warren.

Then there was a second line defensive system, 2,000 to 5,000 yards behind the first, and a partial third line system another 3,000 yards back. Hart's descriptions of what it was like to try to attack these lines, told from the vantage point of the individual soldier through dozens of letters and other eyewitness accounts, makes for heart-wrenching commentary—and his depictions of the cold, mud, lice-infested quarters, sanitation issues, and other venalities of life in the trenches underscore that it was a very tough existence even when fighting was not intense.[160]

The Battle of the Somme did witness the introduction of the tank to warfare by allied forces. But as could be expected with modest numbers of a fledgling technology, the immediate results were of limited significance.[161]

The overall carnage of 1916 was yet again stunning. Many hundreds of thousands perished over the course of the year. All that the British and French ultimately had to show for the Battle of the Somme was a net movement of some 3 to 5 miles in the average position of the front line in the sector of battle.[162] John Keegan again put it dramatically, writing that "the Somme marked the end of an age of vital optimism in British life that has never been recovered."[163] Peter Hart subtitled his seminal work on the battle *The Darkest Hour on the Western Front*.

Meanwhile the years 1915 and 1916 largely cancelled each other out on the eastern front. There were various movements of the front, largely in and around present-day Poland and areas to the south. But given the vast expanses of territory that continued to provide strategic depth and immense resources, the effects were far from decisive.

Germany and Austria-Hungary achieved a huge victory against Russia in the spring of 1915. Bringing to bear forces from the west and benefiting as well from the superiority in materiel that Germany's impressive industry allowed it to establish in the war's early phases, they created an advantage in troops and equipment of 3:2 or more and conducted a successful surprise attack at Gorlice-Tarnow in early May. From that point onward, much of the Russian army was in disarray or retreat, as the tide of battle continued to favor the Alliance powers and Russian Poland continued to fall into German and Austro-Hungarian hands.

That said, what was from one perspective a successful offensive became over time from the position of Russia an improved defensive position. Rather than attempting to defend the whole Polish sector, Russia was able to consolidate its defensive lines by almost half—now defending some 600 total miles of mostly north-to-south perimeter instead of 1,000 miles. Doing so set up some successful if limited counteroffensives in the south, and a protection of Russian interests and territory to the north.[164]

This repositioning also set Russia up for successful offensives in 1916. Its efforts were particularly impressive in the southern sector, near the Carpathian Mountains on Austro-Hungarian territory where Russian General Brusilov showed considerable panache and ingenuity. Though enjoying only about a 4:3 force advantage across the sector, he utilized good tactics, including moving trench lines as close as possible to the enemy before launching his assaults, and conducting the assault across a long front of about 300 miles to prevent the defender from concentrating reserves at a single point of attempted breakthrough. The resulting territorial gains were modest relative to the losses of the previous year—typically 20 to 40 miles of westward motion, at no point more than about 60 miles. But these gains did shift the momentum of battle, and took another huge chunk of losses out of an Austro-Hungarian army that had already been reeling.[165]

These years also witnessed a renewed attack by Austria-Hungary on Serbia. There were new entrants to the conflict as well. Italy joined the war on the Entente side in 1915. Romania signed up with the Entente. Bulgaria joined forces with Germany, Austria-Hungary, and the Ottoman Empire.

In the years 1915 and 1916, the conflict truly became a world war. Beyond the western and eastern fronts, notable battlefields developed in several distinct areas. One was Africa, where Germany was generally unable to hold onto its various possessions—even if this theater was too far away to have much bearing on the core fight. Another was the broader Middle East. That included Egypt, near the Suez Canal, where Britain made sure the canal would not fall into Ottoman hands, as well as the Palestine/Levant region of the Middle East, which was still controlled by the Ottoman Empire of the day, but where Britain sought with eventual success in 1918 to wrest away control. All this helped set the conditions for gradual implementation of the framework of the Sykes-Picot Agreement of 1916, whereby Britain and France agreed in effect on how to divvy up the broader Middle East between them. Major battles occurred in modern-day Turkey, at Gallipoli; along the mountainous Italian-Austro-Hungarian border, where Italy now wished to pursue territorial ambitions; and in the Balkans, where, as noted, Austria-Hungary was again intent on punishing Serbia, and Bulgaria as well as Romania were joining the fight. Then there was the famous Battle of Jutland in the North Sea.

In fact, none of these theaters had a particularly decisive influence on the overall course of the war, with the exception of the great naval battle at Jutland and what it presaged for the competing maritime blockade efforts of Britain and Germany against each other. But a number drained substantial resources from the main fights, and in that sense were relevant to the war's main trajectory, so merit brief discussion here. Italy's attempts to wrest territory from erstwhile ally Austria-Hungary required the latter to use troops it might have otherwise employed elsewhere. Britain's ultimate deployment of some one million soldiers from Egypt to the Middle East to Greece to Gallipoli took away from its strength and potential for the main fight in western Europe.[166]

Gallipoli, near Istanbul, is undoubtedly the most famous of all these campaigns. The basic concept was that, in recognition of the stalemated trench warfare conditions of western Europe, the Entente powers should find a way to change the geographic center of gravity of the war. Winston Churchill was one of the chief architects of the failed concept. One vision was to open up a reliable supply route through the Black Sea to manpower-rich but weapons-poor Russia, by which the Entente powers might improve their position on the eastern front. Perhaps Russia could even realize its dream of controlling Constantinople. Whether these goals were worth the necessary effort remains debatable. Unfortunately for its prospects, London in particular could never quite make up its own mind on the subject at the time.

The Entente failed badly at Gallipoli. First, it surrendered surprise with too much dithering in its preparations, as it debated just how much investment the prize was worth. Allied forces also initially failed to appreciate that ground forces would be needed to control the areas from which ships could be attacked in the straits. The realization that more effort, including substantial ground forces, would be needed came too late—always allowing the Ottomans the opportunity to recover their footing and redeploy forces over the course of a prolonged engagement that took much of 1915. Initial landings in April, and a major new effort in August, were under-resourced and often lackadaisical. Even when they established footholds in ways that surprised the defending forces, Entente commanders missed opportunities for exploitation of initial success, and possible

rapid movement inland. Suvla Bay in August 1915 was a prominent example.[167] Ultimately, Entente forces were unable to make much headway
in ground battles on the narrow, rocky, and mountainous strip of land
known as the Gallipoli Peninsula. Some one million troops may have
fought there, in aggregate, over the course of the campaign, with more
than 100,000 killed and hundreds of thousands more wounded.[168]

The Australian historian L.A. Carlyon wrote about the eight-month
series of battles at Gallipoli—which were so important for his nation and
neighboring New Zealand as well as Britain and Turkey—the following
trenchant and biting summary:[169]

> We should not try to bring too much order to it, beyond noting three
> obvious things about the British strategy, if indeed that is the right
> noun. Churchill, Kitchener and Hamilton [General Sir Ian Hamil-
> ton was the senior British commander at Gallipoli] never had the
> means to reach their end: they were always about five divisions and
> a couple of hundred heavy guns short. Second, the political resolve
> in London was never strong enough. And, third, Gallipoli was al-
> ways an adventure and never a scheme.

Carlyon further observed, reflecting on his visit to the battlefield, "This is
Australia's largest memorial, and it isn't even in Australia. And another
curious thing: the Australians and New Zealanders who died here were,
in truth, fighting for Nicholas II, last Tsar of Russia. He had been promised Constantinople."[170] That was not the only potential benefit that would
have ensued from a successful operation. But success was not in the cards.

Austria-Hungary, having decided that revenge is a dish that can be
served well cold, resumed its efforts to punish the mountainous inland
kingdom of Serbia in late 2015. Aided by Germany and Bulgaria, it made
considerable inroads. It did so despite the efforts of Britain and France to
establish a countervailing Balkans presence by working with (a fraction
of the divided) Greek government to establish major military concentrations of their own to the southwest at Salonika. Serb forces and government were ultimately driven out of their nation, with those who survived
the battle and the arduous wintertime trek through the Montenegrin
mountains making an escape by sea in the winter of 1915–1916.

However understandable Turkey's reaction to wanting to defend its
own core territory at Gallipoli, 1915 also brought a tragedy for which
there can be no defense—the mass killing of Armenians in the empire's

eastern regions. Worried about Armenian loyalties and willingness to collaborate potentially with Russia, Turkey drove huge numbers of Armenian civilians from their homes and into neighboring desert where many
hundreds of thousands perished in what has been called the first genocide of the twentieth century.[171]

Two major naval engagements were important in World War I (in addition to Gallipoli, which had important naval elements itself, as noted).
One was a single great engagement, finite in time and space—the Battle
of Jutland. The other, what might be called the Battle of the Atlantic (even
if that term is more commonly associated with World War II), was a prolonged campaign that continued beyond 1916 and was central to the war's
outcome. And the dynamics of the latter were affected to some degree by
the outcome of the former.

The battle of Jutland occurred off the coast of Denmark in the North
Sea, over a period of about twelve hours on May 31 and into the early
morning of June 1, 1916. With 250 ships involved, it was at that time the
largest naval engagement in the history of warfare.

Key commanders in the battle were Admiral Sir John Jellicoe and Admiral Sir David Beatty on the British side and Admiral Reinhard Scheer
on the German. The German fleet had for some time been conducting raids
and shows of force to draw out a British response, perhaps provoking a
limited engagement that they might win and thereby reduce Britain's overall naval advantage.[172] Unfortunately for Germany, Great Britain had
learned how to decode German maritime communications—taking advantage of its dominance in the realm of undersea cable communication
(which later helped intercept the "Zimmermann Telegram" in which Germany proposed that Mexico attack the United States, thereby helping
bring America into the war in 1917).[173] Thus, despite some initial errors
in internal communication that prevented even greater exploitation of the
information, British forces largely knew what was coming.[174] As such,
Britain sailed its main battle fleet southward, largely from bases in Scotland, keeping a wary eye in anticipation of an ambush.[175]

In this era, guns and torpedoes typically had ranges of 10 miles or less,
and lacked any kind of terminal guidance to home in on targets in final
approach.[176] Optical devices for estimating the range to other ships, and
observing the landing places of shells (of up to 1 ton in weight) to allow
subsequent targeting corrections, were good. But they depended on good
weather and had limited range. Radar did not yet exist. Aircraft were not
plentiful and were easily handicapped by bad weather. Ships like cruisers

and battle cruisers were up to 10 knots (nautical miles per hour) faster than the heavily armed Dreadnoughts that each side possessed, but still had limited search radii over any given time period.[177] As such, general information about a fleet's location did not imply acquisition of tactical targeting coordinates. The latter required more direct contact.

There were five main phases to the battle. First was the southward movement by part of the British Grand Fleet during which initial detection was made by the two parties. Once contact was made, the Germans got the better part of this early fighting.[178] Then in the second part of the overall battle, the British turned northward to tempt the German High Seas Fleet into a chase—and ideally, into an ambush.

That British tactic worked, meaning that the next two phases of battle featured Dreadnought-on-Dreadnought heavyweight engagements. During these, the British fleet successfully "crossed the T" twice against the Germans. That is, it tactically maneuvered its vessels into a single line at the right moment (rather than the parallel shorter lines normally used in cruising), and positioned itself in a way that enabled most of its ships to fire down the line of approaching German vessels from the "top of the T." Admiral Scheer broke off contact with the enemy after each exchange, realizing he was out-positioned and outgunned—though his decision to return for a second round remains controversial, even inexplicable. After the second of these two engagements, Scheer used destroyers to launch a torpedo salvo (at considerable risk to themselves) in a successful effort to buy time for the escape of his main capital ships (knowing Jellicoe would likely turn away from the torpedoes to improve his fleet's odds of outmaneuvering them).[179]

And then finally, there was a phase fought at night by smaller covering ships. Meanwhile, the main German fleet made a beeline for safe port to the southeast, while the British fleet guessed (wrongly) about where it might position itself to fight again the next day. Soon, however, the Germans knew where the British were, due to successful reconnaissance by a zeppelin. In any case, with that incorrect British guess, the Battle of Jutland was effectively over.[180]

The net effect was a near wash in materiel terms. Britain lost more vessels and sailors—15 ships and 6,000 souls, respectively, to Germany's 11 ships and 2,500 sailors. That was an accomplishment for the German underdog. But Germany suffered more damage to surviving ships that required extensive repairs. Compared with expectations, it was not a strong showing by Britain; Admiral Jellicoe described the result as "unpalatable."

A modern historian, John Brooks, similarly wrote that, "the weaker side inflicted much greater losses, while the stronger, although left in control of the battleground, was unable to prevent the enemy fleet from regaining its bases largely intact."[181]

Strategically, however, the battle amounted to a British win—and a major one at that. Realizing that its fleet had escaped a difficult predicament by virtue of some considerable good luck, Germany decided not to attempt to use its surface fleet beyond the North Sea for the duration of the war.[182] Navies of this period cherished their fleets and did not want to take huge risks that could lead to losing large numbers of their impressive ships.[183] They had after all spent preceding decades building up these remarkable testaments to modern science and engineering, propelled by advanced engines, equipped with huge guns, and protected by thick armor.[184]

With this outcome at Jutland, the respective blockade efforts of the two sides started to tilt toward a British net advantage. The basic geography of the maritime competition strongly favored Britain. It had coasts on all sides of its country, of course, some facing the open ocean. Germany, by contrast, could only reach the outside world by water via the North Sea. The latter could be largely closed off by the British navy. It employed ships, submarines, and mines in the English Channel across from France, together with minefields and big capital ships lurking further north near Scotland. Germany's so-called High Seas Fleet was effectively turned into a North Sea Fleet—except, that is, for its formidable submarine force. The latter continued to wreak considerable havoc on shipping in the Atlantic, west of Ireland and elsewhere—especially in those periods in 1915 and from 1917 to 1918 when it resorted to unrestricted submarine warfare, in which submarines gave no fair warning of attack to their prey.[185] The Entente allies would eventually find a partial solution to their U-boat predicament, whereas Germany would never escape the punishment of the blockade that could be imposed on its own shipping.

As 1916 ended, President Woodrow Wilson proposed peace negotiations. But he did so by asking the various parties to clarify in public their core terms—arguably precluding the chance for serious compromise, since few would want to concede anything to archenemies quite so openly and preemptively. Perhaps with better diplomacy, and in light of the war's stalemate to date, there could have been a deal that would liberate Belgium and northern France from German control, return Alsace-Lorraine or at least part of it to France, and create an independent Poland that would also serve as a buffer against Russia for Germany.[186]

Yet it is hard to blame a faraway American president too much for a war in which the European protagonists had by then pounded away fairly pointlessly at each other for two and a half years and still harbored various theories for how they might nonetheless prevail the following year. Wilson's leverage was considerable, but it was largely measured in economic terms, and still lacked a meaningful military element.

1917 and 1918: Revolution, Escalation, War and Peace

The year 1917 began much as the previous two tragic years, with ongoing fighting across the major fronts. But the cumulative effect of so much war, hardship, and economic malaise soon made for a much different course of events.

The historian John Keegan describes 1917 as the year of the "breaking of armies." Specifically, the French, Italian, and especially Russian armies reached or passed their points of exhaustion in one sense or another. Germany and Austria-Hungary were under severe military and societal stress, as well, due to the wide-ranging hardships of such a long and brutal and intense war, but the manifestations would be somewhat slower. That meant they had one last chance to achieve overall victory. In the attempt, they were racing against the entry of the United States into the conflict. Of course, in 1918, they lost that race.

But first, 1917. On the western front, spring offensives were undertaken—growing out of Allied joint planning the previous November in Chantilly, France. (There had also been such a meeting in December 1915 to plan the Somme offensive.). The offensives produced more military failure. There were limited British and Canadian successes around Arras (almost due north of Paris, most of the way to Lille and then the Belgian border, west of Mons) as well as Vimy Ridge. But their progress was measured in the low single digits of miles only, and then bogged down in the cold, rain, and mud of a northern European spring. The Germans had modified the positions of their trenches, consolidating around a new "Hindenburg" set of lines. By this point in the war, they placed a higher percentage of their forces in the second and third lines rather than the front position, and kept mobile reserves even further back. This approach was devastating to the French when they attacked at Chemin des Dames, northeast of Paris (and some 80 miles to the southeast of where the British and Canadians were attempting their attacks as noted above).[187]

The result was Keegan's so-called breaking of the French army. The strong French state survived, to be sure. And in fact, so did its army. But there was nonetheless a limited mutiny of sorts within the ranks. Trench lines were still manned; defensive operations were still within the realm of the possible. But much of the French army made it clear to superiors that it would no longer be thrown into the meat grinder of massive head-first offensive operations. As a result, the French army became more discriminating in when and how it would go on the attack. Perhaps, under the circumstances, that was the better part of wisdom, while awaiting American reinforcements.[188]

Meanwhile, turning attention eastward, the Hindenburg Line also allowed the overall frontage to be protected by a smaller German force. That freed up Berlin to send more forces to its ongoing campaign against Russia.

And in Russia in 1917, there was internal upheaval. Russia did not face the food shortages like those in Germany due to the war. However, inflation became rampant; inequities became more glaring; major cleavages developed across the society.[189] The great Russian revolution then ensued. It took place in two parts, the first centered on February/March and the second on October, ultimately bringing the Bolsheviks into power (though the process would not be consolidated and complete until the early 1920s). The czar abdicated in March, and would be killed, with his family, in July 1918. Each of these steps progressively weakened the Russian resolve to keep fighting. That was underscored in June by the so-called "Kerensky offensive" against Austria-Hungary (again, near Lemberg) which enjoyed a certain success yet quickly petered out. By the end of October Russia was effectively out of the war.[190] Germany then gobbled up elements of Poland, Ukraine, and other areas of eastern Europe, on the battlefield and eventually at the negotiating table in the Treaty of Brest-Litovsk, Poland, in early 1918. With these achievements, Germany dramatically expanded its territorial size, for the moment at least, while also confiscating crops and thus partially alleviating the economic misery inflicted on its citizens by the British-led naval blockade.[191]

In Italy, a renewed effort by Austria-Hungary and Germany broke the longstanding stalemate in the mountains and drove Italian forces deep into their own national territory. Defeat was comprehensive in the fall of 1917.[192]

The United States entered the war in the spring of 1917. There were two proximate reasons for Wilson's, and America's, change of heart. First, Germany tried unsuccessfully to lure Mexico into alliance, with the hope that it would attack the United States so as to distract America. However, Berlin's "Zimmermann telegram" was intercepted by both British and U.S. intelligence, enraging the United States. It is hard to think of something more foolish, when trying to keep the United States *out* of the war, than to risk such a provocation.

Second, and even more consequential, was the resumption of unrestricted U-boat warfare on February 1, now carried out by a much larger German submarine fleet numbering almost 150 vessels. The effects on the Entente were severe. Monthly loss rates for Allied shipping to Britain (which mostly needed food), and France and Italy (which needed coal) increased from less than 100,000 tons in 1915 and 1916 to 520,000 tons in February of 1917, 565,000 tons in March, and 860,000 tons in April. The latter figure easily exceeded what German admiralty thought necessary to win the war within a few months' time. U-boat losses were averaging only about three a month, so trendlines were foreboding for the Entente powers.[193] At this same time, Entente offensives were failing on the western front, and Russia was weakening from within. Most trends seemed clearly in Germany and Austria-Hungary's favor, even if they too were suffering from the cumulative effects of war and prolonged blockade.

The indiscriminate U-boat attacks took American lives as well, however—and proved to be the last straw for the United States. Wilson had a vision for building a new postwar world order that added to his own motivation. Most Americans may not have had such lofty ambitions for the war and its aftermath (explaining why Wilson's League of Nations construct ultimately did not enjoy adequate domestic support to be accepted within the U.S. Senate). But they did agree that there was an unacceptable threat to their own well-being that had developed in Europe, and by 1917 they were very angry about it.[194] In April, the United States declared war, first on Germany and then also on Austria-Hungary, Bulgaria, and Turkey. The question would now become, could the central powers win the war before America's entry turned the tide?

Given how small the American military was at the time, and how potent the U-boat campaign had become, the answer was hardly obvious at first. U.S. ground forces would have to grow enormously—and quickly. From a tiny starting point at around 100,000 soldiers and some 15,000 marines in 1917, they would in fact exceed 4 million in 1918. Of that total, 300,000 American troops would be in Europe by March of 1918, 1.3 million by August, and some 2 million by war's end (most of them army soldiers, plus about 25,000 marines at peak).[195] Wilson was still being criticized, by former president Teddy Roosevelt and some others, for inadequate intensity in his war planning and mobilization efforts in early 1918.[196] However, by that point, the country does appear to have been on a serious path to military buildup and all-out war. By war's end, U.S. military spending as a percent of gross domestic product would rise from roughly 1 to almost 14 percent in the four fiscal years since 1915.[197]

In the meantime, however, things would continue to be difficult for the Entente. In the summer and fall of 1917, the Third Battle of Ypres, known also as the Battle of Passchendaele (in Belgium), led by General Douglas Haig, produced huge losses for no strategically significant gain. So-called bite-and-hold tactics allowed some degree of progress by this point in the war, with tanks part of the offensive mix, but still did little to facilitate major breakthroughs. The limited numbers of protective vehicles, their slow speeds, the presence of defensive fortifications—and the mud!—precluded the sorts of methods and maneuvers that would dominate the German attack on France twenty-three years later. The Fourth and Fifth Battles of Ypres would take place in 1918.[198]

Collectively, Ypres and Flanders became important symbols and summaries of the whole war effort, especially from the British perspective. As two historians put it, reflecting on the cumulative experiences in the Flanders battlespace, "By 1918 Ypres had evolved into an extremely complex narrative.... It was the city of the dead, but infused with an unconquerable, immortal spirit; it was the city of medieval glories now turned to rubble; it was the heart of the horror and filth of war and the site of sublime nobility."[199] Then of course there is the famous poem, "In Flanders Fields," written by John McCrae, a Canadian doctor and military officer grieving over the recent loss of his countryman Alexis Helmer during the Second Battle of Ypres in 1915. It underscores the war's tragedy. But, reflecting the prevalent attitudes of the times, it is not a call to peace by any means:[200]

> In Flanders fields the poppies blow
> Between the crosses, row on row,
> That mark our place; and in the sky
> The larks, still bravely singing, fly
> Scarce heard amid the guns below.
>
> We are the Dead. Short days ago
> We lived, felt dawn, saw sunset glow,

Loved and were loved, and now we lie,
In Flanders fields.

Take up our quarrel with the foe:
To you from failing hands we throw
The torch; be yours to hold it high.
If ye break faith with us who die
We shall not sleep, though poppies grow
In Flanders fields.

A British attack at Cambrai further south, within France, was also initiated, using more than 300 tanks, in November. Despite some initial gains, it ultimately amounted to little, partly because the tanks were unsupported by proximate infantry and were thus vulnerable to various enemy tactics, and because German forces carried out a prompt counterattack to reclaim some of the limited ground they had lost.[201]

Meanwhile, to sustain the ability of the Entente powers to remain in the fight, and to prepare the way for the movement of huge numbers of Americans across the Atlantic in 1918, the submarine threat had to be mitigated directly. The Allied forces decided to use convoys to make it harder for U-boats to find targets randomly on the open ocean. Such convoys could also be supported with an armed escort vessel that could put the U-boats themselves at greater risk. Finally, the Allies used minefields and warships as well as antisubmarine aircraft in key locations—if not always to find and sink submarines, then to complicate their lives and slow their offensive operations. The net effect was favorable. Germany continued to build and launch new submarines at least as fast as existing subs were destroyed. But improved Allied tactics still achieved the chief objective of ensuring safe transit of most ships. Shipping losses in August of 1917 declined to just over 500,000 tons, December losses to 400,000, and spring of 1918 monthly loss rates dropped below 300,000 tons of aggregate ship weight.[202] In the last year of the war, more than 90 percent of Allied shipping sailed in convoy (often fifteen or more ships per group), with a loss rate of just 0.5 percent.[203]

America mobilized its troops faster than its industry. Most weaponry used by American soldiers in World War I was actually manufactured in France.[204] France produced more airplanes in the war than Germany or Britain, in fact, and wound up supplying more than three-fourths of the heavy equipment used by American forces in the course of the campaign.[205]

The year 1918 was a tale told in two parts. In the spring and into July, Germany, with enormous forces from the east now freed up to fight in the west, undertook a massive offensive in France. Berlin enjoyed a modest but noticeable superiority in overall strength, with some 192 divisions to the Allies' 178. With Germany's forces, it took far more territory against allied forces than any previous offensives of the last three years had achieved. Across a broad sector, the distance from starting positions to Paris was typically cut in half or so. Indeed, Germany got close enough to use its new Paris gun (often confused with the "Big Bertha") to fire rounds into the French capital itself from dozens of miles away.

Several innovations, besides an increase in sheer numbers and firepower, contributed to the German successes. Some of these dated back to British innovations in late 1917 that the Brits themselves would not use particularly effectively until later in 1918.[206] German forces assaulted across a broad front that complicated the defender's ability to use reserves against any localized breakthroughs. They increased the odds of such breakthroughs by instructing small elite infantry formations, including "storm battalions," armed with light machine guns, to bypass resistance and penetrate more deeply into enemy rear positions. They also precalibrated artillery so that the initial miss distances would be reduced in preparatory barrages, enhancing the effects of surprise from the first shots.[207] They used intense yet relatively short rolling barrages of artillery against the enemy's front lines and defenses in depth to set up the infantry movements. They made better use of aircraft and other sensors to locate enemy artillery precisely. They trained to make sure they could do all the above in synchronized and discipline fashion, yet also left much tactical initiative in the lands of local commanders.[208]

In recognition of their predicament, and with the ongoing arrival of American forces on the battlefield, the Entente Allies agreed to unity of command in early April 1918. Field Marshal Ferdinand Foch, chief of staff of the French military for roughly a year at that point, was designated as supreme Allied commander for the duration of the war.

The tide soon started to turn. As historian Michael Neiberg wrote, "as long as German casualties remained roughly equivalent to Allied casualties, they only represented attrition on a larger and more mobile scale. Given that Germany could not replace its manpower losses as quickly as could the Allies, the German offensives were actually bringing Germany closer to defeat, not victory."[209]

Geography and logistics concerns slowed down the Germans, too, as they overextended their forces in an effort to drive to the coast and split British and French forces from each other (with the goal of forcing the former to return home).[210] For example, in the Second Battle of the Marne, beginning on July 15 and lasting until August 9, they had an advantage of perhaps seventy-five to fifty-nine in overall divisions. But that advantage was less impressive when corrected for the fact that eight Allied units were American divisions, twice as big as others (of the rest, forty-five were French, four British, and two Italian). By contrast the typical German division was perhaps the smallest on the battlefield by this point in the war. And it was increasingly distant from its supply lines, as a function of the successes from earlier in the year. What's more, the battered and beleaguered British and French forces hung in there. Not only did they fight hard on the defensive, but partly as a result of intelligence breakthroughs that gave them knowledge of German positions and plans, they were able to go on the offensive as well. The Allied forces were also now equipped as well with greater (if still modest) numbers of tanks. By this point in the struggle, the year of the mutiny was over, and the French showed considerable courage, commitment, and fortitude.[211]

In particular, Foch deduced that German forces would approach the Marne, and specifically the town of Rheims with its nearby railroads. He further determined that this action would leave the Germans with exposed flanks that could be counterattacked. Even as the Germans were about to launch a new phase of a successful campaigning in 1918, Foch started to sense that the war was about to turn the Allies' way. The verdict of the Second Battle of the Marne would soon back him up. Not only would the threat to Paris be neutered, but the overall momentum of the fighting along the western front would fundamentally change.[212]

Meanwhile, U.S. troops continued to arrive. They were formed into their own army, the American Expeditionary Forces (AEF), under General John Pershing. Some 2 million U.S. troopers, with a few months' training each on average, would wind up in Europe, their generally safe arrivals in Europe benefiting from the recently expanded use of naval convoys to deal with the German U-boat threat.[213] Upon arrival, they took up positions in the southern sector, on the Allies' right side as they faced the enemy.

The United States contributed to an important success in June at Belleau Wood, about fifty miles northeast of Paris. There, the army's Second Division, which in this case included the U.S. Marine Corps' Fourth Brigade, fought tenaciously and successfully. Some French leaders believed that the American arrival had done much to save Paris.[214] Accordingly, the Fourth's performance earned its way into service lore.[215] With their success, U.S. Army and Marine Corps forces also denied Germany access to key transportation arteries that could have doubled supply flows to deployed forces in that sector.[216]

In September, American-French forces, backed up by a large airpower contingent organized under Colonel Billy Mitchell, achieved a major success in September near the St. Mihiel salient.[217] The U.S. forces might have been directed to press on to sever German logistical access to France. But instead, at French and British insistence, they were brought westward and northward to meet up with the main British effort and thereby attack entrenched German forces, having their own turn at attrition warfare when maneuver might have been the better call.[218] In late October and into November, they moved into the region of the Meuse River and Argonne forest, as well as points closer to the English Channel. American forces suffered substantial losses for modest gain in much of the fighting, as German troops were well dug-in and tenacious. On the whole, most of the U.S. effort in the fall of 1918 was tactically flawed, frustratingly slow, and tragically bloody. American units were too green, and their mission was too challenging.

However, the situation was still not favorable for the German cause at the higher levels of operations and strategy. Their odds were rapidly deteriorating as they faced a growing coalition of British, French, American, Canadian, and Australian forces.[219] The Spanish flu even did its part, hitting famished and thus vulnerable German troops particularly hard.[220]

By November, the combined effects of these military dynamics, combined with economic hardship resulting in large part from naval blockade and political discontent back home, led ultimately to the collapse of the German government, the abdication of the kaiser, and the dissolution of the military. Surviving German forces became more concerned with internal revolt from Bolsheviks than with erstwhile enemies across the border. Similarly, Austria-Hungary and the Ottomans became more concerned about managing their own disintegration than with any further fighting against external foes.

The Peace That Ended Peace

Riffing on English science fiction writer H. G. Wells and his 1914 novel, *The War that Will End War,* Margaret MacMillan described World War I as "the war that ended peace." That is a compelling framing. The process was capped off by the peace conference that ended World War I, setting up the conditions that contributed later to the rise of Nazism. That was the peace that ended peace.

When the allies offered armistice in the fall of 1918 based in part on Wilson's so-called and relatively magnanimous Fourteen Points, Berlin was in no position to refuse, as its ability to resist militarily was rapidly disintegrating. The proposed terms of peace, later formalized and toughened in June 1919 at Versailles, imposed only relatively modest territorial changes on Germany compared with might have been expected, especially in the west.[221] However, they placed strict limitations on German military capabilities, backed up by Allied occupation forces in part of the country. Most of all, and not necessarily consistent with the Fourteen Points, they required enormous payments of reparations, averaging 3.4 percent of GDP a year from 1918 through 1931.[222] These were due in large part to the need of countries like France to service debts to the United States that Washington refused to forgive. All this helped set the stage for the economic woes of the Weimar Republic and thus, after the world economic depression that began in the late 1920s, the rise of Adolf Hitler.[223]

Wilson had spent the first half of 1919 in France trying to shape, and in some cases moderate, the terms of the peace accord. But he could not thwart the huge forces arrayed against his vision, or avoid his own serious diplomatic mistakes as well.[224] Exhibit A was the League of Nations. Having been negotiated without meaningful Republican involvement in the United States, it never gained Republican support. It was seen by many as potentially obliging the country to conduct future military operations based on the decisions of a group of nations rather than its own elected leaders.[225] So the Senate failed to ratify, the United States stayed out, and the league was left mostly toothless. And tough reparations were placed on Germany, even though Wilson would have preferred otherwise, as the price of getting the league.[226]

Even if the United States had joined, the methods of enforcement for a stable world order were unclear. The idea of the League of Nations was to have "armies and navies large enough for self-defense but no more," as Patricia O'Toole wrote in her masterful biography of Wilson. Yet those armies and navies would theoretically also have to be strong enough to reverse any non-compliance with the core principles of the new world order.[227] That is easier said than done. As defense analysts know, it is very hard to construct stable balances of power or ensure that a defensive-minded coalition will be able to impose its will on any aggressor, given the imprecisions and uncertainties of defense analysis. Even a 2:1 advantage—indeed, even a 3:1 advantage—in firepower or other measures of combat power cannot guarantee victory, and certainly not rapid or easy victory.[228] To be sure, if say six or eight main countries of roughly comparable size and capacity undergirded the League, they could probably defeat any one that defected from the collective security arrangement, if acting promptly and in unison. But it is not clear that such conditions were realistically attainable.

Not only was World War I a terrible tragedy unto itself. The way in which it was ended made possible the path to even greater calamity in World War II.

Mistakes Made and Lessons Learned

World War I was the fault of multiple nations and was a tragedy beyond belief due to a sequence of cascading errors. It should never have been fought.

At one level, that latter tautology can be offered about virtually any war. But in this case, the unredeeming senselessness of it all, especially at a time of such human progress in other endeavors, was stunning. The collective responsibility was particularly evident, even if Germany and then Russia arguably deserve special blame. The naivete about likely casualties was jaw-dropping. The failure of generals to devise war plans that promoted security rather than aggression was tragic and unprofessional; diplomats were similarly guilty of stoking crisis rather than seeking to defuse it.

Of the five main initial parties to the conflict, any one of them could probably have found a way to prevent the war occurring on the scale that it did, through steps that were available and evident at the time. Austria-Hungary did not need to spend weeks debating how to punish Serbia or refuse the latter's response to its ultimatum. Russia certainly did not need to enter the war at all; it could have let Austria-Hungary exact a certain revenge without harm to its main interests or its core security. France could have encouraged Russian restraint—and had fewer imperialistic ambitions abroad, as well as less intense preparations for war against Germany closer to home. Germany did not need to egg on Austria-Hungary to war and certainly did not need either to join it or to attack France preemptively. England could have thought harder about its interests, and clarified its commitments, sooner—that is, before the war, when doing so might have furthered the cause of deterrence and persuaded Germany not to attack.

Yet for the strategist, and defense planner, additional and more technical lessons also need to be drawn from a study of World War I. They proceed from questions like these:

- Were alliances too binding, or not binding and credible enough?
- Were war plans, especially but not limited to the Schlieffen Plan,
  too rigid and rapidly escalatory?
- Were strategists of the day guilty of negligence in not foreseeing
  what the technologies of modern war would mean for combat?
  And as the conflict unfolded, were they too stubborn about sticking with previous tactics?

The themes of overconfidence and naivete certainly permeate the lessons of World War I. Government officials and military planners were all
guilty of this cardinal sin of the strategist. Such thinking was especially
prevalent, and consequential, in both the decisions to go to war and the
nature of the early war plans that militaries had developed. It is sometimes said that if you wish peace, prepare for war—but in fact, prior to
World War I, preparations for war helped cause it. There was less naivete
about fighting as the war progressed, and it became obvious what the technologies of the day could do to the human body as well as to organized
armed forces.

By 1915 onward, the main sources of the ongoing carnage were stubbornness, passion, and a desire to justify the enormous sunk costs that
had already been incurred. Leaders should have swallowed their pride and
anger and looked for ways out of the war short of victory—President Wilson was right that peace without victory would have been far better than
what ensued. Human nature being what it is, and the leaders of the day
being who they were, that proved to be far easier said than done. As Fred
Iklé noted in his classic book, *Every War Must End*, "Fighting sharpens
feelings of hostility. . . . More is expected of a settlement because both the
government and the people will feel that the outcome of the war ought to
justify the sacrifices incurred. In addition, various institutional forces will
compound the difficulties of making peace."[229] As such, the most realistically preventable mistake was the decision to go to war in the first place,
and to do so with absurd plans for quick success.

But before getting to a critique of war plans as well as military operational concepts and tactics—especially, though not exclusively, the Schlieffen Plan—there is the matter of the era's alliance systems. The fundamental

problem with the alliances of the day is that their architects had generally discarded Bismarck's emphasis on defense and sought, one way or
another, to further the offensive strategic ambitions of the key parties.[230]
Austria-Hungary and Russia wanted more power and influence in the Balkans, for themselves as well as their friends and proxies, in the context of
the Ottoman Empire's ongoing decline and loss of control over that region. France and Britain wanted to preserve their freedom of maneuver
for colonial and imperial conquest, from Africa to South Asia to China
and beyond; France also hoped that if Russia and Germany someday
fought, it could take advantage of the opportunity to retake Alsace and
Lorraine after they were lost to Berlin in 1870–1871. Germany wanted
to get into that global game, and to improve its position in Europe so that
its navy would not be so bottled up by the North Sea. Others like Japan,
Italy, Serbia, Bulgaria, and Greece had ambitions of their own—as was
evidenced from their aggressions and land grabs in coastal China, Libya,
and the Ottoman areas of the Balkans respectively.

Serbia and Bulgaria lost some of the ground that they had taken in the
First Balkan War of 1912—fought largely to drive the Ottomans out of
the general area—during the Second Balkan War in 1913. The second
conflict was largely a fight to contest the spoils from the first dispute. Serbia did not fully realize its maximalist ambitions over the course of the
two wars, but did wind up twice as large as it had been prior to their
outbreak, and it continued to have greater ambitions including within
Austria-Hungary thereafter.[231] In this sense, its pseudo-alliance understanding with Russia contributed to war by helping Belgrade believe it
had protectors even as it sought to stir trouble in neighboring countries.

More generally, even when couched or camouflaged in defensive terms,
the security partnerships and alliances of the day were not designed to
balance against threats so much as to further their parties' respective
ambitions.[232]

Because of the offensive strategic context in which they existed, alliances of the day were used to magnify and accelerate crises rather than to
help defuse them. Notably, in the summer of 1914, Austria-Hungary and
Germany reinforced each other's instincts to use the punishment of Serbia after the assassination of Archduke Ferdinand as a pretext for a wider
war. The earlier "concert of Europe"—cooperation among the great powers to dampen or resolve problems that arose—weakened as the twentieth
century unfolded and competitive dynamics increased.[233]

Russia's alliance with France made the former more likely to attack Germany. That is because it could do so knowing that any such conflict would likely lead Germany and France to war with each other, drawing away forces that could then not be quickly directed against the Russian legions. On this point, Russia was correct, but the logic was perverse. France allowed itself to be entrapped in this toxic security relationship out of antipathy for Germany and, among other things, a desire to reclaim Alsace and Lorraine. Poincaré, as foreign minister and prime minister in 1912 and then president in 1913, made clear that Paris would support Russia in virtually any war, even one of Russia's own choosing and instigation—a modification of previous understandings of the French-Russian alliance.[234]

The conditionalities, secret clauses, and intentional ambiguities of these treaties contributed to the war's outbreak as well. They flew in the face of what modern deterrence theory tells us about the importance of the clarity and credibility of commitments.[235] The most glaring problem was Germany's uncertainty, and ultimately its incorrect assessment, of whether Britain would fight in defense of France and Belgium. Britain contributed to the problem because it saw alliances primarily in terms of how they would serve its global position and ambitions, and as such sought to preserve maximum flexibility until the last minute.

In summary, the main problem with alliances of the day was not that most existed in the first place. Rather, the difficulties arose because they reflected—and reinforced—offensive foreign policies on the parts of most members. Britain's wishy-washy attitude did not help either.

And now, to war plans, beginning with Schlieffen. To understand how his deeply flawed plan could take hold of the German mind of the day, it is important to acknowledge first that he got lots of things right. Only because the concept for a muscular and highly choreographed movement into France featured creativity, boldness, and impressive logistics could it gain favor with so many. The lesson is to beware of war plans promising rapid and decisive victory that may sound clever, but that have little margin for error.

Schlieffen figured out how to mobilize and position seven-eighths of the German army, including active and reserve divisions (the latter to the surprise of France), on the western front. He then developed a scheme to use roughly two-thirds of those western-front divisions in a giant right hook or wheel—attacking France from the north, through Luxembourg and Belgium and above the Ardennes forest, rather than through the immediate border zone of Alsace-Lorraine.[236] The plan called for the roads through Liege, Belgium to be open by the twelfth day of mobilization, Brussels to fall by the nineteenth, the French border to be crossed on the twenty-second, and Paris as well as France overall to fall by day thirty-nine.[237]

But Schlieffen and colleagues gave insufficient consideration to what might go wrong. Conquering a large neighboring country according to a fixed six-week schedule flies in the face of most of what history teaches about the unpredictability of war.[238] It was at best a highly optimistic concept, requiring exquisite timing and precise execution even in the face of enemy resistance. At a practical level, the plan also focused inadequately on the logistical sustainability of forward forces.[239] It gave short shrift to the fact that an attacked adversary might reinforce its positions using relatively rapid movement on internal railroads while advancing forces would be obliged to move largely on foot.[240]

General Erich von Ludendorff once said that, "A general has much to bear and needs strong nerves. The civilian is too inclined to think that war is only like the working out of an arithmetical problem with given numbers. It is anything but that."[241] But Ludendorff should have directed that criticism even more to his fellow general, Field Marshal Graf von Schlieffen. The Schlieffen Plan was also fundamentally irresponsible in that it required Germany to preempt potential adversaries, thereby depriving policymakers of options for crisis diplomacy.

Other countries had deeply flawed concepts of military operations as well. Take Russia. It elected to turn a relatively minor faraway crisis in the Balkans into not just a single war but a two-front war. It did so on a wing and a prayer. Ironically, its very fear of German power led it to choose to attack Germany preemptively—fearing that its only hope against the German colossus was to strike early, when Germany would likely be preoccupied with the western front. The decision to fight poorly on two fronts, rather than well on just one—or, better yet, not at all—reflected a bureaucratic compromise between two different camps on its general staff. The resulting plan was owned by no one.

Again, there were impressive aspects of Russia's war preparations that contributed to the overconfidence. By 1914, Russia had made considerable progress in figuring out how to call up reservists quickly and move them by internal rail lines. That was enough to prepare the way for early victories against Austria-Hungary. It was not enough to defeat Germany.[242]

France's focus on *offensive à outrance* and on *elan* were problematic as well. They led French leaders to attempt a head-on attack into German forces once the Schlieffen Plan was unleashed. France wanted Alsace and Lorraine back; the plan offered the hope of liberating them, if only confidence and esprit de corps could be enough to gain victory. But the French plan was anticipated by Germany. France effectively played into Germany's hands, therefore—the latter's forces fell back in the initial stretches of battle to separate French units from their logistics support and make them overconfident. Then Germany struck back, with great success—even as its main effort proceeded apace further north and west.

These war plans and concepts were generally deeply flawed. But so was the decision to invoke them—to actually choose to fight. Leaders of the day should have had an awareness of the distinct possibility of extreme carnage. Enthoven and Smith's warnings about developing pessimistic as well as optimistic estimates for how any scenario in military planning, budgeting, or warfighting might play out are to the point. Leaders at the time of World War I did not have the book *How Much Is Enough?* at their fingertips, but they did have Thucydides and Clausewitz, as well as their own common sense. They also had the examples of the American Civil War and the Boer War to suggest what modern weaponry could do to the human body. War colleges were also becoming well institutionalized in the period before 1914. They should have spent a bit less of their time mastering railroad schedules and a bit more wargaming possible dynamics and outcomes from actual combat.

While debate about the offense-defense balance in World War I continues, and admittedly has fodder for both sides of the debate, the weight of evidence tilts in favor of thinking that a defensive advantage persisted throughout the period. Some offensive advantages, or at least possibilities, existed in the military balances, technologies, and geographies of early twentieth-century Europe.[243] But offense was hard, and bound to be bloody.[244]

In light of this poor potential for the weapons and associated tactics of the day to allow a major change in fortunes in the war, should the belligerents have changed their fundamental strategies once the tragedy of 1914 had made itself apparent? At one level the answer must be yes. They could have called a halt to the combat and reverted to prewar territorial arrangements or something similar. But that kind of rethinking, once so much blood has already been shed, is difficult for the human species, with its powerful passions of pride and honor.

Perhaps Britain and France, stymied on the western front, should have tried to use their power projection capabilities to take the war elsewhere.

But of course, they tried that, albeit with only limited conviction. Their joint effort in Greece produced little; together with Australia and New Zealand, the Brits failed miserably in Gallipoli. Partial successes in the Middle East were against the Ottoman Empire, not the main aggressor or enemy—and even these were difficult.

Britain and France might have been on more promising ground in hunkering down on the defensive in France while seeking to win the war at sea through economic strangulation of Germany and Austria-Hungary. But no one could be sure how well that strategy would work in 1915 or 1916 or 1917. Indeed, Germany itself had some prospects of using its U-boats to prevail in any such blockade-based war plan—especially once Russia fell into civil war and revolution, and fell out of the war. And there was nothing particularly foreseeable or inevitable about America's ultimate entry into the conflict.

I conclude that the main mistakes of the participants in World War I were made before the war and at its outset. Arrogance, imperialism and expansionism, extreme nationalism, and almost willful ignorance about the killing potential of the weapons of the day were the chief causes. The leaders of the day were generally mediocre, in intellect and in ethics. The stove-piped and insular ways their governments processed information, developed options, and reached decisions were mediocre as well.

Thucydides wrote that humans go to war based on three main passions: fear, honor, and greed. In 1914, the last two were in more than ample supply. The first was perhaps not present enough. Overconfidence that the powerful forces of war, once unleashed, could be effectively controlled was rampant as well. And it all happened at such an otherwise promising time in history. At the broadest level, that is perhaps the single most striking lesson of all. Wars may not truly be accidental. But they can occur in surprisingly rapid, and stunningly destructive, ways. As Peter Hart wrote about the British attitudes of the time, though he could easily have been talking about any of the main belligerent nations, "War was a risk, casually accepted. When it arrived it was not as they had imagined, but by then it was too late."[245] Some key figures, including in Germany, may have had a sense of foreboding about what they were unleashing. But the sentiments seemed almost subconscious, and did not supersede their overall eagerness to test fate by trying the fortunes of war.[246]

THREE   *World War II*

In so many ways, World War I and World War II were strongly interconnected. Most of the main participants were the same, with similar though not identical alliance relationships. Many senior political and military leaders in World War II had fought in World War I, and had their worldviews shaped by its course as well as its consequences. World War I's badly flawed peace arrangements created the conditions that gave rise to Adolf Hitler's power grab in Germany in 1933 and thus to the outbreak of actual fighting half a dozen years later.

The expectation of rapid victory was different than it had been in World War I, however. Ironically, even though World War II was the war that did witness major and somewhat decisive rapid victories, it was not a conflict in which most participants generally expected a quick end. While the German army's blitzkrieg led to stunningly fast initial successes in the fall of 1939 and spring of 1940, fostering the belief in some quarters that conquest would be relatively easy and quick, it was never a predominant opinion in the collective minds of Hitler and his generals.[1] Hitler himself combined, somewhat oxymoronically, a confidence that creative military planning and good preparation could often achieve rapid victory with a psychopathic willingness to fight even if wars killed millions and took a long time. He saw martial virtue in conflict, and espoused a hypernationalist Darwinism combined with a Hobbesian view of international politics.[2] Japan, too, was led by a passionate and ambitious warrior class.

Accordingly, World War II ultimately dwarfed World War I in scale. Between the wars, world manufacturing capacity roughly doubled. The "great powers" including Germany, Japan, Italy, the United States, Great Britain, and the Soviet Union then typically devoted 20 to 40 percent of their much larger GDPs to their military machines.[3] Average military spending levels on the eve of World War II were about seven times greater

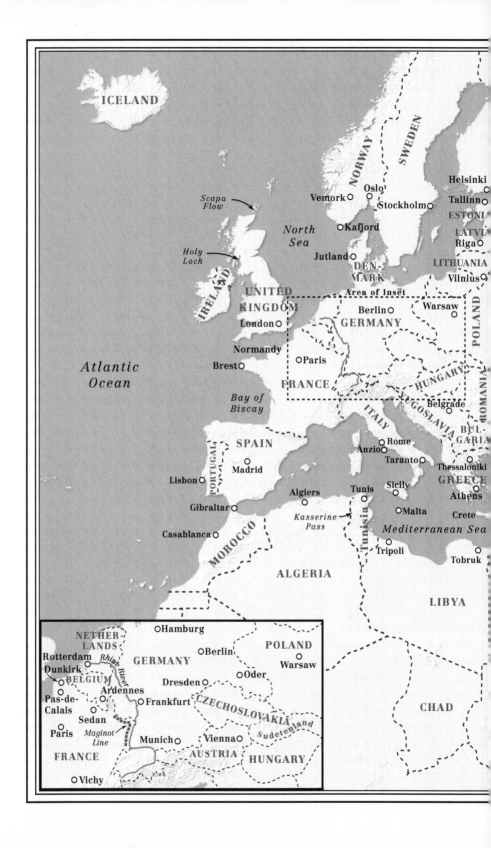

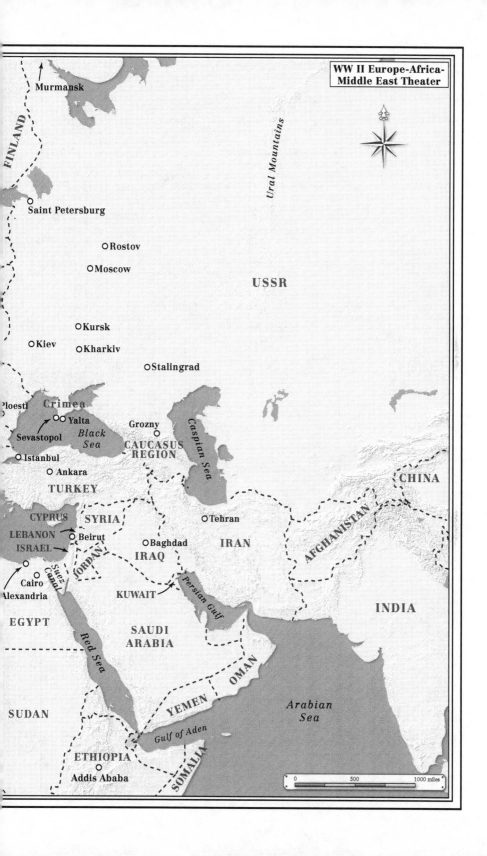

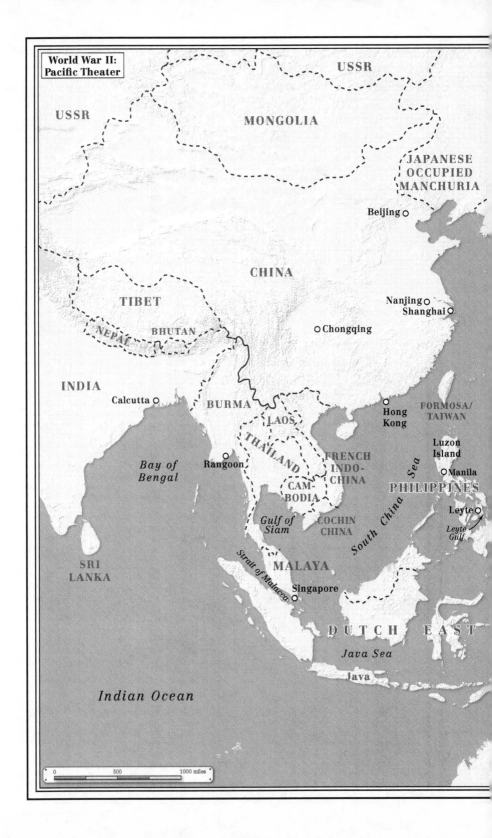

World War II:
Pacific Theater

USSR

MONGOLIA

USSR

JAPANESE
OCCUPIED
MANCHURIA

Beijing

CHINA

TIBET

Nanjing
Shanghai

NEPAL   BHUTAN

Chongqing

INDIA

Calcutta

BURMA

LAOS

Hong
Kong

FORMOSA/
TAIWAN

Bay of
Bengal

Rangoon

THAILAND

FRENCH
INDO-
CHINA

Luzon
Island

Manila

CAM-
BODIA

PHILIPPINES

Gulf of
Siam

COCHIN
CHINA

South China Sea

Leyte

Leyte
Gulf

SRI
LANKA

Strait of Malacca

MALAYA

Singapore

DUTCH   EAST

Java Sea

Java

Indian Ocean

0   500   1000 miles

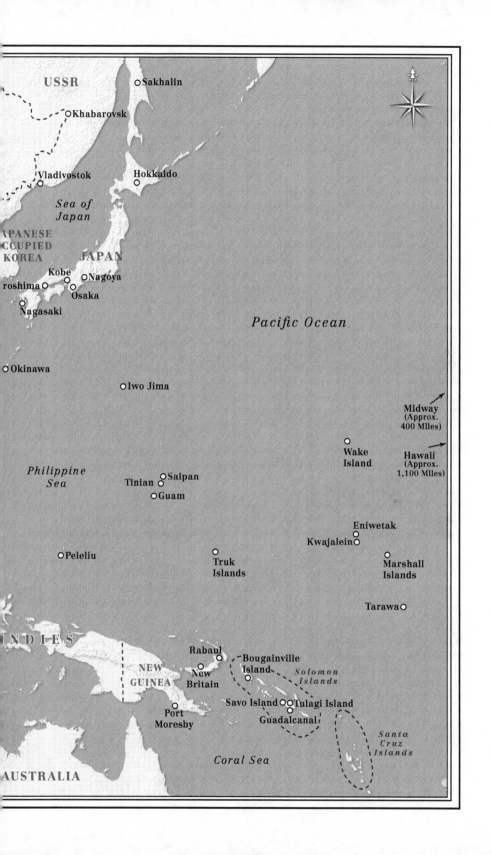

than in 1914.[4] To give just one indicator, during the war's peak years, more than 100,000 military aircraft a year were being produced globally; in 1944, the total topped 200,000.[5] The levels of rapid invention and industrialization achieved were simply beyond any human experience before or since. The war ultimately cost the United States alone about $5 trillion in direct and immediate costs (as measured in today's dollars).[6] Sixteen million Americans would serve in uniform over the course of the war.[7]

Both conflicts were brutal in the bloodletting. But World War II was roughly six times worse in its death toll, and more barbaric. Soldiers killed each other in World War I out of national pride and loyalty, and battlefields largely spared cities and unarmed innocents. By contrast, civilians were frequently targeted and killed in World War II; they constituted about three-fourths of all fatalities, in fact.[8] The Holocaust against Jews claimed ten times as many victims as had the worst mass killing of civilians in World War I, the Ottoman genocide of Armenians in 1915.

Almost half of all estimated fatalities in World War II were citizens of the Soviet Union; perhaps twenty-seven million died. China suffered some fifteen million fatalities. Germany lost nearly seven million; Japan nearly three million. Poland had five million citizens killed. Southeast Asian countries including Indonesia lost some five million in all, and the Philippines another million. Somewhat more than 500,000 Italians and a similar number of French perished; just under that number of Brits died, and nearly a half million Americans lost their lives as well. Between one million and three million Indians died, most due to famine and hardship, some in uniform fighting for the British Crown. More than a million Yugoslavs died, and almost 800,000 Romanians. Others suffered many fatalities as well: some 400,000 Koreans and a similar number of Greeks, more than 300,000 Czechs, some 100,000 Finns, about 45,000 Canadians, a comparable number of Australians, and some 12,000 New Zealanders.[9] More than 20 million were displaced by war and its immediate aftermath.[10] Had he won, Hitler would have sought to shoot or starve many millions more as he made space in central Europe for his vision of an expanded German empire inhabited by the Aryan nation.

In technical terms, World War II probably witnessed—and produced—more military innovation than any conflict in history.[11] Hitler and the recently defeated German nation, anxious to exercise payback for World War I, got the better of it at first, with blitzkrieg. But with air combat, naval warfare, amphibious assault, submarine and antisubmarine operations, code-breaking machines, and, finally, nuclear weapons, other countries, to include of course the United States, were not far behind for long.

The war in Europe began with Germany's invasion of Poland in September 1939 and then of northern France (along with Norway and the Low Countries) in the spring of 1940. Germany failed to coerce Britain into capitulation through aerial attack and the threat of invasion during the summer of 1940. It regained its momentum in the first half of 1941, first with its rapid capture of much of the Balkans and Greece, then with its June 22 invasion of the Soviet Union. But by late 1941 its assault on the Soviet Union slowed, stalled, and ultimately was reversed. In the Atlantic, Germany's submarine force of U-boats wreaked havoc on Allied shipping through 1942 before things shifted decisively in 1943. Japan's remarkable attack at Pearl Harbor made a substantial dent in the American Pacific fleet, and its synchronized aggressions in the Philippines and southwest Asia went far towards making its Greater East Asia Co-Prosperity Sphere a reality. But battles at Midway and Coral Sea as well as the Solomon islands from May 1942 onward changed the course of events, and by late 1943 the United States was poised to begin its inexorable pushes westward and northward (from starting points in Hawaii and Australia) toward the Japanese mainland. The Allies' huge industrial advantages kicked in on all fronts, such that by D-Day in France in June 1944—though perhaps not much before—the outcome of the war became all but inevitable.[12]

The Weapons of War and the Strategies of the Key Protagonists

Probably more than any conflict in history, World War II was a laboratory of innovation at a technical level. Certain military technologies and operational concepts were displayed with a prominence never before witnessed; many new systems and ideas were developed in the course of the conflict. Because the effects of each were so important for the course of the war, more detailed discussion is woven into the chronology below. Yet it can be noted here that the radical changes—perhaps revolutions—in military affairs that occurred just before or during World War II included those of aircraft carrier warfare, large-scale amphibious assault under fire, blitzkrieg, the use of radar in air defense as well as antisubmarine warfare, strategic bombing, and nuclear warfare.[13] Basic weapons of war, including tanks and combat aircraft, went through major improvements in the course of the conflict.[14] Also extraordinary were innovations in logistics and long-range transport. And the scale of industrialization that provided the materiel of war, as noted earlier, dwarfed anything seen before in the history of warfare.[15]

Of course, the concept of a military revolution is grandiose and sweeping, and risks overstating the degree of transformation caused by a given innovation. For example, while few would challenge the importance of their arrival on the scene, aircraft carriers did not cause most naval attrition during World War II except when they fought against each other, in the war's six main carrier battles (four of which occurred in 1942, at the Coral Sea, Midway, the Eastern Solomons, and the Santa Cruz islands, and two in 1944, in the Philippine Sea and Leyte Gulf). Indeed, planes flying from aircraft carriers caused only about 17 percent of ship losses during the war, due largely to the mediocre accuracy and limited lethality of their munitions.[16] Nonetheless, it is hard to contest the idea that there *was* remarkable, disruptive innovation.

The strategies of the main actors were multifaceted. They also evolved considerably over the course of the conflict.

For Germany, and Hitler, the goals emphasized the domination of Europe, including the creation of a great German "living space" (*lebensraum*) for the Aryan peoples throughout much of central and eastern Europe. Only with such acquisitions could Germany establish itself as a great power, strengthen itself as a nation, solidify its long-term security, and fulfill its true destiny.[17] It would require not only the defeat but also the extermination of the peoples living there. For Hitler, so be it.[18] His overall geostrategic goals could be aided by the permanent weakening of France, such that it could no longer be a serious rival or threat, and some kind of accommodation with Britain on Berlin's terms.[19] Hitler would achieve these goals through a combination of military conquest and mass murder that eliminated the peoples (not just Jews) he did not want populating these regions in order to free up their territories, and resources, for his own ethnic countrymen. He did not have quite the detailed timetable of the Schlieffen Plan of World War I. He also sought to pick off victims one by one—making sure France was out of the war before he attacked the Soviet Union (and hoping that Britain would be too, though here he was not as successful of course), and ideally defeating the Soviet Union before facing the possibility of war against America. Certainly, he was motivated by a simple desire for vengeance, and restoration of German pride, after the defeat of World War I and the terms of the Versailles Treaty. But even among the ranks of the most militaristic leaders in history, Hitler was an extremely ambitious and horribly psychopathic case.[20] That said, he also had more support for his vision from his generals and other leaders than is sometimes acknowledged, and he was capable of considerable cleverness as well as stupidity.[21]

The Soviet Union's Joseph Stalin, though perhaps almost as indifferent to the loss of human life as Hitler, was nonetheless somewhat easier to understand. Through the initial alliance with Germany, the 1939 Molotov-Ribbentrop Pact, he sought to carve up eastern Europe with Hitler, taking swaths of Poland and more northerly reaches for the Soviet Union. Astonished by Hitler's turncoat attack against the Soviet Union on June 22, 1941, Stalin fought first for survival, then for restoration of occupied Soviet lands to his control and the defeat of Hitler. After the betrayal, in fact, he felt what Harry Hopkins, a confidant of Franklin D. Roosevelt (FDR), called a "cold, implacable anger" at Hitler.[22] He also of course became opportunistically ambitious with time, creating a Soviet-dominated zone in eastern Europe; his territorial ambitions also reached to northeast Asia by war's end.[23]

Italy's role in the war was, in ideological terms, to advance fascism just as Hitler sought. In territorial terms, Rome was primarily opportunistic.[24] Benito Mussolini admired Hitler and was jealous of his military victories. He sought a share of the spoils for Italy, which led him to attack France and, later (and without consulting first with Hitler), to attack Greece.

For Britain, the goals were . . . Churchillian. First and foremost, of course, was a courageous defense of the homeland in a struggle for survival. Once the most imminent danger of being conquered passed, London developed a strong resolve to reverse Nazi aggression and defeat Hitler. London also sought to preserve the British empire, including India as well as colonies in Africa. For that reason, and because of its need for oil and other traded commodities, it focused strong attention on the Mediterranean and North African theaters throughout the war. This perspective also meant that, while Churchill worked hard to persuade the United States to adopt a "Europe first" approach to the war, London always had a strong interest in the Indo-Pacific as well.[25]

For the United States as an overall polity, initial goals were pragmatic. They included not only preventing the Axis powers—featuring Germany, Japan, and Italy—from gobbling up large chunks of the globe, but staying out of the war itself if possible (at least for most Americans and most political leaders, even if not necessarily FDR). As such, early in the war, America became the "arsenal of democracy," creating the lend-lease program in

March 1941 to provide enormous amounts of supplies to the Soviet Union and Britain in the hope that such a role would possibly suffice. It was not at all clear to the main parties that the United States would enter the war. Harry Hopkins, FDR's close friend and adviser, touched British hearts when he went to London in January 1941 and, speaking in a private meeting with the prime minister, quoted from the Book of Ruth, saying "Wither thou goest, I will go. And where thou lodgest, I will lodge; thy people shall be my people, and thy God my God." The reason such a statement could be so powerful was that it was about the closest Washington came in those days to promising an ironclad commitment to Allied victory.[26] As Churchill's physician later recalled, "Even to us the words seemed like a rope thrown to a drowning man."[27] Still, it is far from certain what America would have done absent the Japanese attack on the United States.

Once ambushed by Japan at Pearl Harbor, staying out of the war was no longer possible; Japan had badly misread the American polity on that score. Germany's declaration of war against America shortly after Pearl Harbor ensured that the United States would fight on two fronts. Roosevelt's, and the country's, motivations were increasingly reinforced by a growing awareness of the sheer scale of the brutality and evil manifested by the Nazi regime, as well as Japan's government under Prime Minister Tojo Hideki. The war became a moral crusade as well.[28] To a large extent, recognizing Germany's size, power, and potential, Washington promulgated a "Europe-first" strategy—though in fact, the allocation of resources was less decisively tilted in favor of the Atlantic and Europe than one might have guessed from that slogan.[29]

For other British Commonwealth countries like Canada, Australia, and New Zealand, World War II was a clear contest of right versus wrong in defense of Mother England—and, especially in Australia's case, its own security in a region increasingly threatened by Japan. For British (and French) colonies, the decision to provide soldiers to fight as part of the allied coalition was less voluntary and often less enthusiastic.[30]

For France, with two competing governments effectively fighting on opposite sides of the war for a time, it is harder to distill its strategy into a single overarching concept. The collaborationist Vichy government sought to preserve some autonomy in southern France and its overseas colonies (mostly in Africa) by cooperating with Germany. In stark contrast, Free French forces under army officer and future president Charles de Gaulle resisted the occupation and fought with Allied forces from North Africa to the Middle East to ultimately France itself.[31]

Smaller east European countries generally followed the maxim dating back to ancient Greek times and Thucydides' Melian dialogue: in international politics, and especially war, the strong do what they will and the weak do what they can. That said, there were noble efforts by countries like Finland (against the Soviet Union) and Yugoslavia (against Germany) to fight against the odds even when that resistance incurred huge suffering for their peoples.[32]

Japan's main goals were to dominate eastern Eurasia and the western Pacific, militarily and economically, through the Co-Prosperity Sphere. The island nation saw its own territory and resource base as inadequate for the kind of power and wealth it sought to achieve, absent dependable access to the resources of the region. In many places, Japan perpetrated terrible brutalities on its victims—such as what is often known as the Rape of Nanking in late 1937.[33] The attack on Pearl Harbor was undertaken in the hope that America's Pacific power could be defanged long enough to allow Japan to establish a bastion of island strongholds throughout Southeast Asia and the Pacific writ large. They would then make any attempt at attacking its Co-Prosperity Sphere or home islands appear too difficult and costly—leading America ultimately to accept Japan's hegemony in the western Pacific (and lift sanctions that interfered with its economy).[34] Meanwhile, Japan would have established sure access to the raw materials, including oil and metals and rubber that it desperately needed, even within that Co-Prosperity Sphere. Thus, tragically, the embargoes imposed on Japan in response to its initial aggressions against China and Korea drove it to escalate rather than relent, to target much of Southeast Asia in its imperialistic sights, and to attack not only British and Dutch holdings in Asia but the United States and its possessions as well.[35] As the Australian historian Geoffrey Blainey put it, "In essence, the economic blockade—designed in the hope that it would halt a Japanese advance—made that advance an urgent priority."[36]

For China, well into a long-standing civil war by the 1930s, the strategies for both Nationalists and Communists were to somehow fend off Japanese aggression—while helping their own odds against the other, so they could seize power in the aftermath of the foreign aggression.[37] Sadly, for many years, that strategy only helped perpetuate the Japanese occupation. For Chinese Communist Party leader Mao Zedong, however, this period provided the crucible for development and application of his theories of insurgent warfare that would eventually bring him to power in China after World War II was over.[38]

The Path to War

The roots of World War II go back directly to World War I, the Treaty of Versailles, the ultimate failure of the League of Nations, and the diplomatic acrimony followed by the economic collapse of the 1920s and 1930s. There is a reason that E. H. Carr's famous book is entitled *The Twenty Years' Crisis,* and that Adam Tooze's history of the period from 1916 to 1931 is called *The Deluge*: this was a time when in so many ways, the world fell apart.

In the years after World War I, Germany was exceptionally weak, verging on a failed state. Communists, monarchists, and others competed for power after the 1918 abdication of the kaiser left a political vacuum. Severe reparations payments averaging about 3 percent of GDP (the size of America's defense budget today) reinforced economic weakness, precluded recovery, and contributed to a severe bout of hyperinflation by 1923. Indeed, in the fourth quarter of 1923, the month-to-month inflation rate exceeded 13,000 percent![39] Hitler's attempted "Beer Hall Putsch" of that same year—by which he sought in effect to overthrow what there was of a functioning government (yet for which he spent only a few months in jail due in large part to a corrupt and rigged legal system)—was emblematic of the state of affairs. It was far from the only example.

For Hitler, like many Germans, a "stabbed in the back" narrative took strong root in the years after the Treaty of Versailles: that the wrong government in Berlin, hastily formed to replace the abdicating kaiser, had treasonably given up on the war effort at a time when no foreign forces had even reached German territory. By this myth, which became entrenched among Germans in the decades between the wars, Germany was never really defeated. Yet it was severely punished. Therefore, it had a score to settle, and honor to restore, in righting the wrong of the war's illegitimate ending, as well as the way it was unfairly blamed for the conflict, including in the "war guilt" language of the Treaty of Versailles. The sense of wounded honor was reinforced not only by the severe reparations payments—for which Germany was granted no reprieve even in the hyperinflation crisis of 1923, for example—but by the strict limitations placed on German military capability. Indeed, the victorious powers granted themselves the right to occupy and control Germany's Ruhr Valley industrial region in the event of German noncompliance with its reparations obligations. That right was exercised by France in 1923, pouring salt on what was already a deep wound of battered national pride.[40]

However, without significant British or American help, France was not well prepared to sustain that kind of enforcement against the more populous Germany, especially because neither Washington nor London was doing very much to stay militarily powerful or active on the European continent.[41]

After the 1923 hyperinflation crisis, however, Germany recovered for a time. As the great journalist and historian William Shirer wrote of Germany in the mid-to-late 1920s:[42]

A wonderful ferment was working in Germany. Life seemed more free, more modern, more exciting than in any place I had ever seen. . . . The old oppressive Prussian spirit seemed to be dead and buried. Most Germans one met—politicians, writers, editors, artists, professors, students, businessmen, labor leaders—struck you as being democratic, liberal, even pacificist.

Yet that spirit was largely destroyed by the global economic crisis that started in 1929. German industrial output declined by almost half over the next three years.[43] When the aversion to the terms of peace was juxtaposed with the economic calamity of the early 1930s, German frustration turned to anger. When it became clear that the victorious powers were themselves tired of or unable to enforce the terms of Versailles, the anger was manifested with a form of aggressiveness. Even though reparations payments were eventually cut back substantially, the relief was too little, too late in light of the broader context.

The terms of Versailles were tough, to be sure, but by themselves they did not cause World War II. It also took the economic crisis of the late 1920s, a sense of historical grievance nurtured and exploited by hypernationalistic politicians, and the uniquely perverse and psychopathic person of Adolf Hitler to create the path to the worst war in human history. As historian Gerhard Weinberg wrote so eloquently:[44]

There was a popular delusion, widespread at the time, sedulously fostered in the 1920s and 1930s by German propaganda, generally believed then and remaining the staple pabulum of history textbooks today, that Germany had been most terribly crushed by the peace settlement, that all manner of horrendous things had been done to her, and that a wide variety of onerous burdens and restrictions imposed upon her by the peace had weakened her into the indefinite future. On the basis of this view, a whole series of modifications was made in the settlement, all without exception in favor of Germany. The occupation was ended earlier than the peace treaty indicated, the commissions to supervise disarmament were withdrawn, the reparations payments were reduced and eventually cancelled, and the trials of war criminals were left to the Germans with predictable results, to mention only some of the most significant changes made.

By 1930, Hitler's National Socialist party won 6.4 million votes, an eightfold increase over the 1928 tally, becoming the second-largest party in parliament.[45] Hitler managed to position himself to become chancellor in 1933, and *fuhrer* the next year (after President Paul von Hindenburg died, with Hitler taking that position over as well). Although Hitler did come to power initially through electoral success, he immediately abused his position and discarded normal democratic constraints. Innuendo, outright lies, the murder of key adversaries by the Nazi storm troopers and by the *Schutzstaffel* (SS) and the Gestapo (secret police), arson at the Reichstag (the parliament building) in late February 1933, establishment of martial law through deceit and false promises, extraconstitutional elimination of the position of president when Hindenberg died in August of 1934—all these ingredients went into the recipe for taking absolute power and consolidating Nazi rule.[46]

Just how this could happen continues to boggle the mind, though clearly the preceding fifteen years of German misery went far toward creating the necessary social and political conditions. As William Shirer wrote about the state of play in 1933:[47]

> The man with the Charlie Chaplin mustache, who had been a down-and-out tramp in Vienna in his youth, an unknown soldier of World War I, a derelict in Munich in the first grim postwar days, the somewhat comical leader of the Beer Hall Putsch, this spellbinder who was not even German but Austrian, and who was only forty-three years old, had just been administered the oath as Chancellor of the German Reich.

Once Hitler came to power, he dramatically increased German military spending. The United States, Britain, and France lagged behind. This new dynamic came after a decade in which Britain and France had already cut back military capabilities enormously. For example, in 1919, while in the process of reducing its military strength by 90 percent over a two-year period, Britain also adopted a policy based on the "Ten Year Rule," which assumed the country would not engage in combat for a decade—even though Britain would presumably have to play a major role in reversing any noncompliance with the terms of the Versailles Treaty.[48]

Historian Paul Kennedy estimates that, in the year 1930, Germany spent the equivalent of less than $200 million on its military, while the United Kingdom and France each spent about $500 million and the United States $700 million. By 1936, the year Germany militarily reoccupied its Rhineland region in blatant violation of the terms of the Treaty of Versailles that required its demilitarization, its military budget was some $2.3 billion. Meanwhile, the United States, Britain, and France were each only approaching $1 billion. By 1938, Germany was up to $7.4 billion; the United Kingdom was nearing $2 billion, and France and the United States were each still only around $1 billion. In other words, by that year, Germany was itself spending twice as much as Britain, France, and the United States combined. (Japan was nearing $2 billion at this point; the Soviet Union was spending more than $5 billion; Italy was nearing $1 billion.)[49] By 1938, Germany was devoting at least 15 percent of GDP to its armed forces. By contrast, Britain and France were spending 6 to 7 percent of GDP on their militaries; the United States clocked in at 2 percent.[50]

In Asia, the militarization was ever further along by some measures; by 1938, Japan was spending more than 20 percent of GDP on its armed forces. The overall situation had begun to fall apart by 1931, when Japan invaded the Chinese province of Manchuria—yet it suffered no major reprieve under the League of Nations framework or other international organizations or mechanisms.[51] That lapse undercut the league's credibility not only in Asia but globally.[52] After a period of relatively cooperative and nonaggressive behavior in the 1920s, Japan returned to its militaristic and expansionist ways of the late nineteenth and early twentieth centuries, when it first took the island of Formosa, Korea, parts of Manchuria (northern China) and Sakhalin Island (in Russia), and numerous smaller islands in the western Pacific as well.

In the 1930s, Japan's highly nationalistic and aggressive military took advantage of the malaise and chaos of the Great Depression period to assert itself domestically as well.[53] Right-wing assassins killed numerous moderate leaders. Extremists seized increasing control, motivated by the ideology that dominating much of East Asia was central to Japan's future economic prospects. Resources like oil, rubber, copper, iron ore, and coal, as well as agricultural land and more space for Japan's growing population, were among the major drivers motivating the extremists. The thinking was more akin, however, to traditional European imperialism than to anything like the *lebensraum* goals of Hitler. Genocide was not seen, therefore, as a necessary part of deliberate strategy—though in the years to come, many episodes of mass killing would result, especially in China.[54] Because China was beset by ongoing civil conflict, between Communists and Nationalists and warlords, it was a tempting target for Japanese imperialists, and they met little resistance in the early 1930s in Manchuria.[55] As noted, for the most part, Mao and Nationalist leader Chiang Kai-shek worried more about each other than Japan, helping to explain why China was unable to effectively resist the occupation.[56]

From the early 1930s onward, Japan's pursuit of this Greater East Asia Co-Prosperity Sphere, suffused with elements of Japanese racial superiority and glorification of battle, increasingly dominated the thinking and policies of its government. (Meanwhile, many in countries like Australia, Britain, and the United States were arguably guilty of a different type of racism too—for example, underrating the quality of Japanese military equipment and fighting forces due to outdated beliefs that they were innately inferior to western capabilities.)[57] The dye was cast for expansionism not only into Manchuria but also French Indochina and eventually the Philippines, the Dutch East Indies, and beyond.[58] Japanese production of warships, aircraft (including the impressive "Zero" fighter), aircraft carriers, excellent torpedoes, and other key armaments accelerated considerably in this period.[59]

Back in Europe and neighboring regions of Africa and the Middle East, the tick-tock of events leading to war was roughly as follows. In 1935, Italy invaded Ethiopia. Italy's strongman leader, Prime Minister Benito Mussolini, thought it time to satisfy some of his own imperial ambitions in one of the relatively few parts of Africa not dominated by Britain or France (or Belgium or Portugal). On this matter the League of Nations did respond—but only to impose economic sanctions of modest bite.[60]

In 1936 and 1937, Germany, Italy and Japan reached agreements that together created the Axis alliance.[61] From roughly this time period onwards, Mussolini became less concerned about German ambitions toward Austria, with "Il Duce" increasingly smitten with the German dictator and willing to tolerate German imperial ambitions more than he had been in prior periods.[62]

In March 1936, citing the supposedly unfriendly Franco-Russian security accord as pretext, Hitler violated Versailles and sent three battalions
into the Rhineland of Germany. His generals were nervous, expecting that
some part of France's 100 divisions, perhaps backed up by Britain, would
attack them as was their right. But Hitler was correct in his reading of
Paris and London. Perhaps the last clear chance to stop Hitler easily—
since he might well have fallen from power with the embarrassment of a
military fiasco in the country's west—was lost.[63] In this case, some combination of enduring war fatigue, political irresoluteness, and military un-
derconfidence on the part of France and Britain produced inaction.

Then the aggressions began. Germany absorbed Austria through a con-
trived series of events and a bloodless military grab—a hostile takeover
to be sure, even if done in connivance with Austrian Nazis—in March 1938.
This *Anschluss* ("joining") was later approved by referendum in Austria,
but only after Germany had created a climate of extreme fear and intimi-
dation.[64] Germany then took a chunk of Czechoslovakia—the Sudeten-
land, where the 3 million or so ethnic Germans comprising 30 percent of
the country's population mostly lived—in the fall of that same year, with
British prime minister Neville Chamberlain's and French prime minister
Edouard Daladier's infamous acquiescence at Munich in September 1938.
In this period of renewed economic vitality and bloodless conquest, Hitler is believed to have enjoyed overwhelming support among the German
people.[65] At this time, even though German military spending had already
grown enormously, the army was not large enough to put more than five
active and seven reserve divisions in the west as it prepared to overrun
Czechoslovakia. That meant France and Britain, the former of which itself had 100 divisions on its own, likely still had an opportunity to achieve
a decisive military outcome if they had chosen to back up Czechoslovakia's security with a direct response to any aggression in Germany's east.[66]
They did not. Given trends in military spending, perhaps that was not so
surprising, since by now Germany was catching up fast to the victorious
powers of World War I. It is doubtful that any enforcement action against
Germany at this juncture would have been smooth or easy.

After stoking and funding separatist movements in other parts of
Czechoslovakia, Hitler then seized the entirety of the country in early
1939. In so doing, he for the first time extended Germany's aggression beyond areas where ethnic Germans predominated. As Donald Kagan wrote
of how this came to be:[67]

In the Munich agreement Britain, no less than Germany, had guaranteed the independence of Czechoslovakia. To honor its word Britain would need to take up arms at once in defense of the victims of German aggression. Hitler, however, had arranged things so that it might appear to those who desperately wanted to believe it that Czechoslovakia had suffered a collapse that was largely internal and that Germany was only picking up the pieces. This was the view seized on by Chamberlain, who told Parliament that Britain could not be bound to guarantee a state that no longer existed.

This was still not quite the beginning of the war, because these blatant acts of treachery and aggression did not involve high-end combat or involve Britain and France—or the Soviet Union—just yet. But on September 1, 1939, that all changed. Hitler was in a hurry by then. He had taken the measure of the leaders arrayed against him and was not impressed. He had achieved a good chunk of his military buildup, and felt empowered. Yet he also viewed that new superiority as a potentially wasting or declining asset that others would quickly seek to challenge—meaning that the time for action was now. After claiming to have attempted a final peace overture—after months of making territorial demands on the Poles—Hitler then had S.S. operators dressed as Polish army officials carry out a mock attack on a German radio station. While the attack was fake, the bullets and casualties were not (the latter were drugged concentration-camp inmates). The stage was set for the September 1 invasion of Poland and the launching of World War II, since that tragic act would bring many combatants into the fight for the first time.[68]

Things were heating up in Asia too; Japan had undertaken increasingly brazen and horrific acts of aggression against China, including by now in Shanghai and Nanking.[69] But that remained, for the moment, a localized war. It would not for too much longer.

Fall 1939 and Spring 1940: Blitzkrieg in the East and West

On September 1, 1939, two large armored formations led the German army's move into Poland, from north and south, ultimately converging on the nation's center and rapidly decimating the infantry-heavy and horse-heavy Polish army. Germany deployed sixty-two divisions, including six armored and ten mechanized, against Poland's forty, none of them armored or mechanized. Many Poles fought bravely. Polish forces were so underarmed, belatedly mobilized, and poorly positioned in the country's westernmost exposed regions (with German forces effectively on three sides of them) that they could not realistically offer sustained resistance. Some did reposition to defend Warsaw, and some even valiantly counter-attacked, but the odds were too strongly tilted against them.

The fighting was effectively over within a month—by which point the Soviet Union had gotten in on the act as well, slicing off a segment of eastern Poland by previous arrangement with Hitler in the infamous Molotov-Ribbentrop Pact. Specifically, Warsaw was encircled by Germans by September 17, the same day Soviet forces moved into the country's east. Warsaw was bombed heavily for ten days and by September 27, Poland had surrendered. This was certainly a "blitzkrieg" or lightning war, but it was such a mismatch—in terms of the weaponry of the forces, as well as Poland's enormous geographic disadvantages—that it is remembered in military terms mostly as a walkover.[70] Germany lost just under 15,000 military personnel killed in action in Poland. Poland suffered 100,000 fatalities, but another 1 million military personnel were taken prisoner. Many would suffer terrible treatment and often death at German or Soviet hands in the ensuing months and years.[71]

Between the fall of 1939 and the spring of 1940, while Hitler pushed his generals to undertake the main attack against France through the Ardennes as soon as possible, but had to wait for the right weather conditions, another fascinating conflict took place. It was "the hundred-day winter war" between Finland and the Soviet Union, brilliantly described in a book of the same name by Gordon Sander.[72] Finland had been part of Russia from 1809 through 1917. Whether Stalin really felt he needed it back,[73] he did decide that he needed a longer strategic buffer near Leningrad (St. Petersburg) and the Baltic states (which the Soviet Union would annex in 1940). Stalin demanded territorial adjustments in October 1939, the Finns refused (even though at this stage, Germany and the Soviet Union were still allies, so no hope could be forthcoming from any nearby power). War ensued on November 30. Ultimately, the Finns' total armed strength of 175,000 could not fend off 1 million Soviets—and Moscow got its desired territory, at least for a time—but the war was quite a fight until the Soviets fully geared up and brought their overwhelming numbers to bear. As John Keegan described it:[74]

Perhaps the most warlike of all European peoples, and certainly the hardiest, the Finns made circles around their Russian attackers in the snowbound wastes of their native forests, employing so-called *motti* or "logging" tactics to cut off and encircle their enemies, who were regularly disorientated and demoralized by a style of warfare for which their training had not prepared them.

Once the spring of 1940 arrived, Hitler took Denmark and Norway. Much of his motivation was to menace the British fleet and access the North Atlantic region from ports on Norway's coast. Access to the Norwegian ports would also allow for wintertime transport of iron ore from mines in northern Sweden over to Norway and then via ship through the Norwegian Sea to Germany—and preempt any designs Allied forces might have had in the Nordics. Denmark was seen as part of a German "land bridge" to Norway. The attack began on April 9. A shell-shocked Denmark quickly capitulated. Norway did its best to fight, receiving limited help from British and French forces for a time (until the following month, when Germany's assault on France changed their priorities and led to their withdrawal). But it fell to German control, partly due to a homegrown Nazi party that betrayed its country. As Gerhard Weinberg wrote, "In making their preparations, the Germans took advantage of internal Norwegian support, led and symbolized by the man who would give his name to the concept of selling your own country to the tender mercies of another, [Prime Minister] Vidkun Quisling."[75]

On May 10, 1940, Germany initiated its blitzkrieg against France. (In the aftermath of the Norway catastrophe, Chamberlin resigned as prime minister of Britain that same day, to be replaced by Churchill.) Germany sent a modest force northward through Belgium and Luxembourg, retracing the path of the famed right or westernmost wing of the Schlieffen Plan—and duping British as well as French forces into believing the main attack would come from there, leading them to move huge forces northward into position to resist.

Instead of concentrating its assault to the west, Germany surprisingly sent most of its armored forces through the topographically challenging Ardennes forest, where Belgium meets France's northeastern corner. These forces then bypassed the Maginot Line of defensive fortifications (which was attacked by a smaller and much less armored force), and crossed the Meuse River through various means including pontoon bridges. French forces were separated from each other, logistics lines were interrupted, headquarters and communications networks were severely disrupted, and the whole military machine was generally paralyzed.

There was one major silver lining. Twice German forces paused, unnecessarily, in their rapid forward movement, on May 17 and May 24–26. The latter occasion provided time for British and French troops to prepare for a fighting withdrawal. The Dunkirk evacuation moved one-third of a million troops, though not their heavy equipment, on an improvised fleet of troop transports. German airpower was only able to sink about 1 percent of the nearly 800 ships that contributed to the evacuation, despite the much different expectations of many.[76] Indeed, given the respective locations of available airfields, the geography of the Dunkirk fight actually favored the Royal Air Force. From May 26 through June 3, the Luftwaffe lost 240 planes to Britain's 177.[77]

But by May 27, Germany had forced the capitulation of Belgium, with the latter's army surrendering in a pocket near the sea north of Dunkirk. As June began, German forces controlled not just Belgium but northern France as well, extending all the way to the English Channel.[78]

To achieve such dramatic effects, Germany also used stunning special force operations. They included a glider-borne attack on the roof of an otherwise impregnable fortress of Eben Emael in Belgium to disable the fort's guns and thereby ensure access to key bridges needed for invading forces—as recounted brilliantly by Admiral William McRaven (later of Osama bin Laden raid fame) in his riveting book of case studies, *Spec Ops*.[79] Summing up the operation, which had been planned and rehearsed meticulously, and then carried out with extreme audacity, employing innovative technologies including shaped charges to destroy key structural elements of the fort, McRaven wrote the following:[80]

> There is little debate that the assault on Eben Emael was one of the most decisive victories in the history of special operations. Sixty-nine German glidermen [on nine aircraft] engaged and soundly defeated a Belgian force ten times their size protected by the largest fort of its day.

More generally, the Ardennes assault defied all reasonable expectations, given the ruggedness of the forest terrain and relative scarcity of roads. Yet once Germany figured out that it could manage the necessary movements on the necessary timelines, those very conditions combined with the forest provided cover and enhanced surprise. It is worth noting that many German commanders doubted the plan would work. The concept depended not just on the tank, but motorized support to allow entire divisions to move fast—often 30 or 40 miles a day, twice that of a typical foot soldier on the march. Infantry was still crucial, too; it created breakthrough points for armored units, and then covered the flanks of ensuing tank movements, while also defeating isolated enemy forces in detail. German unit commanders were given the prerogative to follow their own tactical instincts, exploit initial successes, keep moving forward, and bypass enemy strongpoints initially when possible. Their ideas built on those that had become successful by the end of World War I. The tank was often second to the fight rather than first, despite the common historical depiction of blitzkrieg as a panzer-led armor-dominant concept. Armored reconnaissance battalions, engineers, and infantry often led the way.[81] Well-integrated combined-arms warfare was the real watchword.[82] Popular lore notwithstanding, the enemy's forces were the objective every bit as much as its command headquarters; the goal was to isolate, encircle, and ultimately destroy them, as in most previous conflicts.[83]

Even as their victories accumulated in 1939 and 1940, German forces continued to improve the concepts undergirding blitzkrieg.[84] By contrast, French and British strategists did not study the Polish campaign as well as they might, or deduce correctly its main lessons prior to May 1940.[85]

Blitzkrieg's success was also due in very large part to air operations— and their close coordination with ground movements. Aircraft did not generally destroy armor, but they played many other important roles, for example against exposed soldiers.[86] The Germans did many things to achieve effectiveness with their Luftwaffe. They co-located air and ground headquarters and placed the Luftwaffe in clear support of the ground campaign. They also made excellent use of radios and tactical intelligence to ensure timely and effective close-air support.[87]

The Luftwaffe's role in the spring of 1940 excelled in other ways, too. German planes attacked enemy aircraft and airfields early, often, and hard, and thereby achieved air superiority quickly. They not only provided integrated close-air support for armored forces in contact, but also protected the flanks of armored units when the latter outpaced their infantry support.[88]

Luftwaffe success was due in large part to smart and efficient logistics as well. The Germans realized the importance of moving airplanes forward to operate off seized airfields so that the aircraft would not be out of range of the ground action.[89] Their fighters averaged four sorties a day, to France's 0.9. The Luftwaffe also provided heavy supporting fire for ground forces, contributed protection against enemy aircraft, and carried out effective airborne operations as well, notably in Holland in the early days of the campaign.[90]

Summing it all up, Max Boot put it insightfully as well, noting how French general Maurice Gamelin sent his best and largest forces northward into the German trap:[91]

> The Ardennes region was regarded as a backwater. It was held by the French Ninth and Second Armies, composed mainly of older, "B-series" reservists who had done their military service many years earlier and had received scant training or new equipment in recent years. These troops had been called up in September 1939, but they did not use the next nine months to make up for their serious deficiencies. (The Germans, by contrast, spent this period correcting mistakes made during the Polish campaign.) Most of them were put to use digging fortifications, not learning to maneuver and fight in the open field. Their equipment remained for the most part antiquated, and they had few antitank guns, much less tanks. With this troop deployment, General Gamelin could not have done more damage to his country if he had been a paid Nazi agent.

After Dunkirk, as well as the surrender of Belgium, German forces quickly turned southward. France attempted a makeshift defense along what it called the "Weygand Line," named for the commander, General Maxime Wegyand, who on May 20 had replaced the ineffective Gamelin. The line stretched from the English Channel over to the Maginot Line, and included about two-thirds of the original French army of 100 divisions. Of these surviving 66 divisions, 17 were still within the Maginot Line positions, and the others were formed into a long perimeter through northern France.

The Weygand Line sought to use a stationary "hedgehog" defense by employing both natural and man-made terrain to create fixed and reasonably well-defended points of resistance. But French forces were too few and far between, had no viable concept to employ strategic reserves, had no clear concept of operations, and were still half dazed by what had already befallen their nation and their comrades.[92] By mid-June, German forces had not only penetrated the line, with armor often simply bypassing the hedgehog strongholds, but reached Paris. That led to the rapid surrender of the French government on June 25, and along with it the establishment of the Vichy regime that henceforth would govern southern

France and French colonies semiautonomously, while Germany ran the north of the nation directly. The six-week battle of May 10–June 25 cost the French about 90,000 dead, and Germany 25,000.[93]

What transpired in France in the spring of 1940 stood in stark contrast to what had occurred there with such bloodshed and maiming and devastation from 1914 through 1918. In 1940, Germany only had 10 armored divisions, each with some 250 tanks—and its total tank inventory was neither notably larger than, nor superior to, that of France. Indeed, Germany's overall strength of some 150 divisions (with 10 armored and four mechanized) was roughly comparable to the aggregate of those arrayed against it—8 Dutch, 18 Belgian, 10 British, and 100 French divisions. The differences were that the German army was organized for rapid exploitation of any success, and tightly linked in with the nation's air power as well.[94]

The battles also demonstrated the advantage of unpredictability. Germany's war plans made it hard to foresee the next move of its army, the Wehrmacht (supported tactically by its air force, the Luftwaffe).[95] In the case of Poland, it was never clear when and where the northern and southern pincers of the German invasion force would pivot, turning inward toward the center of the country. In so doing they would create a giant envelopment, often analogized in military literature to the ancient battle of Cannae in Roman times, that would cut up Polish armies and trap large elements of them within its grasp. In the case of France, Paris was more inclined to expect a repeat of World War I, when the Schlieffen Plan had kept Germany's "right wing strong" as it marched through Belgium. Instead, a feint from the north led French and British forces to move into Belgium, leaving their supply and communications lines exposed to an armored force that would cut through them from the east and south. The effectiveness of this approach, decided only in the months just before it was attempted, surprised even Hitler and his generals.[96] Indeed, it left them a bit off balance, contributing to the indecision and delay that allowed the Dunkirk evacuation halfway through the overall campaign in northern France.[97]

A challenge to the traditional narrative of the defeat of France, argued by historian John Mosier, offers a different perspective at the tactical and campaign levels of combat. Mosier argues that in tank-on-tank engagements, German forces did not win but in fact took big losses in the early going (including in their short war against the Netherlands at the beginning of that broader campaign, in which they lost nearly 300 transport

aircraft among other assets). Yet they were saved in part by their air defenses, which caused enormous attrition to Allied aircraft, and by their
Luftwaffe, which in addition to good tactical concepts for close air support possessed forward airfields permitting multiple sorties per aircraft per
day. Most of all, they were helped by French and British unwillingness to
commit reserves after initial incursions surprised their senior leadership
and left them in a defeatist mentality. Indeed, by this perspective even the
Dunkirk evacuation was a mistake, for it conceded defeat at a time that
was hardly inevitable, and also forced exposed Belgian forces to surrender subsequently, once their flank was left unguarded. France then fought
on for another month, but deprived of Allied help, ultimately could not
recover from the mistakes of May.[98]

But before getting to the fateful year of 1941, there is a whole additional story to be told about the second half of 1940, most notably the
Battle of Britain. Blitzkrieg had had its heyday for the moment; now, the
critical elements of combat turned overwhelmingly to the air, and to some
extent the water as well.

Summer 1940, the Battle of Britain, and Early Phases of the Battle of the Atlantic

If the fall of 1939 and the spring of 1940 were the seasons of successful German blitzkrieg, the summer of 1940 would be the season of a
failed German strategic bombing campaign—and the first serious setback
to the German military juggernaut. Yet other trends in the war, including the Battle of the Atlantic by which Britain sought supplies from the
United States and German U-boats tried to intercept them, were still
going largely the German way at this point in the war.

With 1940 only half over, Hitler had half of France under direct occupation and the other half in the palm of his hand through the collaborationist Vichy government. He also had already conquered lands to the
east and south, with big additional ambitions for the east the following
year. But now the actual fighting turned to the skies over southeastern
England including London.

Hitler partly expected Britain to agree to terms after the defeat of
France. When London refused any such capitulation, Hitler threatened
invasion, to be preceded by a period of bombardment. That created the
conditions for a protracted battle for the air, pitting British Hurricane and
Spitfire aircraft against German Messerschmitts.

The invasion was to be known as Sea Lion. In contrast with his plans for the earlier blitzkrieg operations on the continent, however, all of this thinking about conquering Britain was sloppy, underdeveloped, and logistically and otherwise unrealistic. Sea Lion was indefinitely postponed by the early fall, never to be attempted in the end.

The air campaign was carried out, also rather sloppily. Germany was feeling its oats after numerous easy wins and felt confident that Britain could be coerced into surrender. To the extent any plan existed for attacking Britain, it assumed only four days would be needed to defeat the Royal Air Force in southern England, followed by four more weeks for a comprehensive nationwide win including the destruction of British aircraft industry.[99] The actual operation proceeded through several different, largely improvised phases, starting with more tactical attacks on military targets, before escalating to direct bombardment of cities. In that sense, it was not really the test case for a theory of warfare put forth by Giulio Douhet, an Italian military strategist, whose 1921 book, *Command of the Air,* argued that future wars could be won by pounding an enemy's homeland, people, and government into submission.

The Germans consistently overestimated their advantages over Britain in the campaign, and in aircraft production that was so crucial to replace losses at this stage of the war—just as the Brits also overestimated relative German strength.[100] Germany also failed to consider tactics that might have been more successful, like the complementary use of commando raids against the radar towers along the British coast that were a crucial part of the overall defensive network.[101]

A preliminary phase started on July 10 and involved broad, somewhat unfocused attacks on shipping, on coastal military sites, and on British aircraft. British defenses, and English resilience, proved better than Berlin expected, however, and the attacks did not achieve their political goal.

The next phase, called the "Eagle" part of the campaign, began on August 12–13. Recognizing the importance of weakening British air defenses, it targeted radar installations, airfields, and other British military assets in southeastern England. During this phase, British losses were considerable—but they were also less than new production of aircraft, with 204 planes lost and some 476 built from August 8 through 23, for example. German losses meanwhile exceeded production over the same period, with 397 planes lost to 313 built. Britain lost 104 of an even scarcer commodity—pilots—in the same time period. However, Germany lost more than 600, killed or captured. British pilots who were shot down could hope to parachute safely onto home territory; downed German pilots had no such recourse.[102]

Luckily, Britain had many advantages in this fight. Even if Britain's political leaders had badly misread Hitler until the invasion of Poland, its scientists and military planners had not been asleep at the switch. The basic concept and technology of radar, and then the Chain Home system of radar stations ringing the British coast, were doggedly developed, manufactured, and deployed in preceding years. So were excellent air defense aircraft, the Hurricane and especially the Spitfire.[103]

Still, the Battle for Britain was a competitive endeavor. British advantages in radar, aircraft production, and the technology of the Spitfire interceptor aircraft were matched up against Germany's strong Luftwaffe, including its menacing (if underutilized) bomber force.[104] Germany had more pilots—but Britain was producing airplanes at three times the pace, belying to an extent the caricature of Germany as the predominant military-industrial power of the day.[105]

Geography played both ways. It was a tactical advantage for Britain in the sense that air battles were conducted near its bases, so aircraft did not need to waste time or fuel getting to the fight. But at a strategic level, that very fact meant any damage done on the ground was to its own territory, economy, and people. And bombers did consistently get through throughout, even if they suffered losses in the process.[106]

With every week that Britain held on, its prospects improved—not only due to its advantages in aircraft production capacity, but because of the looming change in weather, which would complicate any attempted German invasion of Britain as autumn and then winter set in.[107] Germany might have done better had it concentrated more attacks on the linchpins of British capability, to include radar towers along the coast, as well as aircraft production industries.[108] It is far from clear, however, that it could have presented a plausible invasion threat that year regardless of how the air campaign was run.

In any event, as the weeks went by and London held firm, Hitler's frustration grew. So did his anger, when Berlin was attacked from the air by Britain in late August. He then shifted course, turning to terroristic aerial bombardment of London starting on September 7. These daytime attacks caused considerable damage and loss of life—but did relatively little to weaken the British air defenses, other military assets, and military-industrial facilities that were crucial to the defense of the home isles. And British pluck did not give out. After ten days of intensive fighting involving hundreds of daily sorties by each side in the fight, Hitler concluded that the numbers were not working in his favor, and postponed Sea Lion (effectively canceling it, as it turned out).

In the final phase of the Battle of Britain, stretching through fall and even into winter, German aircraft sustained the attack—but now primarily at nighttime, to avoid British fighter aircraft. However, German aircraft had a hard time locating their targets at night, despite guidance from their own radar beacons mounted on land in nearby continental Europe. What had become known in Britain as "the Blitz" therefore gradually petered out. Although it continued at some level through the ensuing winter, the outcome was no longer in doubt.

In the Battle of Britain, about 43,000 British civilians ultimately lost their lives. But Britain was not brought to its knees from the air, and the British Isles were not made vulnerable to invasion, thanks to its pilots and their teammates on the ground. German aircraft losses totaled nearly 2,000, British losses a bit over 1,500. Net trendlines were even more important. Notably, Britain was adding pilots and planes as the months went by, whereas Germany was losing them; for example, available British pilots increased by 40 percent or so from July into early November, whereas German totals dropped almost 25 percent.[109] Thus was inspired Churchill's famous line that never had so many owed so much to so few.[110] In fact they were not so few. Yes, the pilots were. But the system of observing, supporting, maintaining, repairing infrastructure, and otherwise carrying out all the functions of the air force involved almost half a million people.[111]

It would be a mistake, however, to view this period as exclusively one of air combat. Another Churchill quote, not made public at the time: "the only thing that really frightened me during the war was the U-boat peril." Britain depended on supplies sent from America, and Africa, to sustain the war effort; the lend-lease program to the Soviet Union required sea lanes as well; ultimately, sending American troops and equipment to Britain in preparation for D-Day and the invasion of Germany would, too. But for a considerable part of the war, safe access to the Atlantic shipping lanes was in serious doubt.

Once France fell, German submarines were no longer easily bottled up in the North Sea, where their limited range (and the mining of the English Channel) made it hard for them to threaten Atlantic shipping. Using France's Atlantic ports, however, they dramatically increased the loss rates for Allied shipping—roughly double what it had been in 1939, and roughly triple the rate at which allied shipping was being replaced by new construction. They benefited as well from "wolfpack" tactics, with U-boats acting in teams that could monitor a wide swath of ocean, and then be cued by shore-based radio to intercept Allied shipping. This meant that several subs would be in position to sink transport ships in any given convoy once it had been detected.

German leaders themselves apparently had doubts about just how effective the submarine campaign could prove strategically.[112] But these early phases of the Battle of the Atlantic worked quite badly against the Allies.[113] There were big boosts of U-boat effectiveness. The first was in the second half of 1940, after the fall of France. The second was in 1942, once the United States was in the war. At this point, Germany no longer felt any reservations whatsoever about attacking American ships wherever they might be (though it had previously targeted shipping in what the United States called its Neutrality Zone in the western Atlantic where the United States reserved the right to attack submarines on the prowl).[114] Yet in early 1942, America had not yet figured out or prioritized the convoy escort concept, even in and near home waters (largely due to the preference of chief of naval operations Admiral King to prioritize the Pacific theater despite official grand strategy that stated the opposite).[115] Changing the momentum of the Battle of the Atlantic would be essential if the Allies were to keep Britain and the Soviet Union provisioned and to get U.S. forces across the ocean in preparation for an eventual direct assault on Germany.

The Fateful Year of 1941

Germany and Japan were each in a strong position as 1940 ended. To be sure, Germany had not brought England to its knees despite several months of concerted attempts. And Japan was suffering from economic shortages as a result of the tightening western blockade, in opposition to its actions in China in particular. Something would need to be done to alleviate the problem. But in military terms, the two Axis powers had achieved enormous gains, and Italy was starting to pick up gains for its part as well.

Then, in 1941, arguably the two biggest mistakes in the history of twentieth century warfare were committed, one by Berlin and one by Tokyo. On June 22, Germany attacked the Soviet Union, completely betraying its erstwhile ally in a move that even one of the century's great cynics, Joseph Stalin, could not believe possible. And on December 7, Japan attacked

Pearl Harbor—with other near-simultaneous attacks on the Philippines, Guam, Wake Island, Hong Kong, Malaya, and Midway Atoll as well.

Things would go well for the attackers for a time—for a few weeks in the case of Germany, once it invaded the Soviet Union, and perhaps for a few months for Japan. Yet the tides would turn. Defeat for Berlin and Tokyo was not yet inevitable, in either case, but became increasingly likely with time. With these attacks, Germany and Japan collectively ensured that the two countries collectively accounting for almost half of all world manufacturing output would be their enemies (46 percent of the global total in 1938, according to estimates by Yale historian Paul Kennedy). Adding in the British Empire as well, the world's three largest GDPs would now be aligned against them in battle—indeed, in increasingly existential struggle.[116]

In the spring of 1941, Mussolini sought to emulate Hitler and grab up nearby territory. Already controlling Libya and Ethiopia, he turned his attention to Greece, seeking grandeur and some degree of historical redress for unhappy outcomes in wars of yesteryear. But Mussolini was largely unsuccessful, as his poorly prepared military was not up to the task of defeating Greek forces. Hitler then faced a dilemma. He sensed potential vulnerability on his southern flank. In psychological and political terms, moreover, any setback for fascist nations would redound negatively to the geopolitical tectonic shift he was seeking to lead. In military terms, Greece might cozy up more closely to Britain—conceivably providing bases for longer-range airpower that could threaten German interests in Romanian oil, Yugoslav minerals, and other mainstays of the German economy and war machine. So Hitler decided to settle matters in Greece himself—and, as discussed more below, to rescue Italy's armies when they faced possible defeat by Britain in North Africa at the same time. When Serbian nationalists undertook a coup against their own collaborationist Yugoslav government in late March, Hitler decided to seize Yugoslavia as well. The showdown of German combat forces against Yugoslavia's large but obsolescent, dispersed, and badly led forces produced an even more lopsided result than had the invasion of Poland a year and a half before. Germany attacked Greece at the same time, meeting somewhat more resistance but quickly emerging victorious there as well.[117] With a somewhat costly and imperfect airborne assault on the island of Crete in May, taking it from British-led forces there, Germany completed the spring campaign to the southeast.

As historian and strategist (and one-time Nazi sympathizer) J. F. C. Fuller wrote of this string of victories:[118]

With the occupation of Crete, Hitler had to his credit a series of conquests which no general in history had gathered in so brief a space of time. He had conquered Poland in 27 days, Denmark in one, Norway in 23, Holland in five, Belgium in 18, France in 39, Yugoslavia in 12, Greece in 21, and Crete in 11.

On June 22, 1941, Germany attacked the Soviet Union across a wide front in a blow that caused shock and even paralysis in the Kremlin. It is not clear that the Balkans campaign really delayed this operation much; soggy terrain may have been just as important a reason.[119] Three million German troops and more than half a million soldiers from countries allied with Germany attacked in three directions—toward the Baltics, toward eastern Poland and the road to Moscow, and toward Ukraine. They faced some 2.5 million Soviet soldiers, out of a military almost twice that total size, with 10,000 tanks and 8,000 aircraft (providing roughly a 3:1 quantitative edge over Germany, which wielded some 3,000 tanks in the operation).[120]

The basic operational concept for the German attack was relatively simple—blitzkrieg-style rapid maneuver and encirclement of various elements of the Soviet front-line forces, profiting from the ability to operate off-road in the warm and dry Russian summer. Once panzer and mechanized divisions had cut them off, German infantry could follow to carry out the destruction in detail of isolated Soviet divisions. But as in the campaign in France, infantry and engineers, supported by artillery and airpower, often created the initial breakthroughs against prepared defenses.[121]

In the early hours and days, when Soviet forces were unprepared and Stalin was incredulous about Germany's betrayal, the results were devastating. Enormous numbers of Soviet planes were destroyed and hundreds of thousands of Soviet troops were killed or taken prisoner. By mid-July, Hitler was so encouraged that he instructed the German military industry to focus on building the ships and aircraft needed to strike at Britain and its supply lines, believing the armor and shorter-range planes needed to defeat the Soviets were already well on the way to completing the job without further need of assistance. He expected victory in the course of August.[122] He was not alone in his assessment; as a young Condoleezza Rice wrote back in the 1980s, "In the early days, Soviet forces fought so poorly that Western intelligence estimated the fall of Moscow in four weeks."[123] Hitler's heinous plans to dismember and destroy Russia, occupy its territory all the way to the Ural Mountains, and kill off part of its population while leaving much of the rest to starve seemed well on the way to successful completion as well.[124] And even if things began to slow down a bit later in the summer, they still were going Germany's way. The battle of Kiev, fought from roughly August 25 to September 26, was also a huge German success. By the end of the summer, in addition to those killed or wounded, Soviet forces had had a staggering 1.5 million soldiers taken prisoner by the Germans.[125]

But in displaying frequent indecision, then trying to have it all—Leningrad and the Baltics, Kiev and Ukraine and the farmlands, the Caucasus and their oil fields, Minsk and finally Moscow, with the planned coup de grace against the Soviet government—Hitler and his generals overextended their forces. Then they ran out of time, as well as good weather. Stalin finally found a few good surviving generals, starting with Marshall G. K. Zhukov, who organized major defensive preparations around Leningrad and Moscow. Despite terrible hardship, the civilian populations in those cities contributed to the building of trenches, and surviving Soviet soldiers were mustered to stand strong. Better dressed and equipped than the German units that were increasingly far from their homes and supply bases, and that were slowed first by rain then by frostbite, Soviet forces held. The German offensives of October and November did not quite have the time, supplies, or strength they needed—or, again, the winter coats (and boots, and gloves, and warm tents, and places to store and repair equipment like tanks where skin did not freeze to metal, or engine oil and hydraulic fluid coagulate, or water in batteries freeze, and rubber piping inside vehicles crack . . . the list goes on). Eventually, the Soviets were able not only to hold, but even to counterattack around Moscow.[126]

By the end of the year, German casualties were in the range of 1 million killed and wounded. Soviet losses were much higher—including those taken prisoner, as well as killed and wounded, they may have approached a staggering 3 million.[127] But by forestalling a complete collapse in 1941, the Soviets were able to enlist the vastness of their resources—geographic depth, manpower, industry, plus the help provided by allies through lend-lease. It was not a good idea to pick a fight with the Russian bear unless you could finish the kill in timely fashion. And Hitler failed by that standard.

Hitler's huge gamble to attack the Soviet Union with an expectation of victory within months almost worked. That is, Germany almost reached the capital before winter. (On the flip side, while Hitler has often been criticized in military terms for dividing his forces into three main lines of effort inside the Soviet Union instead of just one, it is not clear that the successful seizure of any single region or city, even Moscow, would have guaranteed Soviet capitulation.) The outcome of World War II was not inevitable, and it certainly was far from inevitable at this juncture. However, the fact that the Soviet Union survived 1941 can now be seen as the beginning of the end for Hitler.[128]

On the other side of the world, Japan was about to conduct one of the most tactically brilliant yet perhaps most strategically foolish acts of the twentieth century in attacking the United States of America on December 7, 1941.

The Pacific war was already well underway by this point. Indeed, it might be dated to 1937, when Japanese hypernationalists took advantage of a minor incident at the Marco Polo Bridge near Beijing to invade northern and coastal China (not content to dominate Manchuria north of the Great Wall, where they had already ruled for half a dozen years). Extremely brutal and bloody battles, including massive slaughter of Chinese civilians by Japanese forces, ensued that calendar year and into 1938 in Shanghai and Nanking.[129]

Through the late 1930s, America sought to minimize its involvement in the Far East but felt strong sympathies for China and growing anger at Japan.[130] As Japan's aggressiveness intensified, so did western sanctions, leading fatefully to the Dutch-British-American ban on oil and iron ore exports to Japan in July 1941 after Japan seized Indochina.[131] These sanctions threatened Japan's basic functioning as a modern industrial economy. Rather than rethink its aggressiveness or reverse any of its conquests, Tokyo chose a huge cosmic roll of the dice.

Electing to attack Pearl Harbor, along with numerous other American territories and key regions in the western Pacific and Southeast Asia, Japan's leaders gambled that they could knock America out of the Pacific long enough to then consolidate a hold on key island chains throughout the broader region. By the time America could build back its navy (so went the logic), Japan would have constructed a virtually impregnable system of fortifications that would make it very hard for the United States to retaliate. Seeing as much, Washington would view tactical defeat, and subsequent restraint, as the better part of valor, and concede the broader region to Japan. Whether the United States and its allies then lifted sanctions or not, Japan would have oil and other crucial inputs for its economy in the Greater Co-prosperity Sphere it envisioned regionally. It would also retain control over enough land to expand its population beyond the Japanese islands to parts of China in the years and decades to come in its own more muted but still brutal and cynical form of *lebensraum*.[132] Some

Japanese leaders preferred a more cautious strategy that would not include attacking Pearl Harbor, believing that an attack on American territory made any compromise outcome to the war impractical. But Admiral Iso-ruku Yamamoto, commander of the Japanese navy, and his more aggressive compatriots carried the day.[133]

This grand strategic vision was backed up by impressive new military capabilities. Japan had made great strides in developing aircraft carriers and aircraft in the interwar period. Fortunately, the United States had as well. Unlike the situation in Britain, the U.S. Navy had not been suppressed in its pursuits of such capability by an independent U.S. Air Force (which did not yet exist). The leadership of key individuals like Admiral William Moffett led to the trial, error, and development of technologies like cata-pults and arrester systems, further improvements to the technologies, con-struction of significant numbers of carriers and planes prior to 1941—and in the end, perhaps a military revolution.[134] But Japan would have the first say as that revolution unfolded.

Germany was not informed of the planned attack by its Axis partner (carried out by the Tojo government within two months of coming to power). Ironically, due to decoding of Japanese communications by the "Magic" program and its decrypting devices, the United States knew more. It had deduced that something big was coming—even if cognitive disso-nance (or a "lack of imagination," to use the phrase coined by the 9/11 Commission half a century later) prevented it from believing the attack could be against U.S. soil. Hitler had not necessarily advised this attack. But he believed it offered advantages for dividing America's attentions be-tween Atlantic and Pacific theaters, and for allowing unrestricted Ger-man antisubmarine warfare against allied convoys in the Atlantic.[135]

Having tightened his security pledges to Japan and Italy under the Three-Power Pact of September 1940, Hitler believed that if Japan became involved in a war against the United States, Germany was honor-bound to join in. His emotional side reinforced such thinking, because by now he had developed considerable contempt for the United States and its pres-ident. (Interestingly, Japan never felt an obligation to attack the Soviet Union just because the latter was at war with Germany.)[136]

In addition to its breakthroughs in carrier operations, Japan had fig-ured out other aspects of a long-range naval ambush operation. Recon-naissance systems of the day were still centered on medium-range aircraft using visual sensors. That meant that fleets in open-ocean waters, far from land, and hidden within cloud formations, could go undetected indefinitely—especially if they stayed out of major shipping lanes. Japan had mastered the art, in fact, of having armadas hide themselves within storm systems that conveniently moved eastward across the Pacific at a pace the fleet could match. It had also worked hard on refueling operations at sea.

With such methods and tactics, Admiral Yamamoto could send a radio-silent task force including six aircraft carriers halfway across the Pacific undetected. (Japan had ten carriers in all, the most modern weighing about 30,000 tons or almost one-third that of a modern U.S. carrier, with a range of 11,000 miles and top speed of nearly 40 miles per hour). The armada possessed 360 planes, including the famed "Zero" fighters as well as the "Val" and "Kate" bombers.[137]

Yamamoto's mass of ships approached Hawaii via a northward route starting near the Kurile Islands in northern Japan. It approached within just a couple hundred miles of Hawaii without arousing suspicion. Japanese planes were detected by shore-based radar on Hawaii the morning of December 7. But they were misidentified as B-17 bombers due to arrive that same day from the mainland United States and thus ignored. America had enough advantages in cryptology, with the so-called Magic program, and other forms of intelligence, to suspect that something was up, but expected attacks in Asia, not Hawaii. The whole system of bases on Oahu was left unprepared, it being a Sunday morning when shore leave and late wake-up times were the norm. Japanese submarines contributed as well. Japanese ordnance included innovative types of torpedoes designed to operate in shallow water, as well as new munitions designed to penetrate strong armor.[138]

The only solace is that it could have been so much worse. None of America's three Pacific carriers were in port in Oahu that day (two were normally based at Pearl Harbor; worldwide, the United States had seven at the time).[139] Of eight battleships in the harbor, only two, the *Arizona* and *Oklahoma,* were permanently destroyed in the attack. To be sure, the overall damage was very considerable. Eighteen ships were damaged to some degree; some 350 American aircraft were either seriously damaged or destroyed; more than 2,400 Americans were killed. But shore-based infrastructure was largely unscathed, most big ships and all submarines survived, the Atlantic Fleet was unaffected, and, of course, America's formidable industry on the mainland was untouched as well.[140]

Yamamoto himself could not have been completely pleased. He was always wary that an awakened America—a country he knew well from earlier stints of study in the United States—would by years two and three of any war become a formidable adversary.[141] At least he, and the Japanese war machine writ large, had also successfully attacked other targets throughout the theater—catching General Douglas MacArthur napping in the Philippines, where a large fraction of America's 150 aircraft were destroyed on the runway the day after the Pearl Harbor attacks (to be precise, 10 hours later, local time), taking Guam and Wake Island and Hong Kong, and sinking two British warships, *Prince of Wales* and *Repulse,* with long-range land-based aircraft off the coast of Singapore.

As outraged as President Roosevelt, like most Americans, was because of Pearl Harbor, that attack and ensuing events simplified his leadership task. Roosevelt and Secretary of State Cordell Hull (America's longest-serving secretary of state in history, from March 1933 through November 1944), had prior to the attack a growing conviction that war against both Japan and Germany was inevitable; as William Shirer wrote, "The bombing at Pearl Harbor had taken them off one hook and certain information in their possession led them to believe that the headstrong Nazi dictator would take them off a second hook." That Hitler did with a vicious tirade against Roosevelt, and America, delivered to the Reichstag on December 11 in a speech during which he made the fateful decision to declare war on the United States. As Shirer continued, in writing about Hitler, "He had a growing hatred for America and Americans and, what was worse for him in the long run, a growing tendency to disastrously underestimate the potential strength of the United States."[142] So had Japanese leaders. That same December day, Germany, Italy, and Japan signed an additional agreement not to seek separate peace deals with the United States or Britain. Shirer added this observation: "Adolf Hitler, who a bare six months before had faced only a beleaguered Britain in a war which seemed to him as good as won, now, by deliberate choice, had arrayed against him the three greatest industrial powers in the world in a struggle in which military might depended largely, in the long run, on economic strength."[143]

By December in the European theater, combat was slowing down. Battle lines were largely stationery by late 1941. The weather, known metaphorically as "General January and General February," helped besieged Soviet forces fend off the invading Germans.

But as 1941 turned into early 1942 in the Pacific, the situation remained extremely fluid. Japanese forces, showing toughness and inventiveness, moved well even through deep jungle, seizing the Malay Peninsula and Singapore in January and February. One of the most spectacular defeats in British history, it involved the taking of more than 100,000 prisoners of war from British, Indian, Malayan, and Australian ranks. The Brits had been treating the Southeast Asia theater as an "economy of force" effort. They were badly punished for that approach in late 1941 and early 1942.[144] The Dutch were even less inherently capable of holding onto their possessions in the Dutch East Indies—modern-day Indonesia—and by March the Japanese were successful in seizing the key islands of that archipelago as well. In what became known as the Bataan death march of early 1942, the American forces that had been garrisoned on the Philippines were isolated, outmaneuvered, and effectively starved into capitulation by a modest-sized but highly effective Japanese invading force.

Japanese conquests reached their limits in attacks on Ceylon (Sri Lanka) and Australia, neither of which Japan could seriously threaten. But on the whole the entire western Pacific region into Southeast Asia had become a Japanese protectorate by March and April 1942.[145]

One last theater requires discussion in any review of the year 1941. It was the year when the "Desert Fox," German General Erwin Rommel, appeared on the scene to command German and Axis forces in North Africa. Italian forces had enjoyed some initial successes in the region before British troops gained the upper hand against them. For Britain, this broader theater was the area where it still had colonial possessions it sought to retain, in Egypt and Iraq and Somalia, and where it valued communications links through the Suez Canal to India. Defining itself still largely in terms of global empire, Britain sometimes conflated what would be important for defeating Hitler with what was important for its own pride and imperial dominion. For France, whether the Vichy collaborationist government or the Free French forces of Charles de Gaulle, this was the heartland of much of French colonial dominance, including Morocco, Algeria, and Tunisia—and of course, it was a region that touched France's southern coast directly. For the United States, not yet in the war and not yet in this theater (that would have to await late 1942), the region would become the possible springboard for a southern assault into Europe to defeat Hitler—though Washington tended to care less about this option than did London, or Moscow. For Italy, this region was an arena of colonial ambition, especially in Libya and Ethiopia. For Germany, the absolute stakes were less. But it took interest when Italy got itself into trouble, as Hitler cared about perception and momentum.

After some early successes in 1940, trouble is exactly what Italy managed to create for itself and its main ally. In November, British aircraft struck three Italian battleships in port at Taranto, one of them damaged beyond repair. Britain then reinforced its land power in the broader region, making it possible to overwhelm Italy's positions in the Horn of Africa, and then North Africa.[146] In early 1941, British and free French forces also reversed a coup in Iraq and pushed Vichy French forces out of the Levant.[147]

The arrival of German forces, as well as Rommel, in February 1941 swung the momentum in North Africa in a pro-Axis direction. In late 1941, things shifted again, however, with a successful counterattack led by British commander General Claude Auchinleck, who pushed Rommel westward out of Tobruk and much of Cyrenaica (eastern Libya). There would be back-and-forth swings again in North Africa in 1942 and into 1943, as discussed further below.[148]

These back-and-forth dynamics were not entirely surprising. The major parties to the war viewed North Africa as important but not central or decisive, so they did not fully commit themselves to the effort as a rule. In addition, the terrain allowed for rapid movements and thus rapid shifts in battlefield momentum. The various armies tried to jump from port to port for resupply. They tried to cut off and entrap enemy forces using minefields, feints, and ambushes as their main tactics. It would not be until 1942, when the United States together with Britain chose to make North Africa a major priority, that fundamental factors of national capacity and power would start to tilt the dynamics of combat in the north Africa theater more consistently and decisively in a single direction.

It is worth pausing for a moment to reflect on how the world must have looked to Americans on December 8, 1941, and the days to follow. Until this moment, many in the United States had still been hoping to somehow avoid direct participation in the war. When FDR asked Congress, in the summer of 1941 to extend the twelve-month draft that had been enacted into law in 1940, it passed the House of Representatives by just a single vote.[149] After Pearl Harbor, war against Japan, and soon Germany too, was an inevitability. Americans were angry. They were also afraid. There was even a certain worry that the United States mainland itself might be vulnerable. To be sure, long-range aircraft, nuclear-tipped missiles, and invading armies were either things of the future or geographic impossibilities. Yet attacks by submarine—or perhaps even by carrier task forces that somehow evaded detection and brought along enough supplies to traverse the entire Pacific—could not be categorically ruled out. As a result, the country was jumpy, particularly along the heavily populated coasts, with specific possible targets of Japanese attack such as California's aviation industry of particular concern. Troops were deployed to key infrastructural and industrial sites; ammunition stockpiles were carefully assessed as the possibility of Japanese raids against mainland sites was contemplated; false reports of close approaches by Japanese fleets were issued by U.S. military commands before being recognized as incorrect.[150] People were anxious.

As 1941 turned into 1942, Churchill visited Roosevelt in Washington. They were to take part in what became known as the Arcadia Conference. But during the private visit before the conference, FDR inadvertently surprised Churchill in the bath, and saw the prime minister completely naked. Not to worry, the latter told Roosevelt, because there was nothing he would hide from the American president. At a more substantive and strategic level, it was at Arcadia that the "Germany first" idea was reaffirmed. It had been proposed a year before, in the U.S.-British "ABC" Conference in Washington in early 1941, but even after Pearl Harbor, the United States was still supportive of the idea. Germany's threat to Europe was recognized to be more acute and strategically significant than Japan's threat to any major allied power, hence the logic.

In addition, at Arcadia the Combined Chiefs of Staff system was created. It set up the basis for strong British-American collaboration in the years to come. It also created the venue for many vigorous debates over strategy, including about how soon and where to invade continental Europe. The Americans favored what was then called Operation Bolero—preparation of a major staging base in Britain—followed by Roundup in 1943, when U.S. and British forces would come ashore in northern Europe.[151] That thinking would eventually lead to Operation Overlord in 1944. But in the early years, the British favored focusing on the Mediterranean and perhaps the Balkans as well, and carried the day in the argument. Thus, Operation Torch was undertaken in North Africa in late 1942.[152]

The Great Turning Point of 1942 and Early 1943

By the time 1942 was over, World War II still had two and a half years to go. It was of course far from over. However, by the end of the year, reinforced by further developments in the Soviet Union in the very early weeks of 1943, its overall momentum had clearly shifted. The outcome may not yet have been truly determined, but Germany's ability to achieve a dominant and definitive victory against the Soviet Union had probably been lost for good, especially after battles around Stalingrad and the Caucasus. Japan's streak of victories had clearly ended at Midway, in the Battle of the Coral Sea, and in subsequent fights in and around Guadalcanal and the Solomon Islands. In the Middle East and Mediterranean/North African regions, the Desert Fox's big victories had been followed by big defeats, and by the end of 1942 American and British forces were ashore in substantial numbers. While there was much still to happen in that theater, any possibility of the Axis powers establishing a continuous zone of control from North Africa through the Middle East into the Caucasus had been lost.

The Allied powers, having previously settled on a policy of demanding postwar German disarmament, with the issuance of the Atlantic Charter in August of 1941 before the United States had entered the war, went further and in Casablanca, Morocco, in January 1943 would issue their demand for unconditional surrender.[153] That raised the stakes in the battle. But the alignment of the three big war machines, in terms of industrial power, manpower, and geographic expanse—the Soviet Union, the United Kingdom (and British empire), and the United States—created a juggernaut that Germany and Japan would have been hard-pressed to challenge under any plausible circumstances. And the silver bullet in the mix—the atomic bomb—was being developed most quickly by the United States.

Yet there would be a lot of back-and-forth in 1942 before this overall picture of a clear sense of strategic momentum would develop. For much of the year, the war plans of Germany and Japan still showed considerable promise.

The eastern European and Soviet theater was still far and away the main arena of intensive combat worldwide. A long north-south front extended from the Baltics to the Black Sea, and it was generally holding. The great Soviet industrial war machine, largely relocated east of the Urals by this point, was pumping out huge quantities of combat equipment and the great mass of Russian youth was being mobilized to fit out as many as 400 combat divisions. For its part, Germany remained some 600,000 soldiers short of what its (more modest) order of battle required in the early spring of 1942.[154] Its ambitions to defeat the Soviet Union comprehensively, as attempted the year before, would have to be scaled back.

Still, the Germans had huge advantages. They started with the fact that based on their 1941 attacks they controlled much of western Soviet territory—corresponding to land where almost half the country's population lived and almost half its food was produced, and where 50 to 65 percent of its coal and metals were extracted as well. Hitler's goal for

1942 was to use these existing positions as a springboard for conquest of the main Soviet oil fields between the Black Sea and the Caspian Sea. His most ambitious dreams were to have the armies that took those territories then meet up with Rommel and others moving eastward through Egypt, the Levant, Turkey, and Iran in a great circular movement that would place much of the world's oil under German control. He also sought, by taking or at least approaching Stalingrad, to sever transport routes connecting the region and its oil fields to central and eastern Russia, and the war industry, in the hope of hamstringing the latter severely while ensuring German access to hydrocarbons.[155]

By the summer of 1942, Germany had achieved some limited successes. Its forces reached many oil fields, approaching Grozny as well as the Caspian Sea. They also reached the Stalingrad region. Perhaps some Nazi aims for the year would in fact be achieved.

The Battle of the Atlantic was also going Hitler's way. U-boats were sinking 700,000 tons of Allied ships a month, an enormous rate. Rommel had also made huge gains in North Africa, reversing his losses of the previous fall in May and June 1942 and pushing British forces eastward, all the way to El Alamein in Egypt—only 65 miles from Alexandria and the Nile River. Rommel benefited from easier and more dependable resupply across the Mediterranean, after successful German air campaigns against Malta and the British Mediterranean fleet.[156]

However, these very successes brought their own problems. German supply lines were by now long and exposed, especially in the Soviet Union. A modest-sized western European country was sustaining huge combat operations more than 1,000 miles to its east, in a region where its main adversary had enormous advantages of size and territory. The Soviets had successfully relocated military industry, and were pumping out T-34 tanks as well as improved combat aircraft from eastern regions of the country, with all of that backed up by lend-lease supplies from the United States.[157] (The United States would send allies 37,000 tanks, 800,000 trucks, 43,000 planes, and almost 2 million rifles in the course of the war, and by 1942 American weapons had begun to flow directly to the Soviet Union.[158]) To compensate for the country's limited resources and logistical overextension, German military planners had fatefully built dependencies on unevenly armed Romanian, Hungarian, and Italian forces who were charged with protecting supply lines and long, extended German flanks. Hitler was also increasingly divorced from reality, overconfident, and greedy, believing he could take Stalingrad to the east as well as the overall Caucasus region to the south at the same time. His top generals opposed him but could not change his mind. The result left German flanks even more thinly guarded.

As the year unfolded, Soviet forces launched a successful pincer movement against the flanks of the German positions, encircling the Sixth Army. But Hitler dug in, insisting that positions near Stalingrad be held into the winter of 1942–1943 even after prolonged periods of intense urban fighting produced inconclusive results. All this led to the death or surrender of at least 200,000 German units in that theater by the early weeks of 1943.

Meanwhile, the tide began to turn in Africa as well. The arrival in Egypt of General Bernard Law Montgomery and General Harold Alexander in August, along with reinforcements and more materiel, allowed British forces to reverse the momentum of battle by October and November. Again, Hitler's stubbornness and unwillingness to face unpleasant reality led him to demand that German forces try their best to stand their ground and fight even when the odds had turned badly against them—leading to major unnecessary losses there as well.[159]

Then, American forces sailed eastward in substantial numbers for the first time in the war. The United States and its allies surprised Germany and Italy with Operation Torch. The joint landings of more than 100,000 troops, with total strength ultimately exceeding twenty divisions, occurred in Morocco and Algeria in November. Morocco was chosen as one of the destinations just in case Germany could make trouble for the invaders in the Mediterranean. The Allies met initial resistance from Vichy French forces there but still managed to get ashore.

In February 1943, the Allies had a showdown with German-Italian forces in and around Tunisia and its Atlas Mountains. At the famous Kasserine Pass, German forces gained the upper hand—but were ultimately unable to exploit their successes with follow-on attacks, largely due to the effective use of American artillery as the battle unfolded.[160]

This theater had by now become a significant area of effort for both sides. That partially mollified Stalin, who would have preferred a second front in Europe, but would take what he could get so that Soviet forces would no longer be the only allied armies directing fighting the Wehrmacht. The battles provided experience for green American and British soldiers, as well as a filtering mechanism for testing top leadership. They also created a sort of political pressure valve for Roosevelt, who increasingly sensed that Americans were restless with the delay at getting their own troops into the European fight.

Hitler's insistence on victory and his inability to relegate some theaters to secondary importance, or to conduct strategic withdrawals where necessary, led him to double down when arguably he did not have the resources to do so. (Most notable was the battle for Stalingrad, where German forces ultimately were surrounded.) Germany was able to reinforce its positions in Africa and supply its forces reasonably well across the Mediterranean, at least early in the campaign. But ultimately, the preponderance of Allied force was too much, as was the Allies' ability to constrain the Axis logistics pipeline running from Europe to Tunisia. Killed and wounded from late 1942 through mid-1943 were perhaps 50,000 to 75,000 on each side in North Africa—but crucially, perhaps a quarter million Axis prisoners were taken.[161]

That North Africa victory also set up the conditions for the Allies to move to Sicily and then on to mainland Italy in 1943. The Axis powers no longer had enough strength near or on the Mediterranean or on Sicily to prevent such incursions.[162] The African campaign also contributed to the development and emergence of General Dwight D. Eisenhower, who began Operation Torch largely untested, but struggled through some questionable decisions to become a much more seasoned and confident commander by the operation's end.[163]

Summing up the North Africa fight, Rick Atkinson wrote these incisive words:[164]

> If TORCH provided one benefit above others, it was to save Washington and London from a disastrously premature landing in northern Europe. Given the dozens of Wehrmacht divisions waiting behind the Atlantic Wall, France would have been a poor place to be lousy in. TORCH had been a great risk—"the purest gamble America and Britain undertook during the war," the official U.S. Army Air Forces history concluded—but it deferred the even greater gamble of a cross-Channel invasion until the odds improved.

In the Pacific, 1942 also witnessed a gradual change in momentum. Symbolically, the first big event was the Doolittle Raid in April, when sixteen B-25 aircraft secretly flew off an aircraft carrier a few hundred miles east of Japan and bombed Tokyo. FDR playfully told the press that their flights had originated in "Shangri-La," a fictional location in China in a popular novel of the day. Most of the pilots then bailed out over China, since they had had to launch from a greater distance than intended when a

Japanese picket ship saw the aircraft carrier's approach. Nine of those pilots and crew lost their lives in the effort (three being executed by the Japanese, and several more dying later in Japanese prisoner-of-war camps).[165]

At the Battle of the Coral Sea in May, near Australia and New Guinea, two fleets that never came within sight of each other fought using their respective carrier-borne aircraft. The fight began as Japan sought to strengthen its position in the region, including an aspiration to take Port Moresby on the southeastern tip of the large island of New Guinea from Australian control, perhaps as a prelude to someday attacking Australia or at least the sea lanes connecting it to America. Each side lost one aircraft carrier in what amounted to a draw. Arguably the Japanese got slightly the better of it, in terms of inflicting damage on the enemy's ships, but their southward ambitions toward Australia were stymied. Moreover, any outcome resembling a draw would not work to the advantage of the much smaller Japanese nation and war machine as time went on.[166]

The next big event in 1942 in the Pacific would be far away, at Midway Atoll, relatively near Hawaii. That fight was much briefer, though— at and around Midway on June 4 through June 6. Just as in the Coral Sea case, the United States learned a good deal of Japanese intentions through signals interception and codebreaking. Then, doing an inadvertent favor to the Americans, Admiral Yamamoto divided his fleet and approached Midway island with just four aircraft carriers—thinking that would be enough, because he expected to attack Midway with surface and amphibious ships, produce an American reaction, and sit back in ambush with his carriers as the Americans came forth to protect the endangered U.S. territory.

Instead, knowing roughly where Yamamoto was and what he was up to, the Americans found his ships first (though Japanese aircraft did manage to attack Midway Island, the first blow in the overall engagement). That enabled a surprise attack in the other direction, with the U.S.S. *Enterprise*, *Hornet*, and *Yorktown* launching aircraft to ambush the Japanese fleet. Although the initial American torpedo bombers suffered huge losses while doing very little damage, they achieved one desirable outcome: they focused Japanese air defenses on low-altitude threats. Then, when the higher-altitude American dive bombers approached in a second wave of strikes, they were only lightly opposed. As a result, they destroyed three Japanese carriers (the *Akagi*, the *Kaga*, and the *Soryu*); a fourth, the *Hiryu*, would be lost to an additional round of attack. The United States did lose one more carrier of its own in the process, the *Yorktown*, damaged on June 4 and sunk by a Japanese submarine on June 7.[167] But the United States clearly prevailed overall—eliminating 40 percent of the entire Japanese aircraft carrier fleet, and two-thirds of the larger carriers, in one fell swoop. And that was an amount of attrition that Japan, the far smaller industrial power, could not afford to absorb.[168] It was perhaps because of the success at Midway, almost exactly half a year after Pearl Harbor, that Admiral Chester Nimitz, overall commander of the Pacific fleet, began to relax ever so slightly. When asked later on about his scariest moment during the war, he once replied, "The whole first six months."[169]

Back to the South Pacific. Just a few weeks after Pearl Harbor, Japan had bombed and seized British and Australian positions on the islands of New Britain, Tulagi, and ultimately (in May) Guadalcanal. By July, the Japanese were seen to be building an airstrip there. Once completed, it would have given them the potential to exert influence further south and east thereafter—threatening key Allied shipping lanes to Australia much more efficiently and continuously than naval forces themselves could have done.[170]

Those developments then led the United States to mount a major effort to seize back the islands starting in August. In some ways, the resulting battles became a microcosm of the entire subsequent war in the Pacific. They involved amphibious landings, land-based and sea-based airpower, surface combatants, jungle fighting, and contested resupply and reinforcement efforts.[171] Some of the concepts, and modified equipment, developed by the U.S. Marine Corps in the 1920s and 1930s for amphibious assault against an entrenched enemy were put to the real-world test. The various ideas that had been tested included use of smokescreens, daytime as well as nighttime landings, assaults of varying degrees of troop concentration or dispersal, and various degrees of preparatory bombardment.[172]

About 10,000 American forces came ashore unopposed on Guadalcanal and nearby Tulagi on August 7. But though the landings were not contested, their presence was far from welcomed. They faced inland resistance by Japanese forces thereafter in both cases. In the Battle of Savo Island on August 9, moreover, the United States lost several ships to a Japanese attack designed to prevent the United States from building up its initial positions. The well-executed and successful nighttime attack, using torpedoes and gunfire delivered by surface combatants (with no carriers present or participating), destroyed four Allied cruisers (one of them Australian). Chief of naval operations Admiral Ernest King considered this the darkest day of the war. Still, the United States was lucky because the Japanese vessels, anxious to escape the area and possible American aerial retaliation before daybreak, did not press their attack. The U.S. transport and supply ships survived.[173]

The ensuing days, weeks, and months witnessed considerable fighting. Some of it was near-constant. For example, there were frequent aerial raids from Japan's base at Rabaul on New Britain, sometimes spotted by friendly Australian "coastwatcher" observers, Jack Read and Paul Mason, who were ensconced in the interior of the nearby island of Bougainville, aided by friendly indigenous inhabitants, and equipped with radios. Both sides sought to resupply and reinforce their positions on Guadalcanal and elsewhere on an ongoing basis as well.[174]

In short order Navy engineering and construction teams known as "Seabees" completed construction of a crucial airfield on Guadalcanal they called Henderson Field. World War II was becoming a laboratory not only for new combat tactics, but for breakthroughs in logistics, supply, and mobilization as well.[175]

There were many additional attempts by one side or the other to break the stalemate and gain the military upper hand. Japanese forces, misled throughout this period by bad intelligence that significantly underestimated the American strength on the island, attempted an unsuccessful "banzai" charge on the main U.S. position on August 20.[176] The naval Battle of the East Solomons took place a few days later, on August 24, as a Japanese armada with carriers and troop transports sought to approach Guadalcanal. Japan gained the tactical edge for a time, and the U.S.S. *Enterprise* took several serious hits—but the American carrier was saved due to good firefighting techniques, and land-based airpower at Guadalcanal also helped save the day for the American forces. Another charge of Japanese troops emanated from the jungle near Henderson Field (benefiting from reinforcements gradually snuck onto the island at night over the course of the late summer) on September 13–14. It too was unable to push Americans off the island.[177] Yet the United States did lose the aircraft carrier *Wasp* on September 14 to a torpedo attack, after having temporarily lost both the *Enterprise* and *Saratoga* carriers to previous attack by air and by submarine.[178] The latter two ships were later repaired and returned to duty.

In mid-October 1942, the Japanese undertook a massive overnight bombardment of the Marine camp at Henderson Field, hoping to shut down aerial operations long enough to move large numbers of troops to another part of the island in preparation for a big ground attack.[179] But the effort failed, as did subsequent major efforts at resupply. Japanese forces grew in number on Guadalcanal, but could not be adequately supplied—and many soldiers wound up starving.[180]

There were significant additional U.S. losses, including the *Hornet* aircraft carrier, in maritime fights known as the Battle of the Santa Cruz Islands (October 25–26) and the Naval Battle of Guadalcanal (November 13–15).

Japan attempted to reinforce its troop positions on Guadalcanal as best it could, but was inhibited by American land-based and carrier-based air-power in the vicinity. The United States worked hard, with more success over time, to reinforce and supply its marines on Guadalcanal so they would be safe and secure and in position to contribute to a more north-ward movement through the Solomons, and beyond.[181]

By winning a few and losing a few, the United States was starting to establish a dynamic that, with its overwhelmingly stronger resource base, would ultimately serve it well against Japan. Long slogs of indeterminate outcome were not what a much smaller and increasingly overextended Japan could afford to engage in, unless America's will somehow cracked.[182] Moreover, even though ship and aircraft losses were roughly comparable over the six-month Guadalcanal/Solomons fight, the Japanese lost many more people—whether they were starving or banzai-charging Japanese soldiers, or aviators bailing out far from home base.[183] By establishing and holding its own positions, the United States was beginning to realize the vision of the top navy leader, the commander in chief of the U.S. Fleet and chief of naval operations, Admiral King, who wrote that, "the general scheme or concept of operations is not only to protect the lines of com-munications with Australia but, in so doing, to set up 'strong points' from which a step-by-step general advance can be made . . ." in northwestward direction.[184] Under the broader Pacific regional command of Admiral Chester Nimitz, and the theater command of Admiral Bill "Bull" Halsey from October onward, the U.S. strikes against Japanese ships and other assets forced Japan in effect to concede Guadalcanal by the end of November.[185]

By year's end, counting losses at Coral Sea and in the Solomons, Japan had lost a total of six carriers. Things were starting to look much better for the Allies. American carrier losses were not inconsiderable, but they were fewer—the *Lexington, Yorktown, Wasp, and Hornet*.[186] (Bear in mind that later, *Essex*-class carriers were built and given these same four names.) The U.S.S. *Langley*, America's first aircraft carrier, was also lost (and also in 1942, like the others), but by that point it was effectively a transport ship, not an operational carrier.[187] Japan could not afford such exchange ratios. As 1942 ended, Admiral King flatly declared, "We are going to win this war.[188] (By war's end, the United States would deploy 12 large carriers mostly of the *Essex* class, 8 light but still fast additional carriers of the *Independence* class, and 18 slower but still effective escort carriers including many in the *Casablanca* class in the broader Indo-Pacific region. Japan's aggregate total, having reached thirteen of all types in June of 1944, would drop to just one.[189])

When he made that comment, it may have been one of the few times King was quoted while in a positive mood. Like General MacArthur, he was a particularly difficult individual. His own daughter described King as "the most even-tempered man in the world. He is always in a rage." And MacArthur and King, personifying a larger army-navy interservice rivalry in the Pacific, did not get along well at all. That was a problem as resource allocation and command decisions were made during the war. For example, leadership had to decide whether to prioritize Nimitz and the navy (and the approach to Japan via the Mariana Islands) or MacArthur and the army (and the approach via the Philippines). Thankfully, calmer heads in the form of Army Chief George Marshall, Secretary of War Henry Stimson, Secretary of the Navy Frank Knox, and Chairman of the Joint Chiefs William Leahy ensured that the decisionmaking process did not break down—though there were unresolved problems that had major consequences as late as 1944, in the Battle of Leyte Gulf, as discussed more below.[190]

If King had become optimistic by the end of 1942, that was not quite yet true of everyone on the American and Allied side. Even with the tide turned in the Pacific, and in central Europe, the fights were very much on in both places. The arrival of U.S. forces in North Africa, and their ultimate success there in league with British (and limited numbers of Free French) forces did not necessarily prove that they would find their way ashore eventually in Europe. And definitive Soviet victory over German forces was far from assured in what was still the war's most intensive battlefield of central and eastern Europe.

Moreover, the Battle of the Atlantic was not yet won. Indeed, it continued to go badly for the Allies into 1943. If it failed, the sustainability of the Soviet armies, as well as preparations for the Overlord invasion of Europe through France that would ultimately take place in June of 1944, were in serious doubt.

German U-boat production was way up at this point. Each deployed sub tended to survive a full year against the mediocre tactics and limited technologies of the Allies. That may not have been huge consolation to U-boat crews, who still died in large numbers, but at a strategic level it was advantageous to the Germans. Thus, the overall size of the German submarine fleet grew throughout the year. Monthly sinkings of American, British, other Allied and neutral shipping reached into the range of about 600,000 tons per month. The United States underperformed in this period. At first, it resisted sailing transport ships in convoys, as noted before, or devoting enough escorts to convoy protection. It also failed to prioritize production or use of long-range aircraft against submarines. Its searching methods and weaponry against submarines were also poor, due in part to insufficient appreciation of the looming submarine threat by the U.S. Navy during the 1920s and 1930s.[191] As noted, U.S. ship production was increasing, as the War Production Board fully reoriented American industry away from commercial goods and towards military materiel—but new hulls were not yet numerous enough to make up the losses. Even on the cryptology front, things did not go well; Germany changed its Enigma encrypting machines that year in ways that left the Allies' Ultra decoding program in the dark about the locations of wolfpacks.[192]

Yes, 1942 (and the opening weeks of 1943) were the war's turning point. But it was not true in all domains of combat, and it is easier to say now than it was to know it then. A real feeling of allied confidence would have to await the spring and summer of 1943.

The Slow But Steady Path to Victory: 1943–1945

By the time the spring of 1943 had arrived, the main dynamics of the war had been established and most major strategic decisions had been made. Victory for the Allies was becoming very likely—in contrast to earlier years, when victory was *not* inevitable, as Richard Overy and certain other historians persuasively argue.[193] From 1943 onward, the fighting of course remained intense and the battles numerous.[194] But the main shape of the war's trajectory and likely culmination had become increasingly clear. That is especially true if one focuses on one major theater at a time over the whole time period, consistent with this book's focus on campaigning. I take that approach below—examining the 1943–1945 period theater by theater.

Perhaps the first crucial turning point in early 1943 was a major change of fortune in the Battle of the Atlantic. The Allies gained the upper hand

and would never again lose it. Convoys began to enjoy cover and protection from aircraft (operating off small carriers or land bases) like never before. Retired Army General Monty Meigs gives great credit to the scientists and systems analysts who figured out the importance of airpower in antisubmarine operations, rather than to the admirals who were often slow to understand.[195] By this point, the allies also had better radar technologies for detecting and attacking submarines when the threatening U-boats surfaced—as they had to do either to communicate with each other and shore-based headquarters, or to attain their higher cruising speeds (subs of the day were much faster when surfaced than when submerged). The Allies could also understand many of those German communications through signals intercepts and cryptology. As Princeton professor Harold Feiveson wrote, "By the spring of 1943, all these developments were in place—decisive leadership, greater number of escorts, air cover provided by long-range bombers and escort aircraft carriers, Ultra, HF/DF, centimetric radar." Ultra was, as noted, the code-breaking capability that was restored after Germany had for a time managed to outwit Allied cryptologists, HF/DF (high-frequency direction finding) was a radar receiver that allowed the Allies to detect radio emissions from the U-boats themselves; centimetric radar was a form of shorter-wavelength radar that could be more easily deployed on aircraft or ships and that could not be detected by the U-boat prey.[196] At least as important as all these tactical innovations was the sheer increase in shipbuilding rates for the Allies. They were roughly comparable to loss rates in 1942. By 1943, they had doubled, as loss rates roughly halved.[197]

The transformation was phenomenal. Allied shipping losses, which had been 600,000 tons in March 1943, declined to 327,000 tons in April and 264,000 tons in May. By 1944, total losses were only 170,000 tons for the entire year. Meanwhile, U-boats were going to the bottom in increasing droves—from only three a month in 1939 and 1940, to close to five through most of 1941, to about eight in most of 1942—and then to twenty or more a month over the last two and a half years or so of the war—even though Germany pulled back its submarines to closer waters in that final period.[198]

The bottom line is this: Allied and neutral shipping had totaled about 40 million tons gross weight at the start of the war. When things were at their diciest, in late 1942 and early 1943, that figure was down to about 30 million tons. By war's end, it was over 45 million tons.[199]

By the end of the war, of 1,162 U-boats that had been built, 785 had been sunk.[200] By comparison, the Allies lost almost 2,500 merchant ships in the Atlantic with a grand total of nearly 13 million tons weight, and 175 warships in the effort, most British.[201]

The snorkel appeared in 1944 and allowed U-boats to run their diesel engines when submerged, allowing them to move quickly when completely underwater. However, in the course of that year they lost their French ports; the net effect was not to their advantage.[202] Other naval developments were also going the Allies' way. For example, a brilliant special forces attack using miniature submarines deploying out of Britain against the giant German battleship the *Tirpitz* in the northern Norwegian port of Kaafjord rendered permanently unusable that huge menace to the Norwegian Sea (and Allied shipping routes to the Soviet Union).[203]

On the eastern front, as 1943 began, both sides made preparations for possible offensives, marshaling forces with thousands of tanks and million-plus totals of soldiers. Their goals were to attempt to gain ground along an established front line that ran mostly north-south between Kiev and Moscow. It started in the north around Leningrad/St. Petersburg and went down to Rostov at the northeastern tip of the Sea of Azov near Crimea. These goals were for the most part less grandiose than in earlier years. The Soviets, though strengthening, were a long way from being able to march on Berlin. For his part, Hitler hoped to disrupt the gradually growing Soviet military machine more than to deliver a knockout punch— though he probably entertained dreams, should the initial fight go Germany's way, of ultimately pushing eastward and then northward to someday capture Moscow from below.[204]

That was not to be. The Soviets, expecting an attack, also took care to prepare robust defenses in what was termed the "Kursk salient"—a protrusion of Soviet-held territory jutting westward into a region that was otherwise Nazi-held. Hitler dithered indecisively about whether to authorize a major attack against the salient. Finally, on July 5, 1943, he reluctantly launched Operation Citadel. The resulting battle, though fought with the weapons of World War II like Germany's new Panther and Tiger tanks and the Soviet Union's "Joseph Stalin" tank, more closely resembled the great siege battles of World War I in many ways, with brutal and sustained bombardments in a relatively localized geographic space. German forces hoped to cut off and destroy the million-strong Soviet forces within the salient. But with time to prepare fortifications and lay hundreds of thousands of mines, Soviet forces were ready when the attack came.[205] Within a couple weeks, the German effort had failed decisively. Soviet forces were subsequently soon launching their own offensives—against which the Germans had few proper preparations—with considerably more success.[206]

By this point in the war, Germany was no longer strong enough to threaten a credible war-winning drive into the Soviet heartland. But Hitler was too headstrong and offensive-minded to trade space for time, shorten defensive lines, and in general adopt an elastic-defense campaign concept. Instead, he forced his generals—Erich von Manstein, Walter Model, and Gunther von Kluge—and others to do their best to hold all ground they currently possessed while attempting offensives at the same time. The Soviet behemoth consisted of 6.5 million soldiers by July, twice what Germany could deploy to the theater. By the early days of January 1944, Soviet forces had liberated Kiev and vicinity, were starting to reach prewar Poland, and were lifting the siege of Leningrad and making headway around the Crimea as well.[207]

Although German forces sometimes won tactical victories during this period, the outcome of the fight was in less and less doubt as time went on. At the campaign level, Soviet forces were simply bringing too strong and big of a punch across a huge sector. They were building up the logistical capacity to sustain and extend the effort as well. By this point in the war, Soviet production of weaponry, trucks, and munitions, when combined with lend-lease shipments from the United States, was also working strongly in the Allied favor. By 1943, Soviet war production equaled that of Germany; U.S. war production almost tripled that of the Nazis, with substantial proportions devoted to aiding the Soviet effort.[208] Similar ratios were achieved in 1944 (at which point U.S. armaments and ordnance production represented about two-fifths of the world total).[209]

This was to be the story of the remaining year-plus of battle in the east, as German forces were pushed back further and further toward their own homeland. The main Soviet thrust was in the center, through Poland, but attacks were also launched along the Baltic–East Prussia region as well as through Romania. At this point in the war the Soviet air force enjoyed about a six-to-one numerical advantage over the Luftwaffe in the theater.[210] With the success of Soviet attacks, Germany lost access to the oil fields at Ploesti, Romania, the only major source of natural oil that it had previously enjoyed. Balkan nations were liberated or persuaded to change sides in the fight as a result of the steady Russian forward progress combined with the absence of any credible narrative as to how it might be stymied.[211]

After a pause in the autumn of 1944 to consolidate positions, resupply forces, and wait for the firmer ground of the winter season, Soviet forces resumed their march in early 1945. Germany made a strong stand in places, slowing the Soviet progress, but could not forestall the inevitable for long. The fact that fuel shortages often left many of its aircraft grounded did not help matters.[212] By mid-April, Soviet forces had crossed the Oder River. Atrocities against German citizens were legion—perhaps 2 million women were raped, and many killed.[213] Around April 21, Soviet forces reached Berlin, with some 3 million Soviet troops close to the fight, and a half million ultimately taking part in the final phases of the inner-city siege. There was brutal block-to-block combat in Berlin's wide boulevards and small side streets and everything in between. In the end, the Red Army lost over 300,000 soldiers in the fight for Berlin. But it had several million more where those had come from.

On April 30, recognizing the inevitable, Hitler and his longtime lover (and wife of one day), Eva Braun, committed suicide.[214] With FDR having died earlier that month and Mussolini being killed by fellow Italians earlier that same week, three of the main wartime leaders from World War II had all perished within thirty days of each other. (It is interesting to note that, unlike the other leaders, Roosevelt was never in or near the battle physically. His overseas travels during the war took him far, but never to hot combat zones—he went to Casablanca in January 1943, to Quebec in August 1943 and September 1944, to Cairo and Teheran at the end of 1944, and to Yalta in Crimea in February 1945.[215])

Some German resistance would continue for a few days in parts of Germany, but formal surrender followed within a week. Victory in Europe Day (V-E Day) became May 8 or 9, depending on whether you were affiliated with American/British/Canadian forces or those of the Soviet Union.[216]

Of course, the war was not won entirely in the east. But certainly until June 1944, the vast preponderance of the ground fighting occurred there. And even after that date, the scale of the struggle in the east surpassed that in western Europe or in the Pacific. The Soviet sacrifices deserve a special respect.

To pick up the narrative in another geographic theater, after prevailing in North Africa, the Allies were positioned to move northward starting in mid-1943. American planners, focused on the destruction of German armies, preferred a concentrated effort as soon as possible in northern Europe. But British reluctance to support such an idea, given London's preference to think more globally than continentally, combined with the

impracticality of launching a northern Europe invasion in 1943, ultimately persuaded Eisenhower, Marshall, and Roosevelt to support the
idea of an invasion first of Sicily and then of Italy proper that year.[217]

Starting on July 9, 1943, and proceeding over the following thirty-eight
days under General George Patton and General Bernard "Monty" Montgomery, a U.S.-British invading force some half-million strong would take
Sicily from Italy and Germany in Operation Husky. The invasion was
somewhat plodding, due to the terrain and fierce German resistance as
well as sometimes tentative Allied leadership. But the outcome was only
delayed as a result. American casualties totaled nearly 10,000; British killed
and wounded somewhat more than 10,000; Axis killed and wounded
approached 30,000, but another 140,000 (mostly Italians) were taken
prisoner.[218]

Given battlefield trends, Mussolini was then deposed, and imprisoned.
He would later be liberated by German forces but would not regain meaningful power (and, as noted, would be captured and killed by Italian partisans in April 1945). However, Germany managed to deploy enough of its
own troops to Italy to make the Allied conquest of Rome and other parts
of the peninsula a slow and painful affair. Despite being outnumbered
roughly 2:1, Germany used terrain and geography well, and turned the
fight into a slog rather than a battle of maneuver, with Rome not falling
until June 4, 1944.[219] American and British mistakes contributed to Germany's relative successes. Invasion efforts occurred in predictable locations, since the Allies wanted to land where they had air cover. As Liddell
Hart wrote, "Henceforth the Allied armies were reduced to pushing their
way up the Italian peninsula like a sticky piston-rod in a stickier cylinder
against increasingly strong compression."[220] Yet the outcome was not seriously jeopardized, even if the full fall of Italy would not be complete until
April of 1945. The overall campaign diverted about 10 percent of Germany's total ground divisions from the fight against the Soviet Union.

The Italy campaign also toughened and seasoned American troops and
commanders.[221] That toughening and seasoning led to a much better performance in a much more important effort—Operation Overlord, the
huge American-British-Canadian invasion of northern Europe through
Normandy, starting on June 6, 1944.

Preparations for Overlord had been ongoing for much of the war.
They had picked up considerable steam in the course of the previous
year, dating back to the formal agreement to conduct such an attack in
May 1943 at the U.S.-U.K. Trident Conference in Washington, DC. The

idea was to use at least 100,000 Allied troops in the equivalent of about eight divisions, backed by massive airpower including some 12,000 planes, to seize five beachheads—code-named Utah, Omaha, Gold, Juno, and Sword, from west to east. The Americans would take the first two; the Canadians had Juno; the Brits, the final two. Allied forces would then seize the ports that could bring more than a million troops ashore for the ultimate invasion of Germany.

A major deception campaign was attempted in the hope of fueling German beliefs that the main invasion effort would take place much further east, where the British Channel was narrowest, near Pas-de-Calais. Ship decoys and fictitious radio commands about the preparations being made by fake Allied combat units were used in the ploy. Unfortunately for the Allies, German aerial reconnaissance was sufficient to reveal the actual preparations. Accordingly, German forces in Normandy were considerably strengthened in the very weeks leading up to D-Day, even if German leadership still hedged its bets about where the main Allied effort would occur.[222]

In the operation, more than 100 warships protected troop ships crossing the English Channel to attack German shore positions. Several thousand ships carried a total of some 150,000 soldiers (accounts differ as to exact numbers). They carried 2,000 tanks and another 12,000 vehicles. Upward of 10,000 aircraft were involved.[223] Airborne troops were used against selective locations as well, and to establish positions where they could protect flanks of the amphibious operation. Two mobile harbors known as "Mulberries" were built and towed across the Channel to ease the reinforcement problem. Special vehicles based on a Sherman tank and known as "Hobart's funnies," as well as other devices, were used to traverse, or fill in, antitank ditches and minefields, and other barriers.[224] And that American dominance of the skies meant that, on June 6, the United States flew nearly 9,000 sorties—to Germany's 250.[225]

Airpower was used to destroy bridges and rail lines and otherwise hinder the movement of German reinforcements from the various possible landing areas to the actual ones.[226] The reduction in capacity was substantial, often 50 percent or more relative to previous levels, and the effects were felt on deployed forces that needed basic provisions, fuel, and ammunition.[227] Tragically, many French citizens died as a result of bombing as well—more than 50,000 over the course of the war, and perhaps 37,000 in 1944 alone.[228] Resistance fighters, in France and the Netherlands and eastern Europe and elsewhere, also helped in the transportation sabotage effort. Throughout the war, while they were not decisive, they could sometimes slow German operations or at least require the use of German forces to quell their sabotage efforts, draining resources that Berlin might have preferred to use in conventional operations elsewhere.[229]

D-Day succeeded along its five main beaches of invasion and the subsequent establishment of its breakout sectors. But the fighting was extremely intense and success was far from preordained. This account by Alex Kershaw captures the situation for part of the morning of June 6 at Omaha, before invading troops began to find ways to get off the beach:[230]

> All along Omaha Beach, men were trapped below the bluffs, being methodically picked off by German snipers and machine gunners, their bodies jolting with the impact of bullets and shrapnel. It was all so one-sided. The enemy couldn't be seen, and few men returned fire, not knowing what to shoot at or not wanting to expose themselves. . . . And still, mercilessly, the Germans kept up the massacre, carrying out Rommel's orders that the invaders be defeated, at all costs, on the beach, before they could press inland.

The sheer scale of what the Allies achieved—not only in the early days of June, but throughout the summer and beyond—was astounding. Some twenty-two Allied divisions reached France in June, ten American and the rest British or Canadian. Then thirty-one more, mostly American, arrived over the summer. Seventeen more came in the fall; fourteen more would arrive in the first three months of 1945, as well.[231] American air dominance helped tremendously; from June 6 to June 30, for example, Allied sorties in the theater outnumbered those of Germany tenfold. German aircraft attrition remained very high even as the force dwindled in size and became starved for fuel as fuel production was cut by two-thirds or so relative to the previous baseline.[232]

For all the formidable capacities that were brought to bear, the fight was difficult. Summertime challenges including navigating the hedgerows in the "bocage" country of northern France; those ancient growths of bush and vine, planted 2,000 years earlier by Celtics, made for excellent defensive barriers. Thus the going was sometimes slow, even as it continued. Fortunately, the United States military had developed by this point in the war a culture of study, reflection, and innovation. It analyzed what went well and what did not go so well in Operation Torch in North Africa as well as other operations, including the early going in France in June of 1944. As historian Russell Hart wrote, "The U.S. Army learned from past mistakes, dismissed incompetent commanders, enhanced interarm and interservice cooperation, refined tactics and techniques, and improvised better weapons."[233] In addition to developing new weaponry like various types of armored bulldozers and hedge-cutting tanks, the U.S. military undertook broad and steady offensives across a long front, followed then in Operation Cobra later in the summer with more concentrated assaults on specific parts of enemy lines after intensive aerial bombardment of enemy front-line positions The U.S. Army also improved communications between its armored and infantry units so they could complement each other quickly on the tactical battlefield.[234]

Paris was liberated in late August. A smaller Allied invasion from southern France, Operation Anvil, met up with the main forces originating from Normandy to achieve that emotional milestone, with a French division having the honor of taking the lead in the effort. The Allies had many specific technical advantages in this whole endeavor, too—beyond their overwhelming advantage in airpower—including the fine Sherman tank.[235]

Yet frustrations returned. The approach to Germany was sometimes slowed in the fall and thereafter by shortages of fuel, as German units managed to hold onto a number of ports in France even when surrounding areas were often held by the Allies. Attempting to push German forces out of France across a broad front, Allied forces were of necessity large and dispersed and in need of huge amounts of supplies. Compounding the challenge, the earlier damage done to railroads and roads by Allied air attack, when it was feared the Nazis could otherwise use the railroads for their own maneuver, often hampered the logistics efforts.[236] Summer and fall were when Germany launched the V-1 and then the V-2 (an early cruise missile and ballistic missile, respectively), against targets in Britain. The combination of a slowly developing Allied offensive, logistical and resource constraints, manpower shortages, and this new form of German terror attack against British cities created considerable anxiety.[237] As historian Tami Davis Biddle writes of allied leaders in late 1944, "The tumultuous months between the liberation of Paris in August and the bleak winter battles in the Ardennes delivered a hard blow to their confidence."[238]

By September, the Allied movement eastward had encountered enough frustrations that Operation Market Garden was attempted: an airborne-based attempt to seize simultaneously a number of bridges in Holland that German forces held and could be expected to destroy as they gradually retreated homeward. But four bridges turned out to be a bridge too far, and the Allied attack failed, with a stranded airborne division being lost in the process. There would be no shortcut into Germany, even as the general momentum of battle still clearly favored the Allies.

In this period Allied command carried out a vigorous debate about whether to enter Germany via a narrow front or a broad front. Logistics limitations raised the stakes; it was not clear that several main lines of effort could be sustained all at once. The prickly British General, "Monty," was in command in the northern sector and hoped to lead a narrow-front attack; Eisenhower continued to favor the more patient and conservative approach that employed multiple axes of attack, including through the general vicinity of Frankfurt, Germany. His view carried the day.[239]

Hitler attempted one last great gamble in the winter, with the Battle of the Bulge in the Ardennes forest starting on December 16, 1944.[240] Against military advice, he hoped that this Hail Mary could somehow dispirit the Allies enough that they would reconsider their fundamental invasion plan. Again profiting from its natural cover, from bad weather that handicapped Allied airpower, and most of all from the unexpected nature of the attack, German General Model envisioned a bisection of Allied forces that could have left a large portion cut off and isolated. It was quite impressive that such a beleaguered, weakened, and poorly supplied German military could make such an attempt. But after a month of hard fighting, its underdog offensive plan petered out in the face of superior Allied firepower.[241]

As Rick Atkinson wrote in reflecting on the effects of the Battle of the Bulge on General Eisenhower, supreme commander of the allied expeditionary force in western Europe:[242]

> . . . His timetable had been disrupted by six weeks or so, but his basic scheme for ending the war remained unaltered: Allied forces would continue destroying enemy forces west of the Rhine; they would seize bridgeheads over the river 'when the ice menace is over' in March; and then they would advance into the German heartland.

The Rhine River was a major challenge. As Atkinson put it, "From Switzerland, where the river was fed by 150 glaciers, to the North Sea, the European father of waters formed an extraordinary moat against invasion from the west." So the Allies had to utilize what Atkinson called their "inland navy" to get across it with all sorts of made-to-order small boats and quickly built bridges, together with what little existing bridging the Allies could salvage before German forces blew it up. German engineers demolished most of the thirty-one Rhine bridges within Germany that stood before the Allied invasion; by the time the war was over, the U.S. Army would build fifty-seven new ones.[243]

The unconditional surrender strategy of Washington, London, and Moscow reduced the odds that Hitler would see any advantage in surrendering rather than fighting on. But with the world's three biggest powers all marching on the Reich from different directions, and with Allied dominance of the skies and a preponderance of force on the ground, too many factors worked against Hitler and his generals.[244] Germany was also losing forces far too fast to replenish or recover; 350,000 were killed, wounded or captured in the fight in and around the Rhine, and a comparable number in the early weeks of April as the Americans, Brits, and Canadians pushed eastward. Leaving Berlin's liberation to Stalin and his legions, as noted before, they met up with Soviet forces south of the city.

Meanwhile, the Pacific war in the years 1943 through 1945 was mostly a campaign in two parts—up from Australia, where a considerable number of American forces had been based, and across the Pacific from Hawaii. The goal was to have bastions of land-based airpower, with overlapping ranges to the extent possible, and to take away Japan's own capabilities—either by direct attack, or by isolation and deprivation of supplies (including fuel, and munitions, and food) to island-based air and ground forces. The effort was enormous, and mainly carried out by the United States. Despite the official "Germany first" strategy, the Pacific theater in fact absorbed just as many American military personnel as did the Atlantic/European theater at the end of 1943 and continued to receive major resources of course thereafter.[245]

By this point, it was increasingly clear that China, or Allied airfields and other positions in China, would not be the key to success against Japan.[246] That disappointment was not for lack of trying. Under the military leadership of U.S. general Joseph Stilwell and others, the Allies had attempted to strengthen supply lines from British-run India through Burma into south-central China where Nationalist military forces were centered. Those supplies might in theory allow the Nationalists to control territory and fend off Japanese attacks more successfully, while also providing the tools for U.S. attacks on Japanese troops in China or Japan itself. So went the theory. But by the spring of 1942, Japan had cut the Burma road so that only an aerial route out of India and into south-central China was left.

Alas, subsequent efforts to carve a new road in northern Burma to connect India with China were generally unsuccessful until the very end of the war—by which point a major staging or operational base in China was no longer needed. Part of that was due to the sheer difficulty of the task in the face of Japanese resistance. Part of it was due to frustrations in working with Nationalist leader Chiang Kai-shek, who had other internal priorities besides working with the United States and allies to defeat Japan.[247] It took a while to reach this conclusion, however. Indeed, Chiang was invited to Cairo in late November 1943 for a summit with Roosevelt and Churchill in what seemed like a possible reaffirmation of the Allies' commitment to the Burma and China theaters. But it was not to be. After Roosevelt and Churchill met with Stalin at Teheran a few days afterwards, Chiang learned that there would be no big new Allied effort to emphasize Burma or anything else in the general theater.[248] Other approaches held more promise.

As the war went on, with its enormously expanding navy and other assets, the United States had the capacity to carry out a strategy focused on island-hopping from the Pacific rather than investing in China from the west of Japan. A large-deck Pacific aircraft carrier fleet that numbered only two ships in early 1943 was up to twelve by the spring of 1945 (counting smaller carriers too, the increase was from five to thirty-eight over that same time period). The large-deck *Essex* class of ships could each carry about 100 planes; the smaller but still fast *Independence* class about 35 each. There were, in addition, numerous escort carriers, too slow to keep up with the speedier ships but still useful in aerial support of landing operations among other things.[249] And many other ships as well.

As for the goals of the island-seizing campaign, it was not known until 1945 whether an invasion of the main Japanese islands would be needed. Whether one subscribed to a strangulation strategy, an aerial bombing strategy, or an invasion, it was widely agreed that proximity to Japan was essential. There was still debate about whether Taiwan or Okinawa should be the penultimate goal, and whether the MacArthur approach with the army or the Nimitz approach with navy and the marines should be accorded the lion's share of the resources. To some extent, the United States never really decided on that latter issue.[250]

Technological innovation helped in the island-seizing process. New amphibious landing craft allowed MacArthur to bypass strong Japanese positions on New Guinea with successive landings up the coast (working up from starting points at Guadalcanal and environs). Amphibious tractors allowed coral reefs to be traversed even at low tide. And weapons that had been around for a while, including the battleship, were employed in increasingly polished fashion as experience was gained against defenders. Notably, as time went on, longer preparatory bombardments were used before forces were sent ashore. Mobile repair and supply bases were improvised; these ships could sustain a fleet at sea for months at a time.[251] This was a remarkable innovation.

The progression of American attacks through the central Pacific went like this: Tarawa, now known as Kiribati, in the Gilbert islands (November 1943); Kwajalein and Eniwetok in the Marshall Islands (January/February 1944); Saipan in the Mariana Islands (June 1944); Guam and Tinian in the Marianas (July 1944); Iwo Jima (February 1945); and then ultimately Okinawa (April 1945).[252]

The progression from the south went from the Coral Sea and Solomon Islands to the large island of New Guinea, the midsized island of New Britain (with its huge Japanese bases), the Philippines (Battle of Leyte Gulf and invasion of Leyte Island in October 1944), invasion of the main Philippine island of Luzon in January 1945), and then Okinawa.

The Philippine operations were primarily fought on the ground by U.S. Army soldiers. Tarawa and Iwo Jima were the province of the marines. Okinawa as well as campaigns in the Mariana and Solomon Islands were carried out by the two services together.[253] Of course, the navy was involved in everything. Most of these battles involved one to three U.S. combat divisions, but the Leyte, Luzon, and Okinawa operations involved seven to eleven each.[254]

Taking the Marianas was crucial. Those islands include Saipan, Guam, and Tinian. It would be the latter island from which aircraft carrying atomic bombs would attack Hiroshima and Nagasaki in August 1945. Possession of these islands put Tokyo within range of American bombers. Knowing as much, Emperor Hirohito had issued fantastical commands to Prime Minister Tojo and his military to prevent the islands' loss. That was no longer within Japanese capacity.[255]

Militarily, these assaults were different kinds of operations. Those islands had some strategic depth, with dimensions typically on the order of 10 miles, unlike the atoll islands taken earlier. The United States lost 3,000 killed in taking Saipan and about half of that in taking Guam. These were larger losses than the roughly 1,000 American fatalities earlier at Tarawa and 500 in the entire Guadalcanal campaign (over six months). They were much less than what would be experienced at Iwo Jima and then, especially, Okinawa. The battles for the Marianas stretched through late spring and summer, lasting a few weeks on each island. A less successful attack, later in the year—and also less necessary one given the availability of other footholds—occurred at Peleliu in the Palau Islands, where about 1,500 Americans died in a campaign that stretched into November.

In all these fights Japanese losses were much higher. Initially, the Japanese often launched suicide-charge attacks (with commanders often committing ritualistic suicide or shooting themselves), shouting "banzai" as they went. Later, they adopted more effective but equally suicidal methods, and generally preferred death to surrender.[256] As the official Marine Corps history of the war put it, "By the time the Peleliu operation was launched in mid-September 1944, the Japanese had changed their tactics of defending the beaches and launching a final banzai once the inevitable end was in sight to a far more sophisticated defense that amounted to an extended delaying action conducted from well dug tunnels and cave positions which had to be taken at great cost to the attacking force."[257]

There were also naval raids conducted by an increasingly dominant U.S. fleet against Japanese ships, airfields, and other assets. One was conducted against the Japanese port on Truk in the Caroline Islands (west of the Gilbert Islands, south/southeast of the Marshall Islands). Another during the same month, February 1944, was in the Marianas, several months before the amphibious assaults there. Each time, Japanese losses were substantial, American losses light. There were a variety of small engagements at sea as well, with some losses on both sides, during this general time period of late 1943 through 1944, but the Japanese efforts could not significantly impede U.S. naval or amphibious operations.[258]

There were also two big naval showdowns. The first took place in June 1944 in the context of American invasions of the Marianas and is known as the Battle of the Philippine Sea. The second occurred in October and is called the Battle of Leyte Gulf (since all the action was nearby, if not actually on that body of water), linked naturally to the planned allied invasion of Leyte Island. It became, counting its various pieces, the largest naval battle in history.

In the Battle of the Philippine Sea, U.S. forces outnumbered the Japanese 2:1 and benefited from better radar and other advantages. They decimated Japanese aircraft in the fight, "the great Marianas turkey shoot" as it was nicknamed. U.S. submarines as well as aircraft also sank several Japanese ships. But given that the priority was to protect landing forces rather than seek a grand naval showdown, the ship attrition was modest. In the aftermath of battle, Admiral Raymond Spruance was on the receiving end of criticism for not being offensively minded enough.[259]

The memory of the battle sat badly with Admiral Halsey, who resolved to be more aggressive himself if offered a chance.[260] That new chance would come in October, in the internal Philippine body of water known as Leyte Gulf. Halsey commanded Task Force 38, with its eight large *Essex* carriers and eight smaller carriers, as well as many other ships.[261] Their overarching job was to cover the approach of an enormous landing force—700 ships, more than 170,000 troops—headed for Leyte, a central island in the Philippine archipelago. Here U.S. forces would make a crucial step in their northward advance toward Japan. They would, as plans dictated, begin landing and establishing a ground position from October 20 onward.[262]

But Halsey also had permission to seek out the Japanese fleet and attempt to destroy it if circumstances allowed. Alas, that license nearly proved Halsey's undoing—and could have led to disaster for the amphibious operation.

Halsey sought to follow the grand ideas of America's great naval historian and strategist, Alfred Thayer Mahan—and the precedent of Admiral Horatio Nelson, hero of the British victory at Trafalgar (despite perishing in that 1805 battle himself)—and go for a decisive victory at sea. The Japanese construed a clever tactical innovation, using carriers largely devoid of planes as a lure to attract Halsey's attention and draw his main forces away from protecting the American amphibious armada—leaving the latter vulnerable to attack by a different Japanese naval group led by Admiral Takeo Kurita for a crucial interval as they neared Leyte through its nearby approach known as the Surigao Strait. As historian Ian Toll wrote:[263]

> Halsey had no compelling reason to concentrate his entire sixty-five-ship fleet against the nineteen-ship carrier force to his north, but he had urgent reasons to guard the strait. Moreover, he did not have to pick between alternatives, because he had more than enough strength to deal with Kurita and Ozawa simultaneously.

As Toll colorfully continued, in reflecting on Halsey's nickname:[264]

> The bull chases the matador's cape while failing to notice his sword. Seeing red, the bull lowers its horns and charges, confident of striking down this feeble antagonist. But in the end, it is almost always the bull's bloody carcass that is dragged from the bullring, while the matador leaves on his feet.

Halsey was a lucky "Bull" in this case. Smaller escort carriers and some luck saved the day for the Americans, given Halsey's mistake. The Japanese fleet of a couple dozen ships under Kurita that could, in principle, have made mincemeat of the lightly protected American landing force was harassed, confused, and fatigued sufficiently that it decided to turn back, even though the American naval forces opposing it were significantly overmatched.[265]

As noted, the sum total of these engagements in late October 1944 became the largest naval battle in history, involving nearly 300 ships of all types.[266] Japan gave the United States a great scare in it, and several losses, including the U.S.S. *Princeton* aircraft carrier. But ultimately Japan lost four carriers and more than 20 ships, itself—285,000 tons of shipping to America's 29,000.[267] This was clearly not the kind of outcome Japan could tolerate at this (or any) stage of the Pacific war.[268] In the two big naval battles of 1944, plus a fight featuring aircraft over and around Formosa in October, Japanese forces took a huge pounding, losing hundreds of planes, three battleships, six heavy cruisers, three light cruisers, and seven aircraft carriers in all.[269]

The net effect of all of this was not only to position U.S. forces to threaten the Japanese homeland directly, but just as important, to dominate the seas and shipping lanes. Indeed, by the end of the war, Japanese imports had declined to something in the vicinity of half their previous levels.[270]

Having struggled tactically in the Battle of Leyte Gulf in the fall, Halsey was again almost defeated in the winter, this time by an inanimate force—the weather. Late in 1944 and then again in June 1945, he did a poor job assessing and reacting to weather reports of approaching typhoons. As a result, his task forces wound up badly damaged. Were it not for his war-hero status, the consequences for him could have been serious. But his reputation survived generally intact. Along with Nimitz, Leahy, and King, he remained one of America's four "Fleet Admirals" of World War II. The five stars were intended largely to ensure there would be no appearance of inferiority in dealing with British or Soviet officers who could sometimes reach the five-star pinnacle in their respective armed services. Among army officers, the five-star "General of the Army" honor was accorded to Marshall, MacArthur, Eisenhower, and H. "Hap" Arnold of the Army Air Force (later the only person ever to have that rank in the newly created U.S. Air Force), and in 1950, Omar Bradley.[271] That rank has never been used in the American armed forces since World War II.

It was not yet clear to American planners if they would need to invade the main Japanese islands. Doing so would have risked a million or more casualties to U.S. forces, according to the estimates of the day. In the Battle of Iwo Jima, nearly 7,000 marines died (and some 18,000 Japanese) as the United States sought to deny the island to Japanese aircraft and claim it as an intermediate landing site for bombers attacking Japan out of the Marianas.[272] On Okinawa, 80,000 Americans were killed or wounded, and 110,000 Japanese were killed with 10,000 taken prisoner. An invasion of the home islands augured far worse.[273]

It turned out that such an invasion would not be needed. A major reason was that, throughout this period, much was happening on the American atomic weapons front. In New Mexico, Robert Oppenheimer and a small team moved to Los Alamos in March 1943 to begin full-fledged work on the atomic bomb project there. This came a month after one of the most brilliant special forces operations in history. Six British commandos of Norwegian origin, equipped and deployed to the vicinity by British military aircraft, joined up with four members of the Norwegian resistance, skiing and hiking to approach, infiltrate, and destroy the heavy-water installation at Vemork that the Nazis were operating in a remote area of southern Norway as part of their own nuclear bomb program. They then successfully escaped. Subsequent air raids and sabotage would prevent this facility from ever producing enough heavy water to make a German atomic bomb possible. The sum total of these two developments early in the year contributed to what would ultimately happen in 1945— and what would *not* happen, in regard to the Nazi nuclear program.[274]

But before World War II would ever witness nuclear bombing, there would be terror from the skies in the form of attacks with conventional ordnance. The thinking of the Italian airpower theorist Giulio Douhet, with support from Americans like General Billy Mitchell, argued that airpower had changed warfare fundamentally. According to them, it would no longer be necessary to defeat an enemy according to the classic dictates of Carl von Clausewitz (or Alfred Thayer Mahan, for naval power). Attrition-based warfare would no longer be necessary. What the historian and strategist Russell Weigley called "the strategic tradition of U. S. Grant" would no longer be essential to victory in major war. Instead, airpower theorists argued that a modern society could be brought to its knees by punishment from the air—whether surgical, against its economy and war machine, or indiscriminate, against its cities and populations.[275]

Attempts at strategic bombing had, of course, been made earlier in the war. There was the Blitz, Germany's attacks on Britain in the second half of 1940. Then the Allies attempted their early aerial blows with a British attack on Berlin in August 1940, and the Doolittle raid on Tokyo in early 1942. Yet it was not until 1944 and 1945, when longer-range bombers were supported by long-range fighter escorts to protect them, that strategic bombing really had its heyday (until then, bomber attrition rates could reach or exceed 10 to 15 percent of an attacking force in a single sortie).[276]

Sadly, as historian Tami Biddle argues persuasively in her landmark study, the sophisticated theories of strategic bombing that envisioned hitting ball bearing plants, oil refineries, combat aircraft factories, and other critical industries in an early incarnation of "precision" or "surgical" bombing were, on balance, too optimistic. So were the theories of airpower that suggested populations would quickly be intimidated by attacks from the air, forcing their governments to capitulate promptly. Everything from bad weather, to the fact that bombs were unguided, to the need for high-altitude release of those bombs due to German antiaircraft flak, to a more resilient enemy population than was often anticipated contributed to the dilemma.[277]

But in the end, strategic bombing had a substantial role in the war. Part of it was through the simple destruction of cities. Massive raids produced huge fires and firestorms from Hamburg to Dresden to Tokyo, Nagoya, Osaka, Kobe, and beyond. By 1945, the United States also had basing in Saipan, within the 1,600-radius range of the B-29 superfortress bomber. That allowed it to strike Japan directly and hard. The United States also figured out how to use napalm to set massive urban fires in Japan's cities (consisting largely of wooden structures) deliberately, under the guidance of General Curtis LeMay. As historian Cathal Nolan wrote, about the day when the Japanese capital suffered attacks that produced a firestorm, "The B-29s arrived over Tokyo on March 9–10, 1945, to carry out what remains the single most lethal and destructive act in the history of war, greater than the atomic bombs."[278] Many hundreds of thousands of Germans and Japanese would lose their lives as a result of these attacks; millions would lose their homes.[279]

The effects of airpower on military production, fuel transport, rail transport, and battlefield mobility were certainly less than hoped.[280] German industrial production continued to climb throughout the war—just not quite as fast as it would have absent bombing. According to the most careful recent estimates, strategic bombing reduced German armaments output by about 3 to 5 percent in 1943 and 11 percent in 1944, but against a rising baseline. For example, German monthly production of fighter aircraft *tripled* between 1943 and September 1944. Still, that production rate did then decline some 20 percent by the end of 1944. Production of bombers declined by more than half by that year's end relative to 1943 levels; overall monthly fuel production went down more than half over the course of 1944. Germany also had to devote a large part of its air defenses to the western half of the country to limit the damage; between early 1943 and late 1944, Germany increased its portion of fighters based in the west from roughly 60 to 80 percent of its total capacity. Nonetheless, given the scale of the bombing, and carnage—as well as the enormous effort the Allies put into the bombing campaign and the tens of thousands of their own people lost in its course—this was on balance a rather disappointing set of strategic effects.[281]

An underappreciated reality about World War II is how much all major parties except the Soviet Union prioritized the production of aircraft, and associated ordnance, in their military industries. Roosevelt's recognition of the importance of aircraft production, sometimes in the face of opposition from some military leaders, was quite important in determining the outcome of the war. But the Allies, and especially the United States, could boost production unencumbered by major constraints on the industrial base or on the movement of finished weaponry to the combat theaters. By 1944, the allies had enough airpower (and, in the Pacific, good enough basing) to exact huge costs on their enemies. Perhaps a quarter to half of Axis aircraft production was destroyed en route, before it could even reach the battlefield. Pilot training went way down due to lack of fuel, worsening performance and survivability. Reinforcements for Japan and Germany had to try to deploy to forward locations at night, and could not react fast or strongly enough for challenges like the battle for Normandy in the late spring and summer of 1944.[282]

And then the innovations of modern long-range airpower with nuclear weaponry came together in 1945 with horrifying effect, as strategic bombing delivered atomic bombs on Hiroshima and Nagasaki on August 6 and 9, respectively. The first, "Little Boy," was a uranium-based "gun assembly" weapon of a type that rapidly brought together two pieces of enriched U-235 to form a critical mass; it had never been tested prior to its wartime use. The second, "Fat Man," relied on a sphere of plutonium as its core nuclear fuel, and had in fact been tested in the New Mexico desert earlier in the summer.

The effects of fire bombing, nuclear bombing, and then the Soviet entry into the war against Japan in its closing weeks were powerful. Together, and when combined with the slight modification of "unconditional surrender" terms to allow Japan to keep its emperor, they persuaded the Japanese government to capitulate. That did not prevent some of its members, including its former prime minister, Tojo, from ultimately heading to the gallows after postwar trials.

The main fighting ceased on August 15, though battle continued in Manchuria until August 21 (and the last Japanese units in the broader theater were not disarmed until October 24). Formal surrender to the United States took place on the U.S.S. *Missouri* in Tokyo Bay on September 2.[283]

Mistakes Made and Lessons Learned

The single most important lesson of World War II must surely be to remind us all of man's capacity for evil and to realize that it is not a distant memory.[284] Sixty million dead—at least two-thirds of those noncombatant civilians, many deliberately gassed or starved or burned to death—by any measure of lethality, make it far and away the worst conflict in history, with killing quite literally on an industrialized scale.[285]

Harvard professor Steven Pinker writes that life has indeed gotten better for most people over the course of time, and the future holds promise as we seek to nurture and elevate what Lincoln called "the better angels of our nature."[286] But World War II must surely underscore that any progress is fragile. The devils in our nature are still very much present as well. That Hitler could come to power in a modern industrial democracy, even if it was one ravaged by previous war and economic distress, and in the lifetimes of some of those reading these pages, is one of the most sobering and simply depressing historical realities of all time. It is not ancient history; many people from that period are in fact still alive today.

Remaining at the same broad philosophical level for a moment, the second big-picture takeaway for me is that World War II's outcome was not inevitable. Had Hitler succeeded in the Battle of Britain in 1940, and London felt obligated to surrender to Germany or at least come to terms that precluded further British combat, events would have been far different. Even with Britain's success in that crucial campaign, for which so many owe so much to so few in Churchill's timeless phrase, an Allied win was not yet inevitable.[287] Perhaps it was nearly so by the end of 1941, by which time Germany had attacked the Soviet Union, Japan had attacked the

United States, and Germany had declared war on the United States itself. And yes, Hitler's worldview made an attack on the Soviet Union very likely. Still, there was always the possibility that with successes in the west and in the Balkans, he might have reassessed. Allied planners could not assume he would attack the Soviet Union just because Hitler's *lebensraum* concept so dictated. Nor could they assume that Hitler's generals would leave him in power as he pursued that scheme; it was always possible that he might have been overthrown from within during the war, and of course attempts were made.

Moreover, the war's turning points—the Soviet resistance to German invasion, the American victories at Coral Sea and Midway, the ability to move troops and supplies across the Atlantic—did not come until 1942 or early 1943. They required enormous effort, great bravery, strong political leadership, technological and military innovation, and considerable time to achieve. Even thereafter, it was conceivable that Germany could have gotten the atomic bomb before America. Hitler's vision for a thousand-year Reich and the Japanese militarists' dreams of a China and Korea they dominated into perpetuity, together with a "co-prosperity sphere" they built throughout the broader region, were extremely ambitious concepts. But scaled-back versions of both were possible, had history played out differently.

Had Japan not attacked the United States, America might not have entered the war, at least not anytime soon. Had Germany not attacked the Soviet Union, Hitler and Stalin might have divvied up central and eastern Europe between them (with some scraps for Italy)—though perhaps such a scenario was not consistent with Hitler's personality and extreme ambition. Had Hitler prepared slightly better for the invasion of the Soviet Union, or had just a few more weeks of good weather to attempt his 1941 invasion, he might have succeeded. Then, maybe a decade later Germany could have had the atomic bomb, and with it the capacity to protect its gains or even expand them. Again, these are sobering thoughts.

Yet those outcomes did not occur. By early 1943, even with more than two years left in the fight, even with tens of millions of lives still to be squandered, it became highly probable that the Allies would win. The declaration of the demand for unconditional surrender at the Roosevelt-Churchill Casablanca conference of January 1943 may have made things marginally more difficult. But given the depravity of the Hitler and Tojo governments, only partially understood at the time of Casablanca in fact, it is hard to imagine any other real outcome.

Another set of lessons, already referred to several times, concerns the importance of military innovation and preparation before a possible war. The Germans were impressive on this front with regard to the development of blitzkrieg; the Japanese did very well when it came to aircraft carrier innovation, in technology and tactics and operational concepts; they also fought masterfully at the small-unit level, including in jungle conditions. Americans too were good at aircraft carrier development, as well as the means and methods of amphibious assault. Less impressive, for example, was development of antisubmarine warfare technology and tactics; this was an area, like strategic bombing, in which most innovation took place during the war itself.[288]

Intelligence was of massive importance in World War II. While there were constant strategic surprises about who would attack whom, and when and where such attacks would occur, the tactical achievements of intelligence were extraordinary. In particular, the use of cryptology to read intercepted communications by the other side was of paramount tactical importance at Midway, in antisubmarine warfare campaigns, in the shootdown of Yamamoto in April 1943 near Bougainville island, and in many other situations.

Overall, World War II was not a product of excessive optimism about the possibility of quick wins and easy victories. In that regard, it runs partially counter to one of the prevalent themes in this book that relate to most other wars I have considered.

Beyond these broad observations, several more specific key decisions from World War II are worthy of additional discussion and assessment, two of them already referred to above:

- Hitler's decision to attack the Soviet Union in 1941, and subsequent operational plan for the invasion (and his declaration of war on the United States in December 1941);
- Japan's decision to attack the United States at Pearl Harbor (as well as the Philippines and other Pacific islands);
- The U.S. decision to adopt a "Europe first" strategy, in conjunction with its Allies, as well as its decision to begin implementation of that strategy in Africa rather than Europe, and then in Italy before France;
- The U.S. decision to prioritize two main thrusts in its Pacific campaign, one via Australia and the other via the Mariana Islands;
- The use of strategic bombing against Germany and Japan.

As historian Max Hastings wrote, "Hitler's invasion of the Soviet Union was the defining event of the war, just as the Holocaust was the defining act of Nazism."[289] Hitler and his generals had been planning an attack against the Soviet Union since the year before—and contemplating the general idea for much longer than that, as revealed in key passages from *Mein Kampf* that were so astutely remembered and highlighted by William Shirer. Hitler saw its vast expanses as providing much of the *lebensraum* that he sought for the future Reich. As historian Stephen Fritz wrote, "The fundamental problem, then, was one of grand strategy: Hitler's goal was not merely a revision of the Versailles system, but a complete reordering of Europe—and perhaps the world—for which the conquest of *lebensraum* in the east was the essential first step."[290] Hitler also simultaneously feared and disdained the Soviet Union's people and politics—their Bolshevism, the nation's Jews, and also its primarily Slavic ethnicity. In addition, Hitler believed that if he defeated the Soviet Union, Britain could no longer realistically stand alone in opposition to Nazism and would sue for peace. Hitler may have also believed, as Lawrence Freedman astutely noted, that it would be advantageous to knock the Soviet Union out of the war—and off the map—before the United States could plausibly enter it.[291]

Hitler's decision was further solidified when Stalin took the Baltic states and then parts of Romania. Although the Soviet Union had been granted these territories by the terms of the Molotov-Ribbentrop Pact, their conquest meant that the territorial ambitions of the two tyrants were beginning to overlap. Romania was critical for oil and food for Hitler; the Baltic states, so proximate to Germany's old East Prussia, encompassed land that he sought to annex. And military overconfidence likely played the final key role in Hitler's decisionmaking. (Stalin, having thoroughly purged his officer corps in 1937–1938, appears not to have suffered from similar overconfidence, and to have been content to divide up most of Europe with Germany rather than seek virtually all of it himself.) Hitler believed, in fact, that the Soviet Union could be defeated in no more than five months—and perhaps much less than that—as evidenced by the complete lack of preparation for winter warfare for the 120 divisions that Germany intended to send eastward.

There was some chance that Germany could in fact have defeated the Soviet Union quickly and comprehensively. Yet that outcome was a best-case scenario, and any other scenario would be far more troubling for Berlin. Even successful conquest of St. Petersburg/Leningrad and Moscow might not have sealed the deal had Hitler managed those achievements.

The decision to invade proved reckless, given the huge costs involved, and the murderous intentions behind it. Yes, it was a gamble that stood some chance of success, but the costs of either success or failure would be measured in the many millions of human lives. In military terms, it was his greatest error; it became, literally as well as figuratively, his fatal error.[292] As Colin Gray put it, "The overarching problem for German strategic performance in the Second World War was the political ambition of the Fuhrer."[293] It knew no bounds.

It is also worth revisiting the Japanese decision to attack Pearl Harbor. One could argue that, while extremely risky, it was not without a certain logical underpinning. Knocking the United States, historically a rather isolationist country, out of the war long enough to fortify much of the western Pacific with military bastions in the hope that the Americans would choose to take the hit rather than mount a full mobilization to defeat Japan unconditionally may have sounded plausible. Hoping that trends in military technology, including the development of longer-range land-based aircraft, might make it possible for such an archipelago-based defense to fend off any aircraft carriers and battleships that sought to approach the region was not demonstrably incorrect, either.

On balance, however, the whole concept was the product of a militaristic, racist, and brutal regime that, if it followed a certain logic, also had a badly warped view of reality. Every one of the previous statements can be turned on its head to oppose the attack. Japan could hardly be confident the United States would take a knee in the war, or that trends in technology would *not* allow a combination of amphibious armadas as well as carrier-based and land-based aviation and traditional naval assets to fight their way gradually toward Japan, or that the combined forces of most of the world's largest economies when unified as allies in war would *not* manage collectively to overwhelm the strength of the axis nations with time. World War I also showed that the United States was not a pacifist nation by any stretch.

Consider next the U.S.-U.K. "Europe first" strategy. It is first worth remembering that it was Europe first largely in name only, since the American effort at all levels—including with shipbuilding and with ground troops—was directed toward both the Atlantic and Pacific theaters. Still, even if honored largely in the breach, the strategy made sense. Since the Allies arguably came closest to losing the war when Hitler attacked Britain in 1940, and then again when his armies neared Moscow in the summer of 1941, Germany had to be viewed as the greater immediate menace.[294] So the real debate is less about whether Europe should be prioritized, and more about whether in fact it was prioritized enough. Thankfully, with the tools that it had available at the time, the United States did enough in Europe to help avert these outcomes, even while ramping up the fight in the Pacific against Japan. Had the Battle of the Atlantic continued to go badly beyond 1942 and early 1943, there might have been a stronger case to pull naval forces out of the Pacific to protect convoys. Thankfully, greater ship construction rates, as well as technical and tactical modifications in antisubmarine warfare, shifted the course of the Battle of the Atlantic in time. And it was just as well to delay Operation Overlord until the allies had more experience in ground combat, in Africa and elsewhere, even if in theory it could have been moved up with a more absolute prioritization of the European theater throughout the war. Thus a nuanced "Europe first" strategy like the one followed was probably the best choice for the United States and allies.

Within the broader European theater, extending through the Mediterranean into North Africa, it also probably made good sense to launch an invasion of North Africa in late 1942. No serious attempt could have been made to invade northern Europe anytime soon at that point. More materiel, to say nothing of more combat and leadership experience for what were still very green American forces, were necessary prerequisites.[295] Yet something needed to be done to relieve German pressure on the Soviet Union at a time when Hitler had not yet made his fateful mistakes around Stalingrad that would ensure a successful Soviet defense of the motherland.

Then there is the matter of how the United States chose to attack Japan. Early in the war, planners had to decide—should it do so via the central Pacific, or the Australia-Solomons-Philippines route? Should Admiral Nimitz carry the day, or General MacArthur? Despite the latter's overly emotional and prideful desire to liberate the Philippines as soon as possible in order to keep his own promise to its people, it is not clear that better options existed than the two-pronged approach, including his preferred path. It ultimately culminated in the taking of Okinawa with both arms of the giant pincer movement.[296] Once the great American war machine was in high gear by 1943–1944, there was no need to choose just one of these approaches over the other, and by having two general directions of advance, the enemy was kept guessing about whether one might become the main effort. Moreover, the two different approaches placed somewhat different relative emphasis on different types of technology and combat force structure. Given that so many new technologies were being deployed, and so many new operational and tactical concepts were being developed, it made further sense to keep options open lest one approach wind up working much better than the other.

Was there a simpler way to defeat Japan—perhaps assembling just a single huge armada, with enormous floating logistics assets to back it up, and sailing straight for the large Japanese island of Hokkaido via the northern waterways? In theory, given what we know now, that might have worked. But it could have been vulnerable to a single point of failure (such as a bad storm, or an effective Japanese defense of the home islands with an unweakened air force). And with a multistep approach, the United States built up combat experience and expertise rather than throwing the dice with one big effort.[297] That new-found expertise also came in handy on the beaches of Normandy in June 1944. Moreover, any direct attempt to land a huge force on Japan's main islands without first establishing control of much of the surrounding region would have squandered the chance to place much of the economic pressure and undertake the aerial bombardment campaigns that ultimately made a land invasion unnecessary.

That brings us finally to the matter of strategic bombardment, using both conventional and nuclear means. I remain torn on the issue, especially with regard to Japan. The experiences on Okinawa and elsewhere suggest that land invasion would have been terribly deadly for both sides. The U.S. Joint Chiefs estimated more than 1 million American casualties in any invasion of Japan's main islands, of whom a quarter million would be killed, adding more than 50 percent to the entire American toll from World War II up to that point. Japanese losses would likely have been even greater.[298] Such estimates should always be viewed warily; my own experience suggests that believing casualty estimates can be accurate within a factor of two or three is unduly optimistic in the best of cases. So perhaps half a million to 2 million would be a better way to indicate the likely American casualties.[299] In any case, estimates of losses were high enough in some cases that some American military leaders, notably Admiral Nimitz, felt growing concerns and doubts about the wisdom of any ground invasion—preferring to continue the economic strangulation and aerial bombardment strategies.[300]

Terrible things happen in war, and terrible choices must be made by decisionmakers. As profoundly unsettling as the idea of destroying cities on purpose must be to any human being, the main cause was the onset and trajectory of the broader war itself. Yet in terms of just war theory, strategic bombing violated the precept against attacking civilians deliberately, and on a grand scale.[301] The carnage was enormous. At a minimum, greater attempts might have been made to focus on energy, steel, electricity, and other industrial sectors of the German and Japanese economies.[302] Greater efforts should also have been made to impede the use of railways to take Jews to their deaths in concentration camps when the nature of the Holocaust, and locations of the camps, were better known later in the war.[303]

On balance, given the stakes entailed in this conflict, and the extreme depravity of America's enemies, and the importance of ending these hugely deadly conflicts as quickly as possible, I find it difficult to object strenuously to tactics and methods that in most other wars could be construed as criminal.[304] But it is also hard to defend them.

The conclusion of World War II did, however, lead to one of the most magnanimous peace arrangements in history. To be sure, top Japanese and German officials guilty of war crimes were severely punished for their actions, and often sent to the gallows, in the years to come. But the United States and allies endeavored to help Germany and Japan rebuild their economies while recreating their political systems and rehabilitating their nations' standing in international society. The resulting transformations in those societies and their dependability as American allies have been remarkable—and a large part of the reason why there has been, as of this writing, no World War III to follow the two terrible global wars of the twentieth century.

FOUR   *Korea and Vietnam*

D uring the first half of the Cold War, after the descent of the Iron Curtain in Europe and the fall of China to communism, two very hot and bloody conflicts in East Asia engaged American forces and those of numerous other countries.

The Korean and Vietnam wars were tragic. They are also stunning from a historical perspective. A country, the United States, which only a few years before the outbreak of the Korean war had built and wielded the most impressive military machine in the history of the planet, failed to win two conflicts against economically and technologically much less developed foes. In Korea, one of those foes was China—but at that point it was a largely agrarian society, fielding a "people's army" that generally lacked sophisticated military technology and did not yet possess nuclear weapons. Whether out of hubris at what it had recently achieved, fatigue at the idea of having to wage war again so soon, desperation given its growing fear of a Communist menace, or lack of imagination and ingenuity in fighting two very different types of conflicts from those of World War I and World War II, the United States generally performed far below its earlier standards in these wars. The "greatest generation," an apt nickname for the group of Americans who did so much to win World War II and then came home to contribute to a period of great U.S. economic prosperity, could not alas expand its successes to the hills of Korea or steamy flatlands of Indochina.

The wars were, as noted, bloody. The Koreans, Chinese, and Vietnamese suffered by far the most casualties. But the United States itself lost nearly 100,000—more than 20 percent as many American fatalities as in World War II, and ten times as many as in all conflicts since 1975.

Technologically, the United States introduced numerous innovations, including jet aircraft and the helicopter, in the course of the time period between 1950 and 1975. By Vietnam it also had satellite communications

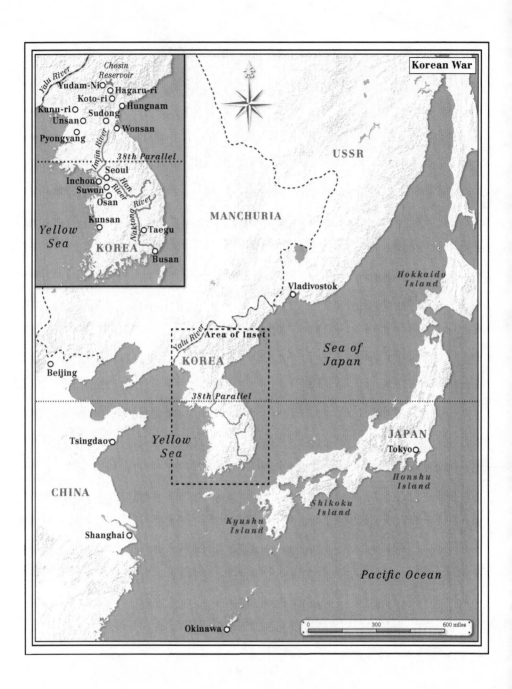

Korean War

Chosin Reservoir
Yalu River
Yudam-Ni
Hagaru-ri
Koto-ri
Kunu-ri
Sudong
Hungnam
Unsan
Pyongyang
Wonsan
Imjin River
38th Parallel
Seoul
Inchon
Han River
Suwon
Osan
Naktong River
Kunsan
Taegu
Yellow Sea
KOREA
Busan

USSR

MANCHURIA

Hokkaido Island

Vladivostok

Sea of Japan

Beijing

Yalu River
Area of Inset
KOREA
38th Parallel

JAPAN
Tokyo

Tsingdao

Yellow Sea

Honshu Island

CHINA

Shikoku Island

Kyushu Island

Shanghai

Pacific Ocean

Okinawa

0   300   600 miles

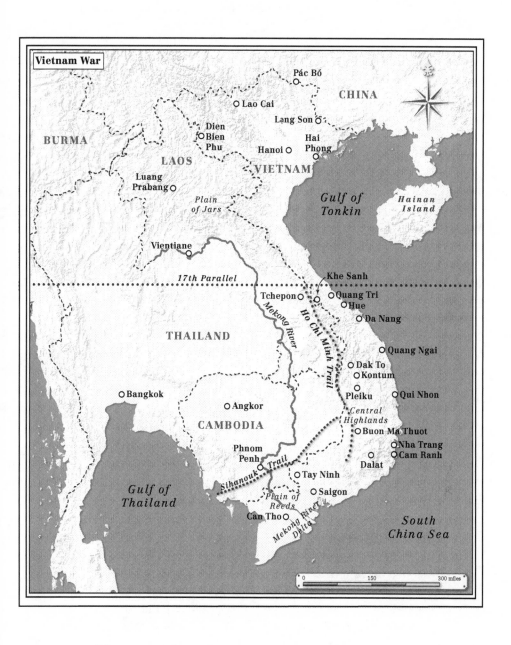

systems, and some precision munitions. But for the most part the United States dusted off modestly improved versions of the weapons of World War II for a kind of fighting that those weapons were generally less well suited to dominate. Meanwhile, irregular forces—America's enemies—profited greatly from the widespread availability of small arms including automatic weapons and widely available explosives.

Picking up a central theme of this book, the United States—like others—was too sanguine about both Korea and Vietnam, and ultimately quite surprised by the difficulty as well as the duration of the two wars. Again, the arguments of scholars like historian Geoffrey Blainey, not to mention Carl von Clausewitz, are vindicated by these conflicts. War is generally unpredictable, unforgiving, and devastating. Overconfidence, the cardinal sin of strategists and policymakers, often proves hard to resist, both before and during combat. For the United States, it has also been a mistake to assume that somehow preparing for the next big war, and living off the legacy of the last, will prove sufficient to be ready for smaller or different kinds of conflicts.

Yet at a grand strategic level, things have not turned out so badly for the United States and its allies. The stalemate and cease-fire that ended the Korean War in 1953 felt like a concession of defeat, or at least exhaustion, at the time. Seventy years later, the Republic of Korea has become a remarkable success story by almost any metric, even if North Korea remains a serious threat. For its part, Vietnam is now more friend than foe of the United States. This counterintuitive result is, in part, a reflection of the overall strength of the U.S. position in the modern era.

These wars are also complex ethically. My goal here is not to examine the morality of the wars in detail, but only to offer several observations and establish context. For the governments of North Korea and North Vietnam, the wars were seen—or at least portrayed—as wars of national liberation and reunification, following extensive periods of colonial subjugation and territorial division in both countries. These narratives, even if self-serving, were probably sincere up to a point. However, the brutal methods that Pyongyang as well as Hanoi were willing to inflict against their enemies, as well as their own peoples, cast a deep humanitarian pall upon their actions. That said, it is only fair to recognize that there was extreme violence, as well as severe corruption, and autocracy, in both Koreas and both Vietnams.

The role of the main outside actors was also morally complex. China had suffered decades, indeed a century of foreign infiltration, domination, and pogroms—and feared the presence of foreign forces near its borders. So its intervention in Korea, after American-led UN forces crossed the 38th parallel headed northward, has a certain logic to it. Yet that narrative cannot explain or justify the extreme ruthlessness and callousness toward human life shown by Chinese leader Mao Zedong, and it cannot change the fact that it was North Korea that started the war. America's role in both wars was understandable as a response to the emergent threat of global communism. But its role also had a strong element of Shakespearian tragedy. The attempt to protect freedom far from home led to firepower-intensive and insufficiently discriminate uses of force, designed to serve what were at least theoretically noble goals, but devastating to local populations just the same. The end results may have justified the means in Korea; it is harder to make that case about Vietnam.

The Korean Conflict

On June 25, 1950, the seventy-fourth anniversary of Custer's Last Stand, tens of thousands of North Korean soldiers flowed south across the inter-Korean border, in tanks and trucks and on foot, in an attempt to reunify the peninsula under the control of Korean leader Kim Il Sung. They almost succeeded.

By November of that year, China was a major part of the war too, providing the preponderance of troops from that point onward in its partnership with its fellow Communist regime, the Democratic People's Republic of Korea (DPRK). They faced off against a coalition made up of the Republic of Korea (ROK), the United States, and some fifteen additional countries fighting under a UN imprimatur.

The fighting occurred nearly exclusively on the Korean peninsula, a land formation some 600 miles long and 150 miles across. Its population at the time was about 30 million, two-thirds of it in South Korea (the same fraction as today, roughly speaking). Chinese aircraft, however, operated out of bases in China, and coalition naval aircraft naturally flew missions from the Yellow Sea and Sea of Japan, so the combat theater was not confined entirely to the peninsula. Some aerial engagements strayed over the China-North Korea border as well.

The end of World War II had established the strategic conditions that led to the Korean War. As Soviet armies moved to liberate Manchuria from Japanese occupation, as the United States prepared to accept Japan's surrender in late summer of 1945, Korea became the meeting ground for the two erstwhile allies who were very quickly transitioning to an adversarial relationship. Still, despite the incipient rivalry between the Soviet Union and the United States, Stalin assented to divide the peninsula in half— along the 38th parallel, roughly where it is divided still today. The purported goal was to allow each half to be governed separately until they could reunify. The two Koreas were formally created as nation-states in 1948; both the Soviet Union and the United States had removed their occupation forces by mid-1949.[1]

But reunification was never to come. When Mao's Communists won the Chinese civil war in 1949, North Korean dictator Kim Il-Sung had another potential ally. When Secretary of State Dean Acheson declared Korea outside the perimeter of America's core strategic interests, in an early 1950 speech, Kim sensed an opportunity as well.[2] Having rejected the idea of war at least twice before when Kim proposed it, Stalin apparently changed his mind in early 1950.[3] He then gave Kim his blessing to launch the war against South Korea and its strongman leader, Syngman Rhee.[4] Since Pyongyang looked to Moscow for doctrinal inspiration as well as more tangible kinds of help, Stalin's approval was important for Kim's calculus.

The war began with major North Korean successes against its South Korean foe. With no American forces on the peninsula initially, only a few hundred advisers, and South Korea's military, such as it was, in poor shape, the North Korean forces made rapid progress southward, capturing Seoul within days. They grabbed most of the peninsula within weeks, even as American forces started to arrive, including the ill-fated Task Force Smith sent to help defend the city of Osan, near Seoul. By late July, only an area in and around the southeastern port city of Pusan (Busan) was still in friendly hands.

That was phase one. Phase two began as the U.S. forces increased, and the Pusan perimeter strengthened. As August unfolded, fears of coalition forces being driven completely off the peninsula began to diminish. One key part of the holding action was an Army unit, the Twenty-fourth infantry regiment of the Twenty-fifth Infantry Division that, despite President Harry S. Truman's 1948 order requiring integration of the armed forces, was still mostly African American.[5]

Then, in mid-September, a third phase began with the great American maneuver success of the war. It played out on the muddy tidal flats of Inchon, west of Seoul, where American amphibious forces came ashore in a daring operation. Achieving great surprise, they sliced through North Korean lines, cut most of the invasion force off from its logistics support, and totally changed the momentum of battle. Liberating Seoul later that month, the Americans then started moving northward, with the intent of reunifying the peninsula forcefully—but now, under South Korean rule. The goal became the Yalu River, where China meets North Korea.

Phase four of the war was the Chinese intervention. Catching coalition forces off guard and widely dispersed, Chinese troops drove them southward, in what some call the biggest retreat in American military history. Enemy forces again took Seoul. There was nonetheless heroic effort by some coalition forces, most notably the First Division of the U.S. Marine Corps in central regions of North Korea near the Chosin Reservoir.

Phase five lasted most of the war. It began with the arrival and growing influence of General Matthew Ridgway, perhaps the main American hero of the Korean War, who helped coalition forces stabilize their units and their positions, and then gradually move northward. Once they liberated Seoul and environs for the second time in early 1951, and fended off concerted Chinese-DPRK attacks that spring, something akin to a military stalemate began to emerge on the Korean peninsula. It would continue for two years as cease-fire negotiations were attempted with varying degrees of seriousness and promise. By the summer of 1953, with now president Dwight D. Eisenhower threatening nuclear attacks (albeit in a calmer and more subtle manner than had General MacArthur, prior to his being relieved of command of U.S. and UN forces for insubordination in early 1951), China and North Korea finally accepted proposed terms of peace.

The Weapons of War and Strategies of the Protagonists

The Korean War was extremely intense and lethal. Widely accepted estimates put Chinese casualties at 900,000 killed and wounded, and North Korean losses at about 520,000. UN forces suffered 400,000 casualties, about two-thirds Korean and most of the rest American. U.S. fatalities totaled almost 34,000.[6]

The carnage resulted from a large number of tanks and large-bore artillery, to be sure. But heavy weapons did not predominate quite as much as in many of the great battles of World War II. Machine guns and other automatic weapons, hand grenades, mortars, man-portable satchel charges, and mines were also among the signature technologies. The rough and wooded Korean terrain, interwoven with rice paddies and otherwise presenting many difficulties for offroad maneuver by heavy vehicles, is a large part of the reason why much fighting involved small arms. Fighting often occurred at night, when North Korean and Chinese forces knew that America's airpower and artillery would be less effective. Enemy forces also often preferred to maintain close contact with the UN coalition so as to limit the ability of the latter to use its overwhelming firepower (for fear of hitting its own people by accident). Many of the crucial battles also took place in the frigid winter that is typical of the Korean peninsula. The cold was itself one of the greatest causes of casualties.

Jet aircraft made their combat debut in Korea. There were other innovations in aerial combat as well; for example, improved navigation radars were developed to facilitate bombing by U.S. aircraft at night. China made huge strides with its own air force, ultimately employing as many as 3,000 planes out of bases on its own territory (given the American ability to destroy airfields within North Korea). It used its fledgling air force to challenge U.S./ROK/UN bombing raids, which were often conducted by two dozen or more bombers. Small numbers of Soviet aircraft, masked as Chinese, also participated in some operations.[7]

In some ways, the use of airpower in Korea resembled practices in World War II (and foreshadowed those in Vietnam). It was brutal, as America and its allies sought to use their overwhelming advantages in technology and firepower to compensate for geographic and topographic disadvantages. Napalm was often used against cities, and the resulting scale of suffering by the civilian North Korean population was considerable.[8] Bomb damage assessment determined that eighteen of twenty-two major cities suffered at least 50 percent destruction in the course of the war.[9] Power plants and irrigation dams were hit as well. Targets in China were never bombed; however, there were numerous U.S. air incursions into its airspace, often in pursuit of Chinese combat aircraft. As one historian, Kenneth Werrell, put it, "Although the Americans did not target Communist airfields in China, the Chinese air space near the Korean border was an unsafe place for Communist pilots."[10]

Airpower was used extensively in an attempt to reduce China's ability to resupply forces by rail and road. In the course of the war, out of perhaps three-fourths of a million U.S. combat sorties, official data showed more than 5,000 hits against bridges, more than 20,000 against rail lines, more than 2,000 against locomotives, some 40,000 against railcars, and more than 100,000 against military vehicles. But these numbers could be inflated, as estimates of the effectiveness of airpower often have been historically. In any event, Communist forces were adept at repairing roads, at using human porters for logistics, even at learning to stand still when airplanes flew overhead so as not to give hints of their presence. They also did not need many supplies: a typical Chinese division was thought to need only 40 tons of supplies a day, and the entire deployed army of around 60 divisions therefore some 2,400 tons daily. As a result, Chinese forces only faced crippling logistical constraints when moving too far southward on the peninsula—airpower did manage to create a certain natural check on their forward progress.[11] Roughly 100,000 U.S. sorties were flown as close-air support, generally against enemy infantry, as well.[12]

The key strategies of the main players are fairly simple to describe—at least, for all parties except the United States, which had a very hard time figuring out what this war was about.

For North Korea, the goal was simply to reunify the peninsula under its control and the dictatorial leadership of Kim Il Sung. The North Koreans almost succeeded, but failed to take account of the U.S. and UN intervention—perhaps largely because the United States had fairly clearly indicated that it would likely not get involved in any Korean War.

For South Korea, the key and initial goal was survival. Once the tide of battle turned at Inchon in September 1950, more ambitious objectives emerged as well, especially since the United States by now also appeared to favor the forcible reunification of the peninsula—now at the expense of North Korea, rather than for its benefit.

For China, the goal was to protect a Communist ally from hostile take-over (regardless of the guilt of the DPRK in starting the war), and per-haps also to ensure that a hostile United States would not have military bases right up against Chinese borders. China also sought to solidify its relationship with the Soviet Union, given that Stalin had green-lit the in-vasion in the interest of furthering the global Communist cause.[13] A rev-olutionary, expansionist ideology guided its foreign policy and, in the eyes of Mao and other Chinese leaders, justified direct support for North Korea's naked aggression. This was a fraught time in world politics, given the global goals of the broader Communist movement and the ways that Moscow as well as Beijing used this extremist worldview to justify the initiation and prosecution of devastating conflicts.

For the United States, and at least some of its fifteen or so other coali-tion partners, the initial goal was to stay out of any war on the remote Korean peninsula. But that position changed almost immediately after the North Korean invasion occurred. Then, the objective became to ensure that there would be no Communist takeover of South Korea by North Korea, with its presumed allies in Moscow and Beijing. After the success at Inchon in September, the objective became much more ambitious, with the goal of punishing the north by taking much or all of its territory and thereby solving the problem of peninsular reunification as well. And then—after the Chinese intervention—the compromise goal was to restore some semblance of a respectable division of the peninsula without allowing the war to distract the United States from broader global concerns.

The North Korean Drive South—and Task Force Smith

At 4 a.m. local time on June 25, 1950, nearly 100,000 North Korean or "Korean People's Army" troops descended quickly southward into South Korea.[14] Including follow-on forces, they comprised about ten divisions with a grand total of some 230 tanks, 200 large-bore artillery pieces, and an air force of some 200 aircraft, featuring Yak-9 fighters and IL-10 attack aircraft.[15]

There were no U.S. forces in Korea at that time, only a few hundred American advisers and trainers.[16] The United States was stunned by the attack. Washington was focused on other scenarios and thought that, if war occurred in Korea, it would likely be in the context of general global war, not intrapeninsular aggression. Also, so many skirmishes had taken place along the Koreas' border in recent years, some rather large, that many onlookers had become inured to the tension. As a result, it took hours for policymakers to recognize the attack for what it was.[17]

South Korean forces, at the beck and call of a corrupt autocratic regime, were poorly led. They were also poorly equipped, since the United States had been wary about providing them the capability to march northward out of fear that Rhee, not Kim, might be the instigator of any internecine violence. South Korea did not have any tanks, combat aircraft, effective antitank weapons, or large-bore artillery.[18] Ammunition stocks might have sufficed for six days of battle at best. And South Korean forces were certainly unprepared for the surprise attack that shook the world.[19]

By 6 p.m., June 25, New York time, just over a day after the invasion had begun, the United Nations Security Council passed a resolution condemning the attack and demanding that North Korea withdraw from South Korea, by a vote of 9–0.[20] The Soviet Union and China were not there to veto the resolution because Moscow had been boycotting the United Nations since January, in light of the fact that the new Communist government in China had not been allowed to assume the Chinese seat at the United Nations or the Security Council. As a result, U.S./ROK/

coalition forces have had formal UN approval ever since, up to this day. More than a dozen other countries soon volunteered forces, but generally at only battalion or brigade strength—hundreds or at most a few thousand soldiers per contributor. Great Britain also sent its Far East Fleet, including a light carrier and total of eight ships.[21] Even with Britain, the total contributions of all these other countries—including Canada, Turkey, Australia, Thailand, the Philippines, France, Greece, New Zealand, the Netherlands, Colombia, Belgium, Ethiopia, South Africa, Luxembourg (plus Italy and Scandinavian nations in the realm of hospital units)—amounted to just one-tenth the U.S. strength.[22]

The U.S. Congress never declared war on North Korea or China. President Truman acted without requesting a declaration of war or other legislative branch authorization, claiming that an emergency "police action" already authorized by the United Nations did not require it. Truman chose such an extraconstitutional approach even though there was little doubt that he could have obtained congressional blessing very quickly. Thus was set the regrettable precedent, to be emulated many times in the years to come, of the United States waging war without Congress authorizing it.[23] Congress did signal support in several other ways—notably, by extending the otherwise-soon-to-expire draft, and by approving a military assistance program for South Korea in the remaining days of June.[24]

Seoul fell in the first week. Almost half of South Korea's army disintegrated and the other half fled southward. Some units simply crumbled upon contact with the enemy. American airpower was available at the outset of the war, but without forward air controllers to find and designate targets, its effectiveness was quite limited. "Friendly fire" tragedies frequently occurred as well, with South Korean forces suffering unintentional losses because of American bombs.[25]

On July 1, 1950, the first contingent of U.S. troops flew to Korea from nearby Japan, where Douglas MacArthur, effectively the viceroy of the U.S. occupation of Japan, had become the first supreme commander of the Korean war effort. Under the tactical command of Lieutenant Colonel Charles "Brad" Smith, they numbered about 400 soldiers, drawn from the B and C companies of the First Battalion of the Twenty-first regiment of the U.S. Army's Twenty-fourth Infantry Division. They were armed only with small weapons, machine guns, 75-millimeter recoilless rifles, a single battery of 105-millimeter howitzers, and 2.36-inch bazooka rockets. They lacked tanks, heavy artillery, and the new 3.5-inch bazooka that could (unlike the earlier, smaller version) actually penetrate North Korea's T-34 tanks.

Arriving from occupation duty in Japan, the units of the Twenty-fourth Division that would make up Task Force Smith were also not well trained for combat. They moved north, dug in, and engaged North Korean forces around Suwon, north of Osan and some 20 miles south of Seoul. Tragically, they were short not only on firepower and numbers, but ammunition as well. Other elements of the Twenty-fourth Infantry Division were no more successful. Things were off to a very bad start.[26] Given South Korea's lack of strategic depth—it is about 200 miles from Seoul to Pusan—the situation did not bode well. Surviving forces retreated to an area soon known as the Pusan perimeter.

Nor did very much improve in the course of July. North Korean forces continued to progress, with the southern tip of the peninsula soon in their sights. As historian Max Hastings wrote, "Terrain, logistics, poor communications, and refugees did more to delay the North Korean advance in the first weeks of July than the American infantry in their path."[27] On July 13, the Eighth U.S. Army, under General Walton Walker, was formally created for the Korean theater, but he had little more than the Twenty-fourth Division under his command. He would only benefit from the gradual arrival of other undermanned, underequipped, and undertrained occupation forces based in Japan, notably the Twenty-fifth and Second Divisions, in the weeks to come.

The Pusan Perimeter

Yet, perhaps imperceptibly at first, the tide was beginning to turn. In addition to the gradual arrival of U.S. and coalition reinforcements, North Korea's military was taking a beating as it drove south. It had suffered 50,000 or more casualties by early August—greater attrition than an army with a total size of less than 150,000 could absorb.[28] The length of logistics lines made it harder for North Korea to supply forces so far from its home territory. And American airpower, while not optimized for the kind of fighting seen in Korea, had a better chance of helping the cause once frontline positions began to stabilize somewhat.

These dynamics converged to create the conditions for a successful coalition defense in the southeast of South Korea, surrounding the port city of Pusan. The overall land area of what was soon known as the Pusan perimeter was a generally rectangular region, some 75 by 40 miles in size. Its northwest corner was located just beyond the city of Taegu, itself 50 miles northwest from Pusan.[29] The battles in this crucial region stretched over a six-week period, beginning around July 31 and continuing until the U.S. landing at Inchon on September 15.

This was to be the last stand for U.S. and coalition forces. As General Walker put it to his troops, "There will be no more retreating, withdrawal, readjustment of lines or whatever you call it. There are no lines behind which we can retreat."[30] Fortunately for him, by this point he had almost 100,000 troops under his command—half American soldiers, half Korean, with marines and British soldiers soon to arrive, a total force that now outnumbered the North Koreans.[31]

In the ensuing fighting, much of it along the Naktong River and often in difficult, hilly terrain, North Korean forces sometimes pushed through U.S./ROK/UN lines. But there were increasingly enough reserves to plug the gaps, as well as enough effective airpower to slow enemy movements. Max Hastings described the fighting as "an interminable series of short, fierce, encounter battles."[32]

As time went on, North Korean forces recognized that their piecemeal attacks were not producing breakthrough or encirclement opportunities. So they reassessed and regrouped. Then, on the night of August 31, they mustered a broad attack across much of the front. For several days, they made progress, at one point forcing General Walker to relocate Eighth Army headquarters to Pusan from Taegu. But U.S. airpower and interior lines of communication were ultimately enough to fend off the DPRK attempt.[33]

Inchon and Beyond

What had seemed likely defeat earlier in the summer changed completely in mid-September, in one of the most brilliant maneuver operations of the twentieth century, the landing at Inchon west of Seoul. With this operation, U.S. and coalition forces completely changed the battlefield momentum. They also cut North Korean supply lines and set themselves up for a counterattack on Seoul. The capital would, by month's end, be liberated.

What made the operation so brilliant, and brave—and what made most other senior American military leaders besides MacArthur so wary of the idea—was the nature of the maritime approach to Inchon. Tidal mud flats dominate the region, meaning that only at certain moments of the highest of high tides would a landing be possible. Storms, mechanical failures, or other unexpected developments could have easily thwarted the entire effort, and caused great peril to the shipborne troops, in a waterway with some of the biggest tidal swings in the world (32 feet from low to high tide). Only three dates were suitable over the month-long period starting on September 15; fortunately, conditions cooperated on that exact date, the 15th.[34]

Some 260 ships, largely of World War II vintage (like most other weapons and vehicles used in this war), were assembled to transport 70,000 American and South Korean troops over a two-day voyage from Japan to Inchon, on Korea's west coast, via the Yellow Sea. After several days of preparatory bombardment, they seized a key island in the approaches to Inchon on September 15, then came ashore over sea walls (using ladders) the next high tide later that same day. They encountered only light resistance and achieved great success with modest casualties.[35] A new formation, the X Corps, conducted Operation Chromite, as it was known, featuring the First Marine Division, including the First, Fifth, and Seventh Marine Regiments, and parts of the Seventh Army Infantry Division. It was put under the command of General Edward "Ned" Almond, directly reporting to MacArthur.[36]

The X Corps soon made its way to Seoul. It faced some resistance en route and then had to cross the Han River, using improvised rafts and makeshift bridging for its tanks. A multipronged attack to liberate the city sector by sector began on September 25. The liberators had to contend with many obstacles emplaced by North Korean forces, as well as a moderately effective active resistance. Within roughly three days, however, the city was back in U.S.-ROK hands.[37]

By September 22, the Eighth Army had broken out of the Pusan perimeter. Many North Korean units then retreated or dissolved. On September 27, the X Corps and the Eighth Army linked up near Osan, south of Seoul.

However, a great catch-22 then presented itself. After such a brazen North Korean attack on South Korea, it seemed inadequate simply to restore the prewar status quo ante. Moreover, the post-1945 discussions about Korea had presumed the peninsula would ultimately be reunified. So going back to the 38th parallel and stopping there seemed a bad idea. But it was also dangerous for coalition forces to move into North Korea. Doing so raised the question of where, if anywhere, coalition forces might stop—and whether Chinese forces might enter the war, out of defensive or offensive motives (or both).[38] Flush with Inchon success, MacArthur found the decision an easy one, however, and Washington did not stand in his way.[39]

The Eighth Army crossed the 38th parallel on October 9. Pyongyang fell on October 19. On October 24, MacArthur issued an edict that U.S. forces could move and occupy any and all regions within North Korea

up to the Yalu River at the Chinese border. With coalition forces now out-
numbering North Korean troops 2:1, that did not seem particularly difficult.

Indeed, the coalition's advantage in the west was great enough that
MacArthur put many U.S. forces back on ships and sent them to Wonsan
on the east coast of North Korea. Expecting to meet resistance in another
Inchon'ish operation, the troops discovered, upon their October 25 arrival,
that comedian Bob Hope had beaten them there.[40]

In any event, things were going well—so well, in fact, that MacArthur
himself summarily rejected a British proposal to create a buffer zone just
south of the Yalu where Chinese and UN forces might patrol, declaring
the idea akin to appeasement.[41] Somehow MacArthur was making these
decisions, and statements, not Secretary of Defense George Marshall (who
served in that role from September 1950 until September 1951), and not
President Harry Truman. Still, they did not overrule him.

Yet China had indirectly warned the United States on October 2,
through an Indian intermediary, that it would intervene in the war if U.S.
and ROK forces crossed the 38th parallel.[42] Indeed, on October 14 it appears that Chinese forces began to enter North Korea; on October 25, they
attacked a South Korean army corps. In the course of November, it became increasingly clear that the People's Republic of China (PRC) had sent
tens of thousands of troops across the Yalu and into North Korea. Skirmishes with Chinese forces were becoming common; Chinese prisoners
were even being taken.[43]

Throughout it all MacArthur stayed dogged in his offensive mindset,
however, and never reversed his October 24 authorization for a general coalition advance to the Yalu River as quickly as possible.[44] As Max Hastings
wrote of the general and his inner circle, devastatingly but persuasively:[45]

> They persisted in their conviction that their armies could drive with
> impunity to the Yalu. They continued to believe that the Chinese
> were either unwilling or unable to intervene effectively. . . . .They had
> created a fantasy world for themselves, in which events would march
> in accordance with a divine providence directed from the Dai Ichi
> building [in Tokyo]. The conduct of the drive to the Yalu reflected a
> contempt for intelligence, for the cardinal principles of military pru-
> dence, seldom matched in twentieth-century warfare.

As the U.S. military machine started to scrape off the World War II dust
and arrive in force, and as airpower mushroomed to the point where

coalition aircraft were flying around a thousand sorties a day by late 1950, it was understandable at one level that MacArthur would feel confident.[46] It is also worth bearing in mind that he had strong support in Washington for moving across the 38th parallel—and it was probably that decision to move into North Korea, more than his ambitions to reach the Yalu fast, that provoked the Chinese intervention.[47] Rare at that point were the voices like that of George Kennan's, who advocated simply restoring the status quo ante bellum at the 38th parallel.[48] That said, the rather undisciplined race for the Yalu, and the complete and utter conviction that unconditional victory was the proper goal for coalition forces, were driven by MacArthur.

The Chinese Intervention: Catastrophe, Chosin, and More Catastrophe

The skirmishing with the Chinese in November did not lead to major sustained combat. David Halberstam described one such incident in early November as "a warning at Unsan," a town in the northwest of North Korea (just north of another town that would soon become memorable, Kunu-ri, located on the Chongchon River).[49] This may have been less deliberate warning than an initial attack that encountered obstacles, however. As such, the Chinese regrouped, and tried again a few weeks later, this time with greater follow-through.

The Chinese had in fact started to move some 120,000 troops onto the Korean peninsula by October 19.[50] Their ability to position forces so secretly was facilitated by moving at night, avoiding the use of radios, limiting their dependence on vehicles or even animals, and minimizing supply requirements—a Chinese soldier typically needed only 8 to 10 pounds of supplies a day, versus 60 pounds for a typical coalition soldier.[51]

In mid-November, the *Korea Times* was celebrating the return to life as normal in Seoul. On Thanksgiving Day, U.S. forces were treated to a nice meal—even those of the Eighth Army, by now in forward positions inside North Korea and still unaware of the looming threat. MacArthur's promise that troops would be home by Christmas was still in effect. The Eighth Army was to continue its movements up the west coast of the peninsula, with the X Corps on its own route up the east side, both with instructions to reach the Yalu as soon as possible, and perhaps meet up with each other along the way to complete an encirclement of any remaining DPRK forces.[52]

But then disaster struck, from November 25 onward. Soon, the war would see yet another dramatic shift in momentum, as coalition forces would be driven entirely out of North Korea and indeed below the Han River, again losing Seoul—this time principally to Chinese forces.

The aggregate sizes of the two main protagonists in the fight were similar. China fielded nearly 400,000 troops in North Korea by this point.[53] Perhaps three-fifths were on the western side of the peninsula, near the Eighth Army, and two-fifths further east, near X Corps. North Korea had about 100,000 personnel at this point. The United States fielded 175,000 troops, its foreign allies another 20,000, and South Korea more than 200,000. So the fight should not really have been so lopsided to the PRC/DPRK's advantage. But the element of surprise, the unprepared posture of coalition forces, effective Chinese tactics that worked very well in Korea's difficult terrain, and the poor condition of most U.S/UN/ROK units augured badly for coalition forces.[54]

China's tactics included ambushes against vehicles confined to the country's narrow and twisting roads. They also featured small-unit attacks, usually at night. Chinese troops had mortars, up to and including 122-millimeter varieties but mostly smaller-bore systems.[55] In their close-combat attacks they typically wielded just machine guns, grenades, and satchel charges as they sought to find an isolated position, or turn the flank of dug-in forces, or just sacrifice themselves while delivering a grenade or satchel charge against a trench.[56] The attacks would be initiated by a flare or bugle call or musical sound—"Like the enemy was watching us and serenading us and mocking us all at the same time."[57]

The Chinese forward movements would seek to find and envelop enemy flanks, and rapidly exploit initial successes with follow-on contingents.[58] They would also typically seek to get behind U.S./ROK/UN lines to attack any forces that chose to attempt a retrograde movement. Not until the arrival of General Ridgway some weeks later did U.S. and coalition forces reduce their vulnerabilities to these methods. Rather than retreat when attacked, they would attempt to create more defensible 360-degree perimeters and request resupply by air, for example.[59]

The PRC-DPRK attacks occurred in two main sectors. In the west, Chinese attacks were launched against the Eighth Army, inflicting huge casualties and essentially dissolving South Korea's II Corps. At battles in and around Kunu-ri, an inland town about halfway between the Yalu and Pyongyang, the Americans found their positions unsustainable and, by November 30, began a southward retreat. Pyongyang was abandoned by December 5.[60] Chinese forces were further aided by the fact that by now, the Yalu River was freezing, making it possible to cross even as UN-coalition aircraft damaged or destroyed some of the bridges across it. Resupply was not yet a major problem for China and North Korea.[61]

In the center of the peninsula, things were also tough, as the Chinese attacked there on November 27.[62] The X Corps, including two battalions of the Seventh Army Division and the First Marine Division, were, unbeknownst to them, facing as many as 100,000 Chinese troops in their sector of the broader battlefield—and were thus outnumbered severalfold.[63]

Army forces that were initially positioned on the eastern side of the Chosin Reservoir were now far too spread out and outnumbered to resist attack; they were decimated in the ensuing battle. Lieutenant Colonel Donald Faith and the other battalion commander, Colonel Allan MacLean, were both killed in the ensuing overrun of their positions and frantic uncontrolled retreat of their forces, with Faith's forces suffering some 90 percent attrition.[64]

On the west side of the Chosin Reservoir, the First Division of the U.S. Marine Corps was about to pull off one of the most impressive and storied retrograde actions in American military history. It too, like the Seventh, had been attacking northward in previous days; it too was dispersed and vulnerable, though less so than nearby U.S. Army forces. As of November 27, the marines held three main positions: in Yudam-ni to the north, Hagaru to the south (at the base of the reservoir), and Koto-ri, ten miles further below Hagaru. Then the Chinese and North Koreans struck. The marines attempted to use tanks and airpower to compensate for their smaller numbers, but to limited effect given the nature of the terrain.[65] The region was very hilly, with roads that were few in number and so narrow that when individual vehicles were disabled by enemy action or the cold or other factors, a whole column could be bottled up. Resupply and retreat were difficult.[66]

Yet it was retreat that was soon deemed essential—even if the X Corps commander, General Almond, resisted giving Marine commander O. P. Smith orders to do so for a couple days after the attack had begun. An effort to resupply the northern positions, known as Task Force Drysdale, under the command of a British marine by that name, was mostly destroyed in what became evocatively known as Hellfire Valley.[67] It was decided that the parts of the division that had been halfway up the reservoir at Yudam-ni would have to work their way back to the base at Hagaru-ri. The remnants of Army units in "Task Force Faith" joined the marines there. Then the whole group moved further southward to a base at Koto-ri. From there the aggregate forces moved over what was known as the Funchilin Pass—where a blown bridge had to be replaced by air-dropped bridge sections that were assembled on the spot. The marines then continued, via a town named Sudong, on to the port of Hungnam.[68]

As the lore goes, when asked by a reporter if his units were retreating, General Smith replied, "Retreat, *hell!* We're just attacking in a different direction." Given the bravery and intensity of the American fighting, and the tens of thousands of enemy casualties that resulted from the battle, there was some truth to this comment.[69] The marines displayed great tenacity and fighting spirit as well as many sound tactical methods—for example, often deploying infantry on hilltops to cover vehicle columns moving on roads on valley floors, with airpower covering their movements as well.[70]

In the end the marines alone suffered more than 4,000 casualties in battle—and another 7,000-plus from frostbite and other related ailments.[71] But they did great damage to attacking enemy forces, while managing an orderly retreat that preserved most of their equipment. Once the marines reached port, they conducted an orderly and unhurried redeployment southward by ship to Pusan. The facts that the First Marine Division, unlike Army occupation forces from Japan, was near full strength when the war began, that it did not need to depend on Korean fill-ins for its combat units, that it had not experienced quite as sustained hard combat to date as had many Army units, and that it had organic airpower at its direct beck and call, collectively made a big difference. So did good leadership and better use of intelligence about the looming enemy threat.[72]

But the brilliance of the marine operation could not hide the fact that it was, geographically and tactically, a retreat. And back on the western side of the peninsula, after the loss of Pyongyang, U.S., ROK, and Allied forces were consistently routed, ultimately winding up below the 38th parallel in the face of the relentless enemy attacks.

Ridgway, Recovery, the Exit of MacArthur, and Stalemate

On December 23, the commander of the Eighth Army, General Walton Walker, was killed in a traffic accident. MacArthur requested General Matthew Ridgway as Walker's successor. It would prove a fortunate choice, and maybe the best thing that MacArthur did in the months after Inchon. Ridgway brought a toughness and confidence. He also brought to the job an attention to detail, including on simple matters like the acquisition of winter gear for troops. Tactically, he insisted on basic infantry skills and practices—for example, that units get off the roads, gain the high ground, and dig in when appropriate.[73] Commanders who would not do these things, and who did not properly reconnoiter their areas or do their basic tactical homework, he sacked. Ridgway did not lord over enlisted soldiers, but he could be ruthless with other senior officers. In his first three months, he relieved a corps commander, five of six division commanders, and fourteen of nineteen regimental commanders.[74]

Eliot Cohen and John Gooch make a point of underscoring how Ridgway himself viewed the situation, quoting him in this passage:[75]

> What I told field commanders in essence was that their infantry ancestors would roll over in their graves could they see how road-bound this army was, how often it forgot to seize the high ground along its route, how it failed to seek and maintain contact in its front, how little it knew of the terrain and how seldom took advantage of it, how reluctant it was to get off its bloody wheels and put shoe leather to the earth, to get into the hills and among the scrub and meet the enemy where he lived. As for communications, I told them to go back to grandfather's day if they had to—to use runners if the radio and phones were out, or smoke signals if they could devise no better way.

Meanwhile, MacArthur was himself headed more and more deeply into trouble. Increasingly fatalistic about the course of the war, he publicly advocated escalation as an alternative to defeat—specifically in regard to bombing targets inside China, and considering the use of nuclear weapons.

On December 6, with MacArthur on his mind, President Truman had issued a directive to theater commanders to show greater caution in their public statements, and to clear them in advance with the Department of Defense and Department of State. So MacArthur simply went off the record with his assessments, prognostications, complaints, and policy recommendations—but kept up the barrage just the same.[76] Neither Secretary of Defense Marshall, by now a somewhat fatigued and aging hero from another decade, nor anyone else could figure out how to corral him.[77]

Thus, it would be up to Ridgway to challenge the false dichotomy that MacArthur propagated—that the war either needed to be abandoned or dramatically escalated.[78] Although the Chinese and North Korean forces together may have had almost 500,000 troops under their control, the coalition total approached 400,000 and benefited from an enormous advantage in airpower—even as MacArthur was frustrated by not being allowed to attack the hundreds of Chinese aircraft when operating north of the Yalu.

The coalition forces were also by now benefiting from the somewhat easier terrain further south on the peninsula. And China was suffering from hyperextended supply lines, trying to sustain forces south of the 38th parallel, hundreds of miles from their national territory. The challenge was magnified by ongoing coalition air campaigns, which may have reduced train capacity on the peninsula as much as 90 percent. Even the spartan Chinese and North Korean forces needed some supplies, and even their muscular human porters needed some help from road and rail.[79]

Those more southerly regions would not remain in Communist hands for long. Coalition forces began to reclaim smaller cities like Inchon, strengthened their lines, reached the Han River, and then crossed it to liberate Seoul in March. Tactically they had not only improved their general combat readiness, and attention to the high ground and to fortifications, but also created field positions that were defended on all sides so as to deny Chinese and North Korean forces options for surprise flank attacks. That gave coalition forces a better opportunity to wait for airpower to soften enemy positions before they were attacked (and to be resupplied by air if they temporarily surrounded). By late March, coalition troops reached the 38th parallel.[80]

Meanwhile, MacArthur's dispute with Truman was intensifying further. The former saw the war in Korea as the chief focal point of the global struggle against communism and favored escalation not only to win the Korean war but to weaken the Chinese government more systematically. Truman along with his top advisers, including Secretary of Defense Marshall and Secretary of State Acheson, favored limiting America's commitments and obligations in Korea and pursuing a peace process that more or less sought to restore the prewar boundary between the two Koreas. They wished to avoid increased expenditure of scarce military resources or increased risks of escalation. They were more focused on Europe, and the threat of the Soviet Union, than on Korea and China. As the chairman of the Joint Chiefs, General Omar Bradley, famously put it, extending or expanding the Korean conflict would be "the wrong war, at the wrong place, at the wrong time, and with the wrong enemy." These disagreements played into a domestic political context where McCarthyism was strong and Truman rather weak. On April 11, MacArthur was fired, replaced in Tokyo by his erstwhile subordinate, Matthew Ridgway, who was himself replaced at Eighth Army by General James Van Fleet.[81]

The Korean War was now headed for military stalemate. But first, it would witness one more season of intense fighting, before it was clear that battle lines would largely solidify. Pushed back above the 38th parallel, Chinese and North Korean forces developed a plan to try to reverse their losses and regain Seoul. That battle opened on April 22, 1951, near the "Kansas Line" as it was called. The First Marine Division, and then further west the British Twenty-ninth brigade (including a Belgian battalion), were heavily engaged. The latter fought along the Imjin River, some 30 miles north of Seoul; British forces took heavy casualties but stymied the Chinese advance. One of the Brits' famous regiments, from Gloucestershire, defended what became known as "Gloster Hill."[82] (Other countries have their important stories from specific battles in Korea, too, like the Turkish brigade's role in the November 1950 battle at Kunu-ri.[83])

In mid-May, enemy forces launched a major attack, this time with twenty-one Chinese and nine North Korean divisions. Again they achieved some success against South Korean forces but no overall breakthroughs. By June, Van Fleet directed coalition forces to pursue some tactical gains to shorten and strengthen his lines. By this point, under Ridgway's command, coalition forces had developed a concept of attrition warfare that sought to maximize enemy losses, minimize coalition losses, and not worry so much about territorial gains.[84]

In July 1951 peace talks began and fighting diminished. By late August, however, it became clear that the peace talks would not reach a rapid conclusion. Fighting again intensified, for example near the Hwachon Reservoir that provided water and electricity for Seoul. Battles along Heartbreak Ridge and Bloody Ridge, as they would become known, ensued in the following weeks until the region and reservoir were secured by the U.S. Second Division in mid-October.

Peace talks began again. During the negotiations, Communist forces began digging in. By the end of the year a solid line of fortifications stretched across the entire peninsula. That new demarcation line would not change appreciably for the remainder of the war.[85]

There was plenty of combat in the war's last two years. But the engagements were largely tactical and localized, involving limited maneuver and pursuing only limited territorial stakes. Entrenchments and fortifications resembled the western front of World War I. Some tough fights occurred—with storied names like the battle for Pork Chop, or the battle for "the Hook," or fights to hold onto hills named Carson, Vegas, and Reno.

Over this period Ridgway went to Europe to succeed Eisenhower at NATO, General Mark Clark replacing him in Tokyo. A change of command also took place in Korea. But it was not entirely happy. After General Van Fleet handed Eighth Army reins to General Maxwell Taylor in February 1953, he expressed frustration at just how much his hands had been tied, and his objectives limited, during his command.[86] Van Fleet, like other commanders, had struggled to maintain good fighting spirit and tactical proficiency within an army that was understrength in many ways, dependent on the Korean Augmentation to the U.S. Army (KATUSA) program to fill out its ranks, prohibited from launching large offensive operations—and otherwise the victim of what had become a "forgotten war" for America in a distant and strategically secondary theater.[87] But at least the battle lines held; Seoul was not lost a third time.

Eisenhower himself wound up as president of the United States. Once elected in November 1952, but before inauguration, he made a secret trip to Korea to tour the battlefield and size up the situation. After taking office, his administration then used a combination of threats, including the purported willingness to use nuclear weapons, to secure a cease-fire. (America's nuclear arsenal had grown from 300 to 1,000 bombs over the course of the three years of combat, and now also included more easily deliverable tactical weapons.)[88] Stalin had died on March 5 as well, though it is not clear how important that development was to the war's outcome, as China's role was more central by far.

Thus, under Eisenhower at least, MacArthur wound up having more support for his proposed policy of escalation than many tend to remember. Like Eisenhower, the U.S. Joint Chiefs were also supportive of the idea of using nuclear weapons if an armistice could not be secured.[89]

Communist forces largely conceded on the issue of whether prisoners of war had to be returned to their country of origin. The cease-fire line was established largely along the 38th parallel, with only small net benefit to ROK/U.S./UN forces relative to the prewar dividing line between the two Koreas. The cease-fire was formalized on July 27, 1953.[90] Seven decades later, despite several brutal incidents and major scares along the way, it remains in effect—even as a formal peace remains elusive.

War in Vietnam

The Korean War was a major blow to American confidence, and a clear demonstration that the world had descended into a dangerous Cold War than was anything but cold in East Asia.

The Vietnam War was much worse than Korea. Vietnam was an outright defeat for the United States. Moreover, if Korea was a blow to America's confidence, Vietnam was a frontal assault against America's very cohesion as a nation, as well as the spirit and sense of purpose of its armed forces.[91] The tumult and turmoil that emerged in the 1960s, largely because of Vietnam, tore at the fabric of the country over a longer period and in deeper ways than even Joseph McCarthy's red-scare witch hunts of the early 1950s. The experience haunted American foreign policy elites and leaders for decades thereafter.[92] And there would be no Eisenhower to emerge as a unifying national figure to end the war and restore the nation's sense of self—indeed, on Vietnam, Eisenhower was himself part of the problem, counseling Presidents John F. Kennedy and Lyndon Johnson to double down on the war effort lest dominoes fall to Communist aggression in Southeast Asia and beyond.

The war was enormously violent and deadly, with some 58,000 American fatalities. Some 300,000 Americans were wounded. Vietnamese losses on both sides were astronomical, perhaps exceeding 3 million.[93] Thousands of South Koreans, hundreds of Australians and New Zealanders and Thais, and many thousands of Laotians and Cambodians died in the war too.[94] The genocidal Khmer Rouge came to power in Cambodia in the aftermath of what the Vietnam War had done to destabilize that ill-fated nation. As another material indicator of the severity of the fighting, some 9,000 U.S. airplanes and helicopters were lost over the full span of the Vietnam war.[95]

Despite improved military performance under General Creighton Abrams in the war's second half, from 1968 onward there would also be no dramatic military leader like Ridgway to rescue the situation for the United States. In broader grand strategic terms, the disaster was ultimately mitigated over ensuing decades as a gradually reforming Vietnamese government saw America as a potential friend and partner. The Cold War itself was ultimately concluded in a successful manner, without too many more "dominoes" falling along the way. But in military terms, the mission was a failure, and the war was a defeat for the United States, its South Vietnamese partners, and the coalition partners who supported them.

Speaking of Ridgway, once back from Korea and in the role of army chief of staff, he had warned against intervention in Vietnam to help salvage the French position there in 1954, estimating that to do so would require seven American divisions—or twelve divisions if China intervened directly in Vietnam as it had in Korea. He and the other American Joint Chiefs stated at that time that "Indochina is devoid of decisive military objectives."[96] Truer words have rarely been spoken. Yet they would be forgotten a decade later, by both military and civilian leaders.

Robert Mason, an American helicopter pilot in Vietnam, wrote in his memoirs the following poignant lines about how he and many other GIs looked at the war they were asked to wage:[97]

> I knew nothing of Vietnam or its history. I did not know that the French had taken Vietnam, after twenty years of trying, in 1887. I did not know that our country had once supported Ho Chi Minh against the Japanese during the Second World War. I did not know that after the war the country that thought it was finally free of colonialism was handed back to the French by occupying British forces with the consent of the Americans. I did not know that Ho Chi Minh then began fighting to drive the French out again, an effort that lasted from 1946 until the fall of the French at Dien Bien Phu, in 1954. I did not know that free elections scheduled by the Geneva Conference for 1956 were blocked because it was known that Ho Chi Minh would win. I did not know that our government backed an oppressive and corrupt leader, Ngo Dinh Diem, and later participated in his overthrow and his death, in 1963.

The nature of the fighting in Vietnam was different than in almost every other war considered in this book. It did not center on major movements of large armies. Its main events and chief turning points did not generally involve the conquest of territory—until the very end. It was guerrilla war, diffused in time and space, even if many of the guerrillas were in fact North Vietnamese soldiers rather than fighters indigenous to South Vietnam. Yes, there were important efforts and events centered on geography: the 1968 Tet offensive's focus on many large South Vietnamese cities, U.S. efforts to create a barrier of sorts along the 17th parallel dividing the two Vietnams, American bombing campaigns in different parts of North Vietnam and ultimately in Cambodia as well, North Vietnam's major assault across the demilitarized zone (DMZ) in March 1972, South Vietnamese army forces forays into Cambodia and Laos. But the story's chapters were for the most part not about maneuver warfare.

Ho Chi Minh, General Vo Nguyen Giap, Le Duan, Le Duc Tho, and fellow insurgent fighters who ultimately became the leaders of North Vietnam and then of all of Vietnam, were extremely dedicated to their cause. They were not only brutal, but smart and tough. They were also often well educated, and some were quite admiring of French culture (if not French colonialism). They believed that the values of freedom and democracy championed by France, and the United States, should have applied to their people as well.[98] Ho's commitment to the cause went all the way back to the Versailles conference at the end of World War I, when he sought (unsuccessfully) a hearing with President Woodrow Wilson to champion Vietnam's claim to self-determination.[99] With such powerful motivations propelling them, they fought Japanese occupation and French colonialism and America's armed forces, as well as their own South Vietnamese brethren, over three decades on the way toward realizing their dream of a unified, independent Vietnam run by a government they led.[100]

The approach of Ho, Giap, and their colleagues does *not* fit my overall observation that most major wars erupt when their instigators develop overconfidence about the prospects for quick and decisive success. Quite the contrary in this case. The Vietminh, later known as the Vietcong, were prepared to do whatever it took for as long as necessary, including the patient form of warfare known as insurgency that avoids pitched battle against a stronger opponent and, in effect, plays for time.[101] Exacting more than 100,000 French casualties, they ultimately drove out the colonial power, first from North Vietnam and then out of Indochina entirely. Even though it was an insurgency, there were times that the Vietcong massed forces, not least of course when they seized the country in 1975. But that was not the first time. Their key battle against the French was a decisive victory in a well-prepared, artillery-backed siege that lasted almost two months in the spring of 1954, at Dien Bien Phu in the mountains of northern Vietnam. Then followed the Geneva Accords that same year, effectively dividing the country in two along the 17th parallel with the expectation of elections to create a government to reunify the country.

But there would be no elections—due to a decision by South Vietnam, backed by its American friends. The government in the south, including the former emperor, Bao Dai, and his choice for prime minister, Ngo Dinh Diem, nixed the terms of the agreement. Then, in fraudulent elections that were organized by his brother Ngo Dinh Nhu (who would be assassinated along with Diem in 1963), Diem cemented his own hold on power, push-ing Bao Dai aside.[102] After observing this turn of events, the Vietminh re-sumed the fight, from 1957 onward, this time against fellow Vietnamese. To their mind, Diem's regime was an American-supported "puppet" that was keeping the nation divided in two while collaborating with the new foreign enemy. By 1958, Ho and company had created new command structures for the Mekong Delta in the south; by 1959 they had created "Group 559" to infiltrate weapons and people over the Ho Chi Minh Trail into South Vietnam; in 1960 they formed the National Liberation Front for South Vietnam, quickly dubbed the "Vietcong" by Saigon.[103] It was about this time that the United States began to realize it had a major prob-lem on its hands.

The Weapons of War and Strategies of the Protagonists

The infantry arms of the Vietnam War were automatic weapons with high rates of fire. The Vietcong and North Vietnamese, armed by China and the Soviet Union, had seemingly limitless supplies of small arms as well as mortars and other guns. They also made booby traps and improvised ex-plosive devices out of dud American munitions. Over time, they developed impressive air defenses within North Vietnam and along the Ho Chi Minh trail as well. They also obtained a great deal of weaponry from South Viet-namese soldiers that they either defeated or convinced to flee in battle.

The United States also had much better intercontinental real-time communications, for better or worse, in Vietnam. As a result, this was a faraway war that was at times literally waged from the White House in Washington, notably in President Johnson's edicts on proper choices for bombing targets. Television brought the war home to American living rooms as well—the first time that had been the case—though not with quite the high-resolution real-time coverage that CNN and others would provide during Operation Desert Storm in 1991.

Air power advanced further in this war, as did counter-air technolo-gies, tactics, and operations. Long-range bombers and helicopters played huge roles. The war also witnessed considerable dogfighting, including with missiles and guns. The combatants employed better jammers, better decoys and chaff to protect aircraft, radar-guided antiaircraft artillery by North Vietnam, and the deployment of radar-guided missile batteries like the SA-2. There was also ongoing evolution in aircraft performance par-ameters and tactics as new planes were introduced by both sides. In the course of the war the United States also developed early versions of precision-guided munitions to drop from its aircraft, including the so-called Walleye glide bomb.

While always the weaker party in the air, North Vietnam inflicted considerable pain and considerable attrition on the United States. Even in dog-fighting, North Vietnam was outmatched but not overwhelmingly so, often shooting down one U.S. plane for every two or three it lost from its own military at various points in the war.

The United States flew hundreds of thousands of sorties and dropped hundreds of thousands of tons of bombs, notably in the Operation Rolling Thunder period of 1965–1968 and then in the Linebacker campaigns against North Vietnam in 1972, the first from May 10 until October 23 and the second from December 18 through December 29.[104]

The United States also developed and increasingly deployed night-vision technology, though there were downsides to these early-generation devices that limited their overall utility. Thus, it is hard to say that in Vietnam the United States "owned the night" the way it would, for example, in the invasion of Panama in 1989 or Operation Desert Storm in 1991.[105] In the Vietnam War it is more accurate to give credit for owning the night to the Vietcong.

Of course, in the Vietnam War the United States had a large number of nuclear weapons, just as in the (latter phases, at least) in Korea. Like in Korea, despite the occasional threat, it never came truly close to using them. In fact, the veiled threats made by President Richard Nixon during the Vietnam War were probably less credible and less meaningful than those issued by Eisenhower in regard to Korea in 1953.[106]

As for the objectives of the various protagonists, the main American goal in the war was to support a South Vietnamese government that could resist guerrilla infiltration and North Vietnamese attack. South Vietnam was increasingly seen as a pillar in the global struggle against communism, and Ho was seen in Washington as a Communist more than a nationalist. A key secondary goal was to strengthen the South Vietnamese government so that it could assume more of the burden for the fight itself. But, at first, the United States assumed it could win the war largely with its own troops.

The main Vietminh/Vietcong and North Vietnamese goals were to undermine that South Vietnamese government and reunify the Vietnamese people as a single polity under their own Communist rule. Although there were some long-standing tensions and divisions between north and south that predated, by decades and centuries, the partition of the country in

Geneva in 1954, that partition was supposed to be temporary from the start. The overall sense of Vietnamese nationalism was strong enough that many (beyond just the Vietminh) did believe reunification to be the correct objective. As such, the South Vietnamese government, led from 1954 to 1963 by the strong-armed and corrupt regime of Ngo Dinh Diem (briefly as prime minister, then as president), was seen by many and certainly by Hanoi as illegitimate since he refused to accept the 1954 UN plan for re-unification of the country.[107]

China, the Soviet Union, and the United States as well all kept wary eyes on each other. Each looked for a win for its overall regional and global causes in Vietnam, to be sure. But all tempered their levels of effort so as to avoid the worst-case scenario of direct combat against each other. That said, during much of the 1960s, China was the more ardent revolutionary power, with a greater emphasis on supporting armed insurgency and pursuing outright victory in places like Vietnam, whereas the Soviet Union at least in relative terms moved into its support for détente and peaceful coexistence (of sorts). This divergence in the Communist bloc had implications for the advice and support each large power gave to the Vietnamese.[108]

The "Advisory Years" of the Early 1960s

The United States began to provide assistance and military training for the Saigon government in Vietnam as soon as 1955. Over the next six years it would give more than a billion dollars in aid.[109]

Vietminh/Vietcong activities in South Vietnam intensified as the late 1950s unfolded. There were thousands of assassinations of local officials, movements of many thousands of trained insurgents from North Vietnam into various positions in the South, and other classic tactics of "phase 2" Maoist insurgencies. Under the guidance of Hanoi, the Vietcong established their command structures, supply lines, and organizing concepts.[110]

Still, when Dwight Eisenhower left office in early 1961, he was ironically more worried about Laos than Vietnam, and he told Kennedy, the young president-elect, to focus considerable energies there. Once in office himself, President Kennedy had a few other things on his mind in the national security domain, not least the Bay of Pigs in Cuba and then the Berlin Crisis of 1961. As Attorney General Robert Kennedy revealingly unloaded, when speaking to journalist and historian Stanley Karnow, "We've got 20 Vietnams a day to handle." Attitudes like that, as well as

President Kennedy's own views that Latin America and Europe mattered more strategically, counseled a minimalist approach to the snowballing insurgency that was unfolding in Indochina. Yet fear of Soviet power and the worldwide Communist threat were palpable throughout the nation, and Indochina increasingly became the key focal point. Kennedy was hardly immune from such fears, having earlier warned when in the Senate that Vietnam was not just "a proving ground for democracy [but a] test of American responsibility and determination."[111]

Where would these contradictory instincts lead the Kennedy administration, as it sought a more effective way to bolster a flailing Diem regime?

Incrementalism was the answer. After a 1961 trip to Vietnam conducted at President Kennedy's request, retired General Maxwell Taylor proposed sending 8,000 American combat troops to Vietnam. Secretary of Defense Robert McNamara and the Joint Chiefs doubled down, recommending 200,000 U.S. troops! Instead, Kennedy expanded the advisory mission, which had numbered some 3,000 Americans in early 1961 and would grow to 16,000 by the end of Kennedy's life in 1963. No ground combat troops were sent during Kennedy's presidency—but some of those "advisers" were in fact American pilots who would conduct bombing raids.

Aid levels from the United States to South Vietnam reached $500 million annually by 1962. More sophisticated equipment, including helicopters, was sent to the South Vietnamese government. From that year onward, the advisers were organized and directed under a formal American Military Assistance Command for Vietnam (MACV).

Meanwhile, a dubious "strategic hamlet" program was hatched. It sought to relocate many South Vietnamese peasants within protected communities where they could be separated and protected from the insidious insurgents. But the suddenness and abruptness with which it was implemented caused more resentment than reassurance among the South Vietnamese civilian populations. The momentum of the struggle continued to favor the Vietminh. As a result of these early frustrations with "pacification" strategies, the idea of protecting enclaves rather than pursuing the enemy was further discredited in the eyes of a U.S. military that was already predisposed to prefer firepower-heavy offensive approaches to war.[112]

A large battle at Ap Bac in South Vietnam on January 2, 1963, famously chronicled by Neil Sheehan in his remarkable book, *A Bright Shining Lie*, underscored the dilemma. Several hundred Vietcong had been located in a place where they could be surrounded and attacked by vehicle and helicopter. Elements of a South Vietnamese division with at least four times the personnel prepared their assault, as the Vietcong dug in. The insurgents were disciplined and patient and used terrain well to improve their tactical position. By contrast, South Vietnamese soldiers, hoping their U.S.-supplied firepower and advisers would carry the day for them, fought abysmally and were defeated, at the price of several downed helicopters, numerous destroyed vehicles, and nearly 200 casualties. Three Americans were killed and another eight wounded.[113]

Generalizing beyond Ap Bac, Stanley Karnow explained the changing combat dynamics that resulted from the large-scale provisioning of American helicopters to South Vietnamese forces with the following passage from his classic history of the war:[114]

> The heliborne deployments initially lacerated the Vietcong, whose remote sanctuaries could now be penetrated, but the guerrillas gradually adapted to the new challenge. They dug trenches and tunnels as shelters against helicopter raids, and they methodically practiced assaults against full-scale mock-ups of choppers constructed in jungle clearings. They also acquired more sophisticated weapons, either infiltrated from North Vietnam or by ambushing South Vietnamese units. Soon they were able to mortar helicopters on the ground or pepper them aloft with automatic fire.

Thus, as the Kennedy years unfolded, Vietnam kept getting worse. American concepts for how to fight better did not work. Forebodingly, a war game carried out at the Pentagon predicted that even if more than half a million U.S. troops were introduced into the battle and airpower used against logistics lines, as would ultimately happen, Vietcong could get enough people and supplies south to keep gaining territory for years. But despite the prescience of this war game, known as Sigma I, its parameters were open to debate—as with any wargame—and most chose not to heed its warnings. A year later, a Sigma II war game, with altered assumptions and more lenient parameters, produced more reassuring—if ultimately less accurate—results.[115]

Meanwhile, America's obsession with Vietnam, and its supposed importance regionally and globally, was not diminishing. That fact made defeat an increasingly unthinkable outcome in the minds of the country's "best and the brightest"—even as victory or even stalemate seemed increasingly unobtainable.[116] South Vietnam's government was increasingly autocratic, and its leaders worried as much about their own perks and their internal competitions with each other as the enemy. That enemy was formidable. It consisted of an indigenous southern resistance actively aided and abetted by supplies and some fighters from North Vietnam, the latter provisioned by China and the Soviet Union.

As 1963 unfolded, all of these elements would together produce a re-markable turn of events: an American-inspired coup d'état within South Vietnam that almost certainly did more harm than good. Having watched President Diem alienate his citizens through increasingly strongman and capricious rule, employ cronyism in his assignment and deployment of military leaders, and otherwise fail to create a military that could keep the Vietminh at bay, American leaders in Saigon and Washington began to think the unthinkable. Perhaps Diem should go—not in the next elec-tion, which was too far in the future to save the day, and which he would surely manipulate in any case, but through a coup. Ideally it would be bloodless and seamless, led by a junta of self-anointed reformist generals who would be seen as improving the quality and legitimacy of the nation's rule. Such is often the hope when coups are hatched. But, as in many other cases, it would prove to be a false hope in the case of Vietnam. As Stanley Karnow pithily wrote of the aftermath, "Inefficient as Diem had been, his successors were worse."[117] And America's culpability in the overthrow and, ultimately if inadvertently, the death of a foreign leader stained its reputation for years to come.

The path to the coup began early that year when the government of the devoutly Catholic Diem refused to give fair treatment to Buddhists. An official in the city of Hue impeded local Buddhists from celebrating the birthday of Buddha in May. Subsequent demonstrations turned vio-lent when police opened fire. Several civilians died. The government botched the response, refusing to conduct independent investigations of the incident or otherwise make amends. Then, in June, a Buddhist monk carried out what would be the first of a number of self-immolations in protest. Not only the Vietminh, but now important parts of the South Viet-namese population were showing just how passionate was their opposi-tion to the Diem government.[118]

As the country began to crumble politically, the U.S. ambassador to Vietnam, Henry Cabot Lodge, began to favor a coup in Saigon and took steps to gain blessing in Washington while planting the idea within ruling ranks in South Vietnam. Americans apparently did not do any of the plot-ting, and certainly did not encourage the killing of President Diem and his brother on November 2, a day after the coup had begun. But few believe that the coup would have happened absent American instigation. Responsibility clearly went all the way up to President Kennedy himself, who know of the idea in advance and took no steps to thwart it.[119]

Three weeks later, Kennedy would himself be dead from an assassin's bullet. And with his demise would also go what some have considered the last best hope to extricate the United States from a losing cause before the damage got too great: the possibility that a President Kennedy who had already faced down his Joint Chiefs of Staff over the Cuban Missile Crisis and been vindicated might, perhaps after being reelected in late 1964, have decided to accept defeat in Vietnam rather than escalation and war.

Then again, maybe not. As Leslie Gelb and Richard Betts argued in their landmark book on the subject, "the system worked" in Vietnam because it kept producing new (if unpromising) ways to pursue an anti-Communist agenda in the Indochina theater, given that almost all policymakers strongly supported that objective. Kennedy may have been part of such thinking himself; it is difficult to know for sure. President Johnson wanted to avoid the political fallout of losing the war, but also did not want to squander resources and attention for his Great Society domestic agenda, so he chose an escalating series of half measures to satisfy military, Republican, and other critics. Gelb and Betts's argument may be slightly overdone, but still captures an important reality. The foreign policy itself failed, to be sure, but the way decisions were made reflected the underlying consensus of the times.[120] Even Eisenhower, in his retirement, counseled President Johnson in 1965 that "We have got to win."[121] At one meeting, he even expressed a willingness to send eight U.S. divisions if need be—and to employ nuclear threats against China and the Soviet Union should they show any inclination to intervene in the war in the way the Chinese had done in Korea.[122] Ike had also used the specter of falling dominoes four years earlier when counseling President Kennedy to be resolute on Vietnam.[123]

In any event, with Johnson now as president in the United States and a junta ruling South Vietnam, the situation continued to worsen. On a fact-finding trip to the region early in 1964, Robert McNamara and Maxwell Taylor found most trends headed in the wrong direction and reported that at least 40 percent of the countryside was under Vietcong control. We now know that, in addition to weaponry, North Vietnamese regulars were traversing an improved Ho Chi Minh Trail through Laos and Cambodia into South Vietnam to the tune of some 10,000 troops in 1964.

That was far less than in subsequent years, when totals may have reached 150,000 annually, but was nonetheless substantial. The junta in Saigon would shuffle and reshuffle itself some seven times in 1964, though often with many of the same names remaining, just in different positions. General Duong Van Minh led it at first, until he was ousted by General Nguyen Khanh. The overall impression was of a government of drift, irresoluteness, and incompetence.[124]

Johnson changed the American ambassador and top military adviser to Vietnam in 1964, replacing Lodge with retired General Maxwell Taylor, and General Paul Harkins with General William "Westy" Westmoreland. Even more consequentially, Johnson approved plans that would start to develop options for striking North Vietnam directly, whether with South Vietnamese ground forces, American airpower, or other capabilities.

As North Vietnam, anticipating such escalation itself, began to buttress its air and coastal defenses with equipment provided by Beijing and Moscow, the United States and South Vietnam sought to track these developments and gain battlefield intelligence. It was this dynamic that produced the showdown in the Gulf of Tonkin in early August 1964. American ships, sailing inside the 12-mile territorial water limits of North Vietnam, wound up in an engagement with North Vietnamese vessels. No American casualties resulted, though the North Vietnamese did suffer some losses. Still, seeking to force the issue, the United States sent vessels back into the same waters the next day. What happened next remains a mystery. A combination of meteorological conditions, complex patterns of boat traffic, and tense American sailors created a "fog of war" that misled the United States into thinking its ships had been fired upon—when in fact they probably had not been. No matter. The sequence of events led to Congress's Gulf of Tonkin Resolution on August 7, while the facts of what had happened were still fuzzy (as they would remain for years). The resolution authorized assertive self-defense measures in such situations. Sadly, it was the only broad authorization measure for Vietnam ever considered by Congress throughout the long conflict.[125]

Johnson, Westmoreland, and War, 1965 through 1968

Although there had been some limited shooting involving American personnel, ships, and aircraft in the Vietnam conflict through 1964, it would be hard to describe as major combat operations. President Johnson in fact had placed severe restrictions on the use of American airpower even after the Gulf of Tonkin incidents.

But the year 1965 would be very different. Vietcong forces attacked American installations at Pleiku in the central highlands of South Vietnam on February 7 of that year. President Johnson then authorized a short bombing reprisal known as Flaming Dart. Operation Rolling Thunder, a sustained bombing campaign of North Vietnam by the United States that would last three years, began on February 24.

A new South Vietnamese government formed on February 18, under Phan Huy Quat, pushing General Khanh out of the country. This new regime would last until being itself replaced in June by a military junta led by Air Vice Marshal Nguyen Cao Ky.

Fatefully, two battalions of American marines, a couple thousand personnel in all, came ashore on March 8. Their immediate mission was to help defend Danang airfield from the Vietcong. That was how it started, in terms of American ground combat troops. Things would take off fast from there. As Secretary of Defense McNamara later put it, referring to things as they seemed around June of that year, "a growing realization of bombing's ineffectiveness intensified the pressure to expand the ground war."[126]

By December, U.S. troops in South Vietnam would total 200,000. A year later, it would be 400,000. A year later still, the figure was 500,000. At the end of 1968, there would be some 540,000 Americans in uniform in the Republic of Vietnam.[127] There might have been 600,000 or more if Westmoreland had had his way, but by that point civilian leadership had soured on the pattern of reinforcing failure with more and more U.S. troops.[128] Meanwhile, U.S. estimates for the total size of enemy forces in South Vietnam in 1967–1968 ranged from 280,000 to 500,000.[129] The South Vietnamese government fielded hundreds of thousands of troops, but most were of mediocre quality and commitment. Their field leadership was also poor.

Although Vietnam like Korea was largely an infantry fight on the ground, the nature of the war was much different. The Korean War was one of major campaigns, with a series of battles linked in chronological and geographical logic in pursuit of territorial conquest. In Vietnam, by contrast, front lines were generally elusive except at the 17th parallel.

Westmoreland's requests for more and more troops were not to create the potential for great maneuvers or invasions but to defeat the seemingly omnipresent enemy within South Vietnam proper. That said, there were specific and sequential purposes to which the huge numbers would be put—defending coastal regions where most of the population lived, then establishing forces further up country to interdict supply lines, and all the while trying to create what were seen as the necessary force ratios to devastate the Vietcong.

As infiltration of North Vietnamese personnel into South Vietnam grew dramatically over the course of the war, and algorithms for sizing necessary U.S. forces were based largely on the estimated size of the enemy, the corresponding American troop "requirements" continued to grow. Since some classic algorithms assumed that at least ten counterinsurgents were needed per individual insurgent, a modest increase in the estimated size of the enemy, however imprecise, could be used to justify a tenfold-larger increase in combined U.S./South Vietnamese forces.[130] Such was the funny math upon which force sizing decisions were largely made. By contrast, modern U.S. counterinsurgency doctrine bases the size of necessary counterinsurgent forces primarily on the size of the civilian population to be protected.[131]

Rather than reassess, the U.S. military and civilian leaders largely either changed their assumptions, or adopted a policy of incrementalism and hoped for the best. Communications channels within the government were often poor, or deliberately muddled by top officials who did not relish a fulsome debate about ends, ways, and means in the Vietnam War. Skeptics about American involvement in the war, like Undersecretary of State George Ball (effectively the deputy to Secretary of State Dean Rusk), Assistant Secretary of State William Bundy, and Vice President Hubert Humphrey were increasingly marginalized in the internal Johnson administration debate. Congressional skeptics like Senate Majority Leader Mike Mansfield, Senate Foreign Relations Committee Chairman William Fulbright, Senator George McGovern of Minnesota, and Senator Frank Church of Idaho fared no better in changing Johnson's mind.[132] Partisan politics and electoral considerations were never far from the minds of those in the White House who worried that perceptions of a losing war effort, or a dramatic need for more troops, or higher taxes to pay for the war, could seriously hurt Johnson.[133]

Asserting that the enemy was moving into "phase 3" of a classic Maoist guerrilla war, which resembles traditional force-on-force combat more than the hit-and-run tactics of "phase 2," American leaders claimed that a 3:1 ratio of friendly forces over the enemy might suffice. But however it was computed, and however much extra edge was imputed to U.S. forces due to technological advantages, even that ratio was hard to achieve. Even if achieved, moreover, it would not compensate for bad tactics. It was a rule of thumb, after all, not a law of physics.[134]

Meanwhile, another assumption on which the attrition-based strategy was based—that Vietcong manpower reserves were not adequate to replace more than some 60,000 casualties a year—was proving incorrect. The artillery officer Westmoreland stuck doggedly to the notion that there must be a "crossover point," where enemy losses would exceed potential replacements. But such a crossover point proved elusive.[135]

Equally flawed was the notion that limiting flows of supplies along the Ho Chi Minh trail could strangle Vietcong forces in South Vietnam. In fact, the latter only needed some 15 tons of supplies a day to arrive from North Vietnam, given how much of their food and even their weaponry and ammunition they could secure right where they were.[136] The short-lived idea, developed in 1966 and approved by President Johnson in early 1967, of building a "McNamara Line" of electronic fencing, sensors, land mines, and other barriers along the inter-Vietnam border and then through Laos to Thailand was ultimately abandoned as requiring too much effort for whatever benefits it might produce.[137]

While much of the Vietnam War was a series of dozens or hundreds of battles of inconclusive character, there were nonetheless several notable individual events. During the Johnson years, perhaps two stand out: the Battle of Ia Drang in October 1965, and the Tet offensive beginning on January 31, 1968.

The fighting in the Ia Drang Valley in the central interior region of South Vietnam was a harbinger of things to come. It demonstrated just how well the Vietcong could employ terrain, and camouflage, while benefiting from approaching and leaving the battlefield on foot. Though a clear U.S. win by casualty counts, it was foreboding in what it signaled about the toughness and character of the enemy.[138]

But that battle, the subject of the famous book *We Were Soldiers, Once. . . . and Young*, was atypical in its size and scale. At most other times, as one would expect given their guerrilla nature, it was Vietcong forces that controlled the nature and intensity of the fighting, as proper "people's war" insurgency concepts would suggest. They generally operated in smaller units, ambushing individual U.S. soldiers, squads or platoons but then backing off when engaged by a major U.S. formation. Alternatively, they might "hug" U.S. forces by approaching them, to make it harder for the Americans to employ indirect fire.[139]

This elusive quality to Vietcong fighters led many American units to try to compensate with the indiscriminate use of artillery and aerial bombardment. The euphemistic, and callous, phrase "prophylactic firepower" was sometimes invoked to explain the overuse of heavy weapons against enemy forces that might or might not actually be present—and that might or might not be co-located with civilian populations. Andrew Krepinevich notes that except during the period of the Tet offensive, 70 percent of U.S. artillery rounds were fired during periods of light or no contact/combat with the enemy.[140]

As for Tet, it was a remarkable example of tactical defeat nonetheless creating a strategic success in war. Launched on January 31, 1968, and continuing into February, it targeted more than 100 South Vietnamese cities with a combined fighting force of 70,000 to 85,000 Vietcong troops. Tet did not come completely out of the blue; it was preceded during the fall of 1967 by a number of substantial Communist attacks against isolated American positions in the central highlands and along the borders with Laos and Cambodia, as well as a siege at Khe Sanh shortly before Tet. (They may have been designed as feints to take the American focus off the cities, the real and subsequent target during Tet.[141]) But to an American public that had been led to believe the war was going passably well, perhaps even being won, it came as a huge shock nonetheless, and a political turning point.

Vietcong losses were huge. As many as half the insurgents carrying out the attacks may have died, in contrast to about 1,000 American and 2,000 South Vietnamese fatalities. Yet the Vietcong demonstrated their geographic reach, their ability to marshal forces throughout the heartland including the cities of South Vietnam, and their mind-boggling if almost suicidal courage. They even managed to threaten the U.S. embassy in Saigon before being stymied. Despite the setback, the Vietcong proved capable of replacing their losses with North Vietnamese troops who moved into the South via the Ho Chi Minh Trail.

Tet was a major factor in President Johnson's decision not to run for reelection. The following summer, General Creighton Abrams would replace Westmoreland, foretelling changes in tactics and strategy (Clark Clifford had replaced McNamara at the Pentagon on March 1, 1968). U.S. troop totals continued to grow somewhat more over the course of 1968, but Johnson was beginning to look for a way out by this point.[142] Shortly after Tet, peace talks between North Vietnam and the United States began in Paris, however unpromising they would prove for several years to come.

Then there was the air war. It had two major components. One part was directed against Vietcong positions, supply lines, and logistics assets in the South, as well as the fields and villages and rice paddies thought to be provisioning the Vietcong.[143] Then there was the campaign against North Vietnam itself. The latter was designed as much for messaging as for direct effect. Massive American aerial attacks on cities were not conducted the way they had been in World War II or even the Korean War. Target sets were authorized in a progressive fashion, apropos the campaign's Rolling Thunder name. The pace of aerial attacks eventually increased roughly fourfold over the 1965–1968 period, from about 25,000 attack sorties in 1965 to 108,000 in 1967, as the annual tonnage of dropped bombs increased from 63,000 to 226,000.[144] Enemy strength and activity over that period grew at least as fast on balance.[145]

Earlier in the period, most bombing targets within North Vietnam were transportation or military assets. As time went on, a wider range of industrial targets was included, too. It was hoped that the enemy could be induced to negotiate, with the goal of pulling its forces out of North Vietnam and accepting partition of the nation, by delivering a certain amount of punishment—and no more. Not only the pain and devastation from what was attacked, but the desire to avoid future attacks, would in theory persuade Ho to accept a deal. A "donut-hole" concept of bombing would spare the cities, most notably the capital Hanoi and the port Haiphong—thereby keeping the "hostage" alive so as to facilitate bargaining.[146] Some Americans, including Air Force Chief General Curtis LeMay, favored a less incrementalist, more intense bombing operation. But they did not win the administration debate—at least not at first.[147]

Regardless, none of it really worked. Despite the gradual escalation of target sets, from transportation and oil assets to industrial facilities and electricity plants, to air defenses and certain military facilities, then to fuel and electricity infrastructure, and despite the occasional bombing pause to improve the atmosphere for negotiations, Hanoi would not agree to abandon its goal of unifying the Vietnamese nation under Communist rule.

Through it all, the South Vietnamese government continued to struggle. This trend continued with the September 1967 election of Nguyen Van Thieu as president and Nguyen Cao Ky as vice president. The former would remain in office for years, but the relative continuity of his rule did not equate to a strengthening of the country he sought to lead. Corruption remained rampant and popular grievances grew.

The weaknesses of the Republic of Vietnam government were doubly troubling because it was that government, and its security forces, that had primary responsibility for what was probably the most important part of the fight. Modern counterinsurgency doctrine emphasizes protecting the indigenous population and gradually enlarging "ink spots" of relative stability and security that can grow and start to merge over time. In Vietnam, this would have meant a major focus on securing the densely populated coastal regions. The task, to the extent it was attempted, was given largely to South Vietnamese forces. They were not up to the job. Counterinsurgency doctrine also argues that popular grievances must be mitigated through some combination of economic opportunity, political voice for a population as well as its various subgroups, and powersharing. Saigon failed by these metrics as well.

In some northern regions of South Vietnam, the U.S. Marine Corps formed Combined Action Platoon teams of about fifteen Marines in an attempt to help. The basic concept was based on previous Marine Corps wartime experiences as captured in the service's famous 1940 *Small Wars Manual*.[148] These CAPs showed the capacity to improve security to a significant degree at roughly half the casualty rate of other U.S. forces.[149] If applied nationwide, this approach could hypothetically have secured most Vietnamese hamlets with fewer than 200,000 American personnel. Even adding in other needed American capabilities, such as quick-reaction forces, the troop requirements for a strategy based around this idea could have been less than the 540,000 troops ultimately deployed to the war.[150] That said, we cannot be sure. The CAP concept was probably not attempted systematically enough to warrant confident assertions about its nationwide potential in Vietnam.[151] General Westmoreland was unwilling to divert American troops to such missions, instead clinging to his stubborn belief that they were more effective in search-and-destroy operations. He was backed up by the chairman of the Joint Chiefs of Staff and the chief of staff of the army in these instincts (the commandant of the Marine Corps, chief of staff of the Air Force, and U.S. ambassador to Vietnam from 1964 to 1965, retired General Maxwell Taylor, disagreed, however).[152]

The American military's focus on brute-strength tactics, attrition warfare, and firepower was deeply ensconced in the military's thinking based on past wars, even if this war was radically different. During the Johnson years, pacification was not systematically or seriously attempted. Instead, the United States used a seriously flawed firepower-centric search-and-destroy concept of operations.

The United States also failed to find a good model for rotating its deployed troops. America's military conscription system tended to prevent
U.S. troops from developing adequate expertise or experience; they generally served 12-month tours before being replaced. As the fabled U.S.
soldier and adviser John Paul Vann put it, looking back on the conflict
shortly before his death in Vietnam in 1972, "The United States has not
been in Vietnam for nine years, but for one year nine times."[153]

Taking all of this in, Secretary of Defense McNamara later wrote about
the flawed assumptions and failed strategy of Vietnam:[154]

> We did not force the Vietcong and North Vietnamese Army to fight
> on our terms. We did not wage an effective antiguerrilla war against
> them. And bombing did not reduce the infiltration of men and sup-
> plies into the South below required levels or weaken the North's
> will to continue the conflict.

By 1968, Johnson had lost a national security adviser, McGeorge Bundy,
and McNamara, his famous secretary of defense, on the Vietnam issue, to
say nothing of his own prospects for reelection. American public support
for the war in Vietnam, which had begun around 65 percent in 1965 before beginning a gradual and inexorable decline, cratered after Tet to less
than 40 percent. It would never recover.[155] Then, Johnson's new secretary
of defense, Clark Clifford, also lost faith in the effort.[156] The political turf
was set for Richard Nixon to win election in part by touting a secret plan
to end the war.

Nixon, Abrams, Geographic Escalation, Disengagement—and Defeat

Richard M. Nixon came to power with, as it turned out, America's combat role in the Vietnam War almost exactly halfway over. About 30,000
American soldiers were already dead. Almost as many would perish even
as Nixon carried out a strategy of "Vietnamization" on the ground, handing more and more of the land fight off to South Vietnamese forces. But
the United States sometimes escalated in the air, including in neighboring
Cambodia, where Prince Norodom Sihanouk gave his tacit blessing to the
effort, before being overthrown in a coup in 1970.[157] The escalatory actions were designed to further the prospects of peace talks with North
Vietnam. Ideally, from Washington's perspective, they would commit the

United States and North Vietnam (including its Vietcong allies) to a mutual withdrawal from South Vietnam.

That was not to be. In the end the United States got prisoner repatriation out of the deal, but not mutual withdrawal. Washington hoped that there would be at least a "decent interval" between its departure and the potential fall of the Saigon government. In the end, just as would prove to be the case nearly half a century later in Afghanistan, the interval would be anything but decent.

As the Nixon administration shifted to its new strategy, the nature of the fighting did not change immediately. For example, in May 1969, U.S. forces fought to take Ap Bia Mountain in northern South Vietnam near the border with Laos in a brutally bloody fight that earned the site the nickname of Hamburger Hill.[158] Tragically, their achievement would last only a month before being reversed, as the mountain was again lost to the enemy.

However, U.S. troops did begin to come home. That achievement was gradual, but lasting. From a peak of 540,000, they were down a bit by the end of 1969 to 480,000. Then the drawdown accelerated. U.S. troop strength in Vietnam stood at 280,000 at the end of 1970, and 140,000 by the end of 1971. After a year of peace talks between Washington and Hanoi in Paris, a peace deal was reached in 1973 that led to the final departure of American troops by the end of March of that year. President Thieu was effectively coerced into accepting it, presented with the alternative that South Vietnam would otherwise lose all American financial and material support, too.[159]

The ground fight was handled differently throughout this period, not only because of Vietnamization and the rapid American troop drawdown but because of the change in command. General Creighton Abrams took a much different view of the situation than had Westmoreland. He rejected earlier tactics that emphasized "search-and-destroy" operations, body counts, and the pursuit of an elusive crossover point at which enemy attrition would exceed its capacity for force regeneration. What had been two largely distinct wars on the ground—the offensive interior missions led mostly by American troops and the enclave protection efforts led mostly by Vietnamese—were merged.

Pacification efforts were transformed. The Civil Operations and Rural Development Support (CORDS) program, started in 1967 under Robert Komer, was taken over by another intelligence officer (and future head of the CIA), William Colby, in late 1968. Abrams and the U.S. ambassador to Vietnam, Ellsworth Bunker, supported it and fostered unity of effort among its disparate agencies. Improved South Vietnamese leadership helped too; Abrams, Colby, and Bunker forged relationships with President Thieu that allowed them to use respectful persuasion to convince the South Vietnamese leader to replace poor security force leaders when appropriate.[160] To the extent one trusts the somewhat subjective statistics, the percentage of villages evaluated as "relatively secure" rose from something in the range of 75 percent to more than 90 percent from roughly 1968 to 1970.[161]

There was also a major offensive into Cambodia, featuring American air power and American as well as South Vietnamese ground troops. Nixon initially undertook the attacks into Cambodia secretly, with a bombing campaign starting in 1969. The aerial attacks went through various phases over the next four years.[162] Nixon also sent U.S. ground troops into Cambodia in 1970. The combined efforts achieved some impressive if fleeting results, in terms of supplies seized and logistics lines interrupted. But spillover from the Vietnam War sadly also caused destructive effects on Cambodia itself that contributed to the widespread outbreak of civil war and rise to power of the genocidal Khmer Rouge by 1975.[163]

By the end of 1970, Congress, angered by the clandestine efforts into another sovereign country, legislated against any further American ground combat beyond South Vietnam's borders. Thus the battle of Lam Son 719 in February and March 1971, a major effort that sought to sever Vietcong supply lines in Laos, could only employ South Vietnamese ground forces (along with lots of American airpower, including helicopter transport). The fighting included not just infantry, but considerable heavy weaponry on both sides. Ultimately, South Vietnamese forces failed in their efforts, suffering substantial losses including more than 100 helicopters destroyed and more than 500 damaged.[164]

During this period, American and South Vietnamese forces created the so-called Phoenix Program to root out Viet Cong leaders and other personnel more effectively within South Vietnam. At one level it was an assassination campaign of sorts, and proved controversial. Yet it attempted to be much more precise than the traditional firepower-heavy approaches to ground combat had been, netting thousands of enemy forces but without killing legions of innocents.[165]

It is not clear that the Vietnam War was becoming winnable. But it certainly was going better on balance in this period. Somewhat wistfully, historian Lewis Sorley entitled one chapter in his impressive book on Vietnam

"Victory." He described late 1970 as perhaps the moment of greatest promise for the U.S. war effort in Vietnam, when the effects of pacification strategies and the Cambodia raids had become evident, and U.S. troop totals were still significant.[166] In 1972, even after major American military downsizing, the Saigon government purportedly "controlled" (at least by day, presumably) some 75 percent of the country's territory, corresponding to regions where 85 percent of its population lived.[167]

North Vietnam tried an "Easter Offensive" in the spring of 1972. However, U.S. air power combined with South Vietnamese ground capabilities fended the North Vietnamese off. Perhaps something similar could have worked again, if the United States had retained the same capabilities in the region thereafter.

Nixon had not authorized major bombing campaigns against North Vietnam in earlier years of his presidency. In 1972, hoping that concentrated and intensive bombardment could create bargaining leverage in Paris, Nixon took the gloves off. The ensuing Operation Linebacker campaigns against targets in North Vietnam were intensive, as were the tactical uses of aircraft against North Vietnamese and Vietcong units in South Vietnam during the Easter Offensive and at other times.[168] Yet their coercive leverage against a battle-toughened North Vietnamese government was still severely limited.

Ho Chi Minh died in 1969. But his fellow leaders—notably Le Duan and Le Duc Tho—retained the grit that had served them so well for a quarter century already. They made mistakes, to be sure, as with the Easter Offensive's attempt to undertake major conventional operations in the presence of still-massive American airpower. But they licked their wounds and regrouped thereafter.[169] Nixon's opening to China, featuring his visit there in early 1972, may have reduced Communist shipments of weaponry to North Vietnam by war's end. But North Vietnam had enough to finish the job, once American forces were no longer part of the equation.[170]

Despite his efforts to cultivate a "madman" image, in the hope that Hanoi would be frightened into concessions and compromise before the American president might do something really crazy like authorizing a nuclear attack, Nixon could not accomplish at the negotiating table what America had failed to do with military power for close to a decade. The terms of peace that emerged in the deal of early 1973 were highly favorable to the Vietcong. They embodied the logic of what Nixon's secretary of state, Henry Kissinger, had advocated as a professor at Harvard before joining the Nixon administration: focusing on the military issues of prisoners of war, a cease-fire, and the U.S. withdrawal, while leaving political matters between the two Vietnams to Hanoi and Saigon thereafter.[171] That may have been an effective way to disengage for the United States, which had larger geostrategic fish to fry—the opening to China, détente and arms control with the Soviet Union, military deterrence in Europe—as it had finally begun to realize by this point in the war. But by removing even the American airpower that had held off (together with South Vietnamese ground troops) the North Vietnamese in the Easter Offensive, it left Saigon with little hope.

The hope would soon dissipate even further. Once Congress cut U.S. dollars to Saigon in half in 1974 and banned any further U.S. military involvement in the war, the house of cards could not stand.[172] By April 1975, Saigon was falling, and Americans were being evacuated by helicopter from the roof of the nation's embassy.

Mistakes Made and Lessons Learned

A number of observations seem reasonable given the difficult history of America's Cold War conflicts in Asia, beginning with Korea:

- Korea showed more vividly than any other experience in American history how quickly a magnificent military can deteriorate, as occurred with the U.S. armed forces from 1945 to 1950.
- Korea also illustrated a type of situation in which weak credibility can lead to deterrence failure. More precisely, the outbreak of the Korean War was not even a case of deterrence failure. Deterrence was not attempted. To the contrary, American leaders went out of their way to declare the peninsula beyond the U.S. security perimeter that they would defend with force if necessary. And it was not any weakness in America's general global credibility that led Moscow and Beijing to bless Pyongyang's aggressive ambitions. Rather, it was specific statements, notably by Secretary of State Dean Acheson, about how little Korea mattered to Washington, that led to war. It turned out that American leaders did not know their own minds very well, because the moment that the attack occurred, they reassessed the importance of Korea to U.S. grand strategy and decided that it needed to be defended.

- The Korean War demonstrated how military advantages for one type of warfare can be much less useful in another type of military geography and another type of combat.
- More specifically, the Korean conflict revealed the limitations of airpower when used against an infantry-heavy and vehicle-light military operating in mountainous and wooded terrain. Some of these limitations persist even today.
- The Korean War also underscored the vulnerability of tanks and other heavy vehicles when operating in terrain where an enemy can approach the vehicles and attack, if not their armor, then their treads and other weak points.
- General Douglas MacArthur, perhaps the most controversial military leader in American history, argued forcefully and wisely for the Inchon landing. But his track record in Korea was otherwise much less impressive.
- Still, not everything was MacArthur's fault. His decision to cross the 38th parallel was probably what brought the Chinese into the war—and the idea of crossing the 38th was widely accepted in Washington in the early fall of 1950. That is more the responsibility of Washington, including President Truman, Secretary of Defense Marshall, and Secretary of State Acheson than of MacArthur.
- Moreover, MacArthur's advocacy of bombing targets in China and threatening the use of nuclear weapons against China was repeated two years later by Eisenhower. Whether that means that Ike was reckless too can be argued, certainly. But at that point, such an approach probably helped secure the cease-fire.
- MacArthur's mistakes, rather, were primarily in the realm of public insubordination to his commander in chief, as he pressed a policy for bombing China in late 1950 and early 1951 that Truman did not want, and in his failure to adapt to clear intelligence by November 1950 that Chinese forces were on the peninsula in substantial numbers. As a result, he left U.S. and coalition troops badly exposed as they sought foolishly to keep moving north when their advances should have been halted and their positions consolidated.
- As for Vietnam, many lessons have been drawn and debated about this colossal failure. The most fundamental is that the United States and allies were facing not just communism but super-

charged nationalism in Vietnam, and one of the most dedicated and competent guerrilla movements in history. Thus, anything smacking of victory would have been extremely hard to achieve, especially given the mediocre quality of America's South Vietnamese allies.

- Another key lesson of Vietnam is that it is easy for policymakers caught up in a crisis or war, pressured by domestic political concerns, and vulnerable to groupthink to exaggerate the strategic importance of a place like Vietnam. It is admittedly also easier to see this with hindsight, given the palpable concerns about the global Communist movement's ambitions during the heart of the Cold War. But Indochina cannot and should not have been viewed as a crucial center of geopolitical significance. As strategist and historian Michael Green convincingly argues, the core U.S. strategic interest in Asia was to prevent a hostile hegemon from dominating the region—but policymakers somehow turned peripheral Vietnam into the central issue of the region.[173]

- There can be no excuse for conducting counterinsurgency operations with such brutal search-and-destroy tactics as were employed by the United States in Vietnam. This *should* have been apparent at the time. But a firepower-oriented American armed forces that had several notable "superhawk" leaders in that period (to quote a young David Petraeus, writing his doctoral dissertation in the 1980s) failed to reach that conclusion, tragically.[174] The country's civilian leadership was to my mind even more at fault on this score, given its ultimate responsibility for policymaking and grand strategy.[175]

- All that said, were there ways to win in Vietnam? A number of authors who have written on Vietnam, including Andrew Krepinevich, Lewis Sorley, and John Nagl, have argued that there were better strategies available. Greater focus on population security, earlier on, as modern counterinsurgency doctrine would tend to advocate, could probably have produced some version of stalemate sooner and at less cost in blood, treasure, and deployed American troop levels.[176]

- The idea of fighting a more conventional war more robustly is on balance less persuasive. Harry Summers advocated a robust and sustained effort to sever the Ho Chi Minh Trail all the way through Laos, for example. The long-standing existence of the

DMZ in Korea suggests that it is possible to construct a fairly impermeable barrier to the movement of people and supplies. But the barrier might have had to be extended, perhaps into Cambodia too, if the North Vietnamese had attempted to outflank any such barrier by moving through Thailand, and it would likely have had to be manned by large numbers of troops just as at the DMZ.[177]

• Any such approach would also have required that a large force continue the interdiction and population security efforts for some time, given the patience and toughness of the Vietcong. Whether the task could have been fully handed off to a capable South Vietnamese military, backed up by legitimate political authority, on any reasonable timeframe is hard to know. It is also hard to know if Nixon's opening to China could have made a significant difference in persuading Beijing to help force North Vietnam to end the war. A better strategy might have required a significant U.S. troop presence for many years. But there is at least a chance it could have worked.

The Korean and Vietnam wars were mind boggling. That the United States and allies could struggle so mightily after achieving such a great military victory in World War II remains a fascinating, and tragic, turn of history. The wars' respective outcomes also underscore the potent battlefield effects of nationalism and ideological fervor, at the political level, combined with the proliferation of small arms, various types of explosives, and other enabling technologies at the military level. Perhaps most remarkable of all is that, for reasons discussed further in the conclusion, the United States and other democracies managed to prevail in the Cold War even as they failed to do so in these two major conflicts, particularly in Vietnam. American grand strategy ultimately succeeded even as military strategies did not.

FIVE   *America's Wars in the Middle*
            East since 1990

*Because this book seeks to provide as objective an account of America's major
wars of the last 162 years as possible, I owe the reader a bit of context. I am
perhaps a less unbiased historian, or at least less removed from this history than
from the conflicts recounted and discussed in earlier chapters. In a nutshell, I
worked at the Congressional Budget Office (CBO) when Senator James Sasser
of Tennessee asked CBO, in late 1990, to predict the budgetary costs of a
possible war to expel Saddam Hussein's Iraqi forces from Kuwait—a conflict
that did in fact occur the following year (and well within the bounds of our cost
estimates—though my bosses were wise enough not to attempt too precise a
prognostication). In the mid-1990s, I moved to the Brookings Institution in
Washington, DC, where I warned that war in Iraq would likely be long and
hard but ultimately did not oppose it, though I was a strong critic of how
unprepared the Bush administration had been for the aftermath of Saddam's
overthrow. Later, I supported the troop surges in Iraq and Afghanistan and
favored keeping a smaller long-term presence in both countries. Thus, I opposed
President Barack Obama's decision to leave Iraq in 2011 and President Joe
Biden's decision to leave Afghanistan in 2021. Throughout much of the last two
decades, though not a Mideast expert by any means, I was a fairly frequent field
researcher (and occasional election observer) in the CENTCOM theater, visiting
the region more than twenty times (most frequently Afghanistan and Iraq, as
well as Pakistan, Qatar, Turkey, and elsewhere). I got some things right and
some wrong over this period, but do hope that I was consistent in always
recognizing the gravity and likely consequences of any decision to use force. I
also hope that I have managed to tell the following history without major bias.*

The United States, along with many partner nations,
has fought three major wars in the broader Middle East since 1990. The
first was Operation Desert Storm in 1991, a huge but relatively short and
circumscribed operation involving more than half a million U.S. troops.

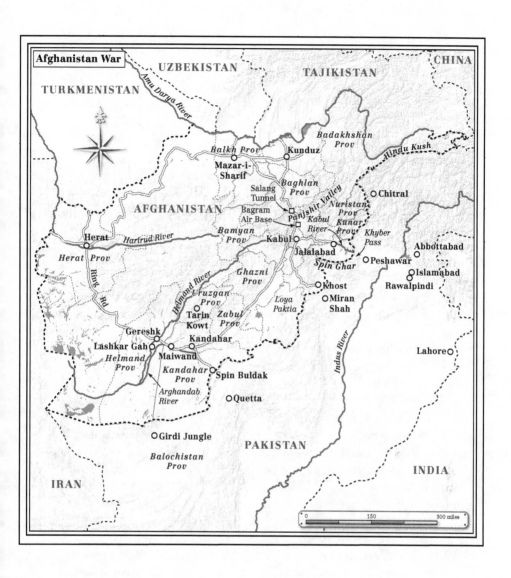

Then came the long wars: Operation Iraqi Freedom, which started in 2003, followed by Operation Inherent Resolve in the same country beginning in 2014; and Operation Enduring Freedom followed by Operation Resolute Support in Afghanistan, from 2001 to 2021. Iraqi Freedom involved as many as 200,000 Americans in uniform; the Afghanistan mission peaked at 100,000 GIs. This chapter attempts to recount their main characteristics and main phases, with an effort to be as pithy as possible given their number as well as their durations.

These conflicts have underscored that war rarely goes as expected. Sometimes, in fact, it goes *better* than first believed—with quick wins accumulating and sometimes causing a fundamental breakdown in an enemy's ability or will to resist. All three of the wars examined here had phases that fit this depiction. Indeed, America's military excellence after the buildup under President Ronald Reagan, and its big breakthroughs in precision-strike weaponry as well as other modern technologies, combined to produce dramatic and positive results in Iraq in 1991, Afghanistan in 2001, and Iraq again in early 2003. But the theme of overconfidence emerges again from these histories. So does the tendency of war to become—rather predictably—tragically difficult.

The decision to carry out Operation Desert Storm was not an obvious choice at the time. Iraqi dictator Saddam Hussein invaded and annexed Kuwait in 1990. That was an outrageous act, to be sure, but Kuwait was not and is not a U.S. treaty ally. Saddam had invaded Iran in 1981, less than two years after a theocratic regime had seized power in Teheran. If nothing else, the Iran-Iraq War diverted Iranian resources that might have otherwise been employed against other Arab countries. At least, that was how Saddam saw it. From his vantage point, a demand that Kuwait adjust borders with Iraq, or share oil and oil wealth, would be reasonable financial compensation for a war that had protected the sheikhdom. When Kuwait refused, he felt entitled to respond with force. In the absence of any U.S. treaty obligations, President George H. W. Bush's decision to reverse the aggression was far from automatic (yes the United States had reflagged oil tankers to protect the export of Kuwaiti oil in 1987–1988 and used force when necessary to do so, but that was a limited maritime operation)[1]. But Bush concluded that such a blatant act of aggression could not stand—especially in those early post–Cold War years, when in Bush's mind a new world order and a global "age of peace" were within reach.

The wars that began in 2001 and 2003 against the Taliban regime in Afghanistan and, again, against Saddam Hussein in Iraq, were different.

Both were initiated soon after the tragic 9/11 attacks, and partly in response to that great tragedy. The Taliban did not perpetrate the 9/11 attacks, but they had invited their ideological kindred spirits, al Qaeda, onto their territory and provided the group sanctuary. Saddam had no role in the 9/11 attacks, either. But his dictatorial and brutal ways, his association with other extremists in the broader Middle East, and his suspected stocks of weapons of mass (WMD) destruction persuaded the Bush administration that he must be required either to disarm verifiably once and for all or lose power. Both the Iraq and Afghanistan decisions had implications that have significantly affected U.S. national security ever since.

In the interest of keeping this chapter finite, I do not address other modern wars of the Middle East in detail—except to the extent I believe those can most usefully inform our understanding of the three big wars at issue. Israel's six-day 1967 war against Arab adversaries foreshadowed the U.S. and Allied use of overwhelming airpower and blitzkrieg-style maneuver warfare in Operation Desert Storm in 1991. The 1973 October War offered a few glimpses into that future operation as well. Israel encountered the kind of irregular resistance to its incursions into Lebanon in the 1980s and beyond that proved to be harbingers of the American and Allied experiences in Iraq and Afghanistan this century. The Soviet Union similarly suffered serious losses and military defeat itself in Afghanistan in the 1980s at the hands of Afghan mujahadeen fighters armed by the United States together with Pakistan.

Outside of the Middle East, the 1982 British-Argentine Falklands/Malvinas War, fought over two modest-sized islands with small populations several hundred miles off the main Argentine coast, demonstrated the lethality of precision-guided munitions against ships, among other things.[2] But I do not otherwise discuss it here. That same lesson was relearned a half decade later in the so-called tanker war in the Persian Gulf in which the United States itself suffered 37 fatalities when a U.S. Navy frigate, the USS *Stark,* was hit by two Iraqi Exocet missiles.[3]

The United States had suffered serious losses from terrorist or irregular forces in Beirut in 1983 and again in Mogadishu, Somalia in 1993. In the first case, American forces came ashore in Beirut in support of an ill-defined peacekeeping mission and became the victims of one of the first mass-casualty truck bombings in history (though the second that year in Lebanon itself). Tragically, 241 marines perished, and the American mission subsequently ended. In the second, American forces in Mogadishu on a humanitarian relief mission were increasingly challenged, in preceding months, by the city's deadly militias. On the night of October 3–4, fighters loyal to the warlord leader Mohammed Farah Aideed used rocket-propelled grenades and small arms to shoot down two U.S. helicopters and kill 18 American soldiers. Again, the United States was unprepared for the viciousness and cleverness of the adversary; again, it responded by withdrawing its forces in following months. There were uncanny similarities between the U.S.-led overthrow of Saddam in 2003 and the U.S./NATO-assisted overthrow of Libyan leader Muammar Qadhafi in 2011. In each case, under two different presidents, the United States was poorly prepared for "the day after." I do not analyze the smaller incidents and conflicts here, but as with the bombing of Khobar Towers in Saudi Arabia in 1996 by Hezbollah, the 1998 bombing of U.S. embassies in East Africa by al Qaeda, and the bombing of the USS *Cole* in Yemen in 2000 by the same, they do help form the historical backdrop and broader context.[4]

Historical Preludes in the Region

Much of what America has experienced tactically in the Middle East since 1990 had precedents and preludes in regional conflicts of earlier decades. Several conflicts stand out in my mind: the 1967 Six-Day War (plus an aside on the 1973 October War), Israel's invasion and occupation of parts of Lebanon at various points starting in the 1980s, the Soviet invasion and occupation of Afghanistan throughout much of the 1980s, and the Iran-Iraq War of that same time period.

The 1967 Six-Day War and the 1973 Yom Kippur War

Although Israel fought a war to defend its existence when it became an independent country in 1948, a more instructive conflict for modern purposes occurred some two decades later. Scholar Ken Pollack described the backdrop to the Arab-Israeli war of 1967 with great pithiness as follows:[5]

> In June of 1967, most of the world thought Israel was a goner. That included most of the population of the State of Israel itself. Another Arab-Israeli war was brewing, and this time it looked like the Jewish state was finished. . . . The Arab coalition threatening Israel had every material advantage. Altogether, the main Arab combatants—Egypt, Jordan, and Syria—would deploy roughly 275,000 men against Israel with about 1,800 tanks, 2,000 armored personnel carriers (APCs), and 1,700 artillery pieces. For its part, the Israel Defense

Forces (IDF) would field about 130,000 troops with roughly 1,000 tanks, 450 APCs, and maybe 500 artillery pieces. In the air, the Israeli Air Force (IAF) had 207 combat aircraft, against 716 Egyptian, Jordanian, Syrian, and Iraqi warplanes.

Pollack argued that Arab equipment was at least as good as that of the Israelis. He further noted that Israel would have to fight on three fronts. It would do so on terrain that was often inhospitable to maneuver warfare and prepared by the Arabs with strong defensive positions (the latter being relevant because, in any conflict, Israel would surely seek to push Arab armies further back from their initial positions, given the clear and present danger they posed to the state of Israel).

Yet Israel won an overwhelming victory against all three of the main Arab belligerents, plus Iraq, and wound up in control of the Sinai Desert, the West Bank of the Jordan River, and the Golan Heights near Syria as well. The latter two areas it controls to this day. How did this happen, against the odds? As Pollack put it, how could it be that "the IDF had also demonstrated a mastery of modern air and mechanized warfare that ironically, but intentionally, rivaled the [Nazi] Wehrmacht at its height."[6]

The Six-Day War began the morning on June 5, 1967, with an extremely successful surprise air strike. The Israeli Air Force launched its planes against planes, runways, maintenance facilities, and storage depots at eighteen Egyptian air bases. The Israeli Air Force had rehearsed the surprise-attack plan repeatedly. Its basic proficiencies contributed to success as well, such as the ability to land, refuel and become airborne again within minutes, allowing repeated strikes.

The Egyptian Air Force lost almost 300 of 420 combat aircraft as a result. Then, its officers sought to cover up the disaster, lying not only to outside world but to their own leader, President Gamal 'Abd al-Nasser. Similar tactics, without the benefit of surprise, took out half the Syrian air forces later the same day. Smaller losses were exacted on the Jordanian and Iraqi air forces after the latter also decided to enter the war (partly due to the misleading Egyptian propaganda that made them think victory was nigh).

The ground war that led to Israel's seizures of the Sinai, West Bank, and Golan Heights began that same day, June 5, at 8:15 a.m. Israeli forces did lots of things right, including envelopment operations, but Arab resistance was poor in most ways. The Arab soldier was not lacking in courage when defending an initial, established position. But there was little tactical flexibility or understanding of proper combined-arms warfare.

Weapons were essentially used as individual set pieces rather than assets for integrated maneuver forces. Whatever the defects of small-unit forces and their local commanders, higher-echelon Arab command was worse, especially in the cases of Egypt and Syria. Commanders became quickly discouraged and disoriented after initial Israeli successes; they did not use reserves well; many of them ultimately fled the battle scene without helping their subordinates organize disciplined retreats. Jordanian troops fought somewhat better in and around Jerusalem but even in their case the outcome was only a matter of time.[7]

On the fourth day of the war, the Israelis blundered with tragic results, accidentally attacking a U.S. ship. (Some think the attack intentional, perhaps conducted out of fear that the United States was for some reason helping Egypt in the fight, but the evidence to substantiate such a theory is lacking.) That morning the USS *Liberty*, an American Navy electronic spy ship, missed a communication to stay away from the Sinai coast and came within 13 nautical miles of the coastline. An Israeli officer was alerted of the ship's presence and recognized it as a US navy boat, marking it neutral on the tactical control board. However, when he left the office at 13:00 he pulled the marker pin, assuming the ship had moved from the area. Earlier that day an explosion had hit the beaches of al-Arish, making Israelis nearby skittish. The Israeli commander in charge of the area sent scout planes to look for Egyptian submarines. They instead found the *Liberty* and concluded from data on the ship's speed, together with its direction, that it was an Egyptian destroyer fleeing toward port after shelling Arish. The Israeli planes received the go-ahead and struck the ship, before noticing that its markings were in English, rather than Arabic and before hearing the subsequent American distress signals. On the ship 34 sailors were killed and 171 injured.[8]

Despite this tragedy—another terrible reminder of the possible consequences of Clausewitz's fog of war—Israeli war aims were achieved. And the price to the Jewish state was not enormous. By the time the war was over, Arab forces had lost some 20,000 dead and another 5,000 captured; Israeli losses were fewer than 1,000 fatalities, and its gains in land as well as reputation were considerable.[9]

A brief note on the October 1973 Arab-Israeli or Yom Kippur War. That conflict was important in the history of the Middle East, helping Arabs restore some of their military pride, inflicting larger losses on Israel than it had suffered in 1967, and ultimately helping set the conditions by which peace between Israel and Egypt was possible a half dozen years later. In military terms, successful surprise strikes by Egypt and Syria were followed by an effective Israeli recovery. The net effect meant little change in territorial holdings in the end, partly because U.S. secretary of state Henry Kissinger effectively imposed terms on the various parties through a combination of threats, inducements, diplomatic engagements, and even an American nuclear alert to dissuade the Soviet Union from intervening militarily.[10] As diplomat and scholar Martin Indyk wrote:[11]

> In this crisis, Kissinger skillfully maneuvered to secure four ambitious and somewhat contradictory objectives simultaneously: to ensure the victory of America's ally Israel over the Soviet-backed Egyptian and Syrian forces; to prevent a humiliating defeat of the Egyptian army so that its leader, President Anwar Sadat, would be able to enter peace negotiations with Israel with his dignity intact; to prove to the Arabs that only the United States could deliver results for them at the negotiating table; and to maintain the "détente" with Moscow, even as he worked to undermine the Soviet position of influence in the Middle East.

Kissinger was aided by the fact that Israel may have already achieved all it wanted and all it realistically could by the time a cease-fire was arranged. In that sense, whatever Kissinger's contributions, a compromise outcome was largely the natural result of the geographic and logistical constraints operating on the two sides.

The war's net effect probably did bring the IDF down a notch or two in prestige, dispelling any myth of the inevitability of its quick and decisive victories in battle. It also underscored the dangers of intelligence failure in modern warfare, since Israel was caught largely unprepared by the initial attacks.[12] And in tactical and technical terms, as Fred Kagan has argued, it informed onlookers around the world about the growing lethality of modern antiarmor weaponry.[13]

Lebanon, 1982–2000 and 2006

Several different types of military confrontations have taken place in the small, complex country of Lebanon just to Israel's north over the last half century. They have included civil war, from 1975 to 1990; Israeli incursions and occupation, from 1982 to 2000 and then again in 2006; and a Syrian occupation from 1976 to 2005. Israel's experiences are most pertinent to this chapter because they mimic in some important ways the kinds of experiences the United States and allies would have in the 2000s and 2010s in Iraq as well as Afghanistan.

To understand the American wars explored later in this chapter, the main military takeaways of this history are perhaps twofold. First, Arab armies generally cannot prevent Israel or the United States and Western allies from prevailing in direct military engagements and achieving specific territorial goals. But second, well-resourced and motivated irregular forces can make any subsequent attempts at occupation extremely difficult. On balance, Israel's experiences in Lebanon have not been happy ones.[14]

In 1982, after a frustrating decade for Israel during which time the Palestine Liberation Organization (PLO) had used Lebanon as a base and effective sanctuary from which to stage terrorist attacks, Israel decided to undertake an operation that would drive it out of the country. With the same operation, it would install a friendlier government in Beirut, and also push Syrian forces out of their positions in the Bekaa Valley in eastern Lebanon—even if the Syrian presence in previous years had in many ways been beneficial for Israel.[15] The IDF did achieve air dominance in the air war against Syrian forces, with a remarkable campaign in which they ultimately shot down 86 Syrian aircraft while suffering no losses of their own.[16] However, some Syrian commando units did better on the ground, and Israel's progress there was slower. As a result, Israel did not achieve all of its aims; the United Nations pressured it to cease operations against Syria before it could complete the process of severing the Damascus to Beirut road, and thereby evict Syrian forces from Lebanon. In addition, while the PLO was displaced, Israel Defense Forces were not so successful as occupiers. Indeed, their presence in southern Lebanon thereafter provided much of the motivation for Iran, together with many Shiite Lebanese, to create the Hezbollah organization.

American efforts to help shape the country's politics were unsuccessful as well, tragically culminating in the October 1983 marine barracks bombing.

Whatever Israel's problems in 1982, the creation of Hezbollah gave it far greater problems in the years to come. Israel's occupation of southern Lebanon through 2000 was painful. The IDF suffered many attacks in which Hezbollah effectively employed improvised explosive devices and other weapons, ultimately killing 300 Israeli troops. Tactically, Israel tended to prevail in most firefights, and Hezbollah suffered several times as many losses as did the IDF. The IDF casualty toll, while not huge, was persistent and politically painful enough that the Israeli government ultimately chose to withdraw its forces from Lebanon. Hezbollah could claim a triumph against Israel, at least at the broad strategic level, as a result.[17]

In 2006, after Hezbollah kidnapped two Israeli soldiers in a crossborder raid, Israel undertook retaliatory airstrikes, especially against Hezbollah's large missile launchers. But when Hezbollah undertook other types of attacks, largely with 122-mm Katyusha rockets that were harder for Israel to find and target from the air, the conflict expanded. Israel launched what became a month-long ground-force operation to establish a zone of control in southern Lebanon and push Hezbollah back from its numerous positions there.

Hezbollah fought back reasonably effectively against the Israeli effort, using well-prepared firing positions in the effort. Its positions were often properly situated so as to provide overlapping fire from multiple locations and directions, with minefields also effectively placed so as to channel or slow Israeli forces in ways that left them more vulnerable. Its discipline in the initiation and use of fire was also often impressive. To be sure, Hezbollah's competence in the use of technologies like antitank weapons was variable, and the ability of Hezbollah fighters to carry out any maneuver operations was limited. But for their purposes in that kind of fight, they did not really need to have such capabilities. They suffered some 700 killed to just over 100 fatalities for Israel, but with only 3,000 or so troops they had managed to fend off an incursion by 10,000 Israeli soldiers. Ultimately, a UN cease-fire left Hezbollah's control of southern Lebanon, and influence throughout the country, largely intact.[18]

At a broader strategic level, the verdict was mixed. Israel took significant losses. Yet it also achieved the goal of reminding Hezbollah and its leaders the pain it could inflict on them—even without achieving comprehensive control of part or all of Lebanon, and even without forcing Hezbollah to change its leadership team or its role in Lebanon's broader political and military ecosystem. Some describe this result as "reestablishing deterrence." Hezbollah has rearmed since, but has not to date again engaged in large-scale provocations or attacks against Israel.

The Iran-Iraq War

After a fundamentalist Shia theocracy came to power in Iran in 1979, the stage was set for war. Across the border, the Iraqi dictator, Saddam Hussein, was both greedy for Iranian oil and fearful of what designs such an aggressive Shia regime might have on his country. So Saddam attacked, in September 1980.

Tragically for his soldiers, he did so with an overtly politicized and incompetent officer corps. Their frontal assault for invasion was far too predictable, plodding, lacking in good tactical intelligence, and badly coordinated. It did not stand a good chance of seizing large chunks of Iranian territory or defeating the armies of the Islamic republic. Although it did reach into Iranian soil, the progress quickly sputtered, and Saddam sued for peace.

But Iran's theocratic leader, Ayatollah Ruhollah Khomeini, was not in a mood to forgive and forget. So the Iranians prepared a counterattack, drove Iraqi forces off Iranian soil, and then developed greater ambitions, just as Saddam had previously feared when making the decision to launch preventive war himself. In 1982, Iran invaded Iraq.

Once fighting in defense of their own country, the Iraqis eventually did better. For starters, they had shorter supply lines and more dependable logistics in general; their capable military engineers also constructed many effective defensive fighting positions. They also became the beneficiaries of international support, even as Iran quickly encountered problems in acquiring spare parts and ammunition from an outside world that was horrified by what it was learning about the extremism of the Islamic Republic.

Saddam also brought back to command many of the officers he had previously fired despite—or in some cases, because of—their competence. It would not have served his purposes to have an army capable of turning against him internally, at least not until the external threat became even more menacing than the possible internal one. And while their approach was ugly, and brutal, and in violation of international law, those officers developed a standard operating procedure that worked passably well—featuring sustained preparatory fire with conventional and chemical weapons followed by highly choreographed movements of forces to take limited nearby objectives. This was inefficient, but moderately effective. It was not unlike the approach that Egypt had used in 1973 to cross the Suez Canal and take a swath of land in the Sinai. Ultimately, Iraqi forces regained the al-Faw peninsula near the Shatt al-Arab waterway that had been lost in 1986. With the region and its petroleum assets now back in Baghdad's control, the two sides were both exhausted, and ready to make peace.[19]

The Soviet Invasion and Occupation of Afghanistan

Over almost exactly the same time period as the Iran-Iraq War, the Soviet Union attempted to shore up a Communist government in Afghanistan despite that country's chaotic and undisciplined politics. Struggles within

Afghanistan had led to the overthrow of a moderately left-leaning government under Mohammad Daoud Khan in 1977, followed by the overthrow of an avowedly Communist but unruly government under Nur
Mohammad Taraki. However, the new leader, Hafizullah Amin, worried
Moscow even more than had his predecessor, and it decided to intercede
to displace him in favor of a more dependent and predictable entity, Babrak
Karmal.[20]

Unfortunately for the Soviets, the fiercely nationalist Afghans did not
welcome foreign invaders in the twentieth century any more than they had
welcome the British in the nineteenth. The original Soviet hope that it
could simply play kingmaker was quickly recognized to be unrealistic.
Moscow's next escalation was to send in enough forces to control the
major cities and roadways so that Afghanistan's own military could combat resistance and impose the government's will throughout the countryside. But that did not work either, leading Moscow to escalate, with a
major buildup of forces, numbering ultimately more than 100,000. The
Soviets then attempted a brute-force type of counterinsurgency of their
own, using aerial bombardment, more targeted attacks with helicopter
gunships, scorched-earth tactics against villages suspected of aiding insurgents, and massive mining, among other tactics.[21] Huge numbers of civilians were inadvertently or deliberately affected as a result of this combat—
out of a population of 15 to 20 million, at least 1 million died, 5 million
became refugees, and perhaps 3 million were internally displaced.[22]

As is often the case in such wars, however, it proved impossible to defeat an insurgency by brute force alone. That became particularly evident
when the United States, working with Pakistan and Saudi Arabia, increased
its aid to the resistance, providing a grand total of close to 1,000 Stinger
missiles from 1986 onward. American aid to the mujahadeen—including
a range of resistance groups, several that would later constitute the so-
called Northern Alliance—which began in the low tens of millions of dollars a year under Jimmy Carter, reached several hundred million dollars a
year.[23] Those Stinger missiles were highly effective against helicopters, the
most effective Soviet platform for supporting ground forces and rapidly
reacting to insurgent attacks. They brought down more than 250 planes
and helicopters by war's end.[24] Indeed, in mid-1987, the Soviets were losing about one aircraft a day to shoulder-fired weapons. In all, the official
tally of Soviet fatalities would reach 15,000, with actual deaths perhaps
two to three times that. Soviet patience would ultimately run out, as new
leadership in Moscow under Mikhail Gorbachev promised not only a

change in Afghanistan strategy but a more thorough overhaul of a struggling Soviet Union itself.[25]

The Geneva Accords of 1988 provided a fig leaf and "decent interval" for Soviet forces to leave, which they did by early 1989. Afghanistan's new government, led by Najibullah, survived in power for three more years, until the dissolution of the Soviet Union and end to Soviet aid deprived it of the wherewithal to fight and to govern. Warlordism then ran rampant until 1996, when the Taliban movement took power in most of the country (in that same year bursting into the UN compound in Kabul and capturing, then executing, Najibullah).[26]

The Soviets were far more brutal and indiscriminate in their use of force than the United States and NATO would be in the early 2000s, but there were nonetheless eerie parallels in the overall trajectory of the Soviet occupation of the 1980s with the NATO-led stabilization mission of the 2000s and 2010s.

Operation Desert Storm in Iraq

The U.S. decision to evict Iraqi forces from Kuwait and restore that nation's sovereignty, while also requiring Iraq to eliminate any nuclear, biological, and chemical weapons of mass destruction as a precondition for regaining its full economic and sovereign rights, was a momentous event in the early post–Cold War period. President Bush hoped to establish the precept that major interstate aggression would not be tolerated—a "new world order," as he termed it—though the Russian invasion of Ukraine has weakened that norm subsequently, at least to a degree.

In military terms, the decision also led to the kind of war that the American military most preferred to fight, using the technologies and tactics it had increasingly perfected in the years since World War II. Operation Desert Storm also profited from improvements to command and control. They included the creation of regional military commands and headquarters under a single commander as a result of the Goldwater-Nichols Department of Defense Reorganization Act of 1986. That led, crucially, to the designation of a single air commander for Operation Desert Storm, able to deconflict operations and adjudicate differences of opinion between various military services.[27] Those changes sought to change the fragmented command arrangements, and sometimes the lack of realistic joint-service training, that contributed to recent American debacles, notably the failed Iran hostage rescue operation of April 1980, the October 1983 Beirut bombing tragedy that killed the 241 marines (despite an earlier attack in April of that same year against the U.S. embassy in Beirut that arguably should have sensitized commanders to the dangers of car and truck bombs), and the rather unimpressive American invasion of Grenada starting two days later.[28] For a brief shining moment, at least, the U.S. military lived in the kind of world it prefers.[29] It would not be so fortunate in the 2000s (or even in much of the rest of the 1990s).[30]

The Path to Desert Storm

The prelude to the war was the ruinous Iran-Iraq conflict, which took a million lives and left both countries a financial and economic shambles. Saddam claimed that he had waged it partly to protect the interests of Sunni-dominant states, and especially the rich Persian Gulf sheikdoms like Kuwait, against the perils of a Shia theocracy that had come to power in Iran. Of course, his assessment of his own goodness and philanthropy was badly exaggerated. As much as anything, Saddam wanted some of Iran's oil, and wished to show off his massive, Soviet-equipped army and air force.[31] Regardless, when the high-flying Kuwaitis refused to help finance Iraqi war debts or share more of the oil wealth within the Rumaylah oil field along the border of the two countries, Saddam chose to invade. Whether it would have made any difference had U.S. ambassador April Glaspie refrained from telling Saddam that the United States had no position on border disputes between Arab countries remains debatable. In any case, Saddam sensed an opportunity to take by force what he had perhaps always wanted.[32] America's history was not (yet) to undertake big military missions in the broader Middle East, and when the United States had attempted them before, as in Beirut in 1983, they had not all gone well. Saddam may have extrapolated this history too linearly into the future—or felt that he could defeat the United States with his own forces even if America responded.

The result was a rapid walkover of the tiny nation of Kuwait and its minuscule military on August 2, 1990, by some 120,000 Iraqi troops.[33] The period during which Saddam threatened the takeover lasted days— during which most analysts at the CIA, though not my future colleague Kenneth Pollack and a couple other prescient observers, thought that Saddam was bluffing in an attempt to coerce concessions out of Kuwait. The subsequent takeover itself took just hours.

Scenes of brutality, including prematurely born babies being ripped out of incubators in hospitals, dominated the airwaves. President George H. W. Bush, differing with the position taken by his own government and articulated by Ambassador Glaspie a week before, and perhaps bucked up by an intense conversation with British prime minister Margaret Thatcher, told the world on August 5 that the Iraqi aggression "will not stand."[34] Concern for oil markets played a role in the calculation as well. Concerns about a possible Iraqi nuclear weapons program were muted after Israel's bombing of the Osirak nuclear reactor in Iraq in 1981; the world had no suspicion that Iraq was in fact making headway on multiple hidden nuclear programs. It was known, however, that Saddam had chemical weapons—he had used them against Kurdish civilians and Iranian troops already in recent years. There were fears too about Iraqi biological weapons programs.[35]

The American military responses by necessity started modestly. Aircraft and lightly armed airborne troops arrived primarily in Saudi Arabia—the country that American policymakers were truly concerned about protecting from any further possible Iraqi ambitions—in the war's first few weeks. Within a couple months, however, the deployment of some 200,000 American troops was complete. American decisionmakers rested more comfortably in the knowledge that they now had a robust defensive position to protect Saudi Arabia and other Gulf partners.[36] Still, Saddam refused to relent in his occupation and proclaimed annexation of Kuwait as Iraq's "19th province." So President Bush announced more than a doubling of the U.S. troop presence on November 8.[37] This decision was in effect an announcement that an American-led war to reverse the Iraqi aggression was now a likelihood; maintaining 550,000 U.S. troops in or near the desert was not sustainable due to the absence of an adequately large rotation base for a U.S. military that was already downsizing after the fall of the Berlin Wall.[38]

The buildup was remarkable. As the U.S. Army's official history put it, the operation "picked up the equivalent of the city of Atlanta, with all its population and sustenance, and moved it more than 8,000 miles to Saudi Arabia. Accomplishment of this feat required the unloading of 500 ships and 9,000 aircraft that carried through Saudi ports more than 1,800 Army aircraft, 12,400 tracked vehicles, 114,000 wheeled vehicles, 38,000 containers, 1,800,000 tons of cargo, [and] 350,000 tons of ammunition." Almost all equipment (95 percent by weight) moved by sealift; almost all people (99 percent) moved by airlift. This buildup benefited from Saudi Arabia's excellent infrastructure, including seven major ports and five secondary ports, as well as two enormous airfields and a number of smaller facilities. Lacking the tools to do so effectively, and still likely hopeful that the United States was bluffing, Saddam chose not to try to obstruct the buildup.[39]

President Bush did not ask the Congress for a declaration of war against Iraq. That continued the post–World War II tradition during which no such declarations have been issued for any American conflict. However, Bush did have the authority of the United Nations, which on November 29 approved the use of "all means necessary" to drive Iraqi forces out of Kuwait. Then, at some political peril of having his request denied, President Bush also asked for a bicameral Congressional authorization to use all means necessary to liberate Kuwait. Congress granted its approval on January 12, 1991.[40] Given how well the ultimate military operation went, it is difficult now to remember just how contentious the debate, and how close the congressional vote, both were.

Initially there were great fears that any war to expel dug-in Iraqi forces, numbering several hundred thousand troops in the Kuwaiti theater out of a total military of 1 million, could resemble World War I. Images of trench warfare, massive artillery bombardments, and perhaps even the use of poison gas haunted leaders. Indeed, according to press reports, the Department of Defense leadership—under Secretary of Defense Dick Cheney and Joint Chiefs Chairman Colin Powell (as well as General "Stormin' Norman" Schwarzkopf, Central Command commander) expected up to 5,000 Americans to be killed.[41]

By contrast, independent scholars, including Joshua Epstein, Barry Posen, Richard Kugler, Trevor Dupuy, and John Mearsheimer, took Israel's successful and short maneuver operations against Arab armies as their model. (In fairness, some in the government did, too.) Accordingly, they predicted a rapid if still bloody victory by U.S.-led coalition forces, within weeks, at a cost of casualties measured in the low thousands of American personnel. They were, as a group, still too high in their predictions, but were nonetheless in the right ballpark. This was a case where the tendency of policymakers to underrate the difficulty of war was *not* validated. The war was much more decisive, at considerably lower cost in lives and treasure, than had been generally expected. Thus, I acknowledge that this book's central theme or lesson about the importance of avoiding overconfidence, while often important, should not be overlearned either. There are some cases in which it does not apply. They can be hard to identify, alas.

By official count, a total of 382 Americans died in the southwest Asian theater in the combined course of Operation Desert Shield, which began in August 1990, and Desert Storm, as that operation was renamed in

January 1991 when the air war began. Of the total, 148 U.S. troops died in combat, including 35 killed accidentally by so-called friendly fire. Others died in accidents of various types, on and off the immediate battlefield.[42] Considering Allied forces as well, and using round figures, the coalition suffered about 240 combat deaths, and about 1,500 total casualties.[43]

The coalition would also lose eighty-six fixed-wing aircraft (forty-eight damaged, thirty-eight lost completely). Somewhat more than two-thirds of the attrition was due to Iraqi infrared-guided surface-to-air missiles or anti-aircraft artillery. Seventeen aircraft were damaged or destroyed on the war's opening day of January 17; after that, daily attrition varied from 0 to 7 planes a day, with 1 or 2 a day the most common outcome. The overall loss rate of one aircraft for every 1,800 combat sorties was very low—five to fifteen times less than key periods of the Vietnam War, for example. It was the result of modern and well-maintained equipment, excellent flying by coalition pilots, and the decision to keep most flights above 10,000 to 15,000 feet—generally out of range of infrared-guided missiles.[44] This high-altitude flight, combined with the limited availability of laser designators, limited amounts of night-vision equipment on airplanes, and a number of stretches of bad weather, impeded many tactical missions. But luckily for the coalition, it could take what time it needed in what became a forty-day air war followed by a four-day ground war.

As noted earlier, the Congressional Budget Office, asked to gauge the likely cost of the American military effort in any war by the Senate Budget Committee, predicted a range of $28 billion to $86 billion. I was part of the research team; we were fortunate that our leadership, under Robert Reischauer, Robert Hale, and Jack Mayer, was prudent enough not to attempt a more narrow range of prediction. The actual outcome fell almost exactly between those endpoints (ultimately being reimbursed by Persian Gulf governments as well as Japan and Germany).[45] Converted to 2023 dollars, that range varies from about $50 billion to $160 billion.

The most important U.S. allies and partners in the operation were the British. They and French troops fought alongside the Americans. Saudi and Syrian forces maintained strong forward positions near their respective borders with Iraq for their own defense and as an implied threat of possible offensive action that prevented the Iraqis from concentrating all forces on Kuwait. Turkey granted coalition troops access to base infrastructure that helped in the north. Israel contributed by staying out of the war, even as it began to suffer Iraqi Scud missile attacks against its cities. Any Israeli role in the conflict would have likely splintered the Arab solidarity with American and British forces that was already weakened by Jordan's political siding with Saddam (though Jordan did not actually fight on the Iraqi side).

The 40-Day War

The military operations associated with Operation Desert Storm included perhaps three main phases—two of them associated with the air war, one of them the final ground war. They were carried out by a coalition of twelve countries that together fielded 1,800 fixed-wing combat aircraft, with another 1,000 fixed-wing aircraft providing support of various kinds (refueling, transport, electronic warfare, command and control, reconnaissance); some 200 naval vessels (127 of them American, and 6 of those aircraft carriers) in the Persian Gulf and Red Sea; and a total force count of 660,000 personnel.[46] The operations ultimately included, among other things, some 120,000 sorties by coalition aircraft.[47]

In the conflict's opening days, starting on January 17, coalition aircraft pounded the fixed Iraqi infrastructure that Saddam and his commanders would need to control their airspace and supply their forces in Kuwait. The coalition hit air defense radar systems, missile batteries, runways, aircraft, command and control sites, major logistics depots, marshaling yards, bridges and other transportation chokepoints, and any suspected weapons of mass destruction sites. The target list included some 723 assets, facilities, or other crucial fixed locations.[48] Substantial numbers of precision-guided warheads, including laser-guided bombs, were used in the process. The attacks were carried out by cruise missiles, stealth jets, attack helicopters, and other aircraft; drones were used to draw the attention of Iraqi air defenses, which when activated could be identified and attacked by high-speed antiradiation missiles (HARM) among other ordnance. Television audiences were treated to the spectacle of laser-guided bombs striking their targets within feet of intended aimpoints, with some weapons even being directed into the chimneys of buildings and through the poorly constructed hardened air defense shelters of the Iraqi air force.[49] The "CNN effect" would from that point onward rivet audiences to TV screens, but also influence real-time decision-making over wartime goals and operations, especially when public opinion was shocked by vivid scenes of violence.

Iraq tried several ways to improve its prospects. For example, it fired Scud missiles at Saudi oil facilities as well as at Israel. The first attacks against Israel were conducted on January 18 and they continued through-out the war, with ultimately forty being fired into Israel; forty-six were fired at Saudi/Gulf targets. Coalition forces had great trouble finding Scud launchers in western Iraq, whether they tried to use airpower—dozens of daily sorties were used in the great Scud hunt in the war's opening ten days, and typically numbered ten to forty flights a day thereafter—or special forces in the searches. Iraqi "shoot and scoot" tactics, with mis-siles launched from unpredictable locations, as well as an effective use of decoys, hampered the anti-Scud efforts. By war's end, despite more opti-mistic earlier reporting, U.S. intelligence could confirm no kills against the mobile missile launchers, and no significant disruption of Iraqi com-munications networks used to direct the launches. That said, these collec-tive efforts slowed and complicated the Iraqi attacks, which fell off sub-stantially after the war's opening days.[50]

Israel almost entered the war as a result of the Scuds, which were di-rected against its cities as well as key military and strategic sites. But Ameri-can diplomacy, the deployment of Patriot missile defense systems to Israel (however imperfectly the latter functioned), and the generally low level of casualties suffered were ultimately enough to keep Israel out of the con-flict.[51] In one event on February 25, a tragically lucky Scud shot—almost surely aimed elsewhere—hit a U.S. troop barracks in Saudi Arabia, killing twenty-eight Americans. That was the single largest U.S. loss of the conflict.[52]

Meanwhile, Saddam's forces in and near Kuwait hunkered down well enough that there were no clear signs the aerial pounding would achieve much headway against deployed Iraqi ground forces. The ground conflict that all expected increasingly loomed, and it still appeared that the ground war could wind up being quite tough.

In the second phase of the air war, which can roughly be defined as occurring within the month of February, coalition aircraft shifted more attacks against the deployed Iraqi army while sustaining the earlier pace of roughly 800 or more strike sorties a day.[53] These and other types of aerial missions—for air-to-air superiority, jamming, reconnaissance, refueling—took place from approximately twenty-three bases in the re-gion, including Turkey. Of those bases, eleven were in Saudi Arabia. Sev-eral U.S. aircraft carriers were employed as well.[54] During this phase the tactic of "tank plinking" was invented, whereby the infrared sensors on combat aircraft were used to locate and target Iraqi vehicles hidden against the desert floor along the Iraq-Kuwait border and elsewhere. Because the vehicles retained the day's heat (and the night's cool) longer than the desert sand, this tactic was often particularly effective in the evening (or morning) hours. It allowed a much more effective tactical use of combat airpower against stationary and partly camouflaged Iraqi armor than had been envisioned at the beginning of the conflict.[55]

There were some shortages and bottlenecks in the coalition air effort—in electronic-warfare or jamming aircraft, in tactical intelligence to carry out prompt bomb damage assessment and to find new targets, in night-vision capabilities and infrared targeting pods for attack aircraft. Some Global Positioning System (GPS) receivers had to be purchased in stores since the military procurement system had not acquired enough to outfit the entire force![56] But the capabilities of the U.S.-led coalition, compared with those of the Iraqi armed forces, were still overwhelming. And the combat readiness of American military equipment, coming out of the Reagan buildup period, was very high, with mission capable rates for major equipment often in the range of 85 to 90 percent or even higher.[57]

Iraq probably had up to 350,000 military personnel in 51 divisions in the broader Kuwait theater at the start of hostilities—much less than the almost 550,000 first believed to be there (because most units were badly understrength).[58] Due to casualties and desertions, around 200,000 to 220,000 Iraqi troops were likely present in the Kuwaiti theater when the ground war began (rounding to the nearest 5,000, based on official estimates from the time). In the course of the ground war, some 82,000 Iraqi prisoners were taken.[59] Total Iraqi fatalities probably numbered in the low tens of thousands.[60]

Over the course of the conflict, almost 15,000 precision-guided air-to-ground munitions (PGMs) were employed by the coalition. They featured, predominantly, laser-guided bombs of various types and Maverick air-to-surface missiles (guided either by infrared or electro-optical systems). Two-thirds were used against equipment in the field, the other third against targets like electricity grids, air-defense networks, transportation choke points, petroleum refining or storage facilities, suspected weapons of mass destruction sites, and military headquarters. Even though such precision weapons became the signature ordnance of the war, they constituted less than 10 percent of total munitions consumed in the conflict.[61] Airpower benefited from open terrain, static and isolated targets, limited Iraqi air defense capabilities (after the opening days of attacks against radars, command centers, and other key assets), and tactics such as tank plinking (from February 8 onward).

Estimates at the time varied greatly as to how much Iraqi equipment was destroyed during the air war—ranging from about 1,000 major pieces of equipment according to the CIA, to several times as high according to CENTCOM. These losses came out of an estimated total of 10,000 to 11,000 such weapons in theater at the start of the war (counting tanks, armored personnel carriers, and large-bore artillery).[62] Frontline units near the Saudi border typically suffered at least 50 percent attrition in the air war, it was estimated, whereas those further back (like most Republican Guard divisions) perhaps lost only half as much. Depending on what total losses actually were, it would appear that ordnance used against armor therefore had a typical kill probability per munition of perhaps 20 percent to 50 percent or more.[63] The original goal of destroying 50 percent of equipment throughout the theater before ground operations began was ultimately recognized to be optimistic and perhaps unnecessary, given how many other ways airpower could weaken the Iraqi military.[64] Coalition bombing also caused huge disruptions for the Iraqis in command and control, in access to roads and rails, in the ability to maneuver, and in the psyche of ground troops.[65]

The ground war finally began, on February 24, and was over by February 28. There was no semblance of World War I trench warfare. The Iraqi military was, in effect, a smaller, less well-trained, and more exposed version of the Soviet military that the United States and allies had just spent decades preparing to fight. Iraqi forces wielded billions of dollars' worth of Soviet equipment but with minimal proficiency in how to operate it. American and British forces took two approaches to conducting the ground operation. Profiting from their dominance of air and space, they moved most forces west to go around the Iraqi positions along the Kuwait border, with the intent of circling around and attacking from the west so as to destroy frontline units as well as much of the Republican Guard. British forces joined in this, the primary effort. Other forces, notably U.S. Marines, rather than simply fixing Iraqi forces as had been expected, went straight through the Iraqi positions en route to Kuwait City. Their use of heavy preparatory fires, armored bulldozers, explosive line charges, and other means of creating narrow channels through which invasion forces could move rapidly to penetrate the initial defenses was extremely effective.[66] Kuwait City was quickly liberated, with all Arab members of the coalition contributing.[67]

What was not attempted was any amphibious assault on Kuwait City. It was determined that Americans' mine-hunting capacity in shallow waters, including its dolphin force (made up of the actual mammals), was not adequate to the task. So amphibious ships were used in a feint operation instead.[68]

Eight Iraqi Republican Guard forces sat north of Kuwait in Iraqi territory as a strategic reserve, but they were outmatched as well, and three were largely destroyed during the ground war. They had to contend, among other things, with the JSTARS—Joint Surveillance Target Attack Radar System—carried aloft on aircraft and capable of spotting moving metal objects quickly at any time of day in any weather.[69] JSTARS had proven its mettle when Iraqi forces attempted an ill-conceived raid into the Saudi town of Al Khafji earlier in the war, between January 29 and January 31.[70] Still, during the ground war, Saddam managed to move some units into blocking positions in the western and southern parts of the theater to allow escape by other forces northward toward Basra.[71]

Overall, Iraqi forces performed less well in the war than predicted. They failed, for example, to post advance guards ahead of their dug-in positions, and did not remove dirt from the vicinity of those positions to keep the locations of dug-in forces secret.[72] Iraqi forces were generally poor at maneuver options; they were also highly limited in their capacities for any kind of tactical improvisation. Whatever improvements they had made in the last parts of the Iran-Iraq War were largely squandered as Saddam again cashiered competent generals and politicized military leadership. As Ken Pollack wrote about the Iraqi performance in Desert Storm, "Combined arms at tactical levels was dismal."[73] Iraqi forces did innovate in some modest ways, for example setting oil wells on fire to obscure the battlefield. But the odds were badly stacked against them overall. They did not wind up using their chemical weapons in offense or defense.[74]

As a result of all these factors, the American-led victory over Iraq was far more lopsided, in terms of relative losses or "exchange ratios," than Israeli victories in previous wars against Syria, Jordan, and Egypt. In those conflicts, Israel typically inflicted three to five times the losses it suffered itself.[75] To give just one revealing metric, the Abrams tank main gun needed only about 1.2 rounds for each enemy tank it would destroy in the war—a remarkable contrast with World War II, where a main gun typically needed 17 rounds for one kill.[76]

Yet that "catastrophic success" came at a price—a potentially premature U.S. decision to agree to a cease-fire. A few massively successful operations, such as American strikes against an Iraqi military convoy on what became the "highway of death," led President Bush to signal his willingness for a cease-fire within 100 hours of the start of the ground war.[77] The terms of the cease-fire that would emerge from this decision proved controversial. Saddam was required to allow the verifiable disarmament of his weapons of mass destruction capabilities. But due to the early end of the ground war, Saddam retained much more of his Republican Guard than intended and perhaps a quarter to a third of its armor in theater survived.[78] Saddam was allowed to keep his helicopters and use them as well against internal opponents.[79] He would do so brutally in the months to come, for example against the "marsh Arabs" who lived near Basra in southern Iraq, and were believed by Saddam to be fomenting some form of revolution during Desert Storm.

The long saga of Saddam obstructing international weapons inspectors from doing their job and verifying the elimination of Iraq's weapons of mass destruction stocks would soon begin. Along the way, inspectors would discover three separate nuclear weapons–related programs that had previously been unknown to the international community.

The Overthrow of Saddam and Attempted Stabilization of Iraq

Desert Storm, with limited aims and massive means, had gone quite well. The U.S. invasion and occupation of Iraq in 2003 would, however, become one of the most difficult and ultimately unpopular military missions in America's history. Two decades later, the results were at best very mixed—and were achieved at very high cost in Iraqi, American, and allied lives.[80]

Iraq had been under international and especially American crosshairs for a decade by the time of the September 11, 2001, tragedy. Despite his many flaws, Saddam was not implicated in the latter plot. The most that could be said is that there had been some limited contact between Iraq and al Qaeda of unknown purpose and consequence. But none of the planning or preparation of the 9/11 attacks occurred on Iraqi soil or with any known Iraqi state assistance. Still, the terrorism argument (or insinuation), along with Saddam's suspected weapons of mass destruction, as well as the CIA's secret prediction that Saddam could acquire a nuclear weapon between 2007 and 2009, were all invoked by the administration of President George W. Bush to justify the war. Fear was palpable in American politics in the early months and years after 9/11, when there was considerable anxiety over another possible catastrophic attack. Decisions were made with a different mentality as a result.

Concerns over Iraqi human rights, as well as the related desire to promote democracy in the Arab world, helped justify the war as well, even if they would not be its main motivation.[81] To help understand the mood of the times, it was in 2002 that Samantha Power published her widely and righty acclaimed Pulitzer Prize–winning book, *A Problem from Hell: America and the Age of Genocide*, in which her treatment of Saddam's Iraq, including his uses of chemical weapons against his country's Kurds, among other atrocities, constituted the second-longest chapter.[82]

Yet another factor, usually unstated, was the desire to demonstrate American power and credibility, in the aftermath of 9/11. The hope was that by doing something big, the United States could deter other would-be extremists by proving American resolve and generating greater respect abroad for American power.[83] All these arguments came together for the Bush administration in the specific case of Iraq and Saddam Hussein. He would be the focal point for the "axis of evil" (also including North Korea and Iran, as President Bush defined the group in his State of the Union speech in early 2002), the poster child for preemption doctrine (which came out of the National Security Strategy of the Bush administration later that same year). Iraq would be the best illustration of how support for terrorism combined with weapons of mass destruction and a willingness to use them could transform the threat environment—and thus the place where a demonstration of American power and resolve was, in Bush's eyes, most logical and appropriate.[84]

Although some called the U.S.-led invasion of Iraq "illegal" under international law, and although false or at least badly exaggerated pretenses about Iraq's supposed rapid progress toward a nuclear bomb were used in the American debate to help justify the war effort, Saddam was in fact in violation of the basic terms of the cease-fire that ended Operation Desert Storm for a full dozen years. Those cease-fire terms had been codified in numerous UN Security Council resolutions, in 1991 and beyond. They insisted that he grant unfettered access to international inspectors and destroy any remaining weapons stocks or related materials.[85] The administration of President Bill Clinton had responded to violations with relative restraint, yet it had sustained economic sanctions on Iraq through the 1990s while also carrying out occasional military strikes against suspected illicit sites.

In November 2002, Saddam was again told by the United Nations to comply or face unspecified, yet presumably quite serious, consequences.[86] A second resolution explicitly authorizing an invasion was never passed in New York—thereby indeed placing the subsequent U.S.-led invasion of

March 2003 on shaky international legal ground. I would describe the war as legally ambiguous, in terms of international law—not clearly illegal *or* legal.

While Congress did not declare war, it did pass a bicameral law with strong bipartisan support—greater, in fact, than the first President Bush received for Operation Desert Storm. In the 2002 vote, the Senate approved, 77–23, and the House, 296–133; in 1991, the respective votes were 52–47 and 250–183. This resolution granted President George W. Bush the prerogative to use force if and when he concluded that the inspection process had failed to ensure the documented destruction of Iraqi weapons of mass destruction.[87]

As such, the United States started to reinforce its positions in the region around Iraq by late 2002, using bases in Kuwait as the main staging area for ground forces, with air and naval facilities also available in Bahrain, Qatar, the United Arab Emirates, Oman, and Saudi Arabia. Ultimately, Turkey would not allow U.S. forces to enter Iraq from its territory, and even resisted combat overflights.[88] But the United States and major allies still had multiple avenues of approach and entry into Iraqi territory.

Shock and Awe

The U.S. and allied deployments continued into early 2003. The war was then launched with relatively little preparatory fanfare sooner than Saddam expected it, in the early morning hours of March 20 Iraqi time (still the evening of March 19 in the United States). Cruise missiles and F-117 fighters were used in this opening blow. Its timing was influenced by the hope that Saddam might be killed in the war's opening raid, when coalition forces wrongly thought they knew his whereabouts at a place called Dora Farms in the outskirts of Baghdad.[89] There was, more generally, a hope that a "shock and awe" attack that involved major air raids throughout Iraq in subsequent days, combined with an unexpectedly early ground invasion, would lead to the rapid collapse of Iraqi security forces. The air raids were aided by the fact that Iraqi air defenses were already in a shambles, after Operation Desert Storm as well as strikes in subsequent years during the Clinton administration (such as Operation Desert Fox, a four-day bombing campaign in 1998). In addition, a dozen years of U.S. conducted "no-fly zone" operations had produced considerable intelligence on the locations of remaining air defense capabilities and other Iraqi military assets.

Lurking in the back of some American minds was also the ultimately successful war over Kosovo in 1999. There NATO decided to act early against the marauding militias of Serbian leader Slobodan Milosevic before they could create the kind of mayhem, ethnic cleansing, and death that similar groups had perpetrated throughout Bosnia and Croatia in previous years. Unfortunately, NATO misread Milosevic at first, and thought a few days of highly selective and limited bombing—not unlike the previous year's Operation Desert Fox, in some ways—could change Milosevic's calculus enough that he would leave the Kosovar Albanian population in peace. NATO started the campaign with fewer than 100 combat aircraft in the region, the United States having just redeployed its only aircraft carrier in the Mediterranean back home shortly before initiating bombing in March 1999. Milosevic likely perceived NATO to be feckless and weak. This was a time, after all, when the United States had shown it would not even risk American casualties in response to massive attacks against two of its embassies in Africa the year before. He calculated that he could drive the ethnic Albanian population largely out of Kosovo (a part of Serbia), repopulate the region with Serbs, and thereby enlarge the broader Serbian-controlled remnants of the former Yugoslavia.

But while NATO did work hard to minimize risks to its personnel, ultimately losing just two in the entire Operation Allied Force by keeping aircraft at altitudes where they were quite safe (yet also ineffective against mobile targets on the ground), it found a way to "win ugly," as Ambassador Ivo Daalder and I argued in a book of similar title. NATO multiplied its aircraft in the region tenfold over a war lasting two and a half months. It ultimately flew a total of some 40,000 combat sorties. It expanded its target set to include many facilities and assets in Belgrade, Serbia, and attacked that target set with a higher percentage of precision-guided munitions—about 30 percent—than had been available eight years before in Operation Desert Storm (including by now the GPS-guided, and inexpensive, Joint Direct Attack Munition, or JDAM). Finally, NATO also began to hint at the possibility of a ground invasion.[90] Milosevic finally relented, allowing autonomy for Kosovo as well as the deployment there of NATO peacekeepers. Some military strategists concluded that technology had finally progressed to the point where it was possible to win wars largely if not entirely from the air.[91]

Such thinking, plus memories of Desert Storm and the ease of overthrowing the Taliban in Afghanistan in the fall of 2001 (discussed below), may have collectively contributed to a certain kind of American overconfidence. Anyone engaging in such thinking risked being guilty of selective memory. War had not really become safe, surgical, or antiseptic. The events of Mogadishu in 1993, or Bosnia in 1993 and 1994 (when America struggled to find viable military options to mitigate the ethnic cleansing and killing), or the Khobar Towers bombing in Saudi Arabia by Iranian-backed Hezbollah in 1996 as well as the Africa embassy bombings of 1998 and the attack on the U.S.S. *Cole* in Yemen in 2000 all underscored U.S. vulnerabilities. But a certain form of hubris may have infiltrated too many minds within the Bush administration—and that hubris, combined with a sense that something dramatic must be done to avenge the 9/11 attacks—show the world that the United States was no paper tiger and shake up the Middle East more sweepingly—may have led the United States astray.[92]

With President Bush clearly set on war by early 2003, a total of about 250,000 U.S. troops deployed to the broader region, about two-thirds of them ground forces. Allies provided another 50,000 personnel. (Perhaps 165,000 coalition ground forces wound up inside Iraq itself in the course of the March-April invasion.) The main U.S. forces on the ground included the First Marine Division, elements of the Second Marine Expeditionary Brigade, as well as some or all of the Army's First Armored Division, Third Mechanized Infantry Division, 101st Airborne Division, Eighty-second Airborne Division, Fourth Mechanized Infantry Division, Second Armored Cavalry Regiment, Third Armored Cavalry Regiment, and 173rd Airborne Brigade. The British First Armored Division was also of central importance.[93] As powerful as this force was, the U.S. component was only about half as large as had been anticipated in Operational Plan 1003 back in the late 1990s, should an invasion of Iraq ever be undertaken.[94]

Approximately 800 fighters and bombers participated (compared with 1,800 in Operation Desert Storm), 90 percent of them American. They flew some 20,000 sorties in all; tankers as well as airlift aircraft and other support flew about another 20,000 over the course of the war. As many as 30,000 bombs were dropped—two-thirds of them guided (almost ten times the fraction of precision munitions used in Operation Desert Storm). More than three-fourths of all targets were mobile land forces in various assigned "kill boxes," in contrast to a fraction closer to two-thirds for that same target category in 1991.[95]

In the invasion, Baghdad itself was the main goal. Most other cities were bypassed in the desire to focus on overthrowing the regime quickly. Other important goals, however, were the Rumaila oil fields, plus Basra in the south, where British forces took main responsibility, and Mosul in the north, where the 101st Airborne Division under Major General David Petraeus ultimately arrived after assisting in the liberation of Baghdad. It became necessary to use the 101st for the northern mission, starting in late April, when Turkey chose not to allow the 4th Infantry Division under Major General Raymond Odierno to traverse its territory. Thus, the 4th Infantry Division ultimately had to enter Iraq via the south like the other main combat formations, delaying its availability.[96]

Most American units went up the main highways. Their movement was rapid, despite having to cope with sandstorms, semi-regular forces known as "Saddam Fedayeen" wielding machine guns and rocket-propelled grenades and mortars, and pockets of more traditional Iraqi military units that sometimes employed tanks, artillery, rockets, and antiaircraft artillery. Coalition forces made special efforts to seize bridgeheads quickly and otherwise anticipate where they could run into trouble at key transportation chokepoints. Of course, coalition dominance of the skies meant that Iraq could not use airpower against advancing ground formations or use aircraft to reinforce any of its main positions.[97]

There were some setbacks. For example, about 60 Apache helicopters suffered considerable damage on March 24 near Karbala (fairly close to Baghdad) when trying to reconnoiter and attack part of Iraq's Medina division, and a combination of concerted Fedayeen resistance with bad weather and tactical mistakes slowed movements and produced numerous American casualties near Nasariyah further south.[98] But overall the campaign moved along very well.

Within three weeks, units reached the outskirts of Baghdad. Despite plans that called for a siege, more aggressive commanders like Buford Blount, Jim Mattis, and David Perkins won the day in advocating more offensive action. On April 5, a battalion of the Second Brigade Combat Team of the Third Infantry Division conducted a "Thunder Run" reconnaissance in force through the main thoroughfares of the Iraqi capital to test defenses in the city, and then followed up with a larger brigade-sized operation on April 7 into the heart of the city. There was considerable fighting, but American forces were able to seize major government buildings quickly, with Saddam leaving for the metaphorical hills.[99]

By April 10, the war seemed over. It was on that date that Secretary of Defense Donald Rumsfeld adviser Ken Adelman wrote in the *Washington Post* that he and others predicting an easy war had been vindicated.[100] Baghdad's main sites were all in U.S. hands. Tikrit, Saddam's hometown to the north, then fell on April 14, and the invasion phase of the war was effectively over.[101] President Bush himself soon celebrated the success with a made-for-TV speech on an American aircraft carrier on May 1, a banner deployed behind him reading "Mission Accomplished." That said, Iraq was far from stable even in this period. Wholesale looting of major government buildings, stores, factories, and anything else with valuables within created a sense of pandemonium and deprived the future government, whoever might lead it, of many of the resources and assets that would be needed to get the country moving forward.[102]

Occupation, Dead Enders, Insurgents—and Mission Not Quite Accomplished

On May 22, 2003, Iraq was placed under a UN mandate. According to the mandate, a U.S.-led occupation force, with the United Kingdom also formally an occupying power, under the leadership of American diplomat Ambassador Paul "Jerry" Bremer, would develop a twelve-month transition plan to hand Iraq to a coalition government known as the Iraqi Governing Council.[103] With Iraq regaining its sovereignty, elections would then ensue as the country became a democracy. Initial thinking in some quarters of the Pentagon that Saddam would simply be replaced by another, more benign strongman leader, like the Shia dissident and longstanding exile Ahmed Chalabi, were shelved by the Bush administration— though only after a protracted period of indecision in the early months of the occupation that cost precious time. As George Tenet sardonically put it, "You had the impression that some Office of the Vice President and [Department of Defense] reps were writing Chalabi's name over and over again in their notes, like schoolgirls with their first crush."[104] Chalabi was a strange person upon whom to crush. His reputation and legacy in previous ventures were not particularly impressive or inspiring, and his potential to help unify Iraq was extremely limited.[105]

This disagreement within the Bush team reflected a common American predicament after toppling nefarious regimes: should we stay long enough to help build a real state and democracy in the aftermath, or try to get forces back home as soon as possible?[106] Ultimately, the Bush administration wrapped the invasion in the banner of new promotion of democracy in the broader Middle East. That message became louder and stronger just as the original official rationale for the war, Iraq's presumed possession of weapons of mass destruction, did not hold water, as inspectors found no WMDs.[107]

The campaign plan such as it was effectively ended with the overthrow of Saddam. Some had hoped that the Iraqi population's relief that Saddam was gone would lead them to "throw flowers at the feet" of U.S. troops as they arrived in country—and presumably collaborate with each other to build a new Iraq thereafter. When the magical stability did not emerge spontaneously, the United States then struggled to make up for lost time, developing an improvised stabilization plan in the summer and fall of 2003. The plan was of rushed and therefore mediocre quality, including a number of half-baked ideas for reviving the economy and building new political structures.[108]

To be sure, building a new and stable Iraq would have been daunting under the best of circumstances. A major part of the problem was Iraq's disenfranchised Sunni minority. It was already feeling marginalized after Saddam was overthrown. It then saw the United States ban most former members of Saddam's Baathist Party, a largely Sunni organization, from positions of responsibility in the new government. That policy was initiated by U.S. ambassador Bremer, the presidential envoy to Iraq from May 2003 to June 2004 during the period of formal American occupation. But then the Shia exile Ahmed Chalabi, even if not accorded the role of top leader in the country as some Americans had wished, was put in charge of the de-Baathification effort. He extended it even to levels of the party typically occupied by the likes of schoolteachers, depriving huge numbers—the Baath Party included perhaps 600,000 to 700,000 members—of their jobs and any influence.[109] Since Saddam had disproportionately favored his fellow Sunnis, the effect of this policy was to disproportionately punish them. That created a seething anger in their ranks. Bremer also formally disbanded the Iraqi army. Even though that policy was largely reversed a couple months later (at which point many former Iraqi soldiers did join the new army), the initial decision exacerbated Sunni angst and anger.

That said, Iraq was such a broken and polarized and corrupt state by 2003, after so many years of abusive rule by Saddam and his henchmen, that straightforward solutions to its difficult political future were bound to be elusive. A country that was only established at the end of World War I, as Britain carved three provinces out of the Ottoman Empire to form a new state, was probably destined to experience centrifugal forces after a strongman dictator was quickly and forcibly removed.[110] Antiforeigner sentiments also placed constraints on how long U.S.-led coalition forces could likely remain in an attempt to stabilize the country. That led to an overly hasty effort.[111]

U.S. domestic politics also argued in favor of minimizing the likely longer-term costs of the operation. What the military calls Phase 4 in such a mission—with Phases 1 and 2 involving buildup and early preparations, Phase 3 the main kinetic action to overthrow the previous political and military order—was therefore poorly planned. Some problems, such as setting of oil well fires by the Iraqi military, or large flows of internally displaced persons, or the need to secure suspected stockpiles of weapons of mass destruction, were anticipated. But general lawlessness and a metastasizing insurgency were not—at least not by the Department of Defense, which ultimately had responsibility for the entire mission. (The Department of State and CIA, though hardly clairvoyant, were closer to the mark in their understanding of the nature of the likely Iraqi resistance to foreign powers and to Shia majority rule.)[112]

Lest there be any doubt about the absence of a serious plan to stabilize the country, one need only consult the Third Infantry Division's after-action report, which reads: "Higher headquarters did not provide the Third Infantry Division (Mechanized) with a plan for Phase IV. As a result, Third Infantry Division transitioned into Phase IV in the absence of guidance." A broader Department of Defense report on the war similarly observed that "late formation of Department of Defense [Phase IV] organizations limited time available for the development of detailed plans and pre-deployment coordination."[113] As a result of the absence of plans for securing the country, and perhaps only half the troops needed to do so, short shrift was given to key tasks—stopping the looting of Iraqi government buildings and stores, sealing the main border crossings to complicate the arrival of extremists, guarding weapons caches so they would not be easy pickings for criminals and insurgents, building up human intelligence networks as well as the trust of the population.[114] Troops were rarely on foot patrol. George Packer wrote, in his outstanding book on the subject, "The American presence in Iraq must be one of the most isolated occupations in history. There was no real way for soldiers and Iraqis to mix outside the context of their jobs."[115]

As democracy expert, and participating member of the Coalition Provisional Authority or CPA (as the occupying mechanism run by Ambassador Bremer was formally known), Stanford professor Larry Diamond put it, "I opposed going to war in Iraq when we did. The largely unilateral rush to war created predictable problems from the outset. But I now believe that the truly cardinal sin was going to war so unprepared for the postwar—despite all the detailed warnings to which the administration had access."[116]

By the summer of 2003 the combination of these broken politics, sectarian divisions, powerful nationalism, criminal elements, and poor planning efforts to stabilize the country set the conditions for a snowballing disaster. The ensuing violence would first be described as the flailing final efforts of "dead enders" and "former regime elements"; soon, however, it would become clear that a powerful insurgency was emerging, and ultimately something akin to a civil war as Iraqi political as well as extremist actors increasingly organized along sectarian lines.[117] Suicide bombings began, including one in August 2003 targeting the UN compound that housed one of the great international public servants of his time, the Brazilian diplomat Sergio Vieira de Mello, who was killed in the blast. A major Shia religious figure, Ayatollah Mohammed Bakir Hakim, was killed later that same month in a bombing of his mosque in Najaf, forebodingly raising the specter of sectarian conflict that would intensify dramatically in the years to come. That fall, eighteen Italian carabinieri lost their lives after another bombing; several shootdowns of aircraft or accidents caused in part by attempts to evade ground fire killed dozens of Americans. Roadside bombs and vehicle-borne bombs killed many as well. The argument of Secretary of Defense Rumsfeld and others that any resistance was composed principally just of "dead enders" and "former regime elements" increasingly fell on deaf ears.[118] Indeed, in mid-July, the new commander at Central Command, General John Abizaid, became the first American official to describe the resistance as a guerrilla-style insurgency, and others joined in his assessment in the months to come.[119]

In the north, under General Petraeus and Colonel H. R. McMaster, some early efforts at counterinsurgency strategy, building on historical models from Malaya to the Philippines, were attempted. They emphasized inclusive governance and economic opportunity and sought to minimize the use of force against most parts of the society—even as Saddam's sons were ultimately tracked down and killed in Mosul in that same time frame. Saddam himself was found and arrested in a region near his hometown of Tikrit in December; imprisoned for three years, he was hanged at the end of 2006 after an Iraqi court found him guilty of multiple capital offenses. Other commanders were not as judicious. They arrested lots of suspects as well as family members of suspects, employed rough interrogation methods, conducted massive search operations, used artillery to respond to incoming fire even in urban areas, and otherwise failed to respect core counterinsurgency principles concerning protection of the population and care in the use of force.[120]

Bush administration hopes that U.S. forces could be reduced by at least two-thirds by fall, and the entire operation kept to $100 billion or less in cost, were gradually recognized to be very optimistic and unrealistic.[121] Later, there were plans—or at least aspirations—to reduce the 130,000-strong U.S. forces in Iraq to 100,000 by 2004 and some 50,000 by 2005. Those hopes too had to be jettisoned.[122]

Fewer than 150 Americans died in the overthrow of Saddam's regime. But nearly 500 overall had died in the Iraq mission by the end of 2003, and 800 or more then died annually in each of the next four years before U.S. fatalities started to decline dramatically in 2008 and thereafter.[123]

As a classic maneuver warfare operation turned into counterinsurgency—a counterinsurgency the United States was initially not well prepared to fight, based either on the war plan for Iraq or the ways in which mostly Army and Marine Corps troopers were trained—the war progressed through several stages in the following years.[124] The year after the creation of the UN mandate through the handoff to a transitional Iraqi indigenous government, in June 2004, featured a growing sense of pessimism that such a strategy could produce a peaceful and stable country—or a significant U.S.-allied troop drawdown. Notably, by spring 2004, terrible firefights occurred in al-Anbar province west of Baghdad, historically a home of Sunnis (south of the Tikrit region, also largely Sunni, from which Saddam hailed). Gruesome television imagery of American contractors shot, their bodies then hoisted on prominent display in public spaces, turned Fallujah and Ramadi, midsized cities of Anbar province, into household words in the United States.[125]

The Post-Occupation Phase: Elections, "Train and Equip," and Civil War

As an increasing number of tragic events unfolded, the American strategy was no longer based on the hope that a simple handoff of formal political power to Iraqis could stabilize the country. Over the next three years the United States had two big ideas. It first thought that a series of elections in 2005—for an Iraqi interim government, then for approval of a constitution, then for a full-term government—could reduce the violence in Iraq through a growing sense of democratic empowerment. Unfortunately, most political parties organized and operated along largely sectar-

ian lines. So winner-take-all elections had the effect of reinforcing polar-
ization and a feeling of disenfranchisement among many Iraqis—especially
Sunnis, who had had their day in the sun under Saddam and, given their
minority status, could not expect to retain it under a one- person one-vote
electoral system.

Second, the United States believed that a much improved—or at least
better trained and equipped—Iraqi security force could take the reins of
responsibility for opposing the insurgency. If the American train-and-equip
program were sufficiently well resourced and rigorous, there might be the
possibility of a handoff in security responsibilities by 2006 or so to complement the handoff of political control that had occurred in 2004. Under
American generals Martin Dempsey, David Petraeus, James Dubik, and
others, the program was much better organized and funded. But making
Iraqi soldiers and police better marksmen with more tactical skills at patrolling and fighting could not change the fact that their leadership was
often corrupt or incompetent. Making security forces stronger therefore
also had the effect of giving them more means to abuse the population as
well as their political enemies.[126] The train-and-equip program also had
few answers to sectarian conflict and the growing sense of a Sunni-Shia
civil war.

By the time the year 2006 arrived, Iraq was a thorough mess, as a wide
spectrum of Iraqis and Americans had come to agree.[127] Yes, the mastermind al Qaeda terrorist Abu Musab al-Zarqawi was tracked and killed
by special forces under General Stanley McChrystal in June of that year.
But by then much of the damage was done in the country. The retaliatory
violence had reached a self-perpetuating and terrible cycle, with sectarian
civil war juxtaposed on top of insurgency as well as terrorism.[128]

Over the course of this period it became clear that neither the transfer
of sovereignty back to Iraqis nor the traditional counterinsurgency emphasis on winning hearts and minds was working in Iraq. Gauging whether
a counterinsurgency campaign is working is difficult even when a conflict
can be understood in such terms. Many considerations enter into this question. That helps explain why the Iraq Index at Brookings, created by
myself and Adriana Lins de Albuquerque in late 2003, included more than
fifty key indicators.[129] Even when some indicators are going well, others
may not be, and it is difficult to know how to weight their relative importance. Information is also typically imperfect, of course. Some things in
Iraq went well after the overthrow of Saddam: availability of consumer
goods to a much larger fraction of the population, proliferation of media,

opening up of political debate, restoration of services like electricity that had suffered during the brief invasion, initial boost to the economy from the large presence of foreign troops and workers. All these positives gave hope. Violence rates, at least as measured, were initially low.

But lurking beneath these positive indicators were brewing problems that turned out to be leading indicators of big trouble ahead. Even if measured violence rates were initially low, crime was spreading, starting with the widespread looting right after the removal of the Baathist regime. Political participation looked good on the surface, but as noted, it wound up inflaming zero-sum sectarian competition for power. Measured violence rates continued to get worse as well. Estimated monthly civilian fatalities from all forms of violence, according to Brookings estimates, approached 2,000 in 2005 and 3,000 in 2006—after having averaged less than 1,000 a month in 2003 and 1,400 in 2004.[130] Truck bombs, Iranian-supplied explosively formed penetrator (EFP) bombs that could penetrate armored vehicles, and small arms killed thousands upon thousands. The nation's economic foundations were not really improving, even if the economy was enjoying some short-term stimulus, and as a result jobs were scarce.

As noted, disaffected Sunnis felt angry about their new place in the political order. Many saw the ruling Shia as unsophisticated, too close to the despised Iran, and not adept at ruling the country.[131] They also feared for their lives, given how Saddam had treated the Shia; many expected that it would now be payback time. That set of attitudes created more animosity, and violence—and not only in Sunni ranks. For example, a Shia group known as Jaish al-Madhi (JAM) was supported and armed by Iran. Teheran followed that policy in order to complicate the American-led mission in Iraq and drive the United States out of the country if possible; at the same time it favored Shia groups within Iraq's multisectarian and complex polity. Led by a firebrand preacher known as Muqtada al-Sadr, JAM's influence was greatest in "Sadr City" in northeast Baghdad, as well as much of central and southern Iraq down to Basra. In Baghdad it was stronger, in terms of ability to maintain territorial control, than any Sunni group—and its use of everything from small arms to mortars and rockets to EFP improvised explosive devices made it deadly.[132] These and other groups generally were most potent and powerful within Iraq's cities. This war was different from many insurgencies of the past, and different from the war in Afghanistan, in which guerrillas often operated out of forests or mountains.[133]

The witches' brew of extremist groups increasingly suggested, as the war went on, that it would not be enough for the Iraqi government or occupying force to provide good governance and a better quality of life to most citizens—even if they had achieved such outcomes. To be successful in calming the environment and fostering stability, a counterinsurgency campaign also typically needs a degree of legitimacy among most or all major groups in a population. Failing that, it needs enough effective power to crush, or at least contain elements that may have no interest in having their hearts and minds won over.[134] And it requires time as well, since counterinsurgency operations typically take years to succeed.

If the intensity of violence reaches too high a level, or a sectarian civil war is superimposed on top of an insurgency, or other complications arise, success may not be possible. Alas, Iraq in this period suffered a number of such additional burdens. Sometimes the general trend toward increasing violence was punctuated with specific events or assassinations, like the al Qaeda bombing of a Shia holy site, the Golden Mosque, in Samarra north of Baghdad in February 2006. Such events further symbolized—and further catalyzed—the country's descent into rampant civil warfare.[135]

The Surge

As Iraq struggled through the years 2004 through 2006, under the leadership of Prime Ministers Ayad Allawi, Ibrahim al-Jaafari, and then Nouri al-Maliki, the need for new ideas became palpable. By September 2006, President Bush asked his advisers for fresh thinking.[136] National security adviser Steven Hadley, with the help of aides including Meghan O'Sullivan and William Luti, as well as outside advisers including notably Fred Kagan of the American Enterprise Institute as well as retired General Jack Keane, and army generals including David Petraeus and H. R. McMaster, all drew on their technical and historical knowledge to devise better tactics and more adequate force levels that might give counterinsurgency, or "COIN," operations a chance.[137]

Petraeus was then tapped to succeed General George Casey and lead the military effort in Iraq, beginning in February 2007, after President Bush had recently announced the new strategy (under Rumsfeld's successor, Secretary of Defense Robert Gates) in January. Key COIN concepts included dispersal of foreign and Iraqi forces into many more small "combat outposts" and "joint security stations," patrolling on foot, protecting the civilian population as a top priority, and gaining intelligence from that population about the identities and whereabouts of threatening actors. Reconciliation with those actors who may have previously been violent adversaries, but were willing to turn over a new leaf, also became crucial. This took place most notably in al-Anbar province, where al Qaeda's depravities had soured much of the population on the idea of any trans-Sunni opposition to the government and the coalition. Many tribal loyalists in Anbar in fact became "Sons of Iraq," patrolling their neighborhoods and keeping al Qaeda fighters at bay. They received a government payment in return, eventually, but had their own very good reasons for conducting these patrols simply out of survival instinct.[138] The new strategy included a "civilian surge" as well, with many more development specialists embedded with military forces, even in dangerous forward locations, to try to jumpstart economic activity and foster longer-term growth as well."[139]

The surge added more than five brigades—about 30,000 soldiers and marines, including support—to the existing U.S. presence. American troop tallies increased from 140,000 at the end of 2006 to 170,000 by the summer of 2007. It is worth noting, when discussing these numbers before, during, and after the surge, that comparable numbers of private-sector contractors from the United States, Iraq, and other countries worked directly for the U.S. and multinational missions as well. The 1:1 ratio was a far higher proportion, relative to the number of uniformed troops they were supporting, than in previous conflicts.[140]

Petraeus lobbied hard and successfully to have all the available additional troops deployed more or less at once, rather than to have to request them continuously in a piecemeal and potentially defeatist process. Meanwhile, Iraqi forces continued to grow—from roughly 323,000 in all at the start of 2007 to about 440,000 by year's end.[141] U.S. military leadership, including Petraeus's deputies and eventual successors, Generals Raymond Odierno and Lloyd Austin, as well as American Ambassador Ryan Crocker worked with some success to persuade Iraqi Prime Minister Nouri al-Maliki to replace sectarian, corrupt, or incompetent Iraqi military and police leaders with more effective individuals.[142]

The concepts behind COIN were not simply to adopt a kinder, gentler approach to U.S. and coalition and Iraqi military operations. Indeed, Petraeus would often underscore just how crucial the high-tempo and highly effective counterterrorism methods of General Stanley McChrystal and others were to any successful counterinsurgency operation, especially in a place like Iraq where extremist violence had become so all-encompassing and destructive.[143]

McChrystal's methods emphasized collaboration by all different U.S. and coalition intelligence agencies in cavernous common open spaces—rather than the segmented "plywood palaces" where representatives from various agencies had often been stovepiped before. The physical separation reinforced a tendency towards stove-piping and protecting the information that one's own agency had gathered, interfering with collaboration. McChrystal emphasized the creation of a "team of teams" that prioritized the sharing of information across bureaucratic barriers. That approach in the field built on the integration happening stateside as a result of the 2004 Intelligence Reform and Terrorism Prevention Act, along with its associated creation of the Office of the Director of National Intelligence and the National Counterterrorism Center.[144] This improved intelligence in turn allowed for more effective and frequent raids. Efficiencies were introduced into the process as well. A virtuous cycle resulted: captured suspects were often interrogated on the helicopter flight back to a detention facility, and information they provided could be used in real time to allow prompt follow-on action against their associates.[145]

The surge also included more conventional military operations to search and clear areas that had become sanctuaries for the worst of the extremist groups. A three-phased campaign plan was initiated in 2007. It began with a strengthening of coalition positions within Baghdad. Then, starting in June, attacks were launched against extremist strongholds, weapons caches, and truck-bomb factories in the Baghdad belts that encircled the city in an operations that was called Phantom Thunder. Then, additional operations to deprive remaining al Qaeda or militia elements of other sanctuaries were undertaken in Phantom Strike.[146] Over the course of these three phases, major operations were conducted in important cities in al-Anbar province, including Fallujah and Ramadi, and in the so-called triangle of death as well as Sadr city within Baghdad, and elsewhere.

As Petraeus put it, "'Clear, hold, and build' became the operative concept—a contrast with the previous practice in many operations of clearing insurgents and then leaving, after handing off the security mission to Iraqi forces that proved incapable of sustaining progress in the areas cleared."[147] Other methods were used to create a greater sense of security as well. Unmanned aerial vehicles and aerostats (balloons tied to the ground) were employed to improve the intelligence picture of the battlefield. Jersey barriers were erected to complicate the job of car bombers, protecting buildings, markets, and other sites where people congregated.

The net effect of all these changes was astounding. After a period of several months in which casualty levels worsened during the most difficult clearing operations, violence levels began to drop dramatically. Civilian fatalities dropped by half, then 75 percent, then by 2008 closer to 90 percent relative to the horrendous levels of 2004 through 2006. Markets bustled, soccer stadiums filled; hopefulness among Iraqis, as measured in public opinion surveys, began to improve. Eventually, even some protective blast walls and other barriers were dismantled, so much had security improved so fast.

As Kenneth Pollack and I observed during a research trip taken to Iraq in July 2007, many American troops (including friends of ours who had always been honest in private conversations—and who had been skeptical of previous happy talk from the U.S. government about supposed progress in Iraq) expressed amazement at how well the new tactics and new strategy were working. Again, the Anbar awakening, during which local tribes generally changed their minds and chose to work with coalition and government forces against al Qaeda, was just as crucial.[148] By this point in midsummer, civilian casualties were already down by an average of about one third. An air of optimism suffused the troops' work, despite the ongoing dangers.[149]

Progress continued in the following months. To be sure, there were ups and downs. Prime Minister Maliki, in the spring of 2008, ordered a "charge of the knights" to retake the southern city of Basra from Shia militias, without coordination with Petraeus and other American officials. Disaster almost ensued. But in the end the militias were weakened. And at least Maliki had shown he was willing to employ Iraqi security forces against his fellow Shia when necessary, however reckless his approach.

Back home, an American political debate was picking up steam, with many Democrats in Congress and on the presidential campaign trail understandably highly critical of the Bush administration for the war in Iraq. By that point, it was rather clear that Saddam had had no weapons of mass destruction and no role in the 9/11 attacks (even if some people retained doubts on the latter point). It was also clear, to paraphrase the Iraqi dissident Kanan Makiya, that even if some Iraqis were willing to throw flowers at the feet of American soldiers who came to liberate them from Saddam, many others were inclined to lay improvised explosive devices in their future tracks. Makiya's 1989 book, *Republic of Fear,* made vivid, in very personal and humanitarian terms, the depravity and brutality of Saddam's regime. That was a compelling and important message.

Alas, the logical leap from that reporting to the expectation of a peaceful post-Saddam Iraq was ultimately not borne out by actual events.[150]

Any thoughts a Democratic-controlled Congress might have had of cutting off funding for the war, as the new fiscal year 2008 dawned on October 1, 2007, were checkmated by compelling testimony about progress in Iraq by General Petraeus and Ambassador Crocker in mid-September. That did not mean the debate was over, however. Barack Obama secured the Democratic nomination for president in the spring of 2008, in part based on his strident and longstanding opposition to the war in Iraq (and conviction that Afghanistan was the "right war" whereas the 2003 invasion of Iraq, as Richard Haass put it, was a "war of choice"—and a bad choice at that).[151] Obama then pledged to bring home U.S. troops within one to one and a half years of taking office. That promise seemed less necessary or convincing by the time election day rolled around. Iraq was less the decisive issue of the campaign than had at one time been expected. But the 2008 financial crisis, together with the country's deep desire for change, combined with Obama's considerable charisma and vision, vaulted him to the presidency. And he was certainly still a skeptic of the whole Iraq project.

The End of the Combat Mission and the U.S.-Allied Departure

Once in office, Obama would slow down the American troop withdrawal relative to what he had previously promised. Rather than get out in 2010, he took three years to leave (after formally ending the American-led combat mission in 2009). But despite this decision to be more patient and prudent, things went awry. Regrettably, the United States wound up supporting Prime Minister Maliki's efforts to hold onto power after the elections of early 2010. Washington did so even though Maliki had attempted, before the elections, to push many Sunni candidates off the ballots in an act of fairly brazen sectarianism. The U.S. desire to see the confusing electoral situation quickly resolved played a role as well, especially perhaps in the mind of Vice President Joe Biden. It was easier to stick with the son-of-a-gun we knew than any alternative, apparently. But the United States had bet on the wrong horse, and would probably have been much better served to support the less sectarian Shia leader Ayad Allawi, whose party included many non-Shia as well.[152]

Compounding the danger of having an increasingly emboldened Maliki still in office, President Obama then chose to push the Iraqi government to make up its mind about whether it really still wanted American help or not. With a previous agreement governing the status of American forces in Iraq soon to expire, Obama insisted that the Iraqi parliament formally replace the status of forces agreement with an accord that would shield American troops from any possibility of trial within Iraq. Obama had at least two other choices—accept an informal extension of the previous understanding, or simply allow the U.S. military to whisk out of country any trooper accused of a crime by the Iraqi legal system before that person could be arrested. But choosing to elevate the issue to a matter of principle, and to a referendum on how Iraq felt about its overall relationship with the United States, Obama wound up empty handed. Iraq's parliament refused to grant the formal immunity. So the several thousand U.S. military personnel still in Iraq left by the end of 2011.[153]

Calamity then ensued in Iraqi politics. An unchained Maliki sought to arrest many Sunni politicians on trumped-up charges for corruption and similar purported offenses, including a number known for having impeccable credentials. He deposed Vice President Tareq al-Hashemi. He even leveled terrorism charges against the well-regarded finance minister, Rafi al-Issawi, forcing the latter to flee the capital for safer areas in Anbar province. Many Sunnis were furious. Sectarianism was reinforced by nepotism, dramatically setting back the country as well as the integrity and fighting spirit of the nation's security forces.[154] Maliki also himself systematically weakened the Iraqi security forces, dismissing competent commanders and often replacing them with the very people Petraeus, Odierno, Austin, Crocker, and others had worked so hard to have replaced several years before during the surge. As a result, training deteriorated, professionalism was lost. Sectarianism again prevailed within the army and police. An independent judiciary, such as it had been, was a casualty as well.[155]

ISIS and the American Return to Iraq, 2014 to the Present

All this set the stage for the 2014 rise to power of ISIS, or the Islamic State in Iraq and Syria. Sometimes instead called ISIL, for the Islamic State in Iraq and the Levant, ISIS had broken off from al Qaeda in Iraq by 2014 due to personality and ideological disputes. Finding succor and support among angry Sunnis, it favored the near-term creation of a transnational "caliphate" and made great progress toward achieving that very goal.[156] It profited from Syria's civil war to establish control of several cities in Sunni-dominated parts of the country there, then moved into Iraq where the country's security forces crumbled when they encountered the vicious and terrifying new group. Videotaped beheadings, mass executions of prisoners (including soldiers who surrendered), and other atrocities were part of its modus operandi. As it gained territory, it also gained access to banks, to oil fields, and to populations from which it could earn more funds through extortion and kidnapping. Specializing in social media, it drew followers from more than 100 countries around the world. Forgoing al Qaeda's focus on austere living in pursuit of rewards in the afterlife, ISIS promised ecstasy to its followers on Earth as well. Sexual slaves taken from Shia, Christian, or non-cooperative Sunni ranks as well as financial rewards were among its main incentives to those who would join its ranks. Soon, roughly one-quarter to one-third of both Syria and Iraq were under its control, including Iraq's third-largest city, Mosul—with nearly 10 million people forced to live under its heinous governance.[157]

That was not the end of it. ISIS threatened to take cities in Iraqi (and Syrian) Kurdistan as well. It also menaced Baghdad, moving from its new bases and sanctuaries in northern and western Iraq toward the Iraqi capital, ultimately approaching within some 30 miles of its outskirts. But it was fended off by American airpower combined with militias on the ground—be they Kurdish, in Iraq's north, or Shia-based (and often Iran-funded) near Baghdad. Wisely, the Obama administration withheld more than minimal military help until it had forced a change of Iraqi political leadership. Maliki, the clear cause of much of what had transpired, was pushed out in favor of the far more conciliatory and inclusive Shia leader, Haider al-Abadi.[158]

With the immediate threat to the very existence of the Iraqi state now contained, Washington and Baghdad could now develop a joint plan to build up a capability that could roll back and defeat the Islamic State. The main concept worked something like this. First, in Iraq, work with a more cooperative Iraqi prime minister to find military leadership that would cultivate a spirit of multisectarian collaboration within the nation's security forces and promote unit commanders who exemplified that attitude. Second, tighten border controls around Iraq as well as Syria where possible to make it harder for foreign recruits to reach the so-called caliphate. Third, use U.S. airpower to limit further ISIS inroads, then using airpower to attack leadership targets, resource-generating facilities such as oil-production infrastructure, and logistics capabilities. Along the way, tolerate the role of Iranian-backed militias known as Popular Mobilization Forces, which provided some of the necessary manpower on the ground to complement U.S. airpower. This whole process might be broken into three main phases: degrade ISIS into early 2016, then counterattack through mid-2017, and finally defeat through early 2019.[159]

Within Iraq, the strategy also emphasized building up a new army (and police force) from scratch, over a multiyear period. It also involved creation of strong special forces. And it profited from close collaboration with Kurdish peshmerga (paramilitary) units. With this strategy the United States was able to limit its footprint on the ground to about 5,000 troops in Iraq and 2,000 in Syria. By 2018, working with regional partners, it was able to defeat the caliphate. The ISIS leader, al-Baghdadi, was ultimately found, targeted and killed in October 2019—though by that point, the caliphate no longer really existed.[160]

Ironically, perhaps, this U.S. strategy displayed considerable continuity from the Barack Obama through the Donald Trump presidencies. Although successful, it has been criticized on several grounds, starting with its slow pace. By focusing on providing air support to the gradually rebuilding Iraqi security forces, it did not attempt more direct and potentially decisive action against ISIS's key strategic capabilities. This patient approach took a full four years to complete. During that time, tens of thousands of lives on the ground were lost, and ISIS retained a certain aura that contributed to successful recruiting as well as numerous ISIS-inspired attacks in Europe and beyond. The operation has also been criticized for its overwhelming use of precision-guided munitions. As a result, the United States was, in a relatively minor war, consuming precision weapons as fast as it could use them. Ultimately, at least 70,000 were used, out of a total of more than 115,000 munitions employed. Some 200,000 American military sorties were flown (including tanker and reconnaissance flights). Some $20 billion was spent on the effort.[161] On balance, however, the costs were very modest compared with many other battles and wars discussed in this book, and the ultimate success was considerable.

With the defeat of ISIS, the saga of America's generation-long military engagement in Iraq almost came to an end. But only almost. ISIS itself has not gone away and may be modestly and gradually strengthening as of this writing in 2022.[162] Shia militias backed by Iran have recently shelled U.S. military bases in Iraq, sometimes wounding and occasionally killing soldiers and contractors (and Iraqis there).

Indeed, this latter problem was serious enough in 2019, 2020, and 2021 that the United States struck depots and staging bases used by the militias in Iraq. And in the first days of 2020, it carried out a drone strike against the mastermind of Iran's elite and violent operations unit known as the Quds force, Qassam Soleimani, who was killed along with a major militia leader after disembarking from a plane at Baghdad airport. The outcries from not only Iran but Iraq, and its fiercely nationalistic parliament, were loud and persistent. In this tense atmosphere, the administration of President Joe Biden decided to further downsize the remaining U.S. presence in Iraq. Whether this smaller, less visible U.S. military posture has reached a stable equilibrium remains to be seen. So does the question of whether Iraq, still riven by sectarianism and a plethora of militias, as well as economic corruption and weakness, can stabilize itself as a polity.[163]

Afghanistan

When Kabul fell to the Taliban on the weekend of August 14 and 15, 2021, history had come full circle. With even greater rapidity than it was defeated in the fall of 2001 by a group of Afghans known as the Northern Alliance, backed up by American aircraft and special forces, the Taliban seized control of Afghanistan.

That country has been called the graveyard of empires. The British were driven out twice in the nineteenth century, and the Soviet Union was defeated there once in the twentieth. It has also been called ungovernable, and a country in name only, given that most Afghans identify by ethnic group or tribe at least as much as nationality. It has been depicted as a land prone to conflict and doomed to interminable violence. These observations were often used to predict the failure of the U.S. and NATO mission in Afghanistan, or to argue against its expansion or extension, at various times during the 2001–2021 period.

Some of these points are valid, but only some of them, and only up to a certain point. As the acclaimed scholar Thomas Barfield has argued, "Afghanistan is one of those places in the world in which people who know the least make the most definitive statements about it."[164] Afghanistan as a country is slightly older than the United States. It did not have national-level insurgencies or civil wars until the Soviet invasion. Before that invasion, its various peoples had generally tolerated a central government as long as it did not impinge unduly on their way of life or tax them too much. Its peoples do have a collective sense of Afghan identity, even if that identity admittedly competes with others. And whereas the British and Soviets arrived with great plans to change governments to suit their own interests, the United States and NATO arrived at a time when Afghans overwhelmingly welcomed their presence—at least at first.[165] By that point, in 2001, Afghanistan was 22 years into a period of violence and chaos that had largely broken the society. Afghans had in effect helped the West win the Cold War. The Afghan mujahadeen had played a central role in the defeat of the Soviet troops occupying Afghanistan and in thus helping Mikhail Gorbachev institute the huge changes that ultimately brought down the Berlin Wall and dissolved the Warsaw Pact as well as the Soviet Union itself.[166] After that war, they were also effectively deserted by the United States in the 1990s. So was Pakistan, which had helped in the effort to arm the mujahadeen to drive out the Soviet occupiers.[167]

But, as General Mark Milley, chairman of the Joint Chiefs of Staff, told Congress in September 2021, the U.S. and NATO missions in Afghanistan wound up as a strategic defeat for the United States. That is surely true at one level. Somehow, the Taliban, while not widely popular across Afghanistan, developed a certain identity as an authentically Afghan movement, and ultimately derived an edge in inspiration as well as motivation over government forces from that mystique.[168] Still, it is important not to overstate this point. Tens of thousands of Afghans, many of them refugees from earlier periods of unrest or young and inspired patriots for their country, worked hard to build a new country out of the ruins of decades of warfare that was mostly not their people's fault. Tens of thousands of young Afghan men gave their lives wearing the uniform of their country. There were many inspired and inspiring individuals on the losing side of the struggle, as well.

While it is too soon to know as of this writing, it is possible that history's broader balance sheet may be more forgiving. In grand strategic terms, the overall war effort achieved some key goals. The United States did not suffer any further catastrophic attacks originating out of Afghanistan between 2002 and 2021. The Taliban, while hardly an American preference, may now be sufficiently aware of the strength and reach of U.S. military power that they choose to pursue a modus vivendi with the United States. In the interest of avoiding war, gaining diplomatic recognition, and accessing funds, the Taliban may well limit any further collaboration with other extremist groups.[169] At least, that is a possibility.

But again, it is too soon to know that verdict, and in any case it is the military scorecard that most interests us here. By that metric, Afghanistan should probably be viewed as a combination of one quick win followed by one protracted and gradually deteriorating stalemate—capped off by a calamitous collapse and defeat. One win, one tie, and an eventual culminating defeat—and all of that within a twenty-year period.

At a more granular level, the U.S. role in the war went through perhaps five main combat phases. At the time of the 9/11 attacks, the Department of Defense had no war plan for fighting in Afghanistan. That was arguably a major mistake, as Fred Kagan has argued, but it remains the reality of the situation regardless.[170] Improvisation therefore became the guiding principle, as aerial attacks against Taliban positions began in early October. Soon, special forces and CIA teams were on the ground—only several hundred American personnel—working with the Tajik-dominated Northern Alliance of Afghanistan (a group that al Qaeda had attempted to weaken just two days before the 9/11 attacks with the assassination of the Northern Alliance's leader, Ahmad Shah Massoud). The Americans embedded with the Afghan fighters and called in precision strikes from U.S. aircraft against Taliban positions.[171] Several hundred marines flew into southern Afghanistan as well. Together, in a remarkable military operation, these Americans helped the Northern Alliance overthrow the Taliban in the fall of 2001. In military terms, that was the first chapter of the American military involvement.

A second distinct chapter played out over the next half-dozen years or so. During that period, American and other NATO forces made modest efforts to help Afghanistan form a government as well as create security forces in what was sometimes nicknamed the "light footprint" approach. Throughout these years, Washington was preoccupied with Iraq, as were some NATO allies; no one in the alliance really prioritized Afghanistan. As Chairman of the Joint Chiefs Admiral Mike Mullen put it, "In Afghanistan, we do what we can. In Iraq, we do what we must."[172] During these years and beyond, the United States and partners did prosecute a largely successful counterterrorism campaign, including striking al Qaeda leaders in Pakistan with drones. Later, it used bases in Afghanistan to carry out the raid to kill Osama bin Laden in Abbottabad, Pakistan on May 2, 2011 as well.

By the end of the Bush presidency, however, a third main phase of the U.S.-led war effort had begun. It dated back to the immediate aftermath of the success of the surge in Iraq; emboldened by this new approach to counterinsurgency, and worried about growing signs of a Taliban recovery, President Bush and Secretary of Defense Robert Gates began a gradual force buildup in Afghanistan in 2008—even as both major U.S. presidential candidates advocated doing the same. Once elected, President Obama went much further. U.S. forces in Afghanistan roughly tripled on his watch, meaning that the Afghanistan surge was an even more dramatic change relative to earlier force levels than the Iraq surge had been. (In Afghanistan, U.S. forces went from around 30,000 troops at the end of the

Bush presidency to 100,000 by 2010–2011; in Iraq, by contrast, the surge had taken U.S. uniformed personnel from roughly 140,000 to 170,000.)

The surge did not achieve the kind of fundamental transformation of the security environment seen in Iraq. There was no corresponding "awakening" movement to complement the work of official security forces. The Pakistan sanctuary for the insurgency remained a huge hindrance to progress; the Taliban remained resilient and committed. But the surge did slow Taliban momentum and regain key parts of the country's south, like Kandahar. Even as NATO and Afghan forces effectively fought "shoulder to shoulder," the progress was slow and sporadic over the period from 2009 through 2012–2013 under General Stanley McChrystal, General David Petraeus, and General John Allen. Compounding the challenges brought on by the brevity of the American and NATO surge, and the Pakistan sanctuary, the capacities of Afghan forces themselves remained quite limited. Afghan government corruption and ineptness remained huge problems, too, as Afghan citizens began to lose faith with the overall state-building venture.

By the end of Allen's command in early 2013, a fourth phase of the American engagement in Afghanistan was emerging. NATO removed some, then many, then most of its main ground combat units. By the end of 2014, the International Security Assistance Force (ISAF) was formally disbanded, replaced by Operation Resolute Support—the change underscoring NATO's new and more limited role. From 2015 until the withdrawal of 2021, NATO provided airpower, intelligence, training, equipment, mentoring, and some limited on-the-ground capabilities in the form of special forces as well as special advisory teams. Economic development and state-building efforts continued, too, though with less presence in the field and generally lower expectations.

The fifth phase witnessed the collapse of the Afghan government, starting with localized surrenders by political leaders and security forces in provincial capitals and soon also in Kabul. By mid-August 2021, the Taliban was in control of almost all the country. By early September it claimed to have taken the last holdout of opposition forces in the Panjshir Valley. The Taliban then formed a transitional government made up primarily of hardline elements, many of the key individuals having their roots in the organization dating back in the 1990s.

In the end, some 800,000 Americans served in Afghanistan; 2,488 died there, with another 20,000 or more seriously wounded. Afghan casualties totaled perhaps half a million, including 200,000 Afghan army and police

(65,000 of those killed), and comparable or somewhat greater Taliban casualties. Civilians in Afghanistan suffered an estimated 120,000 killed and wounded. But life expectancy across the entire population rose by almost ten years over the twenty-year U.S.-led foreign intervention, and the average child received several years' more education, among other benefits—and the United States as well as its major allies did not suffer another large-scale terrorist attack hatched or coordinated on Afghan soil.[173]

The 2001 Overthrow of the Taliban

After the tragic day of September 11, Congress passed the "Authorization on the Use of Military Force." It went into effect on September 18 and legitimized retaliation against those who attacked the U.S. as well as their collaborators. Armed with this legal and political predicate, President George W. Bush then issued an ultimatum to the Taliban government in Kabul that it either present the al Qaeda perpetrators of the attack or be deemed complicit itself. The Taliban did not respond. NATO, however, did respond, and within twenty-four hours of the attacks at that. The defense pact formally invoked its Article V mutual-defense provision for the first time in its history, thereby committing other allies to help the United States defend itself and prevent any further attacks. Given how al Qaeda trumpeted its great successes on September 11, claiming momentum in its goal to drive the American presence in all its forms out of the broader Middle East, the possibility of further violence seemed palpable.[174]

On October 7, the United States initiated military operations against the Taliban. It did not ask for NATO help in the effort or closely consult with allies. The Bush administration was criticized for this purported unilateralism. But just as likely a cause of its silence was the simple fact that it was entirely improvising in the military campaign. Using the preferred modern U.S. military tool of aerial bombardment—with cruise missiles, as well as long-range aircraft dropping either unguided or guided munitions—would likely not achieve decisive effects against a government that took pride in its spartan ways and lacked meaningful military or economic infrastructure against which ordnance might be directed. The administration might have asked allies for help. However, it did not really yet know what kind of help it needed or wanted.

Fortunately for the United States, it had resourceful midlevel field officers and agents from the Department of Defense and the CIA who had contacts with Afghanistan's Northern Alliance. That Tajik-dominated resistance group had never been conquered by the Taliban in the preceding five years and retained sanctuary in the Panjshir Valley in the country's northeast. So-called A-teams (more formally, Operational Detachment-Alpha) were each made up of twelve Green Beret soldiers from U.S. Army special forces; CIA teams were organized in groups of ten. Under then–Brigadier General James Mattis, the United States also managed to insert several hundred marines based on amphibious ships in the Indian Ocean into southern Afghanistan by overflying Pakistan's Baluchistan province. Aircraft carrier-based aircraft participated as well.[175] Deputy Secretary of State Richard Armitage had previously warned Pakistan's leaders that it was time to choose sides in order to avoid the wrath of an angry and vengeance-minded America; overflights whether of Marine Corps helicopters, bombers, or other aircraft were not opposed by Pakistani forces.[176]

With these building blocks available, a strategy began to emerge within a few weeks. CIA and special forces advisory teams would embed with the Northern Alliance as they sought battle with the Taliban. Northern Alliance fighters, though outnumbered, were good in their own right. But even more important, the embedding enabled American operatives to call in airstrikes precisely at key moments.[177] Laser range finders, GPS devices, and reliable radios allowed these brave U.S. personnel, typically on foot (or in the case of at least one team, horseback) in such engagements, to gain close-air support for the Northern Alliance exactly when and where it was needed—as documented later in excellent field research by Columbia University professor Stephen Biddle.[178] Fears that the Taliban might still have leftover Stinger anti aircraft surface-to-air missiles were mitigated by having many aircraft drop their bombs from above 15,000 feet, as in Kosovo a couple years earlier—but in this case, the presence of Americans on the ground permitted accurate targeting even from such altitudes. Demoralized, and intimidated, the Taliban increasingly went to ground, abandoning positions not only in remote rural areas where they could be easily attacked, but even in cities. Kandahar was the last city to fall, as the Taliban's leader, Mullah Omar, fled that southern city on December 6. The entire war was won within two months.[179]

As they saw what was happening, bin Laden and other al Qaeda leadership, previously holed up in places like their training base near Kandahar or their mountain redoubts near Khost in eastern Afghanistan, took flight. They hoped for sanctuary in the tribal areas of western Pakistan. So they began to move in that general direction, reaching the Tora Bora area near Jalalabad (and the Khyber Pass) by late November. But the United States had few forces on the ground anywhere in the area. Regrettably, Bush administration leaders saw no need to establish an American presence in the Tora Bora region—perhaps by creating a makeshift set of helicopter refueling sites. Instead, the United States bombed mountain passes and paid local militia commanders to watch ingress and egress points. Happy to do so by day but uninterested in suffering the cold of early winter Hindu Kush nights to maintain twenty-four-hour vigil, the latter failed to construct an airtight cordon and bin Laden, along with perhaps a thousand associates, slipped away.[180] The overall operation in the fall of 2001 was a masterpiece, but a flawed masterpiece.[181]

An interim Afghan government was established at the Bonn, Germany, conference in December 2001. Fatefully, no effort was made to include Taliban participation in such a government in light of the group's extremism, and perhaps a certain overconfidence in victors' circles that it could not mount a comeback. On December 20, the United Nations also established the International Security Assistance Force to provide security for Kabul and train Afghan security forces.[182] Some argue that the latter approach was a mistake, and that America and allies would have been wiser just to walk away from Afghanistan, promising to return with lethal effect if anyone affiliated with al Qaeda again took power.[183] However, that was essentially the strategy that was used after America and Pakistan worked with the mujahadeen to defeat the Soviet Union in the 1980s, and its track record was not very good. Nor was it seen as a particularly noble way to treat a people that had suffered for so long, after helping the United States win the Cold War.

The "Light Footprint" Strategy of 2002–2007

For the next five years, the United States and NATO took a minimalist approach to Afghanistan. Doubting it could be strengthened into a modern nation state, believing that the Taliban threat was largely gone for good, it adopted what has often been called a "light footprint" approach to state building. The United States in particular focused primarily on ongoing counterterrorism operations there.

For the United States, much of this logic was reinforced by the desire to make major change in the broader Middle East through the overthrow of Saddam Hussein and building of a new Iraq. The United States military was not large enough to conduct two major and protracted counterinsurgency and stabilization missions at the same time. Indeed, even a large mission in Iraq and much smaller one in Afghanistan would strain it severely in the years to come. Army units would often spend fifteen months at a stretch on deployment (rather than the preferred twelve). Soldiers would often spend only twelve to fifteen months at home on rest, recovery, and retraining before returning to the CENTCOM theater (rather than the preferred cycle of two to three years at home for every one on deployment).

From 2002 to 2007, American allies collectively deployed anywhere from 5,000 to 25,000 troops to Afghanistan. They began at the lower level, and then ramped up by a few thousand a year starting in 2004 (with the biggest increases in 2006 and 2007). These troops, who made up ISAF, were initially restricted to Kabul—after Pentagon officials successfully lobbied against a larger force and broader geographic scope for their mission.[184] That restriction was gradually eased over time. Peacekeepers were first deployed outside of Kabul in 2005 and arrived in the crucial south of the country in 2006.[185] Halfway into 2007, there were some 2,500 Canadian troops in Kandahar, and 6,000 Brits mostly in Helmand. (By the end of 2008, the respective totals would be 2,750 and 8,100, plus another 1,700 Dutch and 1,000 Australian troops in the south.) The ISAF and American military command were unified in 2007 when U.S. Army general Dan McNeill arrived in Afghanistan to lead both.[186]

The United States itself generally deployed troops in the same broad range, starting close to 10,000 and gradually increasing to 25,000 in 2007 as well.[187] But as noted, its primary emphasis was on counterterrorism, and its forces operated under separate command. The main geographic focus of U.S. efforts was the country's Pashtun-majority regions in provinces near or adjoining Pakistan, since it was Pashtuns who made up the preponderance of the Taliban movement (even if most Pashtuns were not Taliban). In March 2002, for example, the fabled Operation Anaconda was conducted in the Shahikot Valley in the country's eastern mountains.[188] Many other operations took place in these early years, and American casualties were considerable—far less than in Iraq, but not dramatically different on a per-troop basis. By 2003, General David Barno, commander of U.S. forces in Afghanistan, set up brigade-level headquarters in the country's east and south. Counterterrorism operations continued thereafter. American forces also began to conduct some preliminary aspects of counterinsurgency operations as well, as the mission's scale and scope creeped upward.[189]

The main state-building efforts centered on forming lightly armed police and army forces of quite modest size. Unfortunately, this task was not taken particularly seriously by NATO. Training programs were minimalist; leaders of the Afghan forces were not particularly well mentored (or selected).[190] Nonetheless, the overall environment was forgiving—in terms of the Taliban threat at the time. The accomplishments of the NATO mission in this period were also limited. But to many, they seemed adequate to the task—especially since schools were opening, lights were coming on, basic health care services were spreading, and living standards for the Afghan people were gradually improving. Electricity production doubled over the first five years of the new Afghan republic; the nation's GDP grew by half; internet use was growing fast. Things seemed okay.[191]

They were not. Programs directed by Germany and the United States to build Afghan security forces, Italian-led efforts to reform the judiciary, and British-led programs to reduce drug production and trafficking were underresourced and generally unsuccessful. The chance to build up the Afghan state during a relatively quiet period was squandered.

The Taliban soon plotted revenge. Angered by its exclusion from the new Afghan government formed in Bonn by the international community in early 2002, supported and provided sanctuary by Pakistan, ideologically committed to similar goals that it espoused before, and impressively patient, it began to prepare a comeback. The ensuing deterioration in security was gradual at first, but unmistakable nonetheless, especially by 2006 or so, when the Taliban mounted offensives under Commander Dadullah from February onward, first in northern Helmand and then also southern Helmand and western Kandahar provinces. Taliban forces attacked police units and stations and other focal points of government presence, and set ambushes when they could anticipate the movements of pro-government personnel.[192] Unfortunately, Afghan political leadership failed to unite the Pashtun tribes in these regions to fight the Taliban, which at this point remained generally unpopular in Afghanistan, and was still rather weak and beatable.[193] American policy also rejected the idea of reaching out to former Taliban members to bring them into the political process in a way that might have taken some wind out of the insurgency.[194]

The statistics of war documented these outbreaks of fighting quantitatively. From 2005 to 2006, suicide bombings quintupled, the use of improvised explosive devices more than doubled, and armed attacks almost tripled. U.S. troop fatalities, having averaged about 50 a year from 2002–2004, topped 100 by 2007; other foreign troop losses, ranging from about 10 to 20 a year in the 2002–2004 period, also topped 100 by 2007.[195]

Major clearing operations were attempted at times, by NATO as well as U.S. forces, as in Operation Medusa and Operation Mountain Fury in southern provinces of the country starting in September 2006.[196] But available resources were not up to the challenge in a country of the size and complexity of Afghanistan.

The Afghan government under President Hamid Karzai—appointed in 2002, elected in 2004, reelected in 2009—did not have much capacity for or many answers to this growing problem, any more than NATO did. By early 2007, NATO and the United States had merged their military commands, so General Dan McNeill (followed by General David McKiernan in 2008) effectively ran the entire military effort. The improvement to the chain of command was welcome, but too little, too late. Otherwise, NATO's response to the growing threat was slow, since the United States remained preoccupied by Iraq.

During this time, despite Karzai's charisma, and his apparent potential to be a unifying figure in Afghan politics, much about the country's politics was not helping the situation. The U.S.-sherpaed Afghan constitution gave great power to the president to appoint local leaders. That generated pushback from those Afghans who favored a considerable degree of regional and local autonomy.[197] Not all regional and local leaders were warlords, or equally corrupt, or unpopular with their own followers, so Karzai often produced resentment when he shuffled people about.[198] Indeed, since Karzai often moved leaders around to strengthen his own political position, he made little net progress against corruption or in favor of better governance. Karzai's own personal charisma notwithstanding, the poor state of political leadership in Afghanistan was creating fertile ground for the Taliban to recruit and grow.[199]

The Taliban itself was hardly popular across most swaths of the Afghan people, but it gained enough followers to become dangerous again, and control of enough territory to increase its revenue from opium production.[200] Counterinsurgent strategist David Kilcullen estimates that Taliban numbers reached about 10,000 hard-core full-time fighters and roughly another 30,000 part-time fighters by 2008—significant numbers, to be sure, but quite modest when compared with many other Afghan militias or the growing Afghan security forces.[201] By one estimate, the Taliban was able to carry out "heavy activity" in only 5 of the country's 34 provinces in 2006, but in two-thirds of them by 2008 (and more than three-fourths by 2009).[202] In the 2006–2007 period, the Afghan people remained generally hopeful for their future and supportive of their security forces—but some of the trends were in gradually more pessimistic directions.[203]

The Afghanistan Surge, Plus Before and After, 2008–2014

It was at this juncture in 2008 that President Bush, Senator John McCain, Senator Barack Obama, and Secretary of Defense Gates all decided that Afghanistan had to be a priority for the United States and especially the next American president. (Obama in particular had felt this way all along.) Under President Bush, the United States decided to add roughly two more brigades, and a total of more than 10,000 troops, to its existing force posture. There would now be more than 30,000 American military personnel in Afghanistan. The two new brigades would deploy in specific geographic zones to ensure greater safety for the Afghan capital and surrounding regions, including parts of the "ring road" that effectively ran like a concentric circle within the country's territorial perimeter.

The coalition now had well over 50,000 troops in country, and under a unified command structure for the first time. To be sure, there were still huge challenges to effective coalition warfare. Some NATO forces were not authorized by their home governments to conduct the full range of counterinsurgency operations, under a policy of national "caveats."[204] All of these forces were dependent on the United States to some degree for intelligence and logistics. But the show of strength and solidarity was nonetheless impressive, with dozens of countries involved on the ground in one way or another.

After Bush authorized the modest buildup, newly inaugurated president Barack Obama asked Brookings scholar and CIA veteran Bruce Riedel, Under Secretary of Defense Michèle Flournoy, and Ambassador Richard Holbrooke to assess the need for any additional forces. That review took place in the first two months of Obama's presidency. Given the need for considerable consultations with allies at the beginning and end of the process, there was about a month for actual development and analysis of options. The debate was considerably influenced by the recent success of modern COIN doctrine during the surge in Iraq. By this point, General David Petraeus was in charge of Central Command. Other veterans of the Iraq surge experience, notably Secretary of Defense Gates (the only person ever to serve as secretary of defense for two different U.S. presidents of two different political parties) and Joint Chiefs Chairman Admiral Mike Mullen, remained in their previous positions.

The Riedel-Flournoy-Holbrooke review led to the deployment of roughly another 30,000 U.S. troops and several thousand more from NATO countries. The review was, as noted, somewhat compressed. More forces were envisioned for Kandahar, for Jalabad, and Khost near Pakistani border regions, and for other places, in what amounted to a general thickening of the U.S. and NATO footprint in key strategic places. Still, typical force densities were far below what had been achieved in Iraq, and for their part the Afghan security forces remained small and underdeveloped compared with those of Iraq. Since Iraq and Afghanistan had comparably sized populations, COIN doctrine suggested the latter would require as many forces as had the former.[205]

In May 2009, General McKiernan was relieved of command, in the hope of injecting more energy and urgency into the operation. His successor was General Stanley McChrystal of Joint Special Operations Command fame. The hope was that, in addition to his demonstrated excellence in special operations, McChrystal could establish a bond with an increasingly obdurate President Karzai—who was starting to lose patience with a United States that seemed bent on depriving him of reelection that same summer, among other affronts real and perceived.

As the Afghan election campaign went into high gear in the summer of 2009, McChrystal was conducting a thorough review of the country's security conditions, developing options for President Obama. Building a substantial analytical team from the U.S. government, NATO and other partner nations, along with the think tank and academic worlds, McChrystal sought to reach an accurate diagnosis of Afghanistan's security challenges. He and his team determined that about 20 percent of Afghanistan's 407 districts were key strategic terrain. After the departure of the assessment team, and applying the precepts of the *U.S. Army/Marine Corps Counterinsurgency Field Manual* (and its guideline that there be 20 to 25 counterinsurgent personnel for every 1,000 civilians being protected in an indigenous population), he estimated overall force requirements for coalition and Afghan forces, if they were to stand a good chance of success.[206] Ultimately three options were developed. Regrettably, they were also leaked to the media, complicating White House relations with McChrystal's command, elements of which were suspected by some to have been behind the leak.[207]

After an autumn of numerous policy discussions in the White House Situation Room, Obama chose a variant of the middle option, though he scaled it back slightly from the proposed increase of 40,000 U.S. troops. That "middle option minus" meant a U.S. troop buildup to 100,000 total troops. Allied nations would increase their strength much more modestly, by a combined total of less than 10,000 additional uniformed personnel.

The foreign coalition would then total something approaching 150,000 troops. The mission would also seek to generate Afghan security forces numbering in total around 300,000 soldiers and police as soon as possible. Tens of thousands of additional private contractors, if counted too, would push the grand total of personnel well over 500,000—starting to be within striking range of the counterinsurgency manual's recommended 600,000 or so, to the extent these algorithms were trusted.

But Afghan forces were not yet that strong, and certainly not yet adequately dependable. So standard COIN force-sizing methods could not be applied and implemented throughout the entire country at once. Obama's decision provided enough capacity to get very serious about Kandahar and Helmand provinces. Because he chose the middle path rather than the high-end approach, however, the east of the country would have to wait, perhaps indefinitely. Obama announced the policy in a much-awaited speech at West Point on December 1, 2009. But the president felt obliged to create leverage for political reform as well. Believing that Afghan leaders needed to clean up their act and get serious about their own responsibilities to the Afghan people, Obama coupled the promise to build up with the promise to build down almost as soon.[208] This approach, perhaps motivated by American politics as well, sought to achieve an exquisite, finely calibrated balance of competing policy goals. It was probably never realistic.[209] At the time, however, McChrystal himself was not discouraged by this policy outcome, writing in his memoirs that, "It gave us an opportunity. I strongly believed we could succeed, and committed myself completely."[210]

After U.S. forces had surged into country over the course of 2010, they would surge out starting by the summer of 2011—returning to the pre-existing force levels of some 68,000 U.S. troops by that point. Given the logistical constraints of moving in and out of Afghanistan, this set of bookends to the surge meant that peak force levels would be in position for only a brief time. The east of the country would probably never receive the canonical density of forces believed necessary for success, and the so-called clear/hold/build/transfer process would have to go very quickly in the south.

During this period ISAF established regional commands in the east, south, southwest, west, and north, as well as the capital city. These commands were teamed up with the Afghan Army 201st Corps, based in Kabul and with responsibility for the east; the 203rd Corps, based in Gardez with responsibility for the southeast; the 205th Corps in and around Kandahar, the 207th in and around Herat, the 209th in Mazar-e-Sharif with responsibility for the north, the 215th in Lashkar Gah in Helmand Province and vicinity, and the 111th Division for the capital.[211] About half of the ISAF regional commands were run by Americans by this time period. Germany led the way in the north, Italy in the west, Britain for a time in Kandahar, and Turkey in Kabul.[212]

McChrystal's military plan was to begin clearing operations in Helmand province. ISAF and Afghan forces would then move eastward toward greater Kandahar, in many ways the heartland of the country and the heartland of the Taliban movement historically. However, along with U.K. major general Nick Carter and others, McChrystal's concept was to try to minimize the use of force, except with targeted special forces raids under the general guidance of Admiral Bill McRaven against key targets. Instead, public messaging and maneuver as well as repositioning of forces were to be used to try to intimidate Taliban or other insurgents and criminal elements to flee rather than fight. In Kandahar, the approach would be similar, in the city itself as well as neighboring towns and regions, like the Arghandab district. If the "clear" part of the strategic trinity could be achieved relatively quickly and easily, the "hold" and "build" phases could be emphasized without delay. Someday, the "transfer" of these gains to Afghan security forces could also be attempted—indeed, given the rapid pace of the surging and unsurging of coalition forces, that transfer would presumably have to begin as soon as 2011.

Prior to clearing operations, President Karzai was asked to help prepare each region with town-hall meetings of sorts, providing Afghan leadership and cover for what was otherwise largely a foreign-led military operation. At this point in early 2010, available and well-trained Afghan troops were still in short supply.[213]

The overall campaign concept sought to achieve early and decisive victories in key sectors of the country. That would generate momentum that would convince other insurgents to flee or reconcile, and convince Pakistan to stop aiding and abetting the Taliban. It would also facilitate the improvement of Afghan governance so that it could deliver services to the people. Then the rapidly mobilized, trained, and equipped Afghan security forces would take responsibility, preserving the territorial gains and stability that had been achieved. Such was the theory. On that entire campaign wish list, however, only the first goal was achieved to any significant degree.

Initial ISAF clearing operations in Afghanistan took place largely in towns, small cities, orchards, river valleys, highways, and fields—unlike the largely urban-centric combat of Iraq. These were bare settings. As scholar and policy practitioner Carter Malkasian wrote about these rural areas, "Other than cell phones, cars, and assault rifles, the 21st century was invisible."[214] Taliban tactics in such settings emphasized the use of IEDs that took many American and Afghan lives. Throughout the war, the Taliban also often ambushed Afghan army and police checkpoints, especially in remote areas where security forces were isolated and difficult to reinforce. Clearing operations involved targeting known Taliban leaders and strongpoints, as well as weapons caches, while also physically removing IED belts and taking back towns or regions in Taliban hands—and then responding to ambushes that would often ensue as Taliban forces sought to resist the NATO and Afghan forces attempting these operations. The clearing attempts were slow, given limited intelligence, Taliban elusiveness, plentiful Taliban IEDS, and the sheer scale of the operations geographically. Building larger Afghan police forces or empowering local militias to then hold these gains was difficult as well, given the mixed loyalties and fears of many Afghans in the south, as well as the endemic corruption challenge. The clear and hold operations in Helmand and Kandahar were ultimately fairly successful. But the successes were achieved only on long timelines and at huge cost.[215]

Casualties were heavy in this intensive phase of the combat. American fatalities totaled 499 in 2010 and 418 in 2011, comparable to the highest rates during the Iraq War on a per-troop basis. Other NATO and foreign losses were proportionate: about 200 were killed per year during this same stretch.[216]

Afghan security forces were being greatly expanded, and rigorously trained for the first time, even as this surge and associated clearing operations were taking place. The simultaneity of these efforts was a major albatross for the overall war effort—necessitated by the fact that too little had been done during the "golden window" of NATO's first half-dozen years in Afghanistan. Arguably too much, too fast, was being attempted now. Afghan security forces, counting army and police, had grown to about 125,000 at the start of 2008, and 150,000 at the beginning of 2009. They were expanded quickly during the surge, reaching the goal of 300,000 personnel in aggregate by the summer of 2011—just in time to begin to replace the NATO troops who would start gradually thinning their ranks by then.[217]

One partial band-aid that was frequently attempted in the course of the mission was to somehow harness the local militias in the country (known in Afghanistan as *arbakai*) in support of the broader effort. The idea was to emulate the successful Sons of Iraq program, paying the local militia groups to take care of their own home territories. Various new programs, like the Afghan Local Police, as well as the Afghan Public Protection Program and the Local Defense Initiative, were hatched as a result. They attracted tens of thousands of additional fighters at their peak—but often with insufficient supervision by responsible authorities. Rather than improve, they often worsened, violence and corruption in their regions as a result.[218]

The overall result of the surge was not particularly heartening, either. Some battlefield gains were achieved in the south, though they were slower than hoped. By the spring of 2010, Obama was developing a negative sense of the progress of the surge. Late that year, General Petraeus advocated a slower drawdown to provide more time to clear the east, but Obama was unmoved by the argument.[219] Thus, with the clock ticking on the U.S. and NATO troop buildup, there would not be enough opportunity to solidify or extend the progress.[220] Even when the clear part of COIN was largely achieved, the hold and build parts were shaky—as was a final envisioned stage, the transfer of responsibility to Afghans themselves.

Meanwhile, Afghan security force fatalities reached into the low thousands a year. They only grew further as NATO undid the surge and handed more of the fighting burden to Afghans in ensuing years, with annual fatality levels ultimately reaching perhaps 10,000 a year all told. It was hard to hold onto troops and police when they knew their lives would be at acute risk. As such, turnover rates in the nation's security forces were very high, as was absenteeism.

The Taliban suffered high losses, too. The U.S. and NATO command refused to provide public estimates, trying to avoid any echo of the Vietnam War period's fixation on body counts. But Taliban casualties were probably at least comparable to those of the government's security forces. The United Nations consistently estimated Afghan civilian fatalities from the war in the low thousands per year—tragic tallies, to be sure, but less than those among fighting forces and much less than civilian losses in the Iraq war.[221] In military terms, the Afghanistan war was principally, though certainly not entirely, a fight between opposing military forces. That said, control of the population, and the country's populated areas, was the main objective of both sides throughout.

NATO used fixed-wing and rotary-wing airpower as well as unmanned aircraft extensively in the war. They provided close-air-support as well as tactical mobility. Landing zones for helicopters were built throughout the country, especially in the crucial east, south, and northeast. Their prevalence, combined with outstanding infrastructure built up over the years of America's longest war, made for high-quality medical care—and a very high survival rate among casualties. Nine out of ten wounded GIs would survive their wounds; fatality rates were about half that of most previous recent conflicts. Ultimately, NATO's inability to build up sufficient Afghan airpower, for strike missions and mobility, comprised a major part of the reason for the security forces' collapse in 2021.

As these battlefield dynamics played out, and NATO and Afghan forces sought to take back much of Helmand, Kandahar, and key transportation arteries as well as a few other sites from the Taliban, drama took place at high command. General McChrystal's staff had invited a reporter, Michael Hastings from *Rolling Stone* magazine, to embed with them in an effort to project openness and transparency to the magazine's readership. Breaking confidentiality rules, Hastings wrote a scathing article that suggested McChrystal or at least his staff were contemptuous of American civilian leadership. Although the truly troubling quotes were all attributed to McChrystal's staff and not the general himself, President Obama chose to request McChrystal's resignation. Sadly, the relationship that the latter had begun to forge with President Karzai was therefore also lost— McChrystal had nurtured a trusting relationship with Karzai that many other American officials, notably Ambassador Richard Holbrooke, as well as Ambassador Karl Eikenberry, did not have. Karzai believed some Americans had actively favored his opponents in the 2009 presidential elections, and tired as well of the lecturing about the corruption problem— however justifiable those lectures may have been. Karzai also began to find the lack of military progress hugely frustrating and saddening, and wondered why the world's best militaries could not defeat what he considered a rather unsophisticated insurgency.

In technical military terms, there was a good deal of continuity in the command transition, with McChrystal replaced by his close confidant and direct superior, General Petraeus. Beyond requesting a review of rules of engagement, having heard that some NATO soldiers had felt reluctant to defend themselves out of fear of inadvertently causing Afghan civilian casualties, Petraeus continued much of the earlier plan. He did step up some efforts on the anticorruption front, appointing H. R. McMaster to run a new task force with that mission, and otherwise sought to bring some of the Iraq magic to Afghanistan.

With Richard Holbrooke as the State Department's special representative for Afghanistan and Pakistan, and a succession of excellent ambassadors, including the fabled Ryan Crocker, on-again and off-again efforts were made to try to bring some insurgents out of the Taliban fold and onto the government side. No high-level dialogue was established, so these aspirations went largely to naught. Despite the efforts of McMaster and others, there was also only limited, halting, and often reversible progress on the anticorruption front.[222]

Compounding all the other problems, the Taliban leadership had effective sanctuary in Pakistan. It could move people easily across mountainous borders in Khost, or remote desert in Helmand, or even heavily trafficked roadways.[223] As Joint Chiefs Chairman Mike Mullen put it in 2011, the Haqqani network, a key part of the broader Taliban movement, was a "veritable arm" of Pakistan's ISI or Inter-Services Intelligence directorate.[224] The Taliban had sanctuary, and ample opportunities to recruit more followers, in parts of Afghanistan as well.

Yet, the U.S.-Pakistan relationship was always multi-dimensional, and never entirely either collaborative or rivalrous. Islamabad did allow NATO to conduct a massive logistics operation through its territory during most of the war—except, notably, for a stretch of several months in 2012 when Pakistan denied NATO access to its roads after a tragic exchange of fire at the border with Afghanistan left twenty-four Pakistani troops dead, and in the aftermath of the bin Laden raid, about which Pakistan was not forewarned, as well as the killing of two Pakistani police by a CIA contractor in Islamabad. (Other logistics pathways were available to the mission, but they had their challenges, too, relying on just aircraft to deliver supplies, as well as Russian acquiescence in some cases.)[225]

As a result of territorial gains from the surge, the Afghan government would control perhaps three-fourths of the country's districts. That was an improvement from 2008–2009 levels but not enough to deprive the Taliban of areas of sanctuary within the country as well as in Pakistan. And the gains began to erode soon after the surge ended. In late 2015, U.S. intelligence estimated that the Afghan government controlled 72 percent of the country's 407 districts. That figure declined substantially over the course of 2016, to about 57 percent, and then over the next couple of years to an estimated 54 percent by late 2018. At that point, 63 percent of the nation's population still lived in areas controlled by the government, since the government tended to control cities and larger towns. But the overall trend line was still clearly in the wrong direction.[226]

Acrimony also intensified in the U.S.-Afghan relationship. President Karzai became increasingly distressed by the violence, the accidental bombings of civilians by NATO forces in several high-profile incidents, and the frequency of night raids by U.S. forces. The misbehavior by several American troops that disrespected the Koran only added salt to the wound.[227] For their part, Americans often found Karzai ungrateful and abrasive. They were also enormously frustrated by the endemic corruption in Afghanistan, which sometimes reached monumental proportions in some cases, as when hundreds of millions of dollars were effectively stolen from the Kabul bank around 2009.

So-called insider attacks were also a huge and tragic problem. Renegade Afghan soldiers or police—sometimes Taliban plants, sometimes disaffected individuals acting largely on their own—would open fire on their foreign allies at unsuspecting moments. These acts of cold-blooded murder took the lives of dozens of coalition troops in a wave of violence peaking around 2012—until NATO instituted what it called a "guardian angel" program of constant bodyguard protection for key leaders and otherwise made it harder for individual Afghans to take aim at NATO personnel.

The counterterrorism mission went better. With Afghanistan providing a secure intelligence and operational base, a successful raid was made against the compound of Osama bin Laden. The compound had been discovered in Abbottabad, Pakistan through marvelous sleuthing work by U.S. intelligence. Bin Laden was killed on May 2, 2011, shortly before the ten-year anniversary of the 9/11 attacks. As it would turn out, that was also almost exactly halfway through the overall U.S. military stay in Afghanistan.

American counterinsurgency methods improved further, too—even if they could not reverse the trend line favoring the Taliban. For example, during General John Allen's tenure at the ISAF and thereafter, security force assistance brigades were created. They were comprised of numerous small teams (and some central capacity for intelligence, coordination, logistical support, and quick-reaction) that could embed within major Afghan combat formations to provide advice and intelligence. By the end of 2014, when the ISAF mission was technically ended, to be replaced by Operation Resolute Support, the total U.S. troop presence was down to about 15,000. Only 1 percent of U.S. active-duty military strength was now in Afghanistan; that number would be cut again by two-thirds by 2020.

A peaceful presidential election and transition to a new Afghan leader, President Ashraf Ghani, would occur in 2014. The election was in fact hugely contentious, but American diplomatic intervention under Secretary of State John Kerry brokered a compromise solution that created a new "COO" (chief operating office) position for Dr. Abdullah, the purported runner-up whom many thought had actually won the vote.

Taliban leader Mullah Omar would be prevented from returning in glory to the land he once ruled; he died in obscurity in Pakistan around 2013. Throughout this period, and beyond, Afghan soil was not again used as a base from which to plan, prepare, practice, or stage major terrorist strikes against the United States and its allies. Indeed, by the time the twenty-year anniversary of 9/11 arrived, no more than 100 Americans had died at the hands of extremist jihadis (or Salafists) on American soil over that period (most of those being victims of lone-wolf individuals inspired by al Qaeda or ISIS but acting on their own).[228]

The End of America's Longest War

NATO's ongoing operation in Afghanistan was renamed Operation Resolute Support as of 2015. It was defined as a support mission—though that hardly meant that U.S. forces were no longer part of the shooting war, whatever the attempted cosmetics may have been. Ultimately, there was irony in the name. President Obama and then President Donald Trump threatened to terminate the mission virtually every year of Operation Resolute Support. Then, President Joe Biden ended it—despite NATO's pledge at its 2012 summit in Chicago that allied forces, after ending the ISAF mission in 2014, would commit to supporting the Afghan government through a decade of "transformation."[229]

After 2014, the next half-dozen years amounted to a long, slow grind on the battleground, with the overall military trend continuing to work against the Afghan government, as small additional amounts of territory went over to Taliban control or became contested each year.[230] The cities stayed in government hands, however, with only rare and temporary exceptions, as with the brief fall of Kunduz in the north prior to its recapture by U.S.-backed Afghan special forces in 2015. It is for that reason that, as noted above, even though the Afghan government only fully controlled an estimated 54 percent of the nation's 407 districts by the end of the 2010s, those 54 districts held about 63 percent of the population.[231] The Taliban controlled only about a fifth of the country's districts as late as May of 2021, according to data and estimates offered by Kate Clark and Jonathan Schroden, with remaining districts being heavily contested.[232]

After 2014, NATO further consolidated its positions into a few large bases, where it conducted air operations, positioned intelligence platforms, staged occasional raids, and trained Afghan forces. By the spring of 2015, the U.S. presence was principally in half a dozen main bases—at Bagram (near Kabul), Herat, Mazar-e-Sharif, Kandahar, Jalalabad, and Kabul itself, plus another five smaller bases. The U.S. troop total was soon under 10,000.[233]

NATO's advisory efforts in the field declined dramatically, in a process that in fact dated back to 2012, as the short-lived surge ended. From 2015 onward, embedded advisory teams did not operate below the Afghan corps level except with Afghanistan's special forces. They did not even maintain a consistent presence with the 203rd Corps in Paktika province in the east or the 215th Corps in Helmand province in the south.[234] President Obama also attempted to restrict the use of U.S. airpower to operations in which NATO forces were at risk, or where al Qaeda elements were suspected to populate enemy ranks. That decision weakened the Afghan army's prospects in battle and bred cynicism in some quarters about America's commitment to its Afghan allies[235]

Once Donald Trump was in office, the table seemed set for U.S. withdrawal. But with retired General Jim Mattis now his secretary of defense and former ISAF commander General Joseph Dunford as the chairman of the Joint Chiefs of Staff, Trump went the other way. Heeding a recommendation from his field commander, General Mick Nicholson, to get tougher, Trump took the gloves off regarding airpower and added almost 4,000 U.S. troops for a total of nearly 14,000. This approach also entailed doubling the size of Afghan special forces and increasing pressure on Pakistan, politically and economically. The plan did stem the erosion of government-controlled territory and the loss of provincial capitals; however, it did not reverse the trend lines. Afghan politics was a problem as well. President Ghani attempted to weaken well-regarded Tajik leaders like the governor of Balkh province in the north, Mohammed Atta, and the leadership network of the former minister of defense and army chief of staff Bismillah Khan. Tajiks in general became much less supportive of the government and less numerous within the nation's security forces. Trump grew deeply frustrated with the situation.[236]

Meanwhile, ISIS was becoming a problem too, having formed a chapter in Afghanistan and vicinity known as ISIS Khorasan. The expanding presence of ISIS-K fighters within Afghanistan, in the east and sometimes elsewhere, gave the United States an ongoing motivation to retain counterterrorism capabilities. The Taliban too became even more hard-line under their new leader, Maulawi Haybatullah, who replaced Mullah Akhtar Mohammad Mansour after he had himself replaced Mullah Omar.

Yet these threatening leaders and ISIS-K fighters would not prove motivation enough for Trump to want to keep an ongoing platform in Afghanistan. He instructed his negotiators to look for a way out of Afghanistan through a deal with the Taliban, ultimately finalized on February 29, 2020. That deal required the Taliban to avoid ties with al Qaeda. There was considerable irony in this supposed agreement; the Haqqani network was part of Taliban leadership while also a part of al Qaeda. But both Trump and his successor would choose to overlook that blatant violation of the accord as they complied with America's obligations to leave Afghanistan in 2021.

Over the seven-year stretch, violence levels were higher than ever for Afghan security forces, quite probably for the Taliban as well, and likely for Afghan civilians too. American losses ranged from ten to twenty fatalities a year, much less than in the 2008–2014 period and in fact substantially less than during the 2002–2007 period as well.

America's use of force was still very substantial. More than 20,000 munitions were dropped over the course of this period, with annual totals for 2018 and 2019 each exceeding 7,000 bombs, levels not seen in Afghanistan since the height of the surge.[237] American costs, with an average military footprint in the range of 10,000 troops, were around $20 billion a year—including several billion dollars a year in support for the Afghan security forces, as well as military activities focused on Afghanistan from elsewhere in the region.[238]

Even though American costs in blood and treasure were now much less, the political frustration in Washington remained acute. President Trump teetered frequently on the brink of ending the mission, and in fact the end of his ultimately unhappy relationship with Secretary of Defense Jim Mattis had much to do with Trump's impromptu announcement in December 2018 that he would cut the U.S. military mission in half by the next year. Ironically, for all of Trump's reputation for bluster and contempt for allies and alliances, it was the experienced Biden who actually ended the mission rather precipitously and without much consultation or warning. In doing so, he was complying with the terms of the Taliban-U.S. agreement of February 29, 2020 that required an American-NATO departure by the spring of 2021—even as the Taliban themselves were not complying with their own obligations under that accord to break with al Qaeda and begin serious peace talks with the Ghani government. The Taliban did largely honor their pledge not to shoot at foreign troops; they certainly did not relent in their violence against Afghan forces or government officials (under the accord, they were not required to do the latter, only the former).

Some would point to the unpopularity of the war as providing Biden political cover, and motivation, for the decision. But there was little intensity surrounding the Afghanistan issue in the mission's latter years, or even during the period of maximum effort.[239] It was rarely debated, and it ranked low on lists of the American public's priorities. More likely than any groundswell of popular opposition was Biden's own personal frustration with a mission that he had become disenchanted with over the years, as senator and vice president and finally president. Indeed, Biden along with vice chairman of the Joint Chiefs General Jim Cartwright and U.S. Ambassador to Afghanistan (and retired general) Karl Eikenberry were believed to have been the main internal opponents of the 2009 Afghanistan surge.[240] Even though his view did not prevail then, Biden would have the last say.

And that he did, in April 2021, announcing that U.S. troops would come home by the twenty-year anniversary of 9/11 five months later. That curious choice of target date was later revised to August 31. With America leaving, so would NATO, as other allies did not have the logistical or transport capacity to mount rapid reinforcement efforts (or bombing runs) should a small troop presence get into trouble.

The CIA expected that the Afghanistan government might fall by the end of the year, based on analysis done that spring. The CIA knew that the Taliban had been developing siege positions around the country's cities since 2020, preparing for the possibility of a simultaneous set of attacks against many urban centers once conditions seemed propitious. The Taliban had also benefited from the release of some 5,000 prisoners in 2020 under the terms of the February 29, 2020, deal between Washington and the Taliban. It benefited further from the fact that, even in the face of such developments, the Ghani government had not prioritized certain parts of the country over others in what was undoubtedly a necessary triaging. Instead, Kabul attempted to maintain its previous positions nationwide. This was done even though the government and its American friends knew that the quality of many army and police commanders, as well as the morale of security force personnel, were variable at best.[241]

When the government effectively fell in the first half of August—after Bagram Air Base was abandoned and America's last four-star commander,

General Scott Miller, had departed the country—many were stunned with the rapidity of events. But perhaps it should not have been so surprising. Afghans had again shown themselves the ultimate survivors. They tend not to fight and die for a lost cause—even if they often will fight hard for causes about which they are passionate. The quickness of NATO's departure after so long a stay, combined with the absence of a credible strategy or narrative for how ensuing territorial losses might be limited through a strategic triage, gave few grounds for hope. Afghanistan also lacked an independently viable air force that could provide firepower or mobility to reinforce attacked positions; by that point Afghans were only capable of maintaining their modest fleet of Russian-built Mi-17 helicopters and not those provided by the West.

Once a defeatist mentality became prevalent, the collapse of the government's security forces snowballed. Many were bought off; many were persuaded to surrender with promises of amnesty; others were simply left disoriented and dumbfounded by the rapidity of the general collapse. If there was a silver lining, it was that a Taliban takeover that had become likely by August 2021 (at least for much of the country) wound up happening so fast that few lost their lives in its last phases.[242]

The final main military story—at least for now—in America's military role in Afghanistan involved the controlled exit from the Kabul airport of more than 120,000 Americans and Afghan friends of America. The U.S. military had to send more than 5,000 troops, different in type and specialization than those who had been in Afghanistan just recently, back to Kabul temporarily to protect and control the evacuation. Although it was a humbling scene—with Washington needing the acquiescence of the Taliban to conduct the operation through August 31, as well as the help of the Taliban in providing general site security for the airport—the overall exit went about as well as it probably could have by that point. Tragically, 13 Americans and nearly 200 Afghans died in a truck bombing conducted by ISIS-K on August 26 on the airport's outskirts. And three days later, in a mistaken effort to prevent another attack, the United States erroneously attacked a civilian vehicle in Kabul, killing ten people.[243]

The August 26 victims were the first U.S. fatalities in Afghanistan since President Trump had reached the deal with the Taliban the previous February 29 under which he promised that American forces would soon leave the country. The Taliban failed to break ties to al Qaeda, as documented in the spring of 2021 by the United Nations—so the United States was hardly under any obligation to depart, according to the terms of the agreement.[244] Yet the Taliban did generally comply with its promise not to target Americans. Just what happens with its promises to grant amnesty to former supporters of the previous regime, allow some limited rights for women and minorities, and form an inclusive government remains to be seen—though it has already violated the latter vow in particular (and to some extent the others as well).

The American public, in opinion polls, remained supportive of President Biden's decision to leave Afghanistan but was critical of the pell-mell manner in which the departure actually took place, and was also of course heartbroken over the loss of life.[245] My own view is that once the United States decided to leave, and leave quickly over the course of just a few months, it lost effective control of the situation. The departure could easily have been much bloodier and uglier, given the potential for an intensifying civil war. Whether the future is bloodier and uglier remains to be seen—as does the degree to which the Taliban can prevent Afghan territory or assets from being used to carry out terrorist violence against the United States and its allies.

Mistakes Made and Lessons Learned

The wars I have discussed in this chapter remain recent history. Indeed, to paraphrase William Faulkner, they are perhaps not even past. Future events may reignite conflicts in both Iraq and Afghanistan, adding new phases or chapters to those countries' complex and tragic modern sagas. As such, I will offer only several brief observations here.

- First, deterrence of Iraq did not fail in 1990, for the simple reason that it was not attempted. To paraphrase another prominent, if fictional, figure, Dr. Strangelove, a doomsday machine doesn't work if you don't tell anyone about it. Ambassador April Glaspie, acting under instructions, told Saddam that the United States did not concern itself with internal disputes within the Arab world (even as, to be fair, she advocated the peaceful resolution of disputes). Saddam may have intended to attack Kuwait before that statement, but his anxieties about doing so were presumably mitigated by his exchange with the U.S. diplomat.
- Second, however, I believe that President George H. W. Bush was correct to decide that Saddam must be evicted from Kuwait. To tolerate that action as the first major strategic event of the

post–Cold War world would have largely demolished Bush's hopes for a "new world order." It would have violated the post–World War II principle that no nation can take territory from a second nation (or simply annex it!). Bush was also probably right not to seek to overthrow Saddam at that point—though the United States was wrong to give Saddam the green light to use helicopters and other forms of brutal attack against internal dissidents. That was an unnecessary and unforced error. Depriving Saddam of that terrible instrument of repression might have increased the chances of his being overthrown, but that was a risk well worth tolerating.

• Third, and building on a key recurring theme of this book, none of the key phases of any of these wars went as expected. Desert Storm, as well as the overthrowing of the Taliban and Saddam, went much more easily and faster than had been generally foreseen. The occupation and attempted stabilization of Iraq and Afghanistan went much worse and took far longer. Costs in blood and treasure were at least tenfold greater than many expected. Outcomes were not nearly as good as had been hoped. Indeed, I was one of the most pessimistic about what an occupation of Iraq could entail—predicting more than 100,000 U.S. troops would be needed for several years, at a public panel at the American Enterprise Institute in the fall of 2002—and even I was too optimistic. (After several years of deploying 130,000 to 140,000 American troops in Iraq, the United States ultimately needed 170,000 in year five of the effort—the surge—to make military headway. Even that did not produce lasting stability, of course.)[246] The rapidity of the Taliban's return to power in 2021 was not expected either—by the United States, by the Afghan government, even by Taliban leaders themselves.[247]

The cases here belie any claim that war is *always* harder than expected. As noted, the early phases of most of the conflicts in this chapter went better and faster than anticipated.

But on balance, these efforts were long and costly sagas for the United States, not to mention the peoples of those countries as well as their neighbors. The journalist and author Dexter Filkins coined the memorable phrase "forever war" to describe the missions in Iraq and Afghanistan—in a book published in 2008. That was only roughly halfway through forever, as it turned out; the Afghanistan conflict in particular had anywhere from six to twelve more years to go at that point, depending on how one counts.[248]

- Fourth, with the exception of Desert Storm, these were not really transformational wars in terms of military technology and tactics. Change was impressive in some ways, but not revolutionary. Yes, the United States and allies did innovate throughout these long wars—arming and proliferating drones, building mine-resistant vehicles, making information networks faster. And the enemy innovated, with various types of explosive devices, for example, and with the use of social media for recruiting as well as for combat communications. But most of all, as I argued in a book published in 2000, the nature of infantry, insurgent, and counterinsurgent warfare has been changing only slowly in modern times.[249] That has continued to be the case in the first two decades of the twenty-first century.

  Small arms are easily available to all sides, as are explosives— and that has been true for decades in these kinds of wars. They are also still very deadly. Nonlethal weapons remain a minor factor in the close fight. Sensors still have difficulty seeing through walls, or divining the proclivity of an individual to use violence (facial recognition technology is impressive in some ways, but not for discerning intent). Signals-intelligence networks only work if adversaries are careless enough to use their cell phones or radios, so it is still hard to get inside the communications and decision loops of the adversary. In short, there has been no modern "revolution in military affairs"—change akin to the development of blitzkrieg, aircraft carrier operations, or other historic and transformative developments in warfare—for insurgent and counterinsurgency warfare.

- Fifth, these American experiences in the broader Middle East reinforce the adage that humans prepare to fight the last war rather than think sufficiently creatively about how the future may be different. Ken Adelman, the George W. Bush administration adviser, typified the attitude of many enthusiasts for the 2003 invasion of Iraq by predicting it would be a "cakewalk" or at least a "crushing win" because Operation Desert Storm in 1991, a war with much different goals, had gone so well. Many thought a surge would work in Afghanistan in part because it had worked so well quite recently in a relatively nearby country, Iraq; I confess to being partly guilty of this aspiration myself.

Finally, could these wars have been prosecuted or ended in significantly different ways than what actually occurred?

Desert Storm was impressive on the whole. It is not clear that it could have been fought in a fundamentally more successful way. There were interesting debates about campaign plans—the left hook around Iraqi forces, versus what some called the "hey diddle, right up the middle" option, for example. However, ultimately the coalition forces triumphed decisively on the battlefield regardless of which approach was taken (since the U.S. Marines did go straight through Iraqi lines, whereas the U.S. Army with coalition partners largely wheeled west and around the frontline positions). Given the mission's specific UN and congressional (and strategic) mandate, it is also relatively hard to critique the decision to leave Saddam in power.

In the subsequent Iraq war, the invasion and overthrow of Saddam was a huge success. But the lack of serious preparation for what might come next was a terrible mistake. And the ultimate success of the surge, at least in military terms, suggests that a better stabilization plan might have worked from the outset of the mission.

It is possible that many Sunnis may have opposed coalition forces and a Shia-majority Iraqi government even if there had been a good stabilization plan starting in 2003. Perhaps they needed to be terrified by al Qaeda for several years before they could come around to allying with al Qaeda's other enemies. That said, the severity and strength of the insurgency, and the country's ultimate devolution into civil war, were probably not inevitable. A better start at keeping the country stable and its borders secure would likely have mitigated the problem considerably by, for example, keeping out many foreign al Qaeda fighters who flocked to Iraq when they saw a jihadist opportunity. Perhaps an Iraqi political system that required any party taking seats in parliament to win a certain minimum percentage of votes from each of the three major ethnic/sectarian groups would have mitigated the tendency towards inflammatory, identity-based politics. Greater efforts from the beginning to build an independent and resilient judiciary would likely have helped as well. The United States mistakenly equated democracy with the successful holding of elections in Iraq. In the end, one cannot really prove anything about a counterfactual scenario that never was tested in the real world. But one can see dynamics in Iraq, as elsewhere, that violence tends to beget violence. Much of what took place was almost assuredly path-dependent.

Afghanistan is a tougher case to analyze, in my view. The state and society were so weak in 2001 that it is not clear there were ever enough building blocks to work with to build a viable government, army, and police force that could hold up against the almost inevitable Taliban attempt at a comeback.[250] If Pakistan could not be persuaded to deny the Taliban sanctuary—and many skilled American military and political leaders attempted that persuasion task, to little avail—then Afghanistan itself would have needed to be hardened against attack, with a government and security forces that enjoyed the respect of most of its population. Either that or the Taliban would have had to be brought into a new government, accepting its place as a minority partner after having ruled the country ruthlessly and comprehensively for half a decade. Some have suggested that the latter approach should have been attempted, at the Bonn process and beyond. Perhaps that is right, but it seems that doing a deal with the Taliban would have been a longshot back then—given the correct insistence of most other Afghans and most of the international community that nothing resembling the previous period of extremist rule could be countenanced for a post-Taliban society.

So it seems that the best chance was to have built up a stronger state in the "golden window" of 2002–2005, when the country was quiet and the threat was modest. Afghanistan's tribes were too rivalrous, and not sufficiently hierarchical, to lead the fight against the Taliban in these years—even though they likely had the capacity when the Taliban was still a relatively weak movement.[251] A "medium-footprint" approach, with more rigorous training and better payment systems and an insistence on better field leadership for Afghan soldiers and police, should certainly have been attempted. Developing the kind of combat advisory teams that the United States ultimately created, under the leadership of General John Allen and others, could have been undertaken sooner, as suggested for example by renowned Marine Corps veteran and storied author Bing West.[252] Tougher and more consistent anti corruption efforts should have been instituted as well, with coalition forces denying funding to those known to misuse resources.

Yet I have become more skeptical over the years that even such an approach could have thoroughly defeated the Taliban on any predictable time scale.[253] I agree with parts of Carter Malkasian's perspective (even though he and I disagreed over President Biden's April 2021 decision to pull out forces). Malkasian wrote in 2021 that, "I thought we should have done more early on to build a stronger military, remove bad leaders, and manage tribal infighting. Evidence suggests that such actions may have led to greater stability, though the intervening years [since the writing of his 2013 book, *War Comes to Garmser*] have left me more cynical. I have seen how hard it is to enact decisive new policies on a nationwide scale."[254]

What such policies might have done however is to obviate the need for a large U.S. and NATO surge. Foreign troop totals might have been kept in the low tens of thousands range; a mission more like what NATO wound up conducting from 2012 or 2014 onward could have been initiated sooner. The country might not have been peaceful as a result, but perhaps the American frustration with the mission could have been mitigated enough that no U.S. president would have felt the need to depart as abruptly and unsuccessfully as President Biden ultimately did in 2021. That kind of staying power, rather than any expectation of crushing the insurgency definitively, might have been the attainable goal. And while far from perfect, it would have been much different and arguably far preferable to what has resulted. So in that limited but important sense, there probably was a better overall strategy for Afghanistan as well. As British official Rory Stewart wrote in late 2021, "The Taliban were not on the verge of victory; they won because the United States withdrew, crippled the Afghan air force on its way out, and left Afghan troops without air support or resupply lines."[255] He might have added that his own, and other European nations' militaries were incapable of doing the relatively modest remaining job themselves, even though it surely should have been within their collective means.

For all their hard-line governance to date, however, the Taliban seem not to want to provoke the United States militarily—as demonstrated in Kabul in August 2021, when they did not oppose the Western evacuation effort and in fact even provided limited assistance to it. Perhaps, despite our failure at one level, they realize that the United States is a formidable foe that will fight hard to defend its security interests and allies. Perhaps the mission did not fail so comprehensively after all, at least relative to the goal of "reestablishing deterrence" against Taliban collusion with terrorists who would strike the West. It is, as of this writing, too soon to know.

Finally, a word on where this all leaves us in the 2020s. The United States has evolved its broader Mideast security strategy toward a place where the region is recognized as important, but where it is also seen as strategic quicksand where no amount of American effort can produce predictably good results in terms of stability and safety. A concept of "mowing the grass" or containing the extremist threat until long-term political and economic and social reforms can produce more countries with the apparent stability of states like Jordan, Oman, Tunisia, and Morocco (as well as several Muslim-majority countries in South Asia and Southeast Asia) has emerged as the least bad approach in the eyes of most American strategists. Military footprints of several thousand troops each in a number of places—Turkey, Iraq, Kuwait, Bahrain, Qatar, the United Arab Emirates, Djibouti—combined with seapower in and around the region has created a network of capabilities that allows the United States to sustain typically about 50,000 to 60,000 military personnel in the broader region without depending unduly on any one country for access and support. Focusing on building up partner-nation capacity through training and equipping and mentoring programs, combined with maintaining U.S.-controlled platforms for intelligence, airpower, and occasional special-forces raids, has become the essence of the approach as the United States with allies seeks to manage conflicts and dangers from Somalia and Nigeria to Libya and Mali to Syria and Yemen.

In Iraq, the United States does have a much closer partner at present than it likely would have had otherwise. It remains dubious if that fact will be seen in historical perspective as justifying the huge costs and major mistakes associated with the U.S.-led effort in Iraq since 2003.

The long-term effectiveness of the strategy—better described as a network of "light footprints" than offshore balancing or over-the-horizon counterterrorism—is still open to debate. And specific application of the strategy to individual countries and sub-regions always requires attentiveness as well as adaptation. But in financial and military terms, it does appear sustainable at the moment.

| SIX | *Three Lessons* |

With all this history in mind, I offer three overall observations or lessons that future strategists should consider as they forge future policies for the United States, and other countries as well.

Lesson One: Outcomes in War Are Not Preordained

The process of writing this book has underscored for me how none of America's major wars since 1861 needed to end the way they did—even in the broadest possible sense of who won and who lost. History, written after the fact of course, sometimes makes outcomes seem preordained. Usually, at least in the cases of war, they are not.

The unpredictability of war is partly due to the fact that leaders matter enormously—and they are always human, with the full range of positive as well as negative attributes that make their decisionmaking very hard to forecast. But the uncertainties of war arise at many levels. The scientists who work on a major new weapons or communication or intelligence system, the midlevel tactical innovator who figures out how to make a new type of combined-arms operation more effective, the toughness of a nation's soldiers when faced with extremely demanding conditions (even if many soldiers are impressive for their courage and resilience)—these types of wild cards do much to determine who wins a war.

The Confederacy could very easily have won the Civil War—in the sense of persuading the Union to give up the struggle and allow it to secede, though quite probably only after massive losses on both sides that would have further reinforced the moral bankruptcy of the Southern cause. The clearest path to such an outcome would have been the electoral defeat of Abraham Lincoln in 1864 (or his assassination earlier in the war). Absent Sherman's taking of Atlanta and march to the sea, Lincoln might have lost the election, and his opponent, the very same McClellan who had failed to find a path to victory in 1862 as commanding general of Union forces, might have negotiated an end to the conflict that left the United States divided in two. That might have dramatically changed the entire course of twentieth- (and twenty-first-) century history worldwide, given that a divided United States might not have been able to intercede effectively the way it did in the world wars or the Cold War or the post–Cold War world.

In World War I, the Schlieffen Plan, however unwise in conception given its technocratic precision and extreme ambition, almost worked. That fact does not mean it was strategically sound or morally defensible; failure was always a distinct possibility, if not probability, and enormous costs in lives and treasure were always a high probability. Still, if France had been conquered quickly, the correlation of forces on the eastern front of the war would have favored Germany and its ally, Austria-Hungary. Alternatively, if Germany had been smart enough to leave the United States alone, in the Battle of the Atlantic and in Berlin's encouragement to Mexico to attack the U.S. homeland (as revealed in the Zimmerman Telegram), it might have succeeded in its late-war offensive and forced France to accept a compromise negotiated outcome. As regrettable as such an outcome might have been on its own terms, we can with hindsight argue that it would have likely lowered the odds of the failure of the Weimer Republic, the rise of Hitler, and the outbreak of World War II—a far greater tragedy.

In World War II, if Hitler had not attacked the Soviet Union, and Japan had contented itself with the possessions it already held by 1940 in the western Pacific, the entire course of the conflict could have been radically different. The United States might not have entered the war at all. Stalin, ever the opportunist, might have been content to carve up central and eastern Europe with his fellow dictator sitting in Berlin, as originally envisioned under the terms of the Molotov-Ribbentrop agreement. If not fighting on the eastern front, Germany might have developed a much more robust defensive position on the shores of northern France, discouraging the U.S./UK/Allied D-Day landing even if the United States had joined the conflict by then. Yes, Hitler's war aims centered on eastern Europe and the Soviet Union, but the Allies could not be sure that he might not change those aims as the conflict unfolded, especially given Germany's successes elsewhere. Hitler might also have been overthrown internally during the war. All the remarkable technical innovations that occurred just before and during the war—including aircraft carrier warfare, combined-arms amphibious assault, blitzkrieg (first in Poland, then in improved form in

France), new technologies and tactics in submarine and anti submarine warfare, improved aircraft and missile performance, the invention of nuclear weapons—did not have to happen at all, and did not have to follow the sequence that was ultimately witnessed. Germany might in theory also have been the first country to develop the nuclear bomb, with unknowable and unspeakable implications for history.

Korea could have gone much differently—or at least much more quickly, with smaller losses of life on all sides—if the United States had adopted more modest war aims and fought back to the status quo ante. In such a case, China might not have intervened. It is hard to fault American policymakers for wanting to solve the core problem and reunify a peninsula that was supposed to be reunified, under previous international agreement, but the decision to go north was highly fraught. Either Korea or Vietnam *might* have gone much differently if the United States had been willing to escalate and attack China directly. That such an attack would have been a huge geostrategic gamble, and probably a mistake given America's grand strategic priorities, does not mean that it was unthinkable. The United States also could have—and, based even on information available at the time, should have—avoided the Vietnam War altogether. It was, in my judgment, correct to be willing to fight in Korea, given the strategic importance of northeast Asia. But for the sake of deterrence, and war avoidance, it should have known its own mind, and telegraphed that commitment, prior to the initiation of conflict. Hindsight is admittedly 20/20.

The Iraq and Afghanistan sagas had numerous turning points, featuring many acts of brilliance and many follies on the part of the United States and others. I do not think easy wins were attainable in either place. But the dramatic success of the surge in Iraq in 2007, and the relative tranquility of Afghanistan from 2002 through 2006 suggest that there were better strategies available, and better outcomes within reach at lower cost, in both places.

Lesson Two: War Is Usually Harder and Bloodier Than Expected

Lesson two builds on lesson one and adds a more specific point and a more clear warning: The history of war is rife with overconfident leaders, especially those who choose to start conflicts, who believe they can achieve quick and easy victories. Policymakers must in the future therefore work hard to avoid overconfidence when deciding on matters of war and peace, as well as war aims and appropriate strategies once engaged in combat. Lack of confidence and resolve can be a problem too, as with English and French leaders facing the German threat in the 1930s, and some American leaders considering how to address Saddam's 1990 invasion of Kuwait. But most of the wars addressed here wound up much worse and much longer than generally expected. Indeed, if one views Operation Desert Storm together with the invasion and ensuing stabilization attempt in Iraq as a single whole, all seven of the wars treated here in detail were surprisingly difficult and sanguinary.

Usually in history there is a seductive logic to war plans, especially those that build on new military capabilities and technical or tactical innovation. Such thinking usually has a certain basis in reality. But often it fails to account for how many things can go wrong in war, and also for how adversaries can adapt and endure. Major wars often do have opening phases in which a cunning aggressor does indeed achieve rapid, if partial and reversible results—until the fog of war sets in, the geography and context of combat change, adversaries adapt, or the attacker's initial elan and luck run out. Also, human beings tend to be tenacious and violent once physically assaulted, more so perhaps than we humans tend to remember or perceive about ourselves. Once the fighting begins, and people see their fellow citizens or even friends and family members begin to die, the proclivity of most individuals and most countries is *not* to back down before things get worse, but to pursue revenge—seeking also some kind of victory that might partly redeem the terrible and irreversible losses. These dynamics were evident, for example, in both world wars, in the Korean War, and in the U.S.-led invasions and occupations of Iraq and Afghanistan.

All this fits with human nature. Most leaders do not start wars. But enough do, with sufficiently seismic consequences, that we must take note of the human proclivity to accept high risks at times. Usually, politicians and military leaders who enter into wars expecting to win fast have a theory of victory that has a certain logic and plausibility to it—if things go well. They often have a narrative of success that while optimistic is not absurd. Tragically, their ensuing decisions are often reckless. They frequently forget to reflect as profoundly on what can, and usually does, go wrong in war as on how their plans can succeed.

One must not paint with too broad a brush, of course. Some countries are simply the victims of aggression. Sometimes, they fight for noble causes that are worth high risk and cost.

Yet more often than not, aggressors, and sometimes even their victims, fail to anticipate just how deadly and difficult war will be. That was true for many Union soldiers, and spectators from nearby Washington, DC, who expected a stroll in the park in the Battle of Manassas in July 1861. It was true of European leaders who expected their glorious war of August 1914 to be over by the time the leaves started to fall. It was true of Hitler who thought that the Soviet Union and Britain might collapse as fast as Poland and France in the face of Third Reich armies, and of Japanese leaders when they engineered the surprise attacks at Pearl Harbor and the Philippines. It has been true of Americans as well—after the Inchon landing in Korea, as well as in Vietnam, Iraq, and Afghanistan. Dictators and evil rulers make these kinds of mistakes. So, sometimes, do democracies.

Returning to the crucial insights of Thucydides, in words that ring as true today as they did when he offered them more than two millenia ago: people typically choose war for reasons of fear, interest, and honor. The late Robert Jervis and other modern political scientists have developed the idea of a "security dilemma" by which actions that one country takes to shore up its own defenses are interpreted as threatening by a potential adversary. But these observations explain why war is often *possible*. They do not completely explain why it actually occurs in a given situation— why honor, interest, or fear override other human attributes such as caution, desire for survival, and even kindness. A tendency to underestimate costs and risks, and to overestimate potential gains, seems a crucial part of the explanation. As the great Australian historian Geoffrey Blainey observed, rarely do wars begin without at least one side expecting rapid victory—but rarely are such lasting victories achieved.

We are slow to learn these lessons, as obvious as they may seem today. The great Prussian strategist Carl von Clausewitz warned, 200 years ago, that war generally takes place in a fog of bad information, uncertain communications, wrought emotions, and unpredictable enemies. Yet the bloodiest wars in history occurred after his warnings were issued. The same Europe that gave us an understanding of modern chemistry and of quantum and nuclear physics in the opening decades of the twentieth century experienced the most insane and brutal conflicts ever waged in these same time periods. Civilization got much smarter in some ways— and no smarter or better at all in others.

Can we be so sure that this tragic tendency of leaders is now behind us? Can we be confident that a future China, armed with hypersonic missiles, robotic swarms of weapons guided by artificial intelligence, and quiet submarines, will not attack Taiwan—thinking that it can deter America from responding? Might Vladimir Putin lick his wounds after the Ukraine conflict (or at least its first big phase in 2022), acquire new technologies, and try again—this time perhaps even targeting regions of NATO member states Estonia and Latvia where numerous Russian speakers reside?

Can we Americans be sure that we will avoid overconfidence ourselves—somehow thinking, perhaps, that a new military buildup will reestablish the kinds of lopsided military advantages we enjoyed over China and Russia in certain earlier periods? For example, are those who talk about sinking the entire Chinese navy within a few days of initiation of hostilities today a bit too impressed by America's sensor-shooter networks that allow us to find, track, and destroy enemy targets (what some call the "kill chain")? Have they explained how such a tactical victory, even if possible, would translate to strategic success? In some of these modern musings, one can detect troubling echoes of Germany's highly escalatory and deceptively precise Schlieffen Plan for World War I.

It is important to remember General David Petraeus's haunting question from the early days of the "forever wars" of the Middle East this century: "Tell me how this ends?" We must heed what the great defense scholars of the 1960s, Alain Enthoven and K. Wayne Smith, emphasized—that for every military problem, we think about "plausible worst-case" scenarios as much as happier outcomes.

Military organizations need a certain healthy degree of entrepreneurial spirit and can-do attitude, of course. They are charged with the responsibility of developing war-winning strategies so that, if conflict proves unavoidable, their own nation will be in a position to prevail—or at least to survive. Much of the most interesting literature on military reform and innovation, such as classic works by Steven Rosen and Barry Posen, is about how this process was catalyzed in countries like Britain of the 1930s—countries that might otherwise have found themselves unable to resist an existential attack against their state.

The danger arises, however, when development of plausible war-winning strategies, concepts, and capabilities morphs into high confidence that the plans will work to their maximum plausible degree. Defense Secretary Donald Rumsfeld was not wrong to think that the U.S.-led invasion of Iraq in 2003 *might* go very well. In fact, the opening phases of the war may have exceeded even his expectations. The mistake was in failing to explore what could go wrong. Defense leaders need a degree of confidence. But they also need to remember Murphy's Law. At modest risk of overstatement, sometimes everything that can go wrong *will* go wrong. Or, to paraphrase Clausewitz, in war everything is simple—but even the simple things are hard.

Lesson Three: America's Grand Strategy Is Strong Enough to Absorb Some Setbacks

I would offer another observation that is more specific to the contemporary United States. America's modern wars, those since 1945, have not gone so well. Yet over this same time period, the country, and world, has generally thrived. Despite the challenges and setbacks, as well as the rise of China and resurgence of Russia in recent times, there has never been a comparable sustained period of long-term great-power peace, and spread of democracy and prosperity, as in the overall course of world history since 1945, Russia's recent revanchism, China's rise, and the Covid catastrophe notwithstanding. Nuclear deterrence has helped, though at considerable risk to the survival of the species in several tense crises. So have memories of the enormous devastation wrought by the world wars of the first half of the twentieth century. But the nation's role undergirding an open global economic system, as well as backstopping a network of alliances that unify much of the wealthy and industrialized and generally democratic littoral of Eurasia with North America, has created a structurally favorable distribution of power that is conducive to peace.

With the American and Allied withdrawal from Afghanistan, resulting in what was recently described by Chairman of the Joint Chiefs General Mark Milley as a "strategic failure," we have now again witnessed the post–World War II paradox of U.S. foreign policy: we often fail to win "limited" wars, yet at the same time we sustain the most successful grand strategy of any power in the history of the planet. At least, that has been the case since 1945.

In 1950, after practically green-lighting a North Korean invasion of South Korea by declaring the latter outside our perimeter of strategic concern, the United States put together a military coalition that was twice driven back below the 38th parallel, twice losing Seoul in the process—once at the hands of North Korean troops and once due to Chinese intervention. Ultimately we fought to a stalemate at huge cost in lives and treasure—with the war only being concluded after a newly inaugurated President Eisenhower threatened the Chinese with nuclear attack if they did not accept a reasonable cease-fire.

Then, from 1965 to 1973, the United States suffered its clearest defeat of all in the Vietnam War. By 1975, North Vietnam had taken the entire country, and beyond the immediate battlefield consequences of the war, America's sense of national self was reeling.

Then in the 1980s we had a turning point of sorts, with the Reagan defense buildup combined with a decade of relative peace. That said, we lost 241 Marines in a tragic bombing in Beirut in 1983, and the magnitude of that loss could not be outweighed by a (mostly) successful invasion of Grenada or a bombing run against targets in then-terrorist Libya.

The George H. W. Bush presidency went much better, with a small-scale win in Panama and a big victory in Operation Desert Storm. We then struggled through the rest of the 1990s, however, suffering tragedy in "Black Hawk Down" in Mogadishu, Somalia in 1993, and finding a way to limit genocide in the Balkans only after considerable delay and great tragedy. Meanwhile, Saddam Hussein refused to let weapons inspectors do their jobs, and Iraq remained an ongoing worry. Osama bin Laden, convinced the United States was a paper tiger, prepared al Qaeda's big attack.

Since 9/11, we struggled mightily in both Afghanistan and Iraq. We had big early successes in both places, in 2001 and 2003, but then long and exhausting slogs that failed to produce stability in either place—despite the brilliance of the surge in Iraq in 2007–2008, which brought down violence by 90 percent but could not itself produce a cohesive Iraqi polity. By 2014, ISIS owned a quarter or so of Iraq and in 2021, the Afghanistan government fell.

Viewing four big conflicts of Korea, Vietnam, Iraq and Afghanistan, it would appear that the United States created expensive stalemates in Korea and Iraq, and failed in its missions in Vietnam and Afghanistan. Put crudely, that looks like a record of 0-2-2. Or, if we view the Iraq experience from 1990 to the present as two separate wars, perhaps 1-2-2. This despite having the world's best military throughout that entire post-1945 period.

Yet the United States still leads a coalition of allies collectively wielding two-thirds of all global GDP, and accounting for two-thirds of all worldwide defense spending. None of the countries in that broader alliance network have been the victims of large-scale attack for three-fourths of a century; there has been no great power war on the planet since at least 1953 (depending on how one defines the Korean War). How could we be so successful while failing so often?

Perhaps some of it is luck. As the nineteenth-century German states-man Otto von Bismarck put it, God would seem to have a special provi-dence for fools, drunkards, and the United States of America.

A more serious answer would have to examine our structural strengths—the nation's size and economic fundamentals, its geography within generally safe North American borders (yet close enough to East Asia and western Europe to build strong military alliances with partners in those regions), its melting-pot demography (even if we still wrestle with serious racial tensions domestically), its innovative and entrepreneurial economic system as well as excellent research laboratories and universi-ties, its democratic model of government (however flawed). It is these at-tributes of the United States, more than any innate "exceptionalism," that make America's role in world affairs unique, crucial, and important even given our proclivity to make big mistakes.

It would appear that the nation is powerful and resilient enough to be able to absorb numerous setbacks. It also helps greatly that, at least be-yond North America (more or less), the United States has not been an ex-pansionist power in our history. Other countries may at times dislike us but they tend not to fear us—and in many cases, they find it advantageous to be allied with the United States. As such, a Western alliance system col-lectively wielding two-thirds of world GDP, a similar percentage of global military spending, and a preponderance of the world's top-tier scientific and industrial might (China's rise notwithstanding) has proven durable and generally dependable.

There are also specific mitigating dimensions to most of our military setbacks. In Korea we did hold the line against attempted Communist ag-gression at a crucial moment in the Cold War while giving South Korea a chance eventually to become the prosperous democracy it is today. In Viet-nam, while I can find little to redeem the immediate outcome of the con-flict itself, we have become friends with the regime that wound up in power there, and in fact now collaborate in addressing mutual security concerns about China. The Iraq War did not produce a shining example of Arab democracy—but things may be looking up ever so slightly there, and at least the murderous Saddam Hussein family is no longer in charge, plot-ting its next act (don't forget that behind Saddam there were his now-deceased sons, Uday and Qusay).

That brings us to Afghanistan, and General Milley's purported "stra-tegic failure." At one level, the chairman's bluntness is commendable, as is his acknowledgement that we (all of us) must learn lessons from that difficult and ultimately unsuccessful saga. It is true that we failed to build up a resilient democratic Afghan state, even after two decades of effort. But the Taliban seem not to want another fight with the West. They helped the United States evacuate some 120,000 Westerners in August 2021, and are not engaging in systemic retaliatory bloodbaths against Westerners or even our former Afghan partners despite being firmly ensconced in power. It can be hoped that they will choose not to join hands with al Qaeda in planning new attacks against the West—though achieving that outcome will be more difficult for the United States than before, given the intelligence and military challenges of conducting counterterrorism policy from afar. Beyond wanting to avoid military confrontation with the United States, the Taliban desire diplomatic recognition, access to Afghanistan's bank accounts abroad, and some degree of future assistance as well. None of this will produce the government or society we would have wanted in Afghanistan, and none of it redeems President Trump's and President Biden's decisions to pull out in 2021. But the United States and partners do possess considerable leverage in dealing with the new realities of Afghanistan.

The paradox of American power is that, while we may not be that good at wielding it tactically and operationally, the system of alliances and global leadership itself is so strong at its core that it appears capable of absorbing a number of blows without crumbling.

None of this is to excuse complacency about future challenges and threats. None of it should encourage a cavalier attitude toward war, of course—or any sense that things will always turn out okay, especially in regard to great-power relations and possible conflict.

Indeed, some of this favorable correlation of forces is at risk. Whether Beijing and Moscow truly fear the United States militarily, they do appear to resent America's exercise of power in the post–Cold War period and are prepared to take risks in pushing back. Iran and North Korea may be more committed to their respective, if very different, nuclear ambitions after witnessing U.S.-led regime-change operations from Afghanistan to Iraq to Libya. The United States should not adopt these nations' worldviews, of course, but it does need to acknowledge the realities of these foreign sentiments and motivations.[1]

On balance, we should address national security challenges with a certain underlying confidence about the strength of our position. That reality may counsel a certain restraint, and calm, more often than not. The trick is to sustain resoluteness in defense of core interests, juxtaposed with caution in the use of force and restraint in grand-strategic ambitions.

A final thought: as a veteran of the so-called revolution in military affairs debate that was particularly enthused during the 1990s, I have been reflecting on the proper relative roles of futuristic defense thought, on the one hand, and the study of history on the other. Both are important in the education of any defense analyst or strategist. But each has its distinct place. I would suggest that futuristic writing is the most relevant for developing visions about military innovation and modernization for defense planners today. But for crisis decisionmakers, and those who seek to help top policymakers when they must make fundamental decisions about war and peace, history may be more important. One thing it counsels is that those who get too impressed by the next generation of weapons, technologies, and associated operational concepts often exaggerate their ability to transform warfare once the fighting, and the dying, actually start. Military history is fundamentally sobering. For that reason its value is hard to exaggerate.

Notes

Preface to the Updated Edition

1. I would also like to thank Jack Bradley, Joey Epstein, Alejandra Rocha, and Anton Weintraub for excellent research assistance as I prepared this new part of the book, and Professor Edward Gutierrez for important feedback and very helpful suggestions as well.

2. See Sergei Chernyshov, "The Majority Never Had It So Good," Russia.Post, September 19, 2023, https://russiapost.info/regions/majority.

3. Stephen Daggett, "Costs of Major U.S. Wars," Congressional Research Service, Washington, D.C., 2010, https://fas.org/sgp/crs/natsec/RS22926.pdf. Military fatalities for each conflict are estimated by the Congressional Research Services as follows: about 4,400 for the Revolutionary War, about 2,300 for the War of 1812, about 13,300 for the U.S.-Mexico War (though of these only an estimated 1,700 were described as battle deaths, the rest from disease and other such causes), and about 2,400 for the Spanish-American War (with about 385 battle deaths). See David A. Blum and Nese DeBruyne, "American War and Military Operations Casualties: Lists and Statistics," Congressional Research Service, Washington, D.C., July 2020, https://sgp.fas.org/crs/natsec/RL32492.pdf.

4. John R. Alden, *A History of the American Revolution* (New York: De Capo Press, 1969), pp. 396–97.

5. Don Higginbotham, *The War of American Independence: Military Attitudes, Policies, and Practice, 1763–1789* (Bloomington, Indiana: Indiana University Press, 1971), p. 150.

6. James Kirby Martin and Mark Edward Lender, *"A Respectable Army": The Military Origins of the Republic, 1763–1789*, 3rd ed. (Chichester, England: John Wiley and Sons, 2015), p. 48.

7. Martin and Lender, *"A Respectable Army,"* pp. 1–3.

8. Martin and Lender, *"A Respectable Army,"* pp. 36–39.

9. Rick Atkinson, *The British Are Coming: The War for America, Lexington to Princeton, 1775–1777* (New York: Henry Holt and Company, 2019), pp. 257–71.

10. Alden, *A History of the American Revolution*, pp. 194–200.

11. Alden, *A History of the American Revolution*, pp. 200–210.

12. See Kevin J. Weddle, *The Compleat Victory: Saratoga and the American Revolution* (Oxford, England: Oxford University Press, 2021), p. 4.

13. Alden, *A History of the American Revolution*, pp. 309–27.

14. Weddle, *The Compleat Victory*, p. 301.

15. Weddle, *The Compleat Victory*, pp. 1–6, 361–78.

16. Weddle, *The Compleat Victory*, p. 379.

17. Ron Chernow, *Washington: A Life* (New York: Penguin Books, 2010), pp. 361–62.

18. Martin and Lender, *"A Respectable Army,"* pp. 50, 54, 70.

19. Chernow, *Washington: A Life*, pp. 229–33.

20. Atkinson, *The British Are Coming*, p. 373.

21. Higginbotham, *The War of American Independence*, pp. 158–62; Atkinson, *The British Are Coming*, pp. 348–79.

22. Chernow, *Washington: A Life*, pp. 251–64.

23. Chernow, *Washington: A Life*, p. 264.

24. Joseph J. Ellis, *Founding Brothers: The Revolutionary Generation* (New York: Alfred A. Knopf, 2001), p. 5.

25. Alden, *A History of the American Revolution*, pp. 272–74.

26. Atkinson, *The British Are Coming*, pp. 530–54.

27. Chernow, *Washington: A Life*, pp. 264–84.

28. Martin and Lender, *"A Respectable Army,"* pp. 78–83.

29. Martin and Lender, *"A Respectable Army,"* pp. 78–83.

30. Mark Edward Lender and Garry Wheeler Stone, *Fatal Sunday: George Washington, the Monmouth Campaign, and the Politics of Battle* (University of Oklahoma Press, 2016), pp. xi–xviii.

31. Russell F. Weigley, *The American Way of War: A History of United States Military Strategy and Policy* (Indiana University Press, 1973), pp. 3–17.

32. Martin and Lender, *"A Respectable Army,"* pp. 113–27.

33. John Shy, *A People Numerous and Armed: Reflections on the Military Struggle for American Independence,* revised edition (University of Michigan Press, 1990), pp. 196–212; Higginbotham, *The War of American Independence,* pp. 364–76.

34. John Buchanan, *The Road to Guilford Courthouse* (New York: John Wiley & Sons, 1997), pp. 3–16.

35. Higginbotham, *The War of American Independence,* pp. 352–60.

36. Russell F. Weigley, *The American Way of War: A History of United States Military Strategy and Policy* (Indiana University Press, 1973), pp. 18–39.

37. Lawrence E. Babits, *A Devil of a Whipping: The Battle of Cowpens* (University of North Carolina Press, 1998), pp. 1–10, 81–123.

38. Congressional Research Service, "American War and Military Operations Casualties: Lists and Statistics," Washington, D.C., July 29, 2020, https://sgp.fas.org/crs/natsec/RL32492.pdf; Larry H. Addington, *The Patterns of War Since the Eighteenth Century*, 2nd ed. (Indiana University Press, 1994), pp. 12–19.

39. Martin and Lender, *"A Respectable Army,"* pp. 66–138.

40. See also Dave R. Palmer, *George Washington's Military Genius* (Washington, D.C.: Regnery Publishing, 2012), pp. 224–25.

41. Weigley, *The American Way of War*, pp. 3–17.

42. Martin and Lender, *"A Respectable Army,"* pp. 139–51.

43. Gregory J. Dehler, "Fabian Strategy," Mount Vernon Ladies' Association, Mount Vernon, Va., 2023, https://www.mountvernon.org/library/digitalhistory/digital-encyclopedia/article/fabian-strategy.

44. Charles Boyster, *A Revolutionary People at War: The Continental Army and American Character, 1775–1783* (University of North Carolina Press, 1979), pp. 61–66.

45. Robert Kagan, *Dangerous Nation: America's Foreign Policy from Its Earliest Days to the Dawn of the Twentieth Century* (New York: Alfred A. Knopf, 2006).

46. Donald R. Hickey, *The War of 1812: A Forgotten Conflict* (University of Illinois Press, 2012), pp. 25–27.

47. Michael Beschloss, *Presidents of War: The Epic Story, from 1807 to Modern Times* (New York: Crown, 2018), p. 91.

48. Beschloss, *Presidents of War*, pp. 1–96; Walter R. Borneman, *1812: The War that Forged a Nation* (New York: HarperCollins Publishers, 2004), pp. 1–3.

49. Henry Adams, *The War of 1812* (New York: Cooper Square Press, 1999), p. 3.

50. Hickey, *The War of 1812*, pp. 284–301.

51. Weigley, *The American Way of War*, pp. 40–55.

52. Borneman, *1812: The War that Forged a Nation*, pp. 99–135.

53. Hickey, *The War of 1812*, pp. 230–55.

54. Hickey, *The War of 1812*, pp. 66–99, 123–61, 183–228.

55. Ulysses S. Grant, *The Complete Personal Memoirs of Ulysses S. Grant* (Lexington, KY: Seven Treasures Publications, 2010), p. 27.

56. K. Jack Bauer, *The Mexican War, 1846–1848* (: University of Nebraska Press, 1992), p. xxv.

57. Bauer, *The Mexican War, 1846–1848*, pp. 1–45.

58. Beschloss, *Presidents of War*, pp. 97–120.

59. Bauer, *The Mexican War, 1846–1848*, pp. 52–57.

60. Bauer, *The Mexican War, 1846–1848*, p. 100.

61. John S.D. Eisenhower, *So Far from God: The U.S. War with Mexico, 1846–1848* (University of Oklahoma Press, 2000), pp. 182–86; Bauer, *The Mexican War, 1846–1848,* pp. 208–20.

62. Bauer, *The Mexican War, 1846–1848,* pp. 164–72.

63. Eisenhower, *So Far from God,* pp. 205–32.

64. Grant, *The Complete Personal Memoirs of Ulysses S. Grant,* pp. 52–56.

65. Eisenhower, *So Far from God,* pp. 312–42.

66. Evan Thomas, *The War Lovers: Roosevelt, Lodge, Hearst, and the Rush to Empire, 1898* (New York: Back Bay Books, 2011).

67. Beschloss, *Presidents of War,* p. 259.

68. See David F. Trask, *The War with Spain in 1898* (University of Nebraska Press, 1981), pp. 1–177.

69. Edward M. Coffman, *The Regulars: The American Army, 1989–1941* (Cambridge, MA: Harvard University Press, 2004), pp. 1–5.

70. Graham A. Cosmos, *An Army for Empire: The United States Army in the Spanish-American War* (Texas A&M Press, 1994).

71. Trask, *The War with Spain in 1898,* pp. 388–90.

72. Doris Kearns Goodwin, *The Bully Pulpit: Theodore Roosevelt, William Howard Taft, and the Golden Age of Journalism* (New York: Simon and Schuster, 2013), pp. 227–31.

73. Trask, *The War with Spain in 1898,* pp. 257–69.

74. Trask, *The War with Spain in 1898,* pp. 466–86.

75. Coffman, *The Regulars,* pp. 34–39.

76. David J. Silbey, *A War of Frontier and Empire: The Philippine-American War, 1899–1902* (New York: Hill and Wang, 2007), pp. 207–12.

Preface and Acknowledgments

1. There are several books that survey various eras of past warfare as well. They include Larry H. Addington, *The Patterns of War Since the Eighteenth Century,* second ed. (Indiana University Press, 1994); Jonathan M. House, *Combined Arms Warfare in the Twentieth Century* (University Press of Kansas, 2001); Theodore Ropp, *War in the Modern World,* rev. ed. (Johns Hopkins University Press, 2000); Robert A. Doughty, Ira D. Gruber, Roy K. Flint, Mark Grimsley, George C. Herring, Donald D. Horward, John A. Lynn, and Williamson Murray, *Warfare in the Western World: Military Operations Since 1871* (D.C. Heath and Company, 1996); and Richard Arthur Preston, Alex Roland, and S. F. Wise, *Men in Arms: A History of Warfare and Its Interrelationships with Western Society* (New York: Holt, Rinehart, and Winston, 1991). The West Point history department has created an interactive online text to serve a related purpose, at http://www.westpointhistoryofwarfare.com/; other wide-ranging books by the likes of

Weigley, Fuller, and Liddell Hart are cited in the pages that follow as well. I hope that adding one more book to this short list, with a particular focus on America's wars since 1861 through 2022, and with an emphasis on drawing lessons for today at the levels of national grand strategy, military strategy, military operations, and tactics, can be a worthy addition to the literature.

2. Maura Reynolds, "'Yes He Would': Fiona Hill on Putin and Nukes," *Politico*, February 28, 2022.

3. See Robert Jervis, *Perception and Misperception in International Politics* (Princeton University Press, 1976).

4. See for example Richard E. Neustadt and Ernest R. May, *Thinking in Time: The Uses of History for Decisionmakers* (New York: Free Press, 1988), pp. xix, 15–16, 234; Hal Brands and Jeremi Suri, "Introduction: Thinking about History and Foreign Policy," in *The Power of the Past: History and Statecraft*, edited by Hal Brands and Jeremi Suri (Brookings, 2016), pp. 11–13; Ernest R. May, *Lessons of the Past: The Use and Misuse of History in American Foreign Policy* (Oxford University Press, 1976), p. xi; and Gideon Rose, "Foreign Policy for Pragmatists: How Biden Can Learn from History in Real Time," *Foreign Affairs*, 100: 2 (March/April 2021), pp. 48–56.

5. Viktor E. Frankl, *Man's Search for Meaning* (Boston: Beacon Press, 2006), p. 154.

1. The American Civil War

1. Russell F. Weigley, *A Great Civil War: A Military and Political History, 1861–1865* (Indiana University Press, 2000), pp. 231–36; James M. McPherson, *Battle Cry of Freedom* (Oxford University Press, 1988), pp. 306–07; History.net, "Civil War Battles," Arlington, Va., 2020, historynet.com/civil-war-battles; and National Park Service, "The Civil War," 2020, nps.gov/civilwar/facts.htm.

2. National Park Service, "The Civil War," Washington, DC, 2020.

3. Guy Gugliotta, "New Estimate Raises Civil War Death Toll," *New York Times*, April 2, 2012; Nese F. DeBruyne, "American War and Military Operations Casualties: Lists and Statistics," Congressional Research Service, April 26, 2017, census.gov/history/pdf/wwi-casualties112018.pdf.

4. Michael E. O'Hanlon, *Defense 101: Understanding the Military of Today and Tomorrow* (Cornell University Press, 2021), p. 58; and Stephen Daggett, "Costs of Major U.S. Wars," Congressional Research Service, Washington, DC, 2010, https://fas.org/sgp/crs/natsec/RS22926.pdf.

5. Andrew F. Krepinevich, "From Cavalry to Computer: The Pattern of Military Revolutions," *National Interest*, 37 (Fall 1994); and Eliot A. Cohen, *Supreme Command: Soldiers, Statesmen, and Leadership in Wartime* (New York: Free Press, 2002), pp. 23–29.

6. Cohen, *Supreme Command,* p. 25.

7. Phillip R. Kemmerly, "Rivers, Rails, and Rebels: Logistics and Struggle to Supply U.S. Army Depot at Nashville, 1862–1865," *Journal of Military History,* 84 (July 2020), pp. 713–46.

8. Paddy Griffith, *Battle Tactics of the Civil War* (Yale University Press, 1989).

9. Max Boot, *War Made New: Technology, Warfare, and the Course of History, 1500 to Today* (New York: Gotham Books, 2006), pp. 128–29.

10. Boot, *War Made New,* pp. 174–75.

11. Martin Van Creveld, *Technology and War: From 2000 B.C. to the Present,* rev. and exp. ed. (New York: Free Press, 1991), pp. 181, 191, 208.

12. Krepinevich, "From Cavalry to Computer.

13. Cohen, *Supreme Command,* pp. 23–29.

14. Weigley, *A Great Civil War,* p. 34.

15. Ibid., pp. 279, 283.

16. Joseph G. Dawson III, "Jefferson Davis and the Confederacy's 'Offensive-Defensive' Strategy in the U.S. Civil War," *Journal of Military History,* 73 (April 2009), pp. 591–607.

17. Weigley, *A Great Civil War,* pp. 29–35.

18. Jefferson Davis, *The Rise and Fall of the Confederate Government* (Middletown, DE: Pantianos Classics), p. 140.

19. Daniel T. Canfield, "Opportunity Lost: Combined Operations and the Development of Union Military Strategy, April 1861-April 1862," *Journal of Military History,* 79 (July 2015), 657–90; and Cohen, *Supreme Command,* pp. 31–33.

20. Michael Walzer, *Just and Unjust Wars* (New York: Basic Books, 1977), pp. 32–33.

21. David Petraeus, "Take the Confederate Names Off Our Army Bases," *The Atlantic,* June 9, 2020.

22. Carl Sandburg, *Abraham Lincoln: The Prairie Years and the War Years,* one-vol. ed. (New York: Galahad Books, 1954), p. 250.

23. Bruce Catton, *Mr. Lincoln's Army* (Garden City, NY: Doubleday and Company, 1951), p. 206.

24. McPherson, *Battle Cry of Freedom,* pp. 1–233.

25. David W. Blight, *Frederick Douglass: Prophet of Freedom* (New York: Simon and Schuster, 2018), p. 304.

26. See McPherson, *Battle Cry of Freedom,* pp. 1–233.

27. Davis, *The Rise and Fall of the Confederate Government,* p. 143.

28. William J. Cooper, Jr., *Jefferson Davis, American* (New York: Vintage Books, 2000), p. 366.

29. H. W. Brands, *The Zealot and the Emancipator and the Struggle for American Freedom* (New York: Doubleday, 2020), pp. 1–3.

30. Weigley, *A Great Civil War,* pp. 25–28.

31. Adam Goodheart, *1861: The Civil War Awakening* (New York: Alfred A. Knopf, 2011), pp. 159–60.

32. See McPherson, *Battle Cry of Freedom,* p. 250.

33. Ibid., p. 313.

34. Review by David Welker of Peter G. Tsouras, *Major General George H. Sharpe and the Creation of American Military Intelligence in the Civil War* (New York: Casemate Publishers, 2019), in *Studies in Intelligence,* 64:4 (December 2020), pp. 65–66.

35. Weigley, *A Great Civil War,* p. xx.

36. Stephen E. Ambrose, "America's Civil War Comes to West Point," *Civil War Times Illustrated* (August 1965), historynet.com/americas-civil-war-comes-to-west -point.htm.

37. Weigley, *A Great Civil War,* pp. 24–25.

38. Sandburg, *Abraham Lincoln,* p. 231.

39. Clayton Newell, *The Regular Army before the Civil War, 1845–1860* (Carlisle, PA: U.S. Army War College, 2014), p. 50, https://history.army.mil/html /books/075/75-1/CMH_Pub_75-1.pdf.

40. John Lewis Gaddis, *On Grand Strategy* (New York: Penguin Books, 2018), p. 234.

41. Brands, *The Zealot and the Emancipator,* p. 273.

42. David Herbert Donald, *Lincoln* (New York: Simon and Schuster, 1995), p. 295.

43. Robert Kagan, *Dangerous Nation: America's Foreign Policy from Its Earliest Days to the Dawn of the Twentieth Century* (New York: Random House, 2006), p. 262.

44. Brands, *The Zealot and the Emancipator,* p. 304.

45. President Abraham Lincoln, Second Inaugural Address, Washington, DC, March 4, 1865, quoted in Carl Sandburg, *Abraham Lincoln: The Prairie Years and the War Years, One Volume Edition* (New York: Galahad Books, 1954), p. 664

46. Abraham Lincoln, "Message to Congress in Special Session, July 4, 1861," in John Grafton, ed., *Great Speeches of Abraham Lincoln* (New York: Dover Publications, 1991), p. 69.

47. Weigley, *A Great Civil War,* p. 24.

48. Donald, *Lincoln,* p. 281.

49. Emory M. Thomas, *Robert E. Lee* (New York: Norton, 1997), p. 197.

50. Shelby Foote, *The Civil War, a Narrative: Fort Sumter to Perryville* (New York: Vintage Books, 1958), pp. 73–74.

51. Ibid., p. 60.

52. Kagan, *Dangerous Nation*; and DeBruyne, "American War" pp. 1–2.

53. McPherson, *Battle Cry of Freedom,* pp. 317, 332.

54. Ulysses S. Grant, *The Complete Personal Memoirs of Ulysses S. Grant* (Springfield, MA.: Seven Treasures Publications, 2010), p. 131.

55. McPherson, *Battle Cry of Freedom*, pp. 600–11.

56. Weigley, *A Great Civil War*, pp. xxiv–xxviii.

57. Catton, *Mr. Lincoln's Army*, pp. 15–16.

58. Foote, *The Civil War, a Narrative*, p. 63.

59. Weigley, *A Great Civil War*, pp. 15–18.

60. See for example, Eugene D. Genovese, *The Political Economy of Slavery: Studies in the Economy and Society of the Slave South*, 2nd ed. (Wesleyan University Press, 1989).

61. Adam Goodheart, *1861: The Civil War Awakening* (New York: Alfred A. Knopf, 2011), pp. 174–84.

62. Thomas, *Robert E. Lee*, p. 314.

63. Donald, *Lincoln*, p. 260.

64. McPherson, *Battle Cry of Freedom*, p. 284.

65. Ibid., pp. 297–303.

66. Catton, *Mr. Lincoln's Army*, pp. 55–60.

67. Sandburg, *Abraham Lincoln*, p. 252.

68. Foote, *The Civil War, a Narrative*, p. 93.

69. McPherson, *Battle Cry of Freedom*, pp. 339–68

70. Weigley, *A Great Civil War*, pp. 58–63.

71. Ibid., pp. 72–77.

72. Kevin J. Weddle, "'The Fall of Satan's Kingdom': Civil-Military Relations and the Union Navy's Attack on Charleston, April 1863," *Journal of Military History*, 75 (April 2011), pp. 411–39

73. Weigley, *A Great Civil War*, pp. 72–77, 223–24, 420.

74. McPherson, *Battle Cry of Freedom*, pp. 382, 440.

75. Donald, *Lincoln*, p. 296.

76. McPherson, *Battle Cry of Freedom*, pp. 318–33.

77. Weigley, *A Great Civil War*, pp. 111–18.

78. Bruce Catton, *Grant Moves South, 1861–1863* (Boston: Little, Brown, and Company, 1960), p. 242.

79. Grant, *Memoirs*, p. 131.

80. John MacDonald, *Great Battles of the Civil War* (New York: Collier Books, 1988), p. 31.

81. McPherson, *Battle Cry of Freedom*, pp. 418–20.

82. Ibid., pp. 392–427.

83. MacDonald, *Great Battles of the Civil War*, pp. 80–87.

84. McPherson, *Battle Cry of Freedom*, pp. 324–25.

85. Stephen W. Sears, *George B. McClellan: The Young Napoleon* (New York: De Capo Press, 1999), p. 1.

86. Weigley, *A Great Civil War*, pp. 120–21.

87. McPherson, *Battle Cry of Freedom*, pp. 377–78.

88. MacDonald, *Great Battles of the Civil War*, p. 32.

89. Donald Stoker, "McClellan's War Winning Strategy," *MHQ—The Quarterly Journal of Military History,* 23: 4 (Summer 2011).

90. Weigley, *A Great Civil War,* pp. 93–94.

91. Ibid., pp. 129–34.

92. Sandburg, *Abraham Lincoln,* p. 259.

93. McPherson, *Battle Cry of Freedom,* pp. 454–77.

94. Wiegley, *A Great Civil War,* pp. 135–44.

95. McPherson, *Battle Cry of Freedom,* p. 490.

96. Weigley, *A Great Civil War,* pp. 135–44.

97. MacDonald, *Great Battles of the Civil War,* pp. 48–55.

98. Weigley, *A Great Civil War,* pp. 135–44.

99. MacDonald, *Great Battles of the Civil War,* pp. 56–67.

100. Weigley, *A Great Civil War,* pp. 153–54.

101. Sandburg, *Abraham Lincoln,* p. 324.

102. MacDonald, *Great Battles of the Civil War,* pp. 68–79.

103. Catton, *Grant Moves South,* p. 366.

104. Grant, *Memoirs,* pp. 161–62.

105. Ibid., p. 162.

106. Ibid., p. 169.

107. J.F.C. Fuller, *Decisive Battles of the Western World, Volume III: From the American Civil War to the End of the Second World War* (London: Cassell and Co., 2001), p. 57.

108. Grant, *Memoirs,* pp. 188–203.

109. MacDonald, *Great Battles of the Civil* War, pp. 88–99.

110. Thomas, *Robert E. Lee,* p. 287.

111. Weigley, *A Great Civil War,* p. 229.

112. Thomas, *Robert E. Lee,* p. 288.

113. MacDonald, *Great Battles of the Civil War,* pp. 100–11.

114. Weigley, *A Great Civil War,* p. 277.

115. Ibid., p. 278.

116. Ibid., pp. 277–85.

117. Addington, *The Patterns of War since the Eighteenth Century,* p. 76.

118. MacDonald, *Great Battles of the Civil War,* pp. 112–31.

119. Catton, *Grant Takes Command,* p. 5.

120. Ibid., pp. 1–85.

121. Ibid., p. 93.

122. Ibid., p. 139.

123. Ken Burns, "The Civil War," PBS Documentary Series, 1990.

124. Catton, *Grant Takes Command,* p. 368.

125. McPherson, *Battle Cry of Freedom,* pp. 718–24.

126. Cohen, *Supreme Command,* pp. 15–16.

127. McPherson, *Battle Cry of Freedom,* pp. 726–43.

128. Ethan S. Rafuse, "'Little Phil,' a 'Bad Old Man,' and the 'Gray Ghost:' Hybrid Warfare and the Fight for the Shenandoah Valley, August-November 1864," *Journal of Military History,* 81 (July 2017), 775–801.

129. McPherson, *Battle Cry of Freedom,* p. 757.

130. Ibid., p. 809.

131. Fuller, *Decisive Battles of the Western World,* p. 84.

132. McPherson, *Battle Cry of Freedom,* pp. 811–19.

133. Grant, *Memoirs,* pp. 291–305; Weigley, *A Great Civil War,* pp. 423–34.

134. McPherson, *Battle Cry of Freedom,* pp. 844–50.

135. Weigley, *A Great Civil War,* p. 67.

136. United States Marine Corps, *Campaigning* (Department of the Navy, 1997), pp. 21–30, marines.mil/Portals/1/Publications/MCDP%201-2%20Campaigning.pdf.

137. Weigley, *A Great Civil War,* pp. 358–67.

138. Fuller, *Decisive Battles of the Western World,* pp. 12–52.

139. Jay Winik, *April 1865: The Month That Saved America* (New York: HarperCollins, 2001), pp. 147–72.

140. Weigley, *A Great Civil War,* pp. xx–xxiv, 324–330. See also, Stephen Badsey, Donald Stoker, and Joseph G. Dawson III, "Forum II: Confederate Military Strategy in the U.S. Civil War Revisited," *Journal of Military History,* 73 (October 2009), pp. 1273–87.

141. Carl von Clausewitz, *On War,* edited and translated by Michael Howard and Peter Paret (Princeton University Press, 1976), pp. 117–18.

142. Doris Kearns Goodwin, *Team of Rivals: The Political Genius of Abraham Lincoln* (New York: Simon and Schuster, 2006), pp. 475–80.

143. Sears, *George B. McClellan,* pp. 98–99.

144. Eliot A. Cohen and John Gooch, *Military Misfortunes: The Anatomy of Failure in War* (New York: Free Press, 1990), p. 244.

145. Weigley, *A Great Civil War,* p. 254.

146. Ibid., pp. 29–35.

147. Alain C. Enthoven and K. Wayne Smith, *How Much Is Enough? Shaping the Defense Program, 1961–1969* (Santa Monica, CA: RAND, 2005).

2. World War I

1. Christopher Clark, *The Sleepwalkers: How Europe Went to War in 1914* (New York: HarperCollins, 2013), pp. 3–64.

2. Ibid., pp. 83–87, 254–55, 266–92.

3. See Michael S. Neiberg, *Dance of the Furies: Europe and the Outbreak of World War I* (Harvard University Press, 2011), pp. 1–35.

4. Paul Kennedy, *The Rise and Fall of the Great Powers: Economic Change and Military Conflict from 1500 to 2000* (New York: Random House, 1987), p. 243.

5. Barbara W. Tuchman, *The Guns of August* (New York: Bantam Books, 1976), p. 25.

6. Stephen Van Evera, "Why Cooperation Failed in 1914," in *Cooperation Under Anarchy*, edited by Kenneth A. Oye (Princeton University Press, 1986), pp. 90–92.

7. Clark, *The Sleepwalkers*, p. 173.

8. Adam Tooze, *The Deluge: The Great War, America and the Remaking of the Global Order, 1916–1931* (New York: Viking, 2014), pp. 50–67; U.S. Census Bureau, "Statistical Abstract of the United States," Department of Defense Personnel (www.census.gov/compendia/statab/); and U.S. Army Center of Military History, "American Military History," vols. 1 and 2 (history.army.mil /books).

9. Gerhard P. Gross, "There Was a Schlieffen Plan: New Sources on the History of German Military Planning," *War in History* (November 2008).

10. Shashi Tharoor, "Why the Indian Soldiers of World War I Were Forgotten," *BBC News*, July 2, 2015, bbc.com/news/magazine-33317368.

11. See Joseph S. Nye, Jr., "1914 Revisited?" *Project Syndicate*, January 13, 2014, project-syndicate.org/commentary/joseph-s--nye-asks-whether-war-between -china-and-the-us-is-as-inevitable-as-many-believe-world-war-i-to-have-been ?barrier=accesspaylog.

12. Kennedy, *The Rise and Fall of the Great Powers*, pp. 219–20.

13. Clark, *The Sleepwalkers*, p. 208.

14. Stephen Van Evera, "The Cult of the Offensive and the Origins of the First World War," in *Military Strategy and the Origins of the First World War*, edited by Steven E. Miller, Sean M. Lynn-Jones, and Stephen Van Evera, rev. and exp. ed. (Princeton University Press, 1991), pp. 81–83; and Clark, *The Sleepwalkers*, pp. 326–34.

15. Stephen Van Evera, "European Militaries and the Origins of World War I," in *The Next Great War? The Roots of World War I and the Risk of U.S.-China Conflict*, edited by Richard N. Rosecrance and Steven E. Miller (MIT Press, 2015), p. 152.

16. See for example, John C. G. Rohl, *Kaiser Wilhelm II* (Cambridge University Press, 2015), pp. 135–63.

17. Ibid., p. xvi.

18. See "Stephen Van Evera Revisits World War I, One Century After Its Bitter End," *MIT Center for International Studies Magazine* (Fall 2018), https://cis.mit .edu/publications/analysis-opinion/2018/stephen-van-evera-revisits-world-war -i-one-century-after-its.

19. Clark, *The Sleepwalkers,* pp. 484–87; and Stephen Van Evera, *Causes of War* (Cornell University Press, 1999), p. 133.

20. Tuchman, *The Guns of August,* p. 162.

21. Mark McNeilly, "The Battle of the Military Theorists: Clausewitz versus Sun Tzu," *History News Network,* George Washington University, January 25, 2015, https://historynewsnetwork.org/article/158123#:~:text=Clausewitz%20 then%20stated%20that%20the,would%20end%20the%20war%20favorably; and Tuchman, *The Guns of August,* p. 36.

22. Lawrence Freedman, *Strategy: A History* (Oxford University Press, 2013), p. 124.

23. Hew Strachan, "Clausewitz and the First World War," *Journal of Military History,* 75 (April 2011), pp. 367–91.

24. See Thucydides, *History of the Peloponnesian War* (New York: Penguin Books, 1972), pp. 79–80 (book one, sections 75 and 76).

25. Ibid., pp. 400–02 (book five, sections 84 through 89).

26. Donald Kagan, *On the Origins of War: And the Preservation of Peace* (New York: Anchor Books, 1996), p. 134.

27. See Cathal J. Nolan, *The Allure of Battle: A History of How Wars Have Been Won and Lost* (Oxford University Press, 2019), pp. 1–17.

28. Geoffrey Blainey, *The Causes of War,* third edition (New York: Free Press, 1978), pp. 35–39.

29. Tuchman, *The Guns of August,* pp. 142–43, 221–33.

30. Van Evera, "The Cult of the Offensive," pp. 89, 98–99.

31. Ibid., p. 91.

32. MacMillan, *The War that Ended Peace,* p. 343.

33. Glenn H. Snyder, *Alliance Politics* (Cornell University Press, 1997), pp. 254–60.

34. Clark, *The Sleepwalkers,* p. 93.

35. John Keegan, *The First World War* (New York: Alfred A. Knopf, 1999), pp. 52, 70.

36. Kagan, *On the Origins of War,* pp. 114–19; and Clark, *The Sleepwalkers,* p. 121.

37. Bernadotte E. Schmitt, *Triple Alliance and Triple Entente* (New York: Henry Holt and Company, 1934), pp. 6, 34–37.

38. Robert Jervis, *Perception and Misperception in International Politics* (Princeton University Press, 1976), p. 92.

39. Margaret MacMillan, *The War that Ended Peace: The Road to 1914* (Toronto: Allen Lane, 2013), pp. 49–55.

40. Jervis, *Perception and Misperception,* p. 110.

41. Clark, *The Sleepwalkers,* p. 130.

42. MacMillan, *The War that Ended Peace,* pp. 158–59.

43. Clark, *The Sleepwalkers,* pp. 222–24, 293–313.

44. MacMillan, *The War that Ended Peace,* p. 82.

45. Ibid., pp. 49–53.

46. Clark, *The Sleepwalkers,* pp. 138–39; Macmillan, *The War that Ended Peace,* p. 55; and Kennedy, *Rise and Fall of the Great Powers,* pp. 250–56.

47. Clark, *The Sleepwalkers,* pp. 123, 139.

48. Kennedy, *The Rise and Fall of the Great Powers,* p. 252; Clark, *The Sleepwalkers,* pp. 129–30; and Kagan, *On the Origins of War,* pp. 151–53.

49. See for example, Robert K. Massie, *Dreadnought: Britain, Germany, and the Coming of the Great War* (New York: Ballantine Books, 1991), pp. 890–900.

50. Kagan, *On the Origins of War,* pp. 205–14.

51. Peter Gatrell, *Russia's First World War: A Social and Economic History* (London: Pearson Education Limited, 2005), p. 3.

52. Dale C. Copeland, *Economic Interdependence and War* (Princeton University Press, 2015), pp. 122–33.

53. See for example, Schmitt, *Triple Alliance and Triple Entente.*

54. Dennis E. Showalter, *Tannenberg: Clash of Empires, 1914* (Lincoln, NE: Potomac Books, 2004), p. 219.

55. Hew Strachan, *The First World War* (New York: Penguin Books, 2013), p. 43.

56. See Bodie D. Dykstra, "'To Dig and Burrow Like Rabbits:' British Field Fortifications at the Battle of the Aisne, September to October 1914," *Journal of Military History,* 84 (July 2020), pp. 747–73.

57. Mike Bullock, Laurence Lyons, and Phillip Judkins, "A Resolution of the Debate about British Wireless in World War I," *Journal of Military History,* 84 (October 2020), pp. 1079–96; and Keegan, *The First World War,* pp. 162–63.

58. Max Boot, *War Made New,* pp. 146–195; and Michael Howard, "Men Against Fire," in *Military Strategy and the Origins of the First World War,* edited by Steven E. Miller, Sean M. Lynn-Jones, and Stephen Van Evera, rev. and exp. ed. (Princeton University Press, 1991), pp. 3–19.

59. H. A. Feiveson, *Scientists Against Time: The Rose of Scientists in World War II* (Bloomington, IN: Archway Publishing, 2018), p. 43.

60. Russell F. Weigley, *The American Way of War* (Indiana University Press, 1973), pp. 224–25.

61. Strachan, *The First World War,* p. 313.

62. For a good overview, see Van Creveld, *Technology and War,* pp. 167–97.

63. Strachan, *The First World War,* p. 312.

64. Again, for a concise treatment that puts this period in broader perspective, see Van Creveld, *Technology and War,* pp. 199–216.

65. Norman Van Der Veer, "Mining Operations in the War," *United States Naval Institute Proceedings,* 45: 11 (November 1919), pp. 1857–65.

66. Tuchman, *The Guns of August,* p. 35.

67. Kennedy, *The Rise and Fall of the Great Powers,* pp. 203, 274; and John Keegan, *The First World War,* p. 73.

68. Keegan, *The First World War,* pp. 35–36.

69. Van Evera, "Why Cooperation Failed in 1914," pp. 80–117.

70. Julian E. Zelizer, *Arsenal of Democracy: The Politics of National Security— from World War II to the War on Terrorism* (New York: Basic Books, 2010), pp. 28–38.

71. Weigley, *The American Way of War,* pp. 192–204.

72. Jack Snyder, "Civil-Military Relations and the Cult of the Offensive, 1914 and 1984," in *Military Strategy and the Origins of the First World War,* edited by Steven E. Miller, Sean M. Lynn-Jones, and Stephen Van Evera, rev. and exp. ed. (Princeton University Press, 1991), pp. 24–30.

73. MacMillan, *The War that Ended Peace,* pp. 318–23.

74. Keegan, *The First World War,* pp. 25–28.

75. B. H. Liddell Hart, *Strategy,* second rev. ed. (New York: Meridian Books, 1967), pp. 151–56.

76. Tuchman, *The Guns of August,* pp. 38–44.

77. Ibid., pp. 50–70, 264.

78. Robert A. Doughty, "French Strategy in 1914: Joffre's Own," *Journal of Military History,* 67 (April 2003), pp. 427–54.

79. Robert A. Doughty, *Pyrrhic Victory: French Strategy and Operations in the Great War* (Harvard University Press, 2005), pp. 54–57.

80. Tuchman, *The Guns of August,* pp. 69–70.

81. Ibid., pp. 75–87, 297–325; MacMillan, *The War that Ended Peace,* pp. 587–88, 600–03; Clark, *The Sleepwalkers,* p. 508.

82. Clark, *The Sleepwalkers,* pp. 451–52.

83. Keegan, *The First World War,* pp. 30–47.

84. MacMillan, *The War that Ended Peace,* p. 358.

85. Tuchman, *The Guns of August,* p. 39.

86. Robert Kagan, *Dangerous Nation, Volume II: America and the Collapse of World Order, 1900–1941,* forthcoming.

87. Michael S. Neiberg, *The Path to War: How the First World War Created Modern America* (Oxford University Press, 1916), pp. 66–94.

88. Ibid., pp. 152, 175, 209.

89. Sean M. Zeigler et al., *The Evolution of U.S. Military Policy from the Constitution to the Present,* Vol. II (Santa Monica, CA: RAND, 2020), p. 63; Robert B. Zoellick, *America in the World: A History of U.S. Diplomacy and Foreign Policy* (New York: Twelve, 2020), pp. 147–49; and Kagan, *Dangerous Nation II.*

90. Kagan, *On the Origins of War,* p. 97.

91. Keegan, *The First World War,* pp. 24–28, 33; and Clark, *The Sleepwalkers,* p. 222.

92. MacMillan, *The War that Ended Peace,* p. 325.

93. Ibid., p. 203.

94. Jervis, *Perception and Misperception,* p. 54.

95. Tuchman, *The Guns of August,* pp. 99–100; and Clark, *The Sleepwalkers,* pp. 527–37.

96. Clark, *The Sleepwalkers,* pp. 214–24.

97. Annika Mombauer, *The Origins of the First World War: Controversies and Consensus* (London: Pearson Education Limited, 2002), p. 14.

98. Clark, *The Sleepwalkers,* pp. 451–69.

99. Keegan, *The First World War,* pp. 48–70.

100. Mombauer, *The Origins of the First World War,* p. 204.

101. Van Evera, *Causes of War,* pp. 49, 63, 137.

102. Tuchman, *The Guns of August,* pp. 91–101.

103. Ibid., pp. 102–03.

104. Eric Pace, "Barbara Tuchman Dead at 77: A Pulitzer-Winning Historian," *New York Times,* February 7, 1989.

105. Tuchman, *The Guns of August,* pp. 105–19.

106. MacMillan, *The War that Ended Peace,* p. 622.

107. Tuchman, *The Guns of August,* p. 146.

108. Ibid., pp. 150–57.

109. Keegan, *The First World War,* pp. 69–70.

110. Tuchman, *The Guns of August,* pp. 188–220.

111. Keegan, *The First World War,* pp. 71–89.

112. Tuchman, *The Guns of August,* pp. 234–261; and Keegan, *The First World War,* pp. 89–94.

113. Tuchman, *The Guns of August,* pp. 381–90.

114. Ibid., pp. 408–09.

115. Holger H. Herwig, *The Marne, 1914: The Opening of World War I and the Battle that Changed the World* (New York: Random House, 2011), pp. 51–53, 191–94, 307–19.

116. Keegan, *The First World War,* pp. 100–112.

117. Herwig, *The Marne, 1914,* p. 231.

118. Keegan, *The First World War,* p. 22, 112; and John Keegan, *A History of Warfare* (New York: Vintage Books, 1994), p. 307.

119. Herwig, *The Marne, 1914,* p. xii.

120. G.J. Meyer, *A World Undone: The Story of the Great War, 1914 to 1918* (New York: Random House, 2006), p. 202; and Tuchman, *The Guns of August,* pp. 440–59.

121. Herwig, *The Marne,* pp. xiii, 262.

122. Keegan, *The First World War,* pp. 112–20.

123. Ibid., p. 114.

124. Quoted in Herwig, *The Marne,* p. 311.

125. Herwig, *The Marne, 1914,* p. xi.

126. Ibid., pp. 266–306.

127. Keegan, *The First World War*, pp. 122–27.

128. Mark Connelly and Stefan Goebel, *Great Battles: Ypres* (Oxford: Oxford University Press, 2018), p. 4.

129. Keegan, *The First World War*, pp. 127–37.

130. Ibid., pp. 135–36.

131. Ibid., p. 153.

132. Ibid., pp. 141–51.

133. Ibid., pp. 144, 151.

134. Dennis E. Showalter, *Tannenberg: Clash of Empires, 1914* (Lincoln, NE: Potomac Books, 2004), pp. 292, 323; and Tuchman, *The Guns of August*, pp. 297–346.

135. Showalter, *Tannenberg*, p. 347.

136. Tuchman, *The Guns of August*, p. 345.

137. Showalter, *Tannenberg*, pp. 326–27.

138. Alexander Watson, *The Fortress: The Siege of Przemysl and the Making of Europe's Bloodlands* (New York: Basic Books, 2020), pp. 1–54.

139. Tuchman, *The Guns of August*, p. 345; and Keegan, *The First World War*, p. 245.

140. Keegan, *The First World War*, p. 170.

141. Ibid., pp. 165–71.

142. Michael J. Green, *By More than Providence: Grand Strategy and American Power in the Asia Pacific Since 1783* (Columbia University Press, 2017), pp. 123–31.

143. Tuchman, *The Guns of August*, pp. 161–87.

144. Ropp, *War in the Modern World*, p. 246.

145. Herwig, *The Marne, 1914, p.* 315.

146. Stephen Biddle, *Military Power: Explaining Victory and Defeat in Modern Battle* (Princeton University Press, 2004), pp. 28–51.

147. Paddy Griffith, *Battle Tactics of the Western Front: The British Army's Art of Attack, 1916–18* (Yale University Press, 1994), pp. 199–200.

148. Meyer, *A World Undone*, pp. 291–304.

149. Connelly and Goebel, *Great Battles: Ypres*, pp. 5, 27.

150. Keegan, *The First World War*, pp. 192–203.

151. Doughty, *Pyrrhic Victory*, p. 509.

152. Paul Jankowski, *Verdun: The Longest Battle of the Great War* (Oxford University Press, 2016), pp. 9–10, 119–20.

153. Jankowski, *Verdun*, pp. 111–20.

154. Ibid., p. 114.

155. Ibid., p. 43.

156. Ibid., p. 117.

157. Ibid., pp. ix–xi.

158. Biddle, *Military Power*, pp. 28–51.

159. See Peter Hart, *The Somme: The Darkest Hour on the Western Front* (New York: Pegasus Books, 2010), p. 58.

160. Ibid., pp. 109–210, 538–48.

161. Keegan, *The First World War*, pp. 278–99.

162. See Hart, *The Somme*, p. 530.

163. Keegan, *The First World War*, p. 299.

164. Ibid., pp. 229–34.

165. Ibid., pp. 302–06.

166. Ibid., pp. 217–30.

167. Cohen and Gooch, *Military Misfortunes: The Anatomy of Failure in War* (New York: Free Press, 2006), pp. 133–46.

168. L. A. Carlyon, *Gallipoli* (London: Bantam Books, 2003), p. 645.

169. Ibid., p. 643.

170. Ibid., pp. 19–20.

171. Samantha Power, *"A Problem from Hell": America and the Age of Genocide* (New York: Basic Books, 2013), pp. 1–16.

172. Holloway H. Frost, "A Description of the Battle of Jutland," *United States Naval Institute Proceedings*, 45: 11 (November 1919), p. 1842; and John Brooks, *The Battle of Jutland* (Cambridge University Press, 2016), pp. 131–43.

173. Rush Doshi and Kevin McGuiness, "Huawei Meets History: Great Powers and Telecommunications Risk, 1840–2021," Center on Security, Strategy and Technology Paper, Brookings Institution, Washington, DC, April 2021, brookings.edu/wp-content/uploads/2021/03/Huawei-meets-history-v4.pdf.

174. Jason Hines, "Sins of Omission and Commission: A Reassessment of the Role of Intelligence in the Battle of Jutland," *Journal of Military History*, 72:4 (October 2008), pp. 1117–53.

175. National Records of Scotland, "Battle of Jutland 1916," nrscotland.gov .uk/research/learning/first-world-war/the-battle-of-jutland.

176. John Brooks, *The Battle of Jutland* (Cambridge University Press, 2016), pp. 63–96.

177. Brooks, *The Battle of Jutland*, pp. 36–48.

178. Robert K. Massie, *Castles of Steel: Britain, Germany, and the Winning of the Great War at Sea* (New York: Random House, 2003), pp. 579–605.

179. Ibid., pp. 606–34.

180. See Imperial War Museums, "Battle of Jutland Timeline," 2021, iwm .org.uk/history/battle-of-jutland-timeline; and Massie, *Castles of Steel*, pp. 635–57.

181. Brooks, *The Battle of Jutland*, p. 514.

182. Keegan, *The First World War*, pp. 257–74.

183. Van Creveld, *Technology and War*, pp. 207, 216.

184. Krepinevich, "From Cavalry to Computer.

185. Massie, *Castles of Steel*, pp. 715–38; and Tooze, *The Deluge*, pp. 34–35.

186. Zoellick, *America in the World*, pp. 154–65.

187. Keegan, *The First World War*, pp. 322–30.

188. Ibid., pp. 330–32.

189. Gatrell, *Russia's First World War*, pp. 132–50.

190. Keegan, *The First World War*, pp. 332–43.

191. Tooze, *The Deluge*, p. 108.

192. Keegan, *The First World War*, pp. 343–50.

193. Ibid., pp. 350–54.

194. Neiberg, *The Path to War*, pp. 206–37.

195. Peter T. Underwood, "General Pershing and the U.S. Marines," *Marine Corps History*, 5:2 (Winter 2019), p. 7; and Keegan, *The First World War*, pp. 372–73, 410; and Edward M. Coffman, *The Regulars: The American Army, 1898–1941* (Harvard University Press, 2007), p. 203.

196. Doris Kearns Goodwin, *The Bully Pulpit: Theodore Roosevelt, William Howard Taft, and the Golden Age of Journalism* (New York: Simon and Schuster, 2013), p. 744.

197. Zelizer, *Arsenal of Democracy*, p. 28.

198. Nick Lloyd, *Passchendaele: A New History* (New York: Penguin, 2017), pp. 1–9, 108–09, 143–44, 287–303; and Connelly and Goebel, *Great Battles: Ypres*, pp. 7–8.

199. Connelly and Goebel, *Great Battles: Ypres*, p. 61.

200. John McCrae, "In Flanders Fields," Poetry Foundation, Chicago, 2021, https://www.poetryfoundation.org/poems/47380/in-flanders-fields.

201. Keegan, *The First World War*, pp. 369–71.

202. Ibid., p. 354.

203. Massie, *Castles of Steel*, p. 738.

204. Keegan, *The First World War*, p. 374.

205. Doughty, *Pyrrhic Victory*, p. 511.

206. Griffith, *Battle Tactics of the Western Front*, pp. 84–93.

207. Michael S. Neiberg, *The Second Battle of the Marne* (Indiana University Press, 2008), p. 65; and Biddle, *Military Power*, pp. 78–107.

208. Timothy T. Lupfer, "The Dynamics of Doctrine: The Changes in German Tactical Doctrine During the First World War," *Leavenworth Papers*, 4 (Fort Leavenworth, Kansas: U.S. Army Command and General Staff College, July 1981), pp. 37–58.

209. Neiberg, *The Second Battle of the Marne*, p. 73.

210. Biddle, *Military Power*, p. 82.

211. Neiberg, *The Second Battle of the Marne*, pp. 182–90.

212. Ibid., p. 85.

213. Ropp, *War in the Modern World*, pp. 260–61; and Doughty et.al., *Warfare in the Western World*, p. 601.

214. Doughty et.al., *Warfare in the Western World,* p. 621.

215. See Marine Corps History Division, "Brief History of U.S. Marine Corps Action in Europe During World War I," 2017, https://www.usmcu.edu/Research /Marine-Corps-History.

216. Underwood, "General Pershing and the U.S. Marines," p. 5.

217. Doughty et.al., *Warfare in the Western World,* pp. 624–26.

218. Weigley, *The American Way of War,* pp. 202–03.

219. Doughty et.al., *Warfare in the Western World,* pp. 626–31.

220. Keegan, *The First World War,* pp. 407–11.

221. Michael S. Neiberg, *The Treaty of Versailles: A Concise History* (Oxford, England: Oxford University Press, 2017), pp. 53–68.

222. Tooze, *The Deluge,* p. 369.

223. Patricia O'Toole, *The Moralist: Woodrow Wilson and the World He Made* (New York: Simon and Schuster, 2018), pp. 370–71; and Tooze, *The Deluge,* pp. 333–73.

224. Tooze, *The Deluge,* pp. 218–31.

225. Michael Beschloss, *Presidents of War: The Epic Story, from 1807 to Modern Times* (New York: Crown, 2018), pp. 330–58.

226. Zelizer, *Arsenal of Democracy,* p. 34.

227. O'Toole, *The Moralist,* p. 307; Beschloss, *Presidents of War,* pp. 317–358; and Tooze, *The Deluge,* p. 120.

228. See Alain C. Enthoven and K. Wayne Smith, *How Much Is Enough? Shaping the Defense Program, 1961–1969* (Santa Monica, CA.: RAND, 2005), pp. 31–72; Trevor N. Dupuy, *Numbers, Predictions, and War: The Use of History to Evaluate and Predict the Outcome of Armed Conflict,* rev. ed. (Fairfax, VA: HERO Books, 1985); Joshua M. Epstein, *Strategy and Force Planning: The Case of the Persian Gulf* (Washington, DC: Brookings, 1987); and Michael E. O'Hanlon, *Defense 101: Understanding the Military of Today and Tomorrow* (Cornell University Press, 2021).

229. Fred Charles Iklé, *Every War Must End* (Columbia University Press, 1971), p. 107.

230. Kagan, *On the Origins of War,* pp. 100–119.

231. See Annika Mombauer, *The Origins of the First World War: Controversies and Consensus* (London: Pearson Education Limited, 2002), p. 12; and Clark, *The Sleepwalkers,* pp. 254–55.

232. On balancing versus bandwagoning, especially in the post–World War II Middle East, see Stephen M. Walt, *The Origins of Alliances* (Cornell University Press, 1987); see also, Glenn Snyder, *Alliance Politics,* pp. 368–71.

233. Glenn Snyder, *Alliance Politics,* pp. 201–60, 365–71.

234. Ibid., pp. 287–90; and Clark, *The Sleepwalkers,* pp. 293–308.

235. Alexander L. George and Richard Smoke, *Deterrence in American Foreign Policy: Theory and Practice* (Columbia University Press, 1974); Thomas C. Schelling, *Arms and Influence* (Yale University Press, 1966); and Thomas C. Schelling, *The Strategy of Conflict* (Harvard University Press, 1960).

236. MacMillan, *The War that Ended Peace,* pp. 346–356.

237. Tuchman, *The Guns of August,* p. 43.

238. Ibid., pp. 35–36.

239. Freedman, *Strategy,* p. 123.

240. Gunther E. Rothenberg, "Moltke, Schlieffen, and the Doctrine of Strategic Envelopment," in Peter Paret, ed., *Makers of Modern Strategy: From Machiavelli to the Nuclear Age* (Princeton University Press, 1986), pp. 315–25.

241. Fuller, *Decisive Battles of the Western World,* p. 208.

242. Jack Snyder, "Civil-Military Relations and the Cult of the Offensive," in Miller, Lynn-Jones, and Van Evera, *Military Strategy and the Origins of the First World War,* pp. 45–51; and Stephen Van Evera, "The Cult of the Offensive and the Origins of the First World War," in *Military Strategy and the Origins of the First World War,* rev. and expand. ed., edited by Steven E. Miller, Sean M. Lynn-Jones, and Stephen Van Evera (Princeton University Press, 1991), pp. 88–90, 101.

243. Scott D. Sagan, "1914 Revisited: Allies, Offense, and Instability," in Miller, Lynn-Jones, and Van Evera, *Military Strategy and the Origins of the First World War,* pp. 114–124; and Jonathan Shimshoni, "Technology, Military Advantage, and World War I: A Case for Military Entrepreneurship," in ibid., pp. 134–162.

244. See for example, Stephen Peter Rosen, *Winning the Next War: Innovation and the Modern Military* (Cornell University Press, 1991).

245. Hart, *The Somme,* p. 12.

246. Mombauer, *The Origins of the First World War,* p. 211–12.

3. World War II

1. Stephen G. Fritz, *The First Soldier: Hitler as Military Leader* (Yale University Press, 2018), pp. 1–17, 85–122, 364–75.

2. William L. Shirer, *The Rise and Fall of the Third Reich: A History of Nazi Germany* (New York: Simon and Schuster, 2011), p. 86.

3. Kennedy, *The Rise and Fall of the Great Powers,* pp. 299, 332–60.

4. Tooze, *The Deluge,* p. 514.

5. Kennedy, *The Rise and Fall of the Great Powers,* p. 354.

6. Rick Atkinson, *The Guns at Last Light: The War in Western Europe, 1944–1945* (New York: Henry Holt and Company, 2013), p. 633.

7. Ibid., p. 641.

8. Max Hastings, *All Hell Let Loose: The World at War 1939–1945* (London: HarperPress, 2001), p. 671.

9. Ibid., pp. 669–71.

10. William I. Hitchcock, *The Struggle for Europe: The Turbulent History of a Divided Continent, 1945–2002* (New York: Doubleday, 2002), pp. 16–18.

11. On these matters, see for example, H. A. Feiveson, *Scientists against Time*; Peter Rosen, *Winning the Next War*; Williamson Murray and Allan R. Millet, eds., *Military Innovation in the Interwar Period* (Cambridge University Press, 1996); Barry R. Posen, *The Sources of Military Doctrine: France, Britain, and Germany between the World Wars* (Cornell University Press, 1984); and Montgomery C. Meigs, *Slide Rules and Submarines: American Scientists and Subsurface Warfare in World War II* (Hawaii University Press of the Pacific, 2002).

12. See for example Shirer, *The Rise and Fall of the Third Reich*.

13. Thomas Heinrich, *Warship Builders: An Industrial History of U.S. Naval Shipbuilding, 1922–1945* (Naval Institute Press, 2020).

14. Richard Overy, *Why the Allies Won* (New York: W. W. Norton and Company, 1997), pp. 101–244.

15. See Paul Kennedy, *Engineers of Victory: The Problem Solvers Who Turned the Tide in the Second World War* (New York: Random House, 2013).

16. See James R. FitzSimons, "Aircraft Carriers versus Battleships in War and Myth: Demythologizing Carrier Air Dominance at Sea," *Journal of Military History*, 84 (July 2020), pp. 843–65, especially pp. 852–58.

17. Stephen G. Fritz, *The First Soldier: Hitler as Military Leader* (Yale University Press, 2018), pp. 18–38.

18. Volker Ullrich, *Hitler: Downfall, 1939–1945* (New York: Vintage Books, 2020), pp. 9–189.

19. Hitler expounded on this in the second volume of his polemic and autobiography, *Mein Kampf*. See Shirer, *The Rise and Fall of the Third Reich*, p. 82.

20. Shirer, *The Rise and Fall of the Third Reich*, pp. 82, 256, 283, 305–08, 427–30; and Gerhard L. Weinberg, *A World at Arms: A Global History of World War II*, new ed. (Cambridge University Press, 2010), pp. 44, 165, 213, 305.

21. Fritz, *The First Soldier*.

22. Michael Fullilove, *Rendezvous with Destiny: How Franklin D. Roosevelt and Five Extraordinary Men Took America into the War and into the World* (New York: Penguin Press, 2013), p. 297.

23. John Keegan, *The Second World War* (New York: Penguin Books, 1989), pp. 450–55.

24. Nolan, *The Allure of Battle*, pp. 442–44.

25. See Freedman, *Strategy*, pp. 139–45; and Weinberg, *A World at Arms*, p. 325.

26. Fullilove, *Rendezvous with Destiny* p. 135; and Rick Atkinson, *An Army at Dawn: The War in North Africa, 1942–1943* (New York: Henry Holt and Co., 2002), p. 7.

27. Fullilove, *Rendezvous with Destiny*, p. 135.

28. See for example Atkinson, *An Army at Dawn*, pp. 54, 293–98; and Beschloss, *Presidents of War*, pp. 359–94.

29. See, for example, Green, *By More than Providence*, pp. 188–90.

30. Hastings, *All Hell Let Loose*, pp. 407–16.

31. Ibid., pp. 80–81, 124–28, 375–76.

32. Weinberg, *A World at Arms,* pp. 135–38, 215–24.

33. Ezra F. Vogel, *China and Japan: Facing History* (Harvard University Press, 2019), pp. 248–85.

34. D. Clayton James, "American and Japanese Strategies in the Pacific War" in *Makers of Modern Strategy: From Machiavelli to the Nuclear Age*, pp. 703–08.

35. Blainey, *The Causes of War,* pp. 243–64.

36. Ibid., p. 254.

37. See for example, Barbara W. Tuchman, *Stilwell and the American Experience in China, 1911–1945* (New York: Random House, 2017), pp. 7–12.

38. Freedman, *Strategy*, pp. 183–87.

39. Tooze, *The Deluge*, pp. 369, 444–45.

40. Shirer, *The Rise and Fall of the Third Reich*, pp. 29–32, 57–75.

41. Kagan, *On the Origins of War,* pp. 295–99.

42. Shirer, *The Rise and Fall of the Third Reich,* p. 118.

43. Kagan, *On the Origins of War,* pp. 316–17, 354, 360.

44. Weinberg, *A World at Arms*, p. 15.

45. Shirer, *The Rise and Fall of the Third Reich,* pp. 118–20, 136–38.

46. Ibid., pp. 150–230.

47. Ibid., p. 4.

48. Kagan, *On the Origins of War,* pp. 312–13.

49. Kennedy, *The Rise and Fall of the Great Powers,* p. 296.

50. Tooze, *The Deluge,* p. 514.

51. Kagan, *On the Origins of War,* pp. 332–33.

52. Kennedy, *The Rise and Fall of the Great Powers,* pp. 333–35.

53. Tooze, *The Deluge,* pp. 499–504.

54. Blainey, *The Causes of War,* p. 244.

55. Ezra Vogel with Richard Dyck, "Political Disorder and the Road to War, 1911–1937," in Ezra F. Vogel, *China and Japan: Facing History* (Harvard University Press, 2019), p. 233.

56. Freedman, *Strategy: A History,* pp. 183–87.

57. Blainey, *The Causes of War,* pp. 248–49.

58. James, "American and Japanese Strategies in the Pacific War," pp. 703–08.

59. Kennedy, *The Rise and Fall of the Great Powers,* pp. 300–01.

60. Kagan, *On the Origins of War,* p. 349.

61. Ibid., p. 365.

62. Shirer, *The Rise and Fall of the Third Reich,* pp. 279–347.

63. Ibid., pp. 290–300.

64. Ibid., pp. 322–56.

65. Ullrich, *Hitler,* p. 10.

66. Shirer, *The Rise and Fall of the Third Reich,* p. 424.

67. Kagan, *On the Origins of War,* pp. 410–11.

68. Shirer, *The Rise and Fall of the Third Reich,* pp. 593–96.

69. Nolan, *The Allure of Battle,* p. 531.

70. Keegan, *The Second World War,* pp. 44–47.

71. Weinberg, *A World at Arms,* pp. 48–57.

72. Gordon F. Sander, *The Hundred Day Winter War: Finland's Gallant Stand against the Soviet Army* (University Press of Kansas, 2013).

73. Weinberg, *A World at Arms,* p. 448.

74. Keegan, *The Second World War,* p. 47.

75. Weinberg, *A World at Arms,* p. 114.

76. Keegan, *The Second World War,* p. 80.

77. Williamson Murray, *The Luftwaffe, 1933–45: Strategy for Defeat* (Washington, DC: Brassey's, 1996), p. 39.

78. Keegan, *The Second World War,* pp. 54–83.

79. William H. McRaven, *Spec Ops: Case Studies in Special Operations Warfare Theory and Practice* (New York: Ballantine Books, 1996), pp. 29–69.

80. McRaven, *Spec Ops,* p. 55.

81. Jonathan M House, *Combined Arms Warfare in the Twentieth Century* (University Press of Kansas, 2001), p. 115.

82. Doughty, *Warfare in the Western World,* p. 665.

83. Robert A. Doughty, *The Breaking Point: Sedan and the Fall of France, 1940* (Mechanicsburg, PA: Stackpole Books, 1990), pp. xv–xix, 22–28; and Stephen Robinson, *The Blind Strategist: John Boyd and the American Art of War* (Dunedin, NZ: Exisle Publishing, 2021), pp. 1–156.

84. Williamson Murray, "Armored Warfare: The British, French, and German Experiences," in *Military Innovation in the Interwar Period,* edited by Williamson Murray and Allan R. Millett (Cambridge University Press, 1996), pp. 34–49.

85. Cohen and Gooch, *Military Misfortunes,* pp. 210–30.

86. Doughty, *The Breaking Point,* p. 342.

87. James S. Corum, *The Luftwaffe: Creating the Operational Air War, 1918–1940* (University of Kansas Press, 1997), pp. 275–80.

88. Ibid., pp. 275–80.

89. Murray, *The Luftwaffe, 1933–45,* p. 38.

90. Corum, *The Luftwaffe,* pp. 276–78.

91. Boot, *War Made New,* p. 227.

92. Liddell Hart, *Strategy,* pp. 234–35.

93. Keegan, *The Second World War,* pp. 83–87.

94. Fuller, *Decisive Battles of the Western World,* p. 390.

95. Liddell Hart, *Strategy,* pp. 207–21.

96. Ropp, *War in the Modern World,* p. 318.

97. Fritz, *The First Soldier,* pp. 100–22.

98. John Mosier, *The Blitzkrieg Myth: How Hitler and the Allies Misread the Strategic Realities of World War II* (New York: Perennial, 2004), pp. 116–53.

99. Murray, *The Luftwaffe, 1933–45,* p. 47.

100. Richard Overy, *The Battle of Britain: The Myth and the Reality* (New York: W. W. Norton and Company, 2002), pp. 113–35.

101. Stephen Bungay, *The Most Dangerous Enemy: A History of the Battle of Britain* (London: Aurum Press, 2000), pp. 377–78.

102. Bungay, *The Most Dangerous Enemy,* pp. 186–202, 368–88.

103. Feiveson, *Scientists against Time,* pp. 43–55.

104. Ibid., pp. 57–65.

105. Keegan, *The Second World War,* p. 92.

106. Overy, *The Battle of Britain,* pp. 113–14.

107. Keegan, *The Second World War,* p. 96.

108. Feiveson, *Scientists against Time,* p. 62.

109. Bungay, *The Most Dangerous Enemy,* pp. 368–69; and Overy, *The Battle of Britain,* pp. 159–63.

110. Hastings, *All Hell Let Loose,* p. 93.

111. Bungay, *The Most Dangerous Enemy,* p. 379.

112. Evan Wilson and Ruth Schapiro, "German Perspectives on the U–Boat War, 1939–1941," *Journal of Military History,* 85 (April 2021), pp. 369–98.

113. Keegan, *The Second World War,* pp. 105–19.

114. Keegan, *The Second World War,* p. 107.

115. Phillips Payson O'Brien, *How the War Was Won* (Cambridge University Press, 2018); 230–42.

116. Kennedy, *The Rise and Fall of the Great Powers,* pp. 330–32.

117. Hastings, *All Hell Let Loose,* pp. 120–24; and Keegan, *The Second World War,* pp. 127–58.

118. Fuller, *Decisive Battles of the Western World,* p. 420

119. Fritz, *The First Soldier,* p. 122.

120. Robert Forczyk, *Tank Warfare on the Eastern Front, 1941–1942* (Barnsley, UK: Pen and Sword Military, 2021), pp. 4, 22–37; and Hastings, *All Hell Let Loose,* pp. 141–44.

121. House, *Combined Arms Warfare in the Twentieth Century,* pp. 129–30.

122. Ullrich, *Hitler,* p. 195.

123. Condoleezza Rice, "The Making of Soviet Strategy," in *Makers of Modern Strategy,* p. 671.

124. Weinberg, *A World at Arms,* pp. 264–70.

125. Fuller, *Decisive Battles of the Western World,* pp. 432–34.

126. Forczyk, *Tank Warfare on the Eastern Front,* pp. 169–70; Fritz, *The First Soldier,* pp. 200–34.

127. Fuller, *Decisive Battles of the Western World,* p. 446.

128. Keegan, *The Second World War,* pp. 173–208; Hastings, *All Hell Let Loose,* pp. 165–82.

129. Richard B. Frank, *Tower of Skulls: A History of the Asia–Pacific War, July 1937–May 1942* (New York: W. W. Norton and Company, 2020), pp. 1–127.

130. Nolan, *The Allure of Battle,* pp. 530–32; and Tuchman, *Stilwell and the American Experience in China,* pp. 176–244.

131. Kennedy, *The Rise and Fall of the Great Powers,* p. 303.

132. Weinberg, *A World at Arms,* pp. 166–70.

133. Ibid., pp. 258–60.

134. Geoffrey Till, "Adopting the Aircraft Carrier: The British, American, and Japanese Case Studies," in *Military Innovation in the Interwar Period,* pp. 210–26.

135. Fritz, *The First Soldier,* pp. 218–19; and Evan Mawdsley, *The War for the Seas: A Maritime History of World War II* (Yale University Press, 2020), pp. 154–69.

136. Shirer, *The Rise and Fall of the Third Reich,* pp. 871–87.

137. Frank, *Tower of Skulls,* pp. 275–91.

138. Boot, *War Made New,* pp. 241–67; and Evan Mawdsley, *The War for the Seas: A Maritime History of World War II* (Yale University Press, 2020), pp. 170–85.

139. Boot, *War Made New,* p. 254.

140. Walter R. Borneman, *The Admirals: Nimitz, Halsey, Leahy, and King—the Five-Star Admirals Who Won the War at Sea* (Boston: Little, Brown and Company, 2012), p. 222; and Boot, *War Made New,* pp. 241–46.

141. Mawdsley, *The War for the Seas,* p. 179.

142. Shirer, *The Rise and Fall of the Third Reich,* pp. 894–95; see also, Richard Overy, *Blood and Ruins: The Last Imperial War, 1931–1945* (New York: Viking, 2022), pp. 168–69.

143. Ibid., p. 900.

144. Richard B. Frank, *Tower of Skulls: A History of the Asia-Pacific War, July 1937–May 1942* (New York: W. W. Norton and Company, 2020), pp. 348–84; Mawdsley, *The War for the Seas,* pp. 170–197; and Keegan, *The Second World War,* pp. 256–67.

145. Mawdsley, *The War for the Seas,* pp. 170–97.

146. Weinberg, *A World at Arms,* pp. 205–15.

147. Keegan, *The Second World War,* pp. 320–36.

148. Ibid., pp. 338–39.

149. Fullilove, *Rendezvous with Destiny,* p. 325.

150. Tuchman, *Stilwell and the American Experience in China,* pp. 279–80.

151. Atkinson, *An Army at Dawn,* p. 12.

152. Maurice Matloff, "Allied Strategy in Europe, 1939–1945," in *Makers of Modern Strategy: From Machiavelli to the Nuclear Age,* pp. 677–92.

153. Shirer, *The Rise and Fall of the Third Reich,* p. 904.

154. Keegan, *The Second World War,* pp. 220–21.

155. Shirer, *The Rise and Fall of the Third Reich,* p. 909; and Keegan, *The Second World War,* p. 222.

156. Shirer, *The Rise and Fall of the Third Reich,* pp. 911–14.

157. Overy, *Why the Allies Won,* pp. 1–5.

158. Rick Atkinson, *An Army at Dawn: The War in North Africa, 1942–1943* (New York: Henry Holt and Company, 2002), p. 7; and Keegan, *The Second World War,* pp. 215–16, 311, 539.

159. Shirer, *The Rise and Fall of the Third Reich,* pp. 915–21, 925–33.

160. House, *Combined Arms Warfare in the Twentieth Century,* pp. 156, 165; Atkinson, *An Army at Dawn,* pp. 1–31, 339–92; and Keegan, *The Second World War,* pp. 336–43.

161. Atkinson, *An Army at Dawn,* pp. 159, 536–37.

162. Weigley, *The American Way of War,* pp. 312–25; and Weinberg, *A World at Arms,* pp. 431–47.

163. Atkinson, *An Army at Dawn,* p. 533.

164. Ibid., p. 540.

165. Robert Dallek, *Franklin D. Roosevelt: A Political Life* (New York: Penguin Books, 2018), p. 462; and Borneman, *The Admirals,* pp. 243–45.

166. Weinberg, *A World at Arms,* pp. 333–35.

167. National World War II Museum, "The Battle of Midway," New Orleans, Louisiana, 2022, nationalww2museum.org/war/articles/battle-midway.

168. Weigley, *The American Way of War,* pp. 272–80.

169. Borneman, *The Admirals,* p. 304.

170. Ian W. Toll, *The Conquering Tide: War in the Pacific Islands, 1942–1944* (New York: W. W. Norton and Company, 2015), pp. xxi–54.

171. Borneman, *The Admirals,* pp. 279–305.

172. Allan R. Millett, "Assault from the Sea: The Development of Amphibious Warfare between the Wars—the American, British, and Japanese Experiences," in *Military Innovation in the Interwar Period,* pp. 77–80.

173. Toll, *The Conquering Tide,* pp. 42–55.

174. Ibid., pp. 23–40.

175. E.J. Spaulding, "Seabees," *Proceedings* (December 1942), usni.org /magazines/proceedings/1942/december/seabees; and David A. Anderson, Review of James G. Lacey, *Keep From All Thoughtful Men: How U.S. Economists Won World War II* (Naval Institute Press, 2011), in *Proceedings,* 66:3 (2012), p. 94, ndupress.ndu.edu/Portals/68/Documents/jfq/jfq-66/jfq-66_94_Anderson.pdf?ver =2017-12-06-115734-790.

176. Toll, *The Conquering Tide,* pp. 68–75.

177. Ibid., pp. 55–84.

178. Ibid., pp. 85–112.

179. Ibid., pp. 137–44.

180. Ibid., pp. 145–89.

181. Ibid., pp. 122–33.

182. Mawdsley, *The War for the Seas*, pp. 224–41.

183. Toll, *The Conquering Tide*, pp. 186–87.

184. Borneman, *The Admirals*, p. 258.

185. Ibid., pp. 298–301.

186. Cid Standifer, "Sunk, Scrapped, or Saved: The Fate of America's Aircraft Carriers," *Proceedings*, U.S. Naval Institute, August 18, 2014, usni.org/2014/08 /18/sunk-sold-scraped-saved-fate-americas-aircraft-carriers.

187. Naval History and Heritage Command, National Museum of the U.S. Navy, "U.S.S. Langley," U.S. Navy, Washington, DC, 2022, history.navy.mil /content/history/museums/nmusn/explore/photography/ships-us/ships-usn-l/uss -langley-cv1-av-3.html.

188. Borneman, *The Admirals*, p. 304.

189. Mawdsley, *The War for the Seas*, pp. 74–75.

190. Debi Unger and Irwin Unger with Stanley Hirshson, *George Marshall: A Biography* (New York: HarperCollins, 2014), pp. 244–50.

191. Meigs, *Slide Rules and Submarines*, pp. 3–96

192. Cohen and Gooch, *Military Misfortunes*, pp. 59–73; Feiveson, *Scientists Against Time*, pp. 87–90; Keegan, *The Second World War*, pp. 118–19.

193. Overy, *Why the Allies Won*, pp. 1–5.

194. Hastings, *All Hell Let Loose*, p. 597.

195. Meigs, *Slide Rules and Submarines*, pp. 211–20.

196. Feiveson, *Scientists against Time*, p. 101.

197. Keegan, *The Second World War*, pp. 118–20.

198. Charles M. Sternhell and Alan M. Thorndike, Office of the Chief of Naval Operations, "OEG Report No. 51: ASW in World War II," Washington, DC, 1946, p. 59, ibiblio.org/hyperwar/USN/rep/ASW-51/ASW-8.html; and Keegan, *The Second World War*, pp. 118–21.

199. Sternhell and Thorndike, Office of the Chief of Naval Operations, "OEG Report No. 51."

200. Feiveson, *Scientists against Time*, pp. 101–02.

201. Keegan, *The Second World War*, p. 121.

202. Ibid., p. 120.

203. McRaven, *Spec Ops*, pp. 201–43.

204. Shirer, *The Rise and Fall of the Third Reich*, p. 1006; Keegan, *The Second World War*, p. 467.

205. Martijn Lak, "The Death Ride of the Panzers? Recent Historiography on the Battle of Kursk," *Journal of Military History*, 82 (July 2018), p. 914, https:// www.smh-hq.org/jmh/jmhvols/823.html.

206. Keegan, *The Second World War*, pp. 458–73.

207. Ibid., pp. 467–74.

208. Kennedy, *The Rise and Fall of the Great Powers*, p. 355.

209. Raymond W. Goldsmith, "The Power of Victory: Munitions Output in World War II," *Military Affairs*, 10: 1 (March 1, 1946), pp. 69–80.

210. Murray, *The Luftwaffe, 1933–45*, p. 285.

211. Shirer, *The Rise and Fall of the Third Reich*, p. 1085; Keegan, *The Second World War*, pp. 503–15.

212. Weinberg, *A World at Arms*, pp. 780–802.

213. Hitchcock, *The Struggle for Europe*, p. 15

214. Keegan, *The Second World War*, pp. 516–29.

215. Ibid., p. 541.

216. Hastings, *All Hell Let Loose*, p. 630.

217. Weigley, *The American Way of War*, pp. 312–35.

218. Rick Atkinson, *The Day of Battle: The War in Sicily and Italy, 1943–1944* (New York: Henry Holt and Company, 2007), pp. 172–73.

219. Weigley, *The American Way of War*, p. 327.

220. Liddell Hart, *Strategy*, p. 291.

221. Atkinson, *The Day of Battle*, pp. 577–88.

222. R. J. Lahey, "Hitler's 'Intuition,' Luftwaffe Photoreconnaissance and the Reinforcement of Normandy," *The Journal of Military History*, 86: 1 (January 2022), pp. 77–109.

223. Alex Kershaw, *The First Wave: The D-Day Warriors Who Led the Way to Victory in World War II* (New York: Penguin, 2019), p. 5.

224. Kennedy, *Engineers of Victory*, pp. 250–70; and Keegan, *The Second World War*, pp. 373–87.

225. Boot, *War Made New*, p. 277.

226. James Holland, *Normandy '44: D-Day and the Epic 77-Day Battle for France* (New York: Atlantic Monthly Press, 2019), pp. 18–19, 220.

227. Murray, *The Luftwaffe, 1933–45*, pp. 267–76.

228. Richard Overy, *The Bombers and the Bombed: Allied Air War over Europe, 1940–1945* (New York: Penguin Books, 2013), p. 400.

229. See J. R. Seeger, "Review Essay: Evaluating Resistance Operations in Western Europe during World War II," *Studies in Intelligence*, 65: 1 (March 2021), pp. 27–31.

230. Kershaw, pp. 198–99.

231. Mawdsley, *The War for the Seas*, p. 430.

232. Murray, *The Luftwaffe, 1933–45*, pp. 280–83.

233. Russell A. Hart, *Clash of Arms: How the Allies Won in Normandy* (Boulder, CO.: Lynne Rienner Publishers, 2001), p. 409.

234. Hart, *Clash of Arms*, pp. 271–93, 417–19.

235. Holland, *Normandy '44*, pp. 411–27.

236. Liddell Hart, *Strategy*, pp. 302–08.

237. Tami Davis Biddle, "On the Crest of Fear: V-Weapons, the Battle of the Bulge, and the Last Stages of World War II in Europe," *Journal of Military History*, 83:1 (January 2019), pp. 157–194, https://www.smh-hq.org/jmh/jmhvols/831 .html.

238. Biddle, "On the Crest of Fear," p. 158.

239. Weinberg, *A World at Arms*, pp. 696–702.

240. Atkinson, *The Guns at Last Light*, p. 420.

241. Liddell Hart, *Strategy*, pp. 309–11.

242. Atkinson, *The Guns at Last Light*, p. 491.

243. Ibid., pp. 542–51, 568.

244. Overy, *Why the Allies Won*, pp. 134–179.

245. Weigley, *The American Way of War*, p. 271.

246. Vogel, *China and Japan: Facing History*, pp. 248–85.

247. Tuchman, *Stilwell and the American Experience in China*, , pp. 368–84; 428–81; 617–22; and Weinberg, *A World at Arms*, pp. 631–33.

248. John Pomfret, *The Beautiful Country and the Middle Kingdom: America and China, 1776 to the Present* (New York: Henry Holt and Company, 2016), pp. 300–05.

249. Mawdsley, *The War for the Seas*, pp. 374–75.

250. Mawdsley, *The War for the Seas*, p. 456; and Weigley, *The American Way of War*, pp. 280–92.

251. Weigley, *The American Way of War*, p. 284–87.

252. See the excellent map in Toll, *The Conquering Tide*, p. 241.

253. Mawdsley, *The War for the Seas*, p. 385.

254. Ibid., p. 385.

255. Toll, *The Conquering Tide*, pp. 530–31.

256. Mawdsley, *The War for the Seas*, pp. 384–92.

257. George W. Garand and Truman R. Strobridge, Historical Division, Headquarters, U.S. Marine Corps, *History of U.S. Marine Corps Operations in World War II, Vol. 4: Western Pacific Operations* (Washington, DC: U.S. Government Printing Office, 1971), p. v, marines.mil/Portals/1/Publications/History%20of%20 the%20U.S.%20Marine%20Corps%20in%20WWII%20Vol%20IV%20-%20 Western%20Pacific%20Operations%20%20PCN%2019000262700_1.pdf.

258. Mawdsley, *The War for the Seas*, pp. 392–98.

259. Ibid., pp. 398–406.

260. Ibid., p. 444.

261. Ian W. Toll, *Twilight of the Gods: War in the Western Pacific, 1944–1945* (New York: W.W. Norton and Co., 2020), pp. 246–309; and Mawdsley, *The War for the Seas*, p. 439.

262. Toll, *Twilight of the Gods*, pp. 204–05.

263. Ibid., p. 303.

264. Ibid., p. 309.

265. Weigley, *The American Way of War*, pp. 301–05.

266. Toll, *Twilight of the Gods*, p. 292.

267. Keegan, *The Second World War*, pp. 558–59.

268. Hastings, *All Hell Let Loose*, p. 564.

269. Mawdsley, *The War for the Seas*, p. 456.

270. Hastings, *All Hell Let Loose*, p. 558.

271. Borneman, *The Admirals*, pp. 404–22.

272. National World War II Museum, "The Battle of Iwo Jima," New Orleans, 2020, nationalww2museum.org/sites/default/files/2020-02/iwo-jima-fact-sheet .pdf.

273. Walzer, *Just and Unjust Wars*, p. 266.

274. Richard Reeves, *The Making of the Atomic Bomb* (New York: Simon and Schuster, 1986), pp. 443–85; and Neal Bascomb, *The Winter Fortress: The Epic Mission to Sabotage Hitler's Atomic Bomb* (Boston.: Mariner Books, 2016).

275. Weigley, *The American Way of War*, pp. 333–35.

276. Boot, *War Made New*, pp. 282–83.

277. Tami Davis Biddle, *Rhetoric and Reality in Air Warfare: The Evolution of British and American Ideas about Strategic Bombing, 1914–1945* (Princeton University Press, 2002); see also, Overy, *Blood and Ruins*, p. 751–58.

278. Nolan, *The Allure of Battle*, p. 563.

279. Biddle, *Rhetoric and Reality in Air Warfare*, pp. 188, 217, 224, 227, 237, 239, 243, 246, 255, 269, 274, 276, 287, 291–92; Boot, *War Made New*, pp. 268–94.

280. Overy, *The Bombers and the Bombed*, pp. 276–300.

281. Richard Overy, *The Bombing War, Europe 1939–1945* (New York: Penguin Books, 2014), pp. 386, 406–09, 616.

282. O'Brien, *How the War Was Won*, pp. 17–66, 479–488.

283. Weinberg, *A World at Arms*, p. 892.

284. Reinhold Niebuhr, *The Irony of American History*, reprint ed. (University of Chicago Press, 2008).

285. Victor David Hanson, *The Second World Wars* (New York: Basic Books, 2017), pp. 3, 38.

286. Steven Pinker, *The Better Angels of Our Nature: Why Violence Has Declined* (New York: Penguin, 2015).

287. Bungay, *The Most Dangerous Enemy*, p. 393.

288. See Williamson Murray and Allan R. Millett, eds., *Military Innovation in the Interwar Period* (Cambridge University Press, 1996).

289. Hastings, *All Hell Let Loose*, p. 139.

290. Fritz, *The First Soldier*, p. 369.

291. Freedman, *Strategy*, pp. 142–44.

292. Hanson, *The Second World Wars*, pp. 256–60, 506; and Shirer, *The Rise and Fall of the Third Reich*, pp. 793–800.

293. Colin S. Gray, *The Future of Strategy* (Malden, MA.: Polity Press, 2015), p. 72.

294. Hastings, *All Hell Let Loose,* pp. 199, 432–33; and Keegan, *The Second World War,* pp. 310–19.

295. Edward M. Coffman, *The Regulars: The American Army, 1898–1941* (Harvard University Press, 2004), pp. 373–74.

296. Weigley, *The American Way of War,* pp. 282–83.

297. David Barno and Nora Bensahel, *Adaptation Under Fire: How Militaries Change in Wartime* (Oxford University Press, 2020), pp. 1–6, 31–53; and Rosen, *Winning the Next War,* pp. 107–82

298. Unger, Unger, and Hirshson, *George Marshall: A Biography,* pp. 352–53.

299. Michael E. O'Hanlon, *Defense 101: Understanding the Military of Today and Tomorrow* (Cornell University Press, 2021), pp. 85–133; and Enthoven and Smith, *How Much Is Enough?,* pp. 1–72.

300. Richard B. Frank, *Downfall: The End of the Imperial Japanese Empire* (New York: Penguin Books, 1999), pp. 186–87, 190–93, 194–96, 338–41, 356–58.

301. Walzer, *Just and Unjust Wars,* pp. 263–68.

302. Hastings, *All Hell Let Loose,* p. 484.

303. Beschloss, *Presidents of War,* pp. 420–22.

304. Walzer disagrees; again, see *Just and Unjust Wars,* pp. 263–68, where he argues that some kind of negotiated peace should have been attempted with Japan (even if not with Nazi Germany). I believe this perspective overrates the prospects of such negotiation and underplays the depravity of the Japanese occupation of China in particular.

4. Korea and Vietnam

1. Max Hastings, *The Korean War* (New York: Simon and Schuster, 1987), pp. 27–45.

2. Ibid., pp. 57–58.

3. Don Oberdorfer, *The Two Koreas: A Contemporary History* (Reading, MA: Addison-Wesley, 1997), p. 9.

4. Vogel, *China and Japan,* pp. 304–05.

5. Mitchell Lerner, "Is It for This We Fought and Bled?: The Korean War and the Struggle for Civil Rights," *Journal of Military History,* 82: 2 (April 2018), pp. 515–45.

6. Don Oberdorfer, *The Two Koreas,* pp. 9–10; and Beschloss, *Presidents of War,* p. 488.

7. Xiaoming Zhang, "China and the Air War in Korea, 1950–1953," *Journal of Military History,* 62:2 (April 1998), pp. 335–70.

8. See Bruce Cumings, *The Korean War: A History* (New York: Modern Library, 2011), pp. 149–61.

9. Conrad C. Crane, "Raiding the Beggar's Pantry: The Search for Air power Strategy in the Korean War," *Journal of Military History* 63: 4 (October 1999), pp. 885–920.

10. Kenneth P. Werrell, "Across the Yalu: Rules of Engagement and the Communist Air Sanctuary during the Korean War," *Journal of Military History,* 72:2 (April 2008), p. 470.

11. Robert A. Pape, *Bombing to Win: Air Power and Coercion in War* (Cornell University Press, 1996), pp. 148–50.

12. Ibid., pp. 159–65.

13. Shen Zhihua, "Revisiting Stalin's and Mao's Motivations in the Korean War," Woodrow Wilson Center, Washington, DC, June 22, 2020, wilsoncenter.org /blog-post/revisiting-stalins-and-maos-motivations-korean-war.

14. T. R. Fehrenbach, *This Kind of War* (Dulles, VA: Potomac Books, 2008), pp. 4–9; Hastings, *The Korean War,* p. 53.

15. Allan R. Millett, *The War for Korea, 1950–1951: They Came from the North* (University of Kansas Press, 2010), pp. 29, 85; and Roy E Appleman, *South to the Naktong, North to the Yalu,* (Washington, DC: United States Army Center of Military History, 1998), pp. 7–9, 381, 545.

16. James F. Schnabel, *Policy and Direction the First Year* (Washington, DC: U.S. Army Center of Military History, 1992), pp. 30–35, 70–82, history.army.mil /html/books/020/20-1/CMH_Pub_20-1.pdf.

17. Richard K. Betts, *Surprise Attack: Lessons for Defense Planning* (Brookings Institution, 1982), pp. 51–56.

18. Fehrenback, *This Kind of War,* p. 7.

19. Hastings, *The Korean War,* p. 53.

20. Ibid., p. 55.

21. Ibid., p. 70.

22. T. R. Fehrenbach, *This Kind of War,* pp. 305–06.

23. Beschloss, *Presidents of War,* pp. 444–91.

24. Hastings, *The Korean War,* pp. 60–61.

25. Ibid., pp. 72–73.

26. Ibid., pp. 15–22.

27. Ibid., p. 79.

28. Ibid., p. 82.

29. Ibid., p. 71.

30. Ibid., p. 84.

31. Ibid., p. 85.

32. Ibid., p. 93.

33. Ibid., pp. 97–99.

34. Ibid., p. 100.

35. Oscar E. Gilbert, *Marine Corps Tank Battles in Korea* (Philadelphia: Casemate Publishers, 2007), pp. 60–64.

36. See U.S. Army History, *Korea* (Washington, DC: 2021), pp. 500–05, https://history.army.mil/books/korea/20-2-1/sn25.htm.

37. Gilbert, *Marine Corps Tank Battles in Korea,* pp. 81–99.

38. See Jervis, *Perception and Misperception in International Politics,* pp. 70–71.

39. Cohen and Gooch, *Military Misfortunes,* pp. 169–75.

40. Hastings, *The Korean War,* pp. 123–27.

41. Ibid., pp. 126.

42. Bruce Riedel, "Catastrophe on the Yalu: America's Intelligence Failure in Korea," Brookings Institution, Washington, D.C., September 13, 2017, https://www.brookings.edu/blog/order-from-chaos/2017/09/13/catastrophe-on-the-yalu-americas-intelligence-failure-in-korea.

43. Betts, *Surprise Attack,* pp. 56–62; and Millet, *The War for Korea,* p. 293.

44. Gilbert, *Marine Corps Tank Battles in Korea,* p. 102.

45. Hastings, *The Korean War,* p. 130.

46. Ibid., pp. 256, 266.

47. Cohen and Gooch, *Military Misfortunes,* pp. 169–75.

48. Green, *By More than Providence,* p. 275.

49. David Halberstam, *The Coldest Winter: America and the Korean War* (New York: Hyperion, 2007), pp. 9–44.

50. Millett, *The War for Korea,* p. 297.

51. Hastings, *The Korean War,* pp. 137–38.

52. Halberstam, *The Coldest Winter,* p. 437; and Hastings, *The Korean War,* pp. 139–40.

53. Millett, *The War for Korea,* p. 335.

54. Cohen and Gooch, *Military Misfortunes,* pp. 174, 182.

55. Gilbert, *Marine Corps Tank Battles in Korea,* p. 112.

56. Cohen and Gooch, *Military Misfortunes,* pp. 175–80.

57. Halberstam, *The Coldest Winter,* p. 400.

58. Fehrenbach, *This Kind of War,* pp. 200–223.

59. Halberstam, *The Coldest Winter,* p. 501.

60. Hastings, *The Korean War,* pp. 140–46.

61. Weigley, *The American Way of War,* pp. 389–90.

62. U.S. Army Center for Military History, *The Korean War: The Chinese Intervention* (Carlisle, PA.: 2003), p. 16, https://history.army.mil/brochures/kw-chinter/chinter.htm.

63. Halberstam, *The Coldest Winter,* p. 469.

64. Thomas E. Ricks, *The Generals: American Military Command from World War II to Today* (New York: Penguin Press, 2012), pp. 135–49.

65. Gilbert, *Marine Corps Tank Battles in Korea,* p. 116.

66. Ricks, *The Generals*, pp. 135–49.

67. Gilbert, *Marine Corps Tank Battles in Korea*, pp. 115–34.

68. Ibid., pp. 135–65.

69. Hampton Sides, *On Desperate Ground: The Marines at the Reservoir, The Korean War's Greatest Battle* (New York: Doubleday, 2018), p. 261.

70. Sides, *On Desperate Ground*, pp. 228–80.

71. Hastings, *The Korean War*, pp. 147–64.

72. Cohen and Gooch, *Military Misfortunes*, pp. 186–89.

73. Hastings, *The Korean War*, pp. 188–91.

74. Ricks, *The Generals*, p. 185.

75. Cohen and Gooch, *Military Misfortunes*, p. 189.

76. Hastings, *The Korean War*, pp. 192–93.

77. Halberstam, *The Coldest Winter*, p. 482.

78. Ricks, *The Generals*, pp. 190–91.

79. Weigley, *The American Way of War*, p. 392; and Fehrenbach, *This Kind of War*, pp. 260–61.

80. Hastings, *The Korean War*, pp. 196–98.

81. Weigely, *The American Way of War*, pp. 390–91.

82. Fehrenbach, *This Kind of War*, pp. 307–14.

83. Mesut Uyar and Serhat Güvenç, "One Battle and Two Accounts: The Turkish Brigade at Kunu-ri in November 1950," *Journal of Military History*, 80: 4 (October 2016), pp. 1117–47.

84. Carter Malkasian, "Toward a Better Understanding of Attrition: The Korean and Vietnam Wars," *Journal of Military History*, 68:3 (July 2004), pp. 911–942.

85. Fehrenbach, *This Kind of War*, pp. 344–63.

86. Hastings, *The Korean War*, pp. 270–83.

87. William M. Donnelly, "A Damn Hard Job: James A. Van Fleet and the Combat Effectiveness of U.S. Army Infantry, July 1951–February 1953," *Journal of Military History*, 82:1 (January 2018), pp. 147–79.

88. Pape, *Bombing to Win*, pp. 167–68.

89. Rosemary Foot, *The Wrong War: American Policy and the Dimensions of the Korean Conflict, 1950–1953* (Cornell University Press, 1985), pp. 204–46.

90. Stephen Sestanovich, *Maximalist: America in the World from Truman to Obama* (New York: Vintage Books, 2014), pp. 68–70.

91. For a compelling account, see Robert Mason, *Chickenhawk* (New York: Penguin Books, 1983).

92. Marvin Kalb and Deborah Kalb, *Haunting Legacy: Vietnam and the American Presidency from Ford to Obama* (Brookings Institution, 2011); and David H. Petraeus, "The American Military and the Lessons of Vietnam: A Study of Military Influence and the Use of Force in the Post–Vietnam Era," unpublished Ph.D. dissertation, Princeton University, October 1987, pp. 259–79.

93. Boot, *Invisible Armies,* p. 425.

94. James William Gibson, *The Perfect War: The War We Couldn't Lose and How We Did* (New York: Vintage Books, 1986), p. 9.

95. Stanley Karnow, *Vietnam: A History* (New York: Penguin Books, 1997), p. 669.

96. Karnow, *Vietnam: A History,* p. 213.

97. Mason, *Chickenhawk,* p. 17.

98. Karnow, *Vietnam: A History,* pp. 109–38.

99. Fredrik Logevall, *Embers of War: The Fall of an Empire and the Making of America's Vietnam* (New York: Random House, 2012), pp. 3–19, 87–91.

100. John Shy and Thomas W. Collier, "Revolutionary War," in *Makers of Modern Strategy,* pp. 846–47.

101. Ang Cheng Guan, *The Vietnam War from the Other Side* (Abingdon, England: RoutledgeCurzon, 2002), pp. 1–71.

102. Max Boot, *Invisible Armies: An Epic History of Guerrilla Warfare from Ancient Times to the Present* (New York: W.W. Norton and Co., 2013), p. 412.

103. Karnow, *Vietnam: A History,* pp. 202–56, 688–93.

104. Lon O. Nordeen, *Air Warfare in the Missile Age,* second edition (Washington, DC: Smithsonian Institution Press, 2010), pp. 1–60; and Pape, *Bombing to Win,* pp. 175–76.

105. Richard A. Ruth, "The Secret of Seeing Charlie in the Dark," *Vulcan,* 5 (2017), pp. 64–88.

106. McGeorge Bundy, *Danger and Survival: Choices about the Bomb in the First Fifty Years* (New York: Vintage Books, 1988), pp. 238–45, 538–39, 588.

107. Karnow, *Vietnam: A History,* pp. 229–56.

108. Ang Cheng Guan, *The Vietnam War from the Other Side,* pp. 10, 139–40.

109. George C. Herring, *America's Longest War: The United States and Vietnam, 1950–1975,* 2nd ed. (New York: Alfred A. Knopf, 1986), p. 57.

110. Green, *By More than Providence,* p. 306.

111. Karnow, *Vietnam: A History,* p. 264.

112. Krepinevich, *The Army and Vietnam,* pp. 140–42, 153; and Karnow, *Vietnam: A History,* pp. 270–80, 694.

113. Neil Sheehan, *A Bright Shining Lie: John Paul Vann and America in Vietnam* (New York: Vintage Books, 1988), pp. 201–65.

114. Karnow, *Vietnam: A History,* p. 276.

115. Andrew F. Krepinevich, Jr., *The Army and Vietnam* (Johns Hopkins University Press, 1986), p. 133.

116. This is of course the title of David Halberstam's famous book on the subject, first published in 1969; see David Halberstam, *The Best and the Brightest* (New York: Ballantine Books, 1992).

117. Karnow, *Vietnam: A History,* p. 294.

118. Ibid., pp. 295–97.

119. Neil Sheehan, Hedrick Smith, E.W. Kenworthy, and Fox Butterfield, *The Pentagon Papers* (New York: Bantam Books, 1971), pp. 160–63; and Gordon M. Goldstein, *Lessons in Disaster: McGeorge Bundy and the Path to War in Vietnam* (New York: Henry Holt and Company, 2008), pp. 44, 189, 219, 231.

120. Leslie H. Gelb with Richard K. Betts, *The Irony of Vietnam: The System Worked* (Washington, DC: Brookings Institution, 1979).

121. Goldstein, *Lessons in Disaster,* p. 189.

122. Robert S. McNamara, *In Retrospect: The Tragedy and Lessons of Vietnam* (New York: Vintage Books, 1996), p. 173.

123. Douglas Frantz and David McKean, *Friends in High Places: The Rise and Fall of Clark Clifford* (Boston: Little Brown and Company, 1995), pp. 162–63.

124. Karnow, *Vietnam: A History,* pp. 335–63, 469.

125. Ibid., pp. 372–402.

126. McNamara, *In Retrospect,* p. 186.

127. Karnow, *Vietnam: A History,* pp. 695–97.

128. Weigley, *The American Way of War,* p. 467.

129. Boot, *Invisible Armies,* p. 420.

130. Krepinevich, *The Army and Vietnam,* p. 143.

131. James T. Quinlivan, "Force Requirements in Stability Operations," *Parameters* (Winter 1995), pp. 56–69; and Lt. Gen. David H. Petraeus and Lt. Gen. James F. Amos, *Field Manual 3–24: Counterinsurgency* (Washington, DC: U.S. Army, December 2006). For an empirically based critique, see Jeffrey A. Friedman, "Manpower and Counterinsurgency: Empirical Foundations for Theory and Doctrine," *Security Studies,* 20: 4 (2011), pp. 556–591.

132. Zelizer, *Arsenal of Democracy,* pp. 178–202.

133. See Halberstam, *The Best and the Brightest,* pp. 361–429; H. R. McMaster, *Dereliction of Duty: Lyndon Johnson, Robert McNamara, the Joint Chiefs of Staff, and the Lies that Led to Vietnam* (New York: HarperCollins, 1997); and Zoellick, *America in the World,* p. 360.

134. Krepinevich, *The Army and Vietnam,* pp. 157–63. Phase 1 consists of party formation and organization.

135. Ricks, *The Generals,* p. 232.

136. Karnow, *Vietnam: A History,* pp. 450–69.

137. Edward J. Drea, *McNamara, Clifford, and the Burdens of Vietnam* (Washington, DC: Historical Office of the Office of the Secretary of Defense, 2011), pp. 127–30; and Hastings, *Vietnam: An Epic Tragedy, 1945–1975,* p. 322.

138. Harold G. Moore and Joseph L. Galloway, *We Were Soldiers Once . . . and Young: Ia Drang, The Battle That Changed the War in Vietnam* (New York: Presidio Press, 2004).

139. John A. Nagl, *Learning to Eat Soup with a Knife: Counterinsurgency Lessons from Malaya and Vietnam* (University of Chicago Press, 2005), p. 155.

140. Quoted in Krepinevich, *The Army and Vietnam,* pp. 190, 197–201.

141. Gelb and Betts, *The Irony of Vietnam,* p. 171.

142. Boot, *Invisible Armies,* pp. 422–23; and Karnow, *Vietnam: A History,* pp. 536–81.

143. Krepinevich, *The Army and Vietnam,* pp. 200–01, 210–13.

144. McNamara, *In Retrospect,* p. 244.

145. Alain C. Enthoven and K. Wayne Smith, *How Much Is Enough? Shaping the Defense Program, 1961–1969* (Santa Monica, CA: RAND, 2005), p. 304.

146. Pape, *Bombing to Win,* pp. 183–95.

147. Herring, *America's Longest War,* pp. 146–48.

148. See Boot, *Invisible Armies,* pp. 199–200.

149. Bing West, *The Village* (New York: Pocket Books, 2003).

150. Krepinevich, *The Army and Vietnam,* pp. 172–80.

151. See for example, Cavender S. Sutton, Review of Ted N. Easterling, *War in the Villages: The U.S. Marine Corps Combined Action Platoons in the Vietnam War* (University of North Texas Press, 2021) in *Journal of Military History,* 85: 4 (October 2021).

152. Nagl, *Learning to Eat Soup with a Knife,* pp. 152–57.

153. See Krepinevich, *The Army and Vietnam,* p. 206; and Sheehan, *A Bright Shining Lie.*

154. McNamara, *In Retrospect,* p. 211.

155. Gelb and Betts, *The Irony of Vietnam,* p. 161.

156. Frantz and McKean, *Friends in High Places,* pp. 208, 252.

157. Karnow, *Vietnam: A History,* p. 616.

158. Ibid., p. 616.

159. Ibid., pp. 698–99.

160. Mark Moyar, *A Question of Command: Counterinsurgency from the Civil War to Iraq* (Yale University Press, 2009), pp. 161–67.

161. Petraeus and Amos, *Field Manual 3–24: Counterinsurgency,* pp. 2.12–2.13.

162. Herring, *America's Longest War,* p. 225.

163. Lewis Sorley, *A Better War: The Unexamined Victories and Final Tragedy of America's Last Years in Vietnam* (New York: Harcourt Books, 1999), pp. 204–10.

164. Sorley, *A Better War,* pp. 243–60; and Max Hastings, *Vietnam: An Epic Tragedy, 1945–1975* (New York: Harper Perennials, 2018), pp. 572–84.

165. Karnow, *Vietnam: A History,* pp. 616–17.

166. Sorley, *A Better War,* p. 217.

167. Karnow, *Vietnam: A History,* p. 672.

168. Pape, *Bombing to Win,* pp. 197–205.

169. Lien-Hang T. Nguyen, *Hanoi's War: An International History of the War for Peace in Vietnam* (University of North Carolina Press, 2012), pp. 231–56.

170. Karnow, *Vietnam: A History,* p. 674.

171. Peter W. Rodman, *Presidential Command: Power, Leadership, and the Making of Foreign Policy from Richard Nixon to George W. Bush* (New York: Alfred A. Knopf, 2009), pp. 44–85.

172. Gelb and Betts, *The Irony of Vietnam,* pp. 350–51.

173. Green, *By More than Providence,* pp. 312, 322.

174. Petraeus, "The American Military and the Lessons of Vietnam," p. 263.

175. For a good discussion on this issue, see Walzer, *Just and Unjust Wars,* pp. 186–196.

176. Krepinevich, *The Army and Vietnam;* Nagl, *Learning to Eat Soup with a Knife;* and Sorley, *A Better War.*

177. Summers, *On Strategy,* pp. 108–24.

5. America's Wars in the Middle East since 1990

1. See Martin S. Navias, "The First Tanker War," *History Today,* 2022, historytoday.com/history-matters/first-tanker-war.

2. Martin Middlebrook, *The Falklands War* (South Yorkshire, UK: Pen and Sword Books, 2012), pp. 153–66.

3. Sam LaGrone, "Attack on U.S.S. *Stark* at Thirty," *USNI News,* May 17, 2017, https://news.usni.org/2017/05/17/the-attack-uss-stark-at-30.

4. Bruce Riedel, "Remembering the Khobar Towers Bombing," Brookings Institution, Washington, DC, June 21, 2021, brookings.edu/blog/order-from-chaos /2021/06/21/remembering-the-khobar-towers-bombing.

5. Kenneth M. Pollack, *Armies of Sand: The Past, Present, and Future of Arab Military Effectiveness* (Oxford University Press, 2019), p. 1.

6. Ibid., p. 18.

7. Ibid., pp. 4–20.

8. Memo from Lily Windholz to author, August 3, 2021; and Michael Oren, *Six Days of War: June 1967 and the Making of the Modern Middle East* (New York: Presidio Books, 2003).

9. Pollack, *Armies of Sand,* p. 18.

10. Martin Indyk, *Master of the Game: Henry Kissinger and the Art of Middle East Diplomacy* (New York: Alfred A. Knopf, 2021), pp. 115–99.

11. Ibid., pp. 5–6.

12. Cohen and Gooch, *Military Misfortunes,* pp. 96–112.

13. Frederick W. Kagan, *Finding the Target: The Transformation of American Military Policy* (New York: Encounter Books, 2006), p. 19.

14. See Esther Pan, "Middle East: Syria and Lebanon," Council on Foreign Relations, New York, February 22, 2005, cfr.org/backgrounder/middle-east-syria-and -lebanon.

15. Indyk, *Master of the Game,* pp. 549–50.

16. Kenneth M. Pollock, *Arabs at War: Military Effectiveness, 1948–1991* (University of Nebraska Press, 2002), pp. 532–34.

17. Pollack, *Armies of Sand,* pp. 256–74, 478–92.

18. Stephen Biddle, *Nonstate Warfare: The Military Methods of Guerillas, Warlords, and Militias* (Princeton University Press, 2021), pp. 110–12, 141–44; and Pollack, *Armies of Sand,* pp. 482–85.

19. Caitlin Talmadge, *The Dictator's Army: Battlefield Effectiveness in Authoritarian Regimes* (Cornell University Press, 2015), pp. 139–231; and Pollack, *Armies of Sand,* pp. 144–55.

20. Steve Galster, "Afghanistan: The Making of U.S. Policy, 1973–1990," in National Security Archive, "Volume 2, Afghanistan: Lessons from the Last War," National Security Archive, Washington, D.C., October 9, 2001, https://nsarchive2 .gwu.edu/NSAEBB/NSAEBB57/essay.html.

21. Selig S. Harrison, "Afghanistan: Soviet Intervention, Afghan Resistance, and the American Role," in *Low Intensity Warfare,* edited by Michael T. Klare and Peter Kornbluh (New York: Pantheon Books 1988), pp. 194–95.

22. Philip H. Gordon, *Losing the Long Game: The False Promise of Regime Change in the Middle East* (New York: St. Martin's Press, 2020), p. 66.

23. Ibid., pp. 46–70.

24. Ibid., p. 56.

25. Doughty, *Warfare in the Western World,* pp. 954–99; Bruce Riedel, *What We Won: America's Secret War in Afghanistan* (Washington, D.C.: Brookings, 2014)

26. Charles G. Cogan, "Partners in Time: The CIA and Afghanistan since 1979," *World Policy Journal,* 10:2 (Summer 1993), pp. 73–82.

27. Michael R. Gordon and General Bernard E. Trainor, *The Generals' War: The Inside Story of the Conflict in the Gulf* (Boston: Little, Brown and Company, 1995), pp. 309–12.

28. Susan L. Marquis, *Unconventional Warfare: Rebuilding U.S. Special Operations Forces* (Brookings Institution, 1997), pp. 69–73; Williamson Murray and Major General Robert H. Scales, Jr., *The Iraq War: A Military History* (Harvard University Press, 2003), pp. 51–52; and Representative Les Aspin and Representative William Dickinson, *Defense for a New Era: Lessons of the Persian Gulf War* (Washington, DC: Brassey's, 1992), pp. 4–5.

29. On the Army's disinterest in preparing for low-intensity and counterinsurgency warfare after Vietnam, see for example, Pat Proctor, *Lessons Unlearned: the U.S. Army's Role in Creating the Forever Wars in Afghanistan and Iraq* (University of Missouri Press, 2020), pp. 398–400. Other parts of government were underprepared and under-resourced, too; see Terrence K. Kelly et al. *Stabilization and Reconstruction Staffing: Developing U.S. Civilian Personnel Capabilities* (Santa Monica, CA: RAND, 2008).

30. David Fitzgerald, *Learning to Forget: U.S. Army Counterinsurgency Doctrine and Practice from Vietnam to Iraq* (Stanford University Press, 2013).

31. Kevin M. Woods, *The Mother of All Battles: Saddam Hussein's Strategic Plan for the Persian Gulf War* (Naval Institute Press, 2008), pp. 47–59.

32. Rick Atkinson, *Crusade: The Untold Story of the Persian Gulf War* (Boston: Houghton Mifflin, 1993), p. 28; and Bruce Riedel, *Kings and Presidents: Saudi Arabia and the United States since FDR* (Brookings Institution, 2018), pp. 99–102.

33. Riedel, *Kings and Presidents*, p. 102.

34. H. W. Brands, "Neither Munich nor Vietnam: The Gulf War of 1991," in *The Power of the Past: History and Statecraft,* edited by Hal Brands and Jeremi Suri (Brookings Institution, 2016), pp. 77–79.

35. Atkinson, *Crusade,* pp. 50–90

36. Ibid., p. 54.

37. Riedel, *Kings and Presidents,* p. 107.

38. Aspin and Dickinson, *Defense for a New Era*, pp. 6–7.

39. Brig. Gen. Robert H. Scales, Jr., *Certain Victory: The U.S. Army in the Gulf War* (Washington, DC: Brassey's, 1994), p. 41, 57; and Thomas A. Keaney and Elliott A. Cohen, *Gulf War Air Power Survey Summary* Report (Washington, DC: Government Printing Office, 1993), p. 4.

40. Atkinson, *Crusade,* p. 509.

41. Congressional Budget Office, "Costs of Operation Desert Shield," January 1991, 15; and Dupuy, *Attrition*, 73–74, 131.

42. See Directorate for Information Operations and Reports, "Persian Gulf War: Desert Shield and Desert Storm," Department of Defense, Dec. 15, 2001 (web1.whs.osd.mil/mmid/casualty); Department of Defense, *Conduct of the Persian Gulf War: Final Report to Congress,* April 1992, M-1.

43. See also, Lawrence Freedman and Efraim Karsh, *The Gulf Conflict, 1990–1991: Diplomacy and War in the New World Order* (Princeton University Press, 1993), 409.

44. James A. Winnefeld, Preston Niblack, and Dana J. Johnson, *A League of Airmen: U.S. Air Power in the Gulf War* (Santa Monica, CA: RAND, 1994), p. 169; and Keaney and Cohen, *Gulf War Air Power Survey Summary Report,* pp. 61–62.

45. Congressional Budget Office, "Costs of Operation Desert Shield," Washington, D.C., January 1991, cbo.gov/sites/default/files/102nd-congress-1991-1992/reports/199101costofoperation.pdf; and Government Accountability Office, "Cost of Operation Desert Shield and Desert Storm and Allied Contributions," Washington, D.C., May 1991, gao.gov/products/t-nsiad-91-34.

46. Keaney and Cohen, *Gulf War Air Power Survey Summary Report,* p. 7; Aspin and Dickinson, *Defense for a New Era,* p. 79; and Winnefeld, Niblack, and Johnson, *A League of Airmen,* p. 290.

47. Keaney and Cohen, *Gulf War Air Power Survey Summary Report,* pp. 184–85.

48. Aspin and Dickinson, *Defense for a New Era,* , p. 90.

49. Atkinson, *Crusade,* pp. 13–49.

50. Gordon and Trainor, *The Generals' War,* pp. 227–48.

51. Aspin and Dickinson, *Defense for a New Era,* p. 25.

52. Atkinson, *Crusade,* pp. 416–21.

53. Keaney and Cohen, *Gulf War Air Power Survey Summary Report,* p. 13.

54. Ibid., p. 174.

55. Aspin and Dickinson, *Defense for a New Era,* pp. 10–11; and Keaney and Cohen, *Gulf War Air Power Survey Summary Report,* p. 21.

56. Aspin and Dickinson, *Defense for a New Era,* pp. 21, 34–42; and Winnefeld, Niblack, and Johnson, *A League of Airmen,* p. 271.

57. Aspin and Dickinson, *Defense for a New Era,* p. 17; and Congressional Budget Office, "Trends in Selected Indicators of Military Readiness, 1980 through 1993," Washington, DC, March 1994, pp. 68–71, cbo.gov/sites/default/files/103rd -congress-1993-1994/reports/doc13.pdf.

58. Barry D. Watts, "Friction in the Gulf War," *Naval War College Review,* 48: 4 (Fall 1995), p. 94.

59. Aspin and Dickinson, *Defense for a New Era,* p. 35; and Keaney and Cohen, *Gulf War Air Power Survey Summary Report,* 105–06; and General Accounting Office, *Operation Desert Storm: Evaluation of the Air Campaign,* GAO/NSIAD-97-134, June 1997, pp. 8–10, 105–07, 146–48, 157–59. gao.gov/assets/nsiad-97-134.pdf

60. Civilian casualty estimates based on a briefing by William Arkin of Greenpeace to Gulf War Air Power Survey project members, October 31, 1991, cited in Keaney and Cohen, *Gulf War Air Power Survey Summary Report,* 75; for other data, see Keaney and Cohen, pp. 102–19.

61. Keaney and Cohen, *Gulf War Air Power Survey Summary Report,* pp. 65, 103–17, 203; General Accounting Office, "Operation Desert Storm," p. 178, https://www.gao.gov/products/nsiad-97-134.Air power used in isolation is not always so effective; see Anthony M. Schinella, *Bombs without Boots: The Limits of Air power* (Brookings Institution, 2019). On tank plinking, see Winnefeld, Niblack, and Johnson, *A League of Airmen,* p. 170.

62. Winnefeld, Niblack, and Johnson, *A League of Airmen,* pp. 308–09; and Brig. Gen. Robert H. Scales, Jr., *Certain Victory,* p. 161.

63. General Accounting Office, "Operation Desert Storm," pp. 110–61.

64. Winnefeld, Niblack, and Johnson, *A League of Airmen,* pp. 169–71; Gordon and Trainor, *The Generals' War,* p. 335; Keaney and Cohen, *Gulf War Air Power Survey Summary Report,* p. 106.

65. Gordon and Trainor, *The Generals' War,* pp. 465, 474.

66. Atkinson, *Crusade,* pp. 394–403.

67. Gordon and Trainor, *The Generals' War,* pp. 371–74.

68. Aspin and Dickinson, *Defense for a New Era,* pp. 13, 28–29.

69. Stephen Biddle, "The Past as Prologue: Assessing Theories of Future Warfare," *Security Studies,* 8: 1 (Autumn 1998): 1–74.

70. Keaney and Cohen, *Gulf War Air Power Survey Summary Report,* p. 109.

71. Pollack, *Armies of Sand,* p. 161; Gordon and Trainor, *The Generals' War,* pp. 375–432; and Biddle, *Military Power,* pp. 132–49.

72. Stephen Biddle, "Victory Misunderstood: What the Gulf War Tells Us about the Future of Conflict," *International Security,* 21: 2 (Fall 1996): 139–79; and Biddle, *Military Power,* pp. 132–49.

73. Pollack, *Armies of Sand,* pp. 158–62.

74. Gordon and Trainor, *The Generals' War,* pp. 364–68.

75. See Keaney and Cohen, *Gulf War Air Power Survey Summary Report,* pp. 21, 58–64, 155; and Aspin and Dickinson, *Defense for a New Era,* pp. 1–41; for data on Arab-Israeli wars, see Posen, "Measuring the European Conventional Balance," in Miller, *Conventional Forces and American Defense Policy,* 113; and Dupuy, *Numbers, Predictions, and War,* 118–139.

76. Scales, *Certain Victory,* p. 81.

77. Gordon and Trainor, *The Generals' War,* p. 370.

78. Ibid., pp. 430–31.

79. Atkinson, *Crusade,* pp. 9, 489–90.

80. For some of the most heartfelt accounts of the war at the human level, see C. J. Chivers, *The Fighters: Americans in Combat in Afghanistan and Iraq* (New York: Simon and Schuster, 2018); Kimberly Dozier, *Breathing the Fire: Fighting to Report—and Survive—the War in Iraq* (Des Moines, IA: Meredith Books, 2008); Evan Wright, *Generation Kill: Devil Dogs, Iceman, Captain America, and the New Face of American War* (New York: Berkley Publishing Group, 2004); and Martha Raddatz, *The Long Road Home: A Story of War and Family* (New York: G. P. Putnam's Sons, 2007).

81. Khidhir Hamza with Jeff Stein, *Saddam's Bombmaker* (New York: Simon and Schuster, 2000); Bob Woodward, *Plan of Attack* (New York: Simon and Schuster, 2004), p. 199; and George Tenet with Bill Harlow, *At the Center of the Storm: My Years at the CIA* (New York: HarperCollins Publishers, 2007), pp. 321–358.

82. Power, *"A Problem from Hell,"* pp. 171–245.

83. Gordon, *Losing the Long Game,* pp. 99–144; and Burns, *The Back Channel,* p. 161.

84. Hal Brands, *What Good Is Grand Strategy? Power and Purpose in American Statecraft from Harry S. Truman to George W. Bush* (Cornell University Press, 2014), pp. 144–65.

85. Congressional Research Service, "The United Nations Security Council—Its Role in the Iraq Crisis: A Brief Overview," Washington, D.C., May 16, 2003, everycrsreport.com/reports/RS21323.html; and Congressional Research Service, "Iraq War?: Current Situation and Issues for Congress," Washington, D.C., February 26, 2003, everycrsreport.com/files/20030226_RL31715_58763d3e0fbee06 fdda4064ca2891c14102fdbe5.pdf.

86. William J. Burns, *The Back Channel: A Memoir of American Diplomacy and the Case for Its Renewal* (New York: Random House, 2020), p. 172.

87. Sara Fritz and William J. Eaton, "Congress Authorizes Gulf War," *Los Angeles Times,* January 13, 1991; and GovTrack, "H.J.Res. 114 (107th): Authorization for Use of Military Force Against Iraq Resolution of 2002," govtrack.us/congress /votes/107-2002/s237.

88. Michael R. Gordon and General Bernard E. Trainor, *Cobra II: The Inside Story of the Invasion and Occupation of Iraq* (New York: Pantheon Books, 2006), pp. 337–43.

89. Ibid., pp. 164–81.

90. Ivo H. Daalder and Michael E. O'Hanlon, *Winning Ugly: NATO's War to Save Kosovo* (Brookings Institution, 2000), pp. 1–5, 137–237; and Benjamin S. Lambeth, *NATO's Air War for Kosovo: A Strategic and Operational Assessment* (Santa Monica, CA: RAND, 2001), p. 88.

91. Lambeth, *NATO's Air War for Kosovo,* pp. 220–22.

92. See Ivo H. Daalder and James M. Lindsay, *America Unbound: The Bush Revolution in Foreign Policy* (Brookings Institution, 2005).

93. Walter L. Perry et al., eds., *Operation Iraqi Freedom: Decisive War, Elusive Peace* (Santa Monica, CA: RAND, 2015), pp. 53, 59, 344, https://www.rand.org /content/dam/rand/pubs/research_reports/RR1200/RR1214/RAND_RR1214.pdf; and Bob Woodward, *Plan of Attack* (New York: Simon and Schuster, 2004), p. 329.

94. Woodward, *Plan of Attack,* p. 8.

95. Perry et al., *Operation Iraqi Freedom,* pp. 151–57.

96. Rick Atkinson, *In the Company of Soldiers: A Chronicle of Combat* (New York: Henry Holt and Company, 2004), pp. 297–303.

97. See Thomas Donnelly, *Operation Iraqi Freedom: A Strategic Assessment* (Washington, D.C.: American Enterprise Institute, 2004), pp. 52–84; and Murray and Scales, *The Iraq War,* pp. 99–100.

98. Perry et al., e *Operation Iraqi Freedom,* pp. 60–81.

99. Stephen Biddle, "Speed Kills: Reassessing the Role of Speed, Precision, and Situation Awareness in the Fall of Saddam," *Journal of Strategic Studies,* 30: 1 (February 2007), pp. 3–46; and Gordon and Trainor, *Cobra II,* pp. 374–410.

100. Kenneth Adelman, "'Cakewalk' Revisited," *Washington Post,* April 10, 2003.

101. Perry et al., *Operation Iraqi Freedom,* p. 100.

102. Charles H. Ferguson, *No End in Sight: Iraq's Descent into Chaos* (New York: Public Affairs, 2008), pp. 104–38.

103. Hilary Synnott, *Bad Days in Basra: My Turbulent Time as Britain's Man in Southern Iraq* (London: I. B. Tauris, 2008), p. 250.

104. Tenet, *At the Center of the Storm,* p. 440.

105. King Abdullah II of Jordan, *Our Last Best Chance: The Pursuit of Peace in a Time of Peril* (New York: Penguin Books, 2011), pp. 225–28.

106. Brendan R. Gallagher, *The Day After: Why America Wins the War but Loses the Peace* (Cornell University Press, 2019), pp. 203–26.

107. Burns, *The Back Channel*, pp. 157–78, 196–99.

108. In addition to a number of other books cited already, on this basic situation in 2003 see Rajiv Chandrasekaran, *Imperial Life in the Emerald City: Inside Iraq's Green Zone* (New York: Alfred A. Knopf, 2007); and Don Eberly, *Liberate and Leave: Fatal Flaws in the Early Strategy for Postwar Iraq* (Minneapolis, MN.: Zenith Press, 2009).

109. Thomas E. Ricks, *Fiasco: The American Military Adventure in Iraq* (New York: Penguin Press, 2006), p. 159.

111. Toby Dodge, *Inventing Iraq: The Failure of Nation Building and a History Denied* (Columbia University Press, 2003).

111. Ambassador L. Paul Bremer III, *My Year in Iraq: The Struggle to Build a Future of Hope* (New York: Simon and Schuster, 2006), pp. 161–65, 220–97; and Tenet, *At the Center of the Storm*, pp. 416–30.

112. Tenet, *At the Center of the Storm*, pp. 424–26; and Burns, *The Back Channel*, pp. 162–78.

113. David Rieff, "Who Botched the Occupation?" *New York Times Magazine* (November 2, 2003).

114. Larry Diamond, *Squandered Victory: The American Occupation and the Bungled Effort to Bring Democracy to Iraq* (New York: Henry Holt and Company, 2005), pp. 279–313; and George Packer, *The Assassins' Gate: America in Iraq* (New York: Farrar, Straus and Giroux, 2005), p. 245.

115. Packer, *The Assassins' Gate*, p. 236.

116. Diamond, *Squandered Victory*, p. 292.

117. On the multifaceted insurgency, see Ahmed S. Hashim, *Insurgency and Counter-Insurgency in Iraq* (Cornell University Press, 2006). See also Omer Taspinar, *What the West Is Getting Wrong about the Middle East* (London: I. B. Tauris, 2021), pp. 109–34.

118. Ricks, *Fiasco*, pp. 220–50.

119. Gordon and Trainor, *Cobra II*, p. 489.

120. Ricks, *Fiasco*, pp. 221–41.

121. Gordon, *Losing the Long Game*, p. 125.

122. Ricks, *Fiasco*, pp. 221, 246–47.

123. Ian Livingston and Michael E. O'Hanlon, "Iraq Index: Tracking Variables of Reconstruction and Security in Post-Saddam Iraq," Brookings Institution, Washington, D.C., January 31, 2011, brookings.edu/wp-content/uploads/2016/07/index20110131.pdf.

124. Michael O'Hanlon, "Iraq Without a Plan," *Policy Review*, 128 (December 2004).

125. Michael R. Gordon and General Bernard E. Trainor, *The Endgame: The Inside Story of the Struggle for Iraq, from George W. Bush to Barack Obama* (New York: Pantheon Books, 2012), pp. 56–73.

126. Gordon and Trainor, *The Endgame,* pp. 351–68.

127. See for example, James A. Baker III and Lee H. Hamilton, co-chairs, *The Iraq Study Group Report* (New York: Vintage Books, 2006).

128. General Stanley McChrystal, *My Share of the Task: A Memoir* (New York: Penguin Press, 2013), pp. 231–36.

129. My profuse thanks to Adriana Lins de Albuquerque, Nina Kamp, Jason Campbell, and Ian Livingston for all they did to create and sustain this project, as well as the Afghanistan and Pakistan indices, over the years.

130. Jason Campbell, Michael O'Hanlon, and Jeremy Shapiro, "How to Measure the War," *Policy Review,* 157 (November and December 2009), p. 21, brookings.edu/wp-content/uploads/2016/06/10_afghanistan_iraq_campbell.pdf.

131. Ali A. Allawi, *The Occupation of Iraq: Winning the War, Losing the Peace* (Yale University Press, 2007), pp. 456–60.

132. Biddle, *Non-State Warfare,* pp. 147–78.

133. David Kilcullen, *Out of the Mountains: The Coming Age of the Urban Guerrilla* (Oxford University Press, 2013); and Carter Malkasian, *War Comes to Garmser: Thirty Years of Conflict on the Afghan Frontier* (Oxford University Press, 2013).

134. See Michael Fitzsimmons, "Hard Hearts and Open Minds?: Governance, Identity, and the Intellectual Foundations of Counterinsurgency Strategy," *Journal of Strategic Studies,* 31: 3 (2008), 337–365; and Jacqueline L. Hazelton, "The 'Hearts and Minds' Fallacy: Violence, Coercion, and Success in Counterinsurgency Warfare," *International Security,* 42: 1 (Summer 2017): 80–113. On the surge in Iraq, see Peter R. Mansoor, *Surge: My Journey with General David Petraeus and the Remaking of the Iraq War* (Yale University Press, 2013), especially 36–39; and Kimberly Kagan, *The Surge: A Military History* (New York: Encounter Books, 2009).

135. Emma Sky, *The Unraveling: High Hopes and Missed Opportunities in Iraq* (New York: Public Affairs, 2015), p. 154.

136. Peter W. Rodman, *Presidential Command: Power, Leadership, and the Making of Foreign Policy from Richard Nixon to George W. Bush* (New York: Alfred A. Knopf, 2009), pp. 266–67.

137. Gordon and Trainor, *The Endgame,* pp. 282–311.

138. Frank G. Hoffman, *Mars Adapting: Military Change during War* (Annapolis, MD: Naval Institute Press, 2021), pp. 197–245; Mansoor, *Surge;* and Kagan, *The Surge.*

139. Special Inspector General for Iraq Reconstruction, *Hard Lessons: The Iraq Reconstruction Experience* (Washington, DC: U.S. Government Printing Office, 2009), pp. 295–319.

140. See P. W. Singer, *Corporate Warriors: The Rise of the Privatized Military Industry* (Cornell University Press, 2003); and Congressional Budget Office, "Contractors in Iraq," U.S. Congress, Washington, DC, August 12, 2008, https://www.cbo.gov/publication/24822.

141. Campbell and O'Hanlon, "Iraq Index.https://www.brookings.edu/iraq
-index.

142. Gordon and Trainor, *The Endgame*, pp. 358–365.

143. Mansoor, *Surge*, pp. 148–76.

144. See Peter A. Clement, "Impact of Intelligence Integration on CIA Analysis," *Studies in Intelligence*, 65: 3 (September 2021), pp. 25–33; and Jim Clapper and Trey Brown, "Reflections on Integration in the Intelligence Community," *Studies in Intelligence*, 65: 3 (September 2021), pp. 1–4.

145. Stanley McChrystal, *Team of Teams: New Rules of Engagement for a Complex World* (New York: Portfolio Books, 2015).

146. Kagan, *The Surge*, pp. 97–204.

147. See General David Petraeus, "Foreword," in Mansoor, *Surge*, p. xi.

148. Stephen Biddle, Jeffrey A. Friedman, and Jacob N. Shapiro, "Testing the Surge: Why Did Violence Decline in Iraq in 2007?" *International Security*, 37: 1 (Summer 2012), pp. 7–40,

149. Michael E. O'Hanlon and Kenneth M. Pollack, "A War We Just Might Win," *New York Times*, July 30, 2007.

150. See Kanan Makiya, *Republic of Fear: The Politics of Modern Iraq* (University Of California Press, 1989).

151. Richard N. Haass, *War of Necessity, War of Choice: A Memoir of Two Iraq Wars* (New York: Simon and Schuster, 2009).

152. Sky, *The Unraveling*, pp. 329–42, 360.

153. Gordon, *Losing the Long Game*, pp. 134–44.

154. Joel Rayburn, *Iraq After America: Strongmen, Sectarians, Resistance* (Hoover Institution Press, 2014), pp. 209–64.

155. Sky, *The Unraveling*, p. 360; and Pollack, *Armies of Sand*, pp. 167–68.

156. Daniel Byman, *Al Qaeda, the Islamic State, and the Global Jihadist Movement: What Everyone Needs to Know* (Oxford University Press, 2015), pp. 166–77.

157. See Will McCants, *The ISIS Apocalypse: The History, Strategy, and Doomsday Vision of the Islamic State* (New York: St. Martin's Press, 2015); see also, Jessica Stern and J. M. Berger, *ISIS: The State of Terror* (New York: HarperCollins Books, 2015); and Ash Carter, *Inside the Five-Sided Box: Lessons from a Lifetime of Leadership in the Pentagon* (New York: Penguin Books, 2020), pp. 227–29.

158. Tim Arango, "Maliki Agrees to Relinquish Power in Iraq," *New York Times*, August 14, 2014.

159. Becca Wasser et al. *The Air War Against the Islamic State: The Role of Air power in Operation Inherent Resolve* (Santa Monica, CA: RAND, 2021), p. xiv, https://www.rand.org/pubs/research_reports/RRA388-1.html.

160. Michael R. Gordon, *Degrade and Destroy: The Inside Story of the War against the Islamic State, from Barack Obama to Donald Trump* (New York: Farrar, Straus, and Giroux, 2022).

161. Benjamin S. Lambeth, *Air power in the War Against ISIS* (Naval Institute Press, 2021), pp. 146, 245–46; Wasser et al., pp. 297, 410.

162. Katherine Zimmerman, "Al Qaeda and ISIS 20 Years After 9/11," *Woodrow Wilson Center,* Washington, D.C., September 8, 2021, wilsoncenter.org/article /al-qaeda-isis-20-years-after-911.

163. Vanda Felbab-Brown, "The Pitfalls of the Paramilitary Paradigm: The Iraqi State, Geopolitics, and Al-Hashd al Shaabi," Brookings Institution, Washington, D.C., June 2019, brookings.edu/research/pitfalls-of-the-paramilitary -paradigm-the-iraqi-state-geopolitics-and-al-hashd-al-shaabi.

164. Thomas Barfield, *Afghanistan: A Cultural and Political History* (Princeton University Press, 2010), p. 274.

165. Ibid., pp. 272–350.

166. See Bruce Riedel, *What We Won: America's Secret War in Afghanistan, 1979–1989* Brookings Institution Press, 2014).

167. Ahmed Rashid, *Taliban: Militant Islam, Oil and Fundamentalism in Central Asia* (Yale University Press, 2000), pp. 207–16.

168. Carter Malkasian is convincing on this point; see Malkasian, *The American War in Afghanistan: A History* (Oxford University Press, 2021), pp. 1–10, 454–55.

169. Amy McGrath and Michael O'Hanlon, "Were U.S. Losses in Vain? 'Forever War' in Afghanistan Resulted in Fewer Terror Attacks," *USA Today,* August 15, 2021

170. Kagan, *Finding the Target,* p. 293.

171. Sean Naylor, *Not a Good Day to Die: The Untold Story of Operation Anaconda* (New York: Berkley Publishing Group, 2005), p. 14.

172. Brands, *What Good Is Grand Strategy?,* p. 170.

173. Malkasian, *The American War in Afghanistan,* pp. 450–53.

174. Secretary General Jens Stoltenberg, "We Must Continue to Stand Together," NATO, Brussels, September 11, 2021, nato.int/cps/en/natohq/opinions _186490.htm.

175. Fred H. Allison, "Thunderbolts: Strike First Marine Corps Blow Against Taliban," pp. 9–13, in *U.S. Marines in Afghanistan, 2001–2009: Anthology and Annotated Bibliography,* edited by Major David W. Kummer (Quantico, VA: U.S. Marine Corps, 2014), pp. 9–13; and Arthur P. Brill, Jr., "Afghanistan Diary, Corps Considerations: Lessons Learned in Phase One," in *U.S. Marines in Afghanistan,* pp. 15–21.

176. Jones, *In the Graveyard of Empires,* p. 88; Nathaniel C. Fick, *One Bullet Away: The Making of a Marine Officer* (Boston: Houghton Mifflin Company, 2005); and Captain Jay M. Holtermann, "The 15th MEU's Seizure of Camp Rhino," *Marine Corps Gazette* (March 2016), https://mca-marines.org/wp-content/uploads /The-15th-Marine-Expeditionary-Units-Seizure-of-Camp-Rhino.pdf.

177. See Henry A. Crumpton, *The Art of Intelligence: Lessons from a Life in the CIA's Clandestine Service* (New York: Penguin Press, 2012), pp. 217–61.

178. Stephen Biddle, "Afghanistan and the Future of Warfare: Implications for Army and Defense Policy," Army War College, November 2002, pp. 8–11, https://publications.armywarcollege.edu/pubs/1422.pdf.

179. Jones, *In the Graveyard of Empires*, pp. 86–95.

180. Senate Foreign Relations Committee Majority Staff, "Tora Bora Revisited: How We Failed to Get bin Laden and Why It Matters Today," Government Printing Office, Washington, D.C., November 2009, https://www.foreign.senate.gov/imo/media/doc/Tora_Bora_Report.pdf?; and Boot, *War Made New,* p. 379.

181. Naylor, *Not a Good Day to Die,* pp. 17–21; and Michael E. O'Hanlon, "A Flawed Masterpiece," *Foreign Affairs,* 81:3 (May/June 2002).

182. T.X. Hammes, "Raising and Mentoring Security Forces in Afghanistan and Iraq," in *Lessons Encountered: Learning from the Long War,* edited by Richard D. Hooker, Jr. and Joseph J. Collins (National Defense University Press, 2015), p. 278.

183. Michael Morrell with Bill Harlow, *The Great War of Our Time: The CIA's Fight Against Terrorism from al Qa'ida to ISIS* (New York: Twelve, 2015), p. 74.

184. Jones, *In the Graveyard of Empires,* pp. 110–15.

185. Ambassador James F. Dobbins, *After the Taliban: Nation-Building in Afghanistan* (Washington, D: Potomac Books, 2008), pp. 161–63.

186. Malkasian, *The American War in Afghanistan,* p. 200.

187. Sam Gollob and Michael E. O'Hanlon, "Afghanistan Index: Tracking Variables of Reconstruction and Security in post–9/11 Afghanistan," Brookings Institution, Washington, D.C., August 2020, brookings.edu/wp-content/uploads/2020/08/FP_20200825_afganistan_index.pdf.

188. Naylor, *Not a Good Day to Die.*

189. Jones, *In the Graveyard of Empires,* pp. 142–45.

190. James Dobbins, "Afghanistan Was Lost Long Ago: Defeat Wasn't Inevitable, But Early Mistakes Made Success Unlikely," *Foreign Affairs,* August 30, 2021, https://flipboard.com/article/afghanistan-was-lost-long-ago-defeat-wasn-t-inevitable-but-early-mistakes-made/f-55c16a4c24%2Fforeignaffairs.com.

191. See Michael E. O'Hanlon and Hassina Sherjan, *Toughing It Out in Afghanistan* (Brookings Institution, 2011), pp. 19–30, 129–56.

192. Ronald E. Neumann, *The Other War: Winning and Losing in Afghanistan* (Washington, DC: Potomac Books, 2009), pp. 58, 109; and Malkasian, *The American War in Afghanistan,* pp. 129–156.

193. Malkasian, *The American War in Afghanistan,* pp. 133, 456.

194. Ibid., pp. 101, 129–56.

195. Barfield, *Afghanistan,* p. 319; Gollob and O'Hanlon, "Afghanistan Index."

196. Jones, *In the Graveyard of Empires,* pp. 213–20.

197. Barfield, *Afghanistan,* p. 305.

198. Dipali Mukhopadhyay, *Warlords, Strongman Governors, and the State in Afghanistan* (Cambridge University Press, 2015).

199. Sarah Chayes, *The Punishment of Virtue: Inside Afghanistan After the Taliban* (New York: Penguin Books, 2006).

200. Antonio Giustozzi, "Conclusion," in *Decoding the New Taliban: Insights from the Afghan Field,* edited by Antonio Giustozzi (Columbia University Press, 2009), p. 298.

201. David Kilcullen, *The Accidental Guerrilla: Fighting Small Wars in the Midst of a Big One* (Oxford University Press, 2009), pp. 48–49.

202. See "Strategic Geography" maps in Toby Dodge and Nicholas Redman, *Afghanistan to 2015 and Beyond* (London: International Institute for Strategic Studies, 2011), p. 166.

203. The Asia Foundation, *A Survey of the Afghan People: Afghanistan in 2009* (San Francisco: Asia Foundation, 2009), pp. 15–41.

204. Jones, *In the Graveyard of Empires,* pp. 248–53.

205. Vanda Felbab-Brown, *Aspiration and Ambivalence: Strategies and Realities of Counterinsurgency and State Building in Afghanistan* (Brookings Institution, 2013), p. 25; and U.S. Army and U.S. Marine Corps, *U.S. Army and U.S. Marine Corps Counterinsurgency Field Manual* (University of Chicago Press, 2007).

206. McChrystal, *My Share of the Task,* p. 331; and Petraeus and Amos, *Field Manual 3-24: Counterinsurgency,* p. 1–13. Some believe the range of 20 to 25 should have a substantially higher upper bound; see R. Royce Kneece Jr. et al. "Force Sizing for Stability Operations," Institute for Defense Analysis, Alexandria, Va., March 2010, https://apps.dtic.mil/sti/pdfs/ADA520942.pdf.

207. Felbab-Brown, *Aspiration and Ambivalence,* pp. 27–28.

208. Ibid., pp. 22–32.

209. For one critique, of not only Obama but the policy process writ large, see Daniel P. Bolger, *Why We Lost: A General's Inside Account of the Iraq and Afghanistan Wars* (Boston.: Houghton Mifflin Harcourt, 2014), pp. 420–34.

210. McChrystal, *My Share of the Task,* p. 361.

211. John Pike, "Afghan National Army (ANA)—Order of Battle," Globalsecurity.org, Washington, D.C., 2012, globalsecurity.org/military/world/afghanistan/ana-orbat.htm; and C. J. Radin, "Afghan Security Forces Order of Battle," *Long War Journal,* May 2011, Foundation for Defense of Democracies, Washington, D.C., 2007, longwarjournal.org/oobafghanistan.

212. NATO Headquarters, "International Security Assistance Force: Key Facts and Figures," Brussels, August 1, 2013, https://www.nato.int/isaf/placemats_archive/2013-08-01-ISAF-Placemat.pdf.

213. McChrystal, *My Share of the Task,* pp. 364–78.

214. Malkasian, *The American War in Afghanistan,* p. 1.

215. Ibid., pp. 240–98.

216. Bolger, *Why We Lost,* p. 435.

217. Ian S. Livingston and Michael O'Hanlon, "Afghanistan Index," Brookings Institution, Washington, DC, February 10, 2015, https://www.brookings.edu/afghanistan-index.

218. Seth G. Jones and Arturo Munoz, *Afghanistan's Local War: Building Local Defense Forces* (Santa Monica, CA: RAND, 2010); and Felbab-Brown, *Aspiration and Ambivalence,* pp. 138–60, 268–70.

219. Malkasian, *The American War in Afghanistan,* p. 300.

220. Kimberly Kagan and Frederick Kagan, "We Have the Momentum in Afghanistan," *Wall Street Journal,* June 6, 2011.

221. Livingston and O'Hanlon, "Afghanistan Index." https://www.brookings.edu/afghanistan-index.

222. Felbab-Brown, *Aspiration and Ambivalence,* pp. 94–118.

223. Carlotta Gall, *The Wrong Enemy: America in Afghanistan, 2001–2014* (Boston: Houghton Mifflin Harcourt, 2015), pp. 290–300; and Jones, *In the Graveyard of Empires,* pp. 306–12.

224. BBC, "U.S. Admiral: Haqqani Is 'Veritable Arm' of Pakistan's ISI," BBC News, September 22, 2011, bbc.com/news/av/world-us-canada-15026909; for some of the other linkages between Pakistani actors and the Afghan Taliban, see C. Christine Fair, *The Madrassah Challenge: Militancy and Religious Education in Pakistan* (Washington, DC: U.S. Institute of Peace, 2008), pp. 57, 70.

225. See for example, Aaron Mehta and Matthew Pennington, "U.S. Suspends Security Assistance to Pakistan," *Defense News,* January 4, 2018, defensenews.com/global/mideast-africa/2018/01/04/us-suspends-security-assistance-to-pakistan.

226. Gollob and O'Hanlon, "Afghanistan Index," 2020.

227. Jones, *In the Graveyard of Empires,* pp. 303–06.

228. Hal Brands and Michael O'Hanlon, "The War on Terror Has Not Yet Failed: A Net Assessment After 20 Years," *Survival,* 63: 4 (August–September 2021), pp. 33–53.

229. Felbab-Brown, *Aspiration and Ambivalence,* p. 32.

230. Harleen Gambhir, "Afghanistan Partial Threat Assessment: February 23, 2016," Institute for the Study of War, February 24, 2016, understandingwar.org/sites/default/files/February%202016%20AFG%20Map%20JPEG-01_4.jpg.

231. Arturo Munoz, Rebecca Zimmerman, and Jason H. Campbell, "RAND Experts Q&A on the Fighting in Kunduz," RAND Blog, Washington, D.C., October 2, 2015, rand.org/blog/2015/10/rand-experts-qampa-on-the-fighting-in-kunduz.html.

232. Jonathan Schroden, "Lessons from the Collapse of Afghanistan's Security Forces," *CTC Sentinel,* 14: 8 (October 2021), https://ctc.usma.edu/lessons-from-the-collapse-of-afghanistans-security-forces, based on data from Kate Clark, "Menace, Negotiation, Attack: The Taliban take more District Centers across Afghanistan," Afghanistan Analysts Network, Kabul, Afghanistan, July 16, 2021, ecoi.net/en/document/2057178.html.

233. Malkasian, *The American War in Afghanistan,* pp. 384–403.

234. Special Inspector General for Afghanistan Reconstruction, "Divided Responsibility: Lessons from U.S. Security Sector Assistance Efforts in Afghanistan," Arlington, Virginia, 2019, pp. 19–25, https://www.sigar.mil/pdf/lessonslearned/SIGAR-19-39-LL.pdf.

235. Malkasian, *The American War in Afghanistan,* pp. 384–403, 457.

236. Ibid., pp. 404–22.

237. Air Force Public Affairs, "Combined Forces Air Component Commander 2013–2019 Air power Statistics," January 31, 2020, afcent.af.mil/Portals/82/Doc uments/Air power%20summary/Jan%202020%20Air power%20Summary. pdf?ver=2020-02-13-032911-670; and Jared Keller, "The U.S. Dropped More Munitions on Afghanistan Last Year Than Any Other Time in the Last Decade," *Task and Purpose,* January 27, 2020, https://taskandpurpose.com/news/the-us-dropped -more-munitions-on-afghanistan-last-year-than-any-other-time-in-the-last-decade.

238. O'Hanlon, *Defense 101,* pp. 58–61; and Congressional Budget Office, "Funding for Overseas Contingency Operations and Its Impact on Defense Spending," Washington, D.C., October 2018, cbo.gov/publication/54219.

239. Gideon Rose, *How Wars End: Why We Always Fight the Last Battle* (New York: Simon and Schuster, 2010), p. xiv.

240. Felbab-Brown, *Aspiration and Ambivalence,* p. 25.

241. Schroden, "Lessons from the Collapse of Afghanistan's Security Forces."

242. Susannah George, "Afghanistan's Military Collapse: Illicit Deals and Mass Desertions," *Washington Post,* August 15, 2021, https://www.washingtonpost.com /world/2021/08/15/afghanistan-military-collapse-taliban.; and Michael R. Gordon, et al. "Inside Biden's Afghanistan Withdrawal Plan: Warnings, Doubts but Little Change," *Wall Street Journal,* September 5, 2021.

243. Statement of Secretary of Defense Lloyd Austin before the Senate Committee on Armed Services, September 28, 2021, armed-services.senate.gov/hearings /to-receive-testimony-on-the-conclusion-of-military-operations-in-afghanistan -and-plans-for-future-counterterrorism-operations.

244. Lindsay Maizland, "The Taliban in Afghanistan," Council on Foreign Relations, New York, September 15, 2021, cfr.org/backgrounder/taliban-afghanistan.

245. Pew Research Center, "Majority of U.S. Public Favors Afghanistan Troop Withdrawal; Biden Criticized for His Handling of Situation," Washington, D.C., August 31, 2021, pewresearch.org/fact-tank/2021/08/31/majority-of-u-s-public -favors-afghanistan-troop-withdrawal-biden-criticized-for-his-handling-of -situation.

246. Ricks, *Fiasco,* pp. 64–5.

247. Dan De Luce, Mushtaq Yusufzai and Saphora Smith, "Even the Taliban Are Surprised at How Fast They're Advancing in Afghanistan," NBC News, June 25, 2021, nbcnews.com/politics/national-security/even-taliban-are-surprised -how-fast-they-re-advancing-afghanistan-n1272236.

248. Dexter Filkins, *The Forever War* (New York: Random House, 2008).

249. Michael E. O'Hanlon, *Technological Change and the Future of Warfare* (Washington, D.C.: Brookings, 2000).

250. For a related argument, see Jack Fairweather, *The Good War: Why We Couldn't Win the War or the Peace in Afghanistan* (New York: Basic Books, 2014).

251. Malkasian, *The American War in Afghanistan,* pp. 129–56.

252. Bing West, *The Wrong War: Grit, Strategy, and the Way Out of Afghanistan* (New York: Random House, 2011), pp. 247–54.

253. See comments of Ambassador Ryan Crocker at a virtual conference, "9/11 Twenty Years Later: Legacies and Lessons," Brookings Institution, Washington, D.C., September 10, 2021, brookings.edu/events/9-11-20-years-later-legacies-and -lessons.

253. Malkasian, *The American War in Afghanistan,* p. 7.

255. Rory Stewart, "The Last Days of Intervention," *Foreign Affairs*, vol. 100, no. 6 (November/December 2021), p. 72.

6. Three Lessons

1. Michael O'Hanlon, *The Art of War in an Age of Peace: U.S. Grand Strategy and Resolute Restraint* (Yale University Press, 2021).

Index

al-Abadi, Haider, 281
Abizaid, John, 271
Abrams, Creighton, 214, 228, 232–33
Acheson, Dean, 196, 211, 235–36
Adams, Henry, xxv
Adelman, Ken, 267, 309
Aerostats, 277
Afghanistan: Soviet invasion and
occupation of, 243, 250–52, 283–84;
Taliban retaking control of (2021),
283–85, 287–89, 291, 306, 308, 312;
Taliban take-over of (1996), 252
Afghanistan War, 283–307; beginning
of, 287; casualties of, 286, 290,
297, 304, 306; combat phases of,
284–86; communication during,
309; counterinsurgency strategy in,
289–90, 294, 301; end of, 302–07,
312, 324; insider attacks during,
301; ISIS-K fighters and, 303–04;
military innovation and, 309;
military spending and, 1, 304;
mistakes and lessons from, 308–13;
overconfidence and, xxxvi, 289,
319; precursors to, 283–84;
state-building phase of, 289–92,
311–12; strategy in, 289–91,
293–98, 301; Taliban retaking
control (2021) and, 283–85,
287–89, 291, 306, 308, 312;
uncertainty of war outcome and,
317; U.S. grand strategy and,
322–24; U.S. troop surge and,
293–302, 309–10, 312; weapons of,
288, 291, 297, 304, 309. *See also*
Soldiers of Afghanistan War
Africa in World War I, 58, 93
Africa in World War II. *See* North
Africa in World War II
Aideed, Mohammed Farah, 244
Aircraft: Afghanistan War and, 288,
298–99, 303; Arab-Israeli War and,
245; Iraq War and, 264, 266–67,
277, 282; Korean War and, 191–94,
198–99, 205–06, 211, 236; Kosovo
War and, 265; Operation Desert
Storm and, 254, 256, 257–59;
Vietnam War and, 191–94, 214,
217–18, 221, 225, 229, 233–34;
WWI and, 67, 90, 96, 103; WWII
and, 120, 121–22, 135–42, 149–50,
157–60, 164, 169, 179–81
Aircraft carriers, 121–22, 148–49,
157–62, 174, 177–78
Akagi (Japanese carrier), 158
Albert (king of Belgium), 57, 77
Alexander, Harold, 156
Algeria in World War II, 156